2023 Pro Football Trends and Angles Bible

All Rights Reserved

Steve's Football Bible offers the best and most informative Trends and Angles information for the sophisticated football handicapper in the nation. We don't offer opinions on who is going to win games.

We provide historical facts, and you can use that to form your opinion and handicap games accordingly. We offer Pro and College football handicappers the best and most in-depth books on team trends and angles, Point Spread analysis, plus each team's schedule for the upcoming season. You have everything at your fingertips with the **Pro Football Bible** or the **College Football Bible.** The **Pro Football Bible** includes the complete history of the NFL playoffs, Monday Night Football, Sunday Night Football, Thursday games and Saturday games. The **College Football Bible** includes each team's all-time records in the Polls when they were ranked and versus ranked teams. You won't find this type of information anywhere.

We also have numerous published books on College Football History and well as books on Baseball History. All of these are available on our website at: www.stevesfootballbible.com.

www.stevesfootballbible.com

2023 Pro Football Trends and Angles Bible

Copyright © (Registered) 2023 by Steve's Football Bible, LLC (All Rights Reserved)

Steve's Football Bible also offers the College Football Bible, the football handicapper's best friend for the 2023 football season. If you are a fan of College Football, you need this for the upcoming season.
To Order:

Go to: https://stevesfootballbible.com/

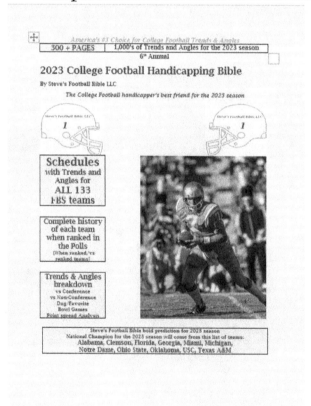

2023 College Football Bible $29.95
To order the College Football Bible go to: https://stevesfootballbible.com/

Books available from Steve's Football Bible LLC

Print Version $34.95 HC/$29.95 Paper	Print Version $34.95 HC/$29.95 Paper

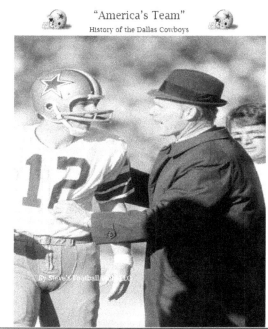

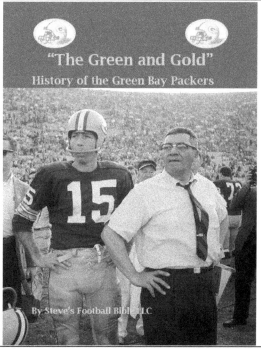

Print Version $34.95 HC/$29.95 Paper	Print Version $34.95 HC/$29.95 Paper

Available at: www.stevesfootballbible.com

Books available from Steve's Football Bible LLC

Print Version $39.95	Print Version $19.95

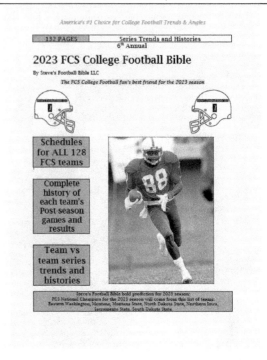

College Football Blueblood Series available at: www.stevesfootballbible.com (Blueblood)

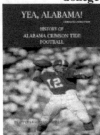  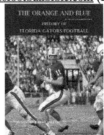 

ALABAMA	AUBURN	CLEMSON	FLORIDA	FLORIDA STATE

College Football Blueblood Series available at: www.stevesfootballbible.com (Blueblood)

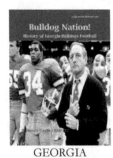    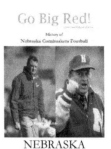

GEORGIA	LSU	MIAMI	MICHIGAN	NEBRASKA

These books are available from numerous online bookstores.

Also available at: www.stevesfootballbible.com

TABLE OF CONTENTS

2022

	Opponent		Surf				Spread		Total	O/U
vs	KANSAS CITY		G	21	44	L	6.5	L	54.0	O
@	Las Vegas Raiders {OT}		G	29	23	W	5.5	W	52.5	U
vs	LOS ANGELES RAMS		G	12	20	L	3.0	L	49.0	U
@	Carolina		G	26	16	W	1.0	W	44.0	U
vs	PHILADELPHIA		G	17	20	L	5.5	W	47.5	U
@	Seattle		A	9	19	L	-2.5	L	50.5	U
vs	NEW ORLEANS	T	G	42	34	W	-2.5	W	44.0	O
@	Minnesota		A	26	34	L	4.0	L	48.5	O
vs	SEATTLE		G	21	31	L	-2.0	L	49.0	O
@	Los Angeles Rams		A	27	17	W	3.0	W	37.5	O
vs	San Francisco (Mexico City)	M	G	10	38	L	9.5	L	43.0	O
vs	L.A. CHARGERS		G	24	25	L	2.5	W	49.0	T
	BYE									
vs	NEW ENGLAND	M	G	13	27	L	2.0	L	44.0	U
@	Denver		G	15	24	L	1.0	L	38.0	U
vs	TAMPA BAY {OT}	Su	G	16	19	L	7.5	W	36.5	U
@	Atlanta		A	19	20	L	6.5	L	40.5	U
@	San Francisco		G	13	38	L	14.5	L	40.0	O

2021

	Opponent		Surf				Spread		Total	O/U
@	Tennessee		G	38	13	W	2.5	W	54.5	U
vs	MINNESOTA		G	34	33	W	-3.5	L	51.0	O
@	Jacksonville		G	31	19	W	-8.0	W	51.5	U
@	Los Angeles Rams		G	37	20	W	3.5	W	54.0	O
vs	SAN FRANCISCO		G	17	10	W	-6.0	W	48.5	U
@	Cleveland		G	37	14	W	3.0	W	48.0	U
vs	HOUSTON TEXANS		G	31	5	W	-20.5	W	47.5	U
vs	GREEN BAY	T	G	21	24	L	-6.5	L	50.5	U
@	San Francisco		G	31	17	W	5.5	W	44.5	O
vs	CAROLINA		G	10	34	L	-7.0	L	41.0	O
@	Seattle		A	23	13	W	5.0	W	45.0	U
	BYE									
@	Chicago		G	33	22	W	-7.5	W	43.0	O
vs	LOS ANGELES RAMS	M	G	23	30	L	-3.0	L	51.0	O
@	Detroit		A	12	30	L	-13.0	L	48.5	U
vs	INDIANAPOLIS	Sa	G	16	22	L	-3.0	L	48.5	U
@	Dallas		A	25	22	W	6.5	W	53.5	U
vs	SEATTLE		G	30	38	L	-5.5	L	49.0	O
@	Los Angeles Rams	M	G	11	34	L	3.0	L	49.0	U

2020

	Opponent		Surf				Spread		Total	O/U
@	San Francisco		G	24	20	W	6.5	W	49.0	U
vs	WASHINGTON		G	30	15	W	-7.0	W	46.0	U
vs	DETROIT		G	23	26	L	-5.0	L	55.0	U
@	Carolina		G	21	31	L	-3.0	L	52.0	T
@	New York Jets		A	30	10	W	-7.0	W	48.5	U
@	Dallas	M	M	38	10	W	1.0	W	56.0	U
vs	SEATTLE {OT}	Su	G	37	34	W	3.5	W	55.5	O
	BYE									
vs	MIAMI		G	31	34	L	-6.0	L	49.0	O
vs	BUFFALO		G	32	30	W	-3.0	L	55.5	O
@	Seattle	T	A	21	28	L	3.0	L	56.5	U
@	New England		A	17	20	L	PK	L	50.5	U
vs	L.A. RAMS		G	28	38	L	2.5	L	49.0	O
@	New York Giants		A	26	7	W	-3.0	W	47.0	U
vs	PHILADELPHIA		G	33	26	W	-7.0	T	49.5	O
vs	SAN FRANCISCO	Sa	G	12	20	L	-5.5	L	49.5	U
@	L.A. Rams		G	7	18	L	1.0	L	42.0	U

2019

	Opponent		Surf				Spread		Total	O/U
vs	DETROIT {OT}		G	27	27	T	3.0	W	45.0	O
@	Baltimore		A	17	23	L	13.0	W	46.0	U
vs	CAROLINA		G	20	38	L	-2.0	L	46.0	O
vs	SEATTLE		G	10	27	L	5.5	L	48.0	U
@	Cincinnati		A	26	23	W	3.0	W	46.5	O
vs	ATLANTA		G	34	33	W	3.0	W	52.5	O
@	New York Giants		A	27	21	W	3.5	W	49.5	O
@	New Orleans		A	9	31	L	12.5	L	48.0	U
vs	SAN FRANCISCO	T	G	25	28	L	10.0	L	43.5	O
@	Tampa Bay		G	27	30	L	5.5	L	51.5	O
@	San Francisco		G	26	36	L	10.0	T	43.5	O
	BYE									
vs	L.A. RAMS		G	7	34	L	2.5	L	47.5	U
vs	PITTSBURGH		G	17	23	L	2.5	L	43.5	U
vs	CLEVELAND		G	38	24	W	3.0	W	49.0	O
@	Seattle		A	27	13	W	8.0	W	50.5	U
@	L.A. Rams		G	24	31	L	7.0	T	46.0	O

Pointspread Analysis Grass/Turf		Pointspread Analysis THU-SAT-SNF-MNF
2-18 S/U on road on grass as 10.5 point or more Dog since 1986		
7-0 O/U on road on grass as 10.5 point or more Dog since 2001		
5-27 S/U on Turf as 10.5 point or more Dog since 1978		
6-32 S/U on Turf as 7.5-10 point Dog since 1980		
6-25 S/U on Turf as 3.5-7 point Dog since 2003		
11-3 S/U on road on Turf as 3.5-7 point favorite since 1978		
Dog		
9-49 S/U as 10.5 or more Dog since 1978		
11-4 O/U as 10.5 point or more Dog since 2001		
9-35 S/U as 7.5-10 pt Dog since 1997		
10-2 ATS as 3.5-7 Point Dog since 2020		
Favorite		
2-11 ATS @ home as 7.5-10 point favorite since 1993		
6-1 S/U as 10.5 or more favorite since 2007		

DATE		OPPONENT	TURF	AZ	OPP	S/U	LINE	ATS	TOT	O/U	Trends & Angles
9/10/2023	@	Washington	G								2-23 S/U @ Washington since 1979
9/17/2023	vs	NEW YORK GIANTS	G								4-0 S/U & ATS vs NY Giants since 2014
9/24/2023	vs	DALLAS	G								7-2 S/U @ home vs Dallas since 1999
10/1/2023	@	San Francisco	G								6-2 S/U @ San Francisco since 2015
10/8/2023	vs	*CINCINNATI*	G								4-0 S/U @ home vs Cincinnati since 1985
10/15/2023	@	Los Angeles Rams	A								2-11 S/U vs Los Angeles Rams since 2017 {2-10-1 ATS}
10/22/2023	@	Seattle	A								6-2 ATS @ Seattle since 2015
10/29/2023	vs	*BALTIMORE*	G								1-4 S/U & ATS @ home vs Baltimore since 1979
11/5/2023	@	*Cleveland*	G								5-0 S/U vs Cleveland since 2007
11/12/2023	vs	ATLANTA	G								11-2 S/U @ home vs Atlanta since 1968
11/19/2023	@	*Houston*	G								vs Houston - HOME team 5-0 S/U since 2005
11/26/2023	vs	LOS ANGELES RAMS	G								0-8 S/U & ATS @ home vs L.A. Rams since 2015
12/3/2023	@	*Pittsburgh*	G								0-3 S/U & ATS @ Pittsburgh since 1985
12/10/2023		BYE									
12/17/2023	vs	SAN FRANCISCO 49ers	G								6-2 S/U @ home vs 49ers since 2014
12/24/2023	@	Chicago	G								3-0 S/U @ Chicago since 2009 {3-0 ATS}
12/31/2023	@	Philadelphia	G								vs Philadelphia - Eagles leads series 60-57-5
1/7/2024	vs	SEATTLE SEAHAWKS	G								1-8-1 S/U @ home vs Seattle since 2013
1/14/2024											NFC Wild Card
1/21/2024											NFC Divisional Playoff
1/28/2024											NFC Championship
2/11/2024											Super Bowl LVIII @ Las Vegas, NV

Pointspread Analysis vs NFC teams		Pointspread Analysis vs NFC teams
6-1 S/U vs NFC teams as 10.5 point or more favorite since 1986		4-0 S/U @ Los Angeles Rams as 3.5-7 point favorite since 2007
5-19 S/U vs NFC East teams as 10.5 point or more Dog since 1978		0-6 S/U vs San Francisco as 7.5-10 point Dog since 2002
4-30 S/U vs NFC East teams as 7.5-10 point Dog since 1980		1-4-1 ATS vs San Francisco as 7.5-10 point Dog since 2002
9-1 S/U vs NFC East as 3.5-7 point favorite since 2015		0-7 S/U @ San Francisco as 10.5 point or more Dog since 1986
0-11 S/U vs Dallas as 10.5 point or more Dog since 1978		0-4 O/U @ home vs San Francisco as 3 point or less Dog since 1999
1-6 O/U vs Dallas as 3 point or less favorite since 1987		3-0 S/U @ San Francisco as 3 point or less favorite since 2005
4-0 S/U vs Dallas as 3.5-7 point favorite since 1989		0-4 ATS vs San Francisco as 7.5-10 point favorite since 2006
0-7 S/U @ home vs New York Giants as 3.5-7 point Dog since 1981		2-11 S/U vs Seattle as 3.5-7 point Dog since 2004
7-1-1 S/U @ home vs NY Giants as 3 point or less favorite since 1978		6-1 S/U & ATS vs Seattle as 3 point or less Dog since 1993
0-3 S/U @ home vs NY Giants as 3.5-7 point favorite since 1994		vs Los Angeles - Los Angeles leads series 50-40-2
3-0 O/U @ home vs NY Giants as 3.5-7 point favorite since 1994		vs San Francisco - San Francisco leads series 33-29
0-5 S/U vs New York Giants as 7.5-10 point Dog since 1986		vs Seattle - Seattle leads series 25-22-1
0-6 S/U vs Philadelphia as 7.5-10 point Dog since 1980		**vs AFC teams**
4-0 S/U vs Philadelphia as 3 point or less favorite since 1993		0-18 S/U vs AFC teams as 7.5-10 point Dog since 1989
0-4 S/U @ Philadelphia as 3.5-7 point Dog since 1993		13-4 S/U vs AFC teams as 3.5-7 point favorite since 1990
3-10 S/U vs Washington since 2000		vs Cleveland - Arizona leads series 6-1
1-6 S/U @ Washington as 7.5-10 point Dog since 1997		2-12 S/U vs AFC North teams as 3.5-7 point Dog since 1979
0-12 S/U @ Washington as 3.5-7 point Dog since 1979		7-1 S/U vs AFC North as 3.5-7 point favorite since 1985
0-11 S/U vs Washington as 3.5-7 point Dog since 1988		3-0 S/U vs Cleveland as 3.5-7 point favorite since 2000
vs Dallas - Dallas leads series 56-34-1		3-0 S/U vs Cincinnati as 3.5-7 point favorite since 1985
vs NY Giants - Giants lead series 80-45-2		0-4 S/U & ATS vs Cincinnati as 3.5-7 point Dog since 1979
1-4 S/U vs NFC North teams as 10.5 point or more Dog since 1999		1-6 S/U vs Pittsburgh as 3.5-7 point Dog since 1979
0-6 S/U vs Chicago as 3.5-7 point Dog since 1979		vs Pittsburgh - Steelers leads series 35-23-3
4-0 S/U & ATS vs Chicago as 3 point or less favorite since 1982		5-2 O/U vs AFC South as 3 point or less favorite since 1994
vs Chicago - ROAD team 6-0 S/U since 2006		**Playoffs**
vs Chicago - Chicago leads series 59-29-6		2-9 S/U on road in Playoffs since 1948
1-12 S/U vs NFC South teams as 3.5-7 point Dog since 2003		5-0 S/U @ home in Playoffs since 1947
vs Atlanta - HOME team 16-1 S/U since 1994		8-3 O/U in Playoffs since 1999
4-0 S/U & ATS @ home vs Atlanta as 3 point or less favorite since 1978		0-2 S/U @ Minnesota in Playoffs since 1974
vs Atlanta - Arizona leads series 17-16		
1-15 S/U vs NFC West teams as 10.5 point or more Dog since 1986		
12-3 O/U vs NFC West as 7.5-10 point Dog since 1996		
1-5 O/U @ home vs San Francisco since 2016		
2-5 O/U @ home vs Seattle since 2015		
0-4 S/U vs Los Angeles Rams as 10.5 point or more Dog since 1989		
7-2 S/U @ Los Angeles Rams as 3.5-7 point Dog since 1988		
8-0-1 ATS @ Los Angeles Rams as 3.5-7 point Dog since 1988		

Last 4 seasons + Pointspread Analysis

2022

	Team	Day	Site	PF	PA	W/L	Spread	ATS	Total	O/U
vs	NEW ORLEANS		A	26	27	L	5.5	W	44.0	O
@	Los Angeles Rams		A	27	31	L	10.0	W	46.0	O
@	Seattle		A	27	23	W	1.0	W	43.5	O
vs	CLEVELAND		A	23	20	W	1.0	W	49.0	U
@	Tampa Bay		G	15	21	L	10.0	W	46.0	U
vs	SAN FRANCISCO		A	28	14	W	3.0	W	45.0	U
@	Cincinnati		A	17	35	L	6.5	L	47.5	O
vs	CAROLINA {OT}		A	37	34	W	-4.0	L	41.5	O
vs	L.A. CHARGERS		A	17	20	L	2.5	L	49.0	U
@	Carolina	T	G	15	25	L	-2.5	L	41.5	U
vs	CHICAGO		A	27	24	W	-2.0	W	48.0	O
@	Washington		G	13	19	L	3.5	L	40.0	U
vs	PITTSBURGH		A	16	19	L	1.0	L	43.0	U
	BYE									
@	New Orleans		A	18	21	L	5.5	W	43.5	U
@	Baltimore	Sa	A	9	17	L	6.5	L	35.5	U
vs	ARIZONA		A	20	19	W	-6.5	L	4.5	U
vs	TAMPA BAY		A	30	17	W	-6.0	W	40.5	O

2021

	Team	Day	Site	PF	PA	W/L	Spread	ATS	Total	O/U
vs	PHILADELPHIA		A	6	32	L	-3.5	L	49.0	U
@	Tampa Bay		G	25	48	L	13.0	L	51.5	O
@	New York Giants		A	17	14	W	2.5	W	48.0	U
vs	WASHINGTON		A	30	34	L	2.5	L	47.0	U
vs	New York Jets {London}		A	27	20	W	-2.5	W	45.5	O
	BYE									
@	Miami		G	30	28	W	-1.5	W	48.0	O
vs	CAROLINA		A	13	19	L	-2.5	L	46.5	U
@	New Orleans		A	27	25	W	7.0	W	43.5	U
@	Dallas		A	3	43	L	7.5	L	55.5	U
vs	NEW ENGLAND	T	A	0	25	L	7.0	L	47.0	U
@	Jacksonville		G	21	14	W	-1.5	W	45.5	U
vs	TAMPA BAY		A	17	30	L	11.0	L	51.0	U
@	Carolina		G	29	21	W	2.5	W	42.0	O
@	San Francisco		G	13	31	L	9.0	L	48.0	U
vs	DETROIT		A	20	16	W	-7.5	L	43.0	U
@	Buffalo		A	15	29	L	14.0	T	46.5	U
vs	NEW ORLEANS		A	20	30	L	4.5	L	40.0	O

2020

	Team	Day	Site	PF	PA	W/L	Spread	ATS	Total	O/U
vs	SEATTLE		A	25	38	L	-1.0	L	49.5	O
@	Dallas		A	39	40	L	2.5	W	54.0	O
vs	CHICAGO		A	26	30	L	-2.5	L	46.5	O
@	Green Bay	M	G	16	30	L	5.0	L	56.5	U
vs	CAROLINA		A	16	23	L	-2.5	L	54.0	U
@	Minnesota		A	40	23	W	4.0	W	53.0	O
vs	DETROIT		A	22	23	L	-1.0	L	55.0	U
@	Carolina	T	G	25	17	W	1.0	W	52.0	U
vs	DENVER		A	34	27	W	-4.5	W	50.0	O
	BYE									
@	New Orleans		A	9	24	L	3.5	L	49.5	U
vs	LAS VEGAS		A	43	6	W	3.5	W	53.0	U
vs	NEW ORLEANS		A	16	21	L	2.0	L	46.0	U
@	L.A. Chargers		G	17	20	L	1.5	L	48.5	U
vs	TAMPA BAY		A	27	31	L	6.0	W	49.5	O
@	Kansas City		G	14	17	L	10.0	W	54.0	U
@	Tampa Bay		G	27	44	L	7.0	L	51.0	O

2019

	Team	Day	Site	PF	PA	W/L	Spread	ATS	Total	O/U
@	Minnesota		A	12	28	L	3.5	L	46.5	U
vs	PHILADELPHIA	Su	A	24	20	W	1.0	W	53.0	U
@	Indianapolis		A	24	27	L	1.0	L	47.0	O
vs	Tennessee		A	10	24	L	-3.0	L	46.0	U
@	Houston		G	32	53	L	4.0	L	49.0	O
@	Arizona		G	33	34	L	-3.0	L	52.5	O
vs	L.A. RAMS		A	10	37	L	3.0	L	54.5	U
vs	SEATTLE		A	20	27	L	7.5	W	48.5	U
	BYE									
@	New Orleans		A	26	9	W	14.0	W	51.5	U
@	Carolina		G	29	3	W	3.5	W	48.5	U
vs	TAMPA BAY		A	22	35	L	-3.5	L	52.0	O
vs	NEW ORLEANS	T	A	18	26	L	7.0	L	48.0	U
vs	CAROLINA		A	40	20	W	-3.5	W	48.0	O
@	San Francisco		G	29	22	W	10.0	W	50.0	O
vs	JACKSONVILLE		A	24	12	W	-7.5	L	48.0	U
@	Tampa Bay		G	28	22	W	PK	W	48.0	O

Pointspread Analysis — Grass/Turf

Grass/Turf
1-17 S/U on grass as 10.5 point or more Dog since 1988
4-19 S/U on Turf as 10.5 point or more Dog since 1985
0-18 S/U on Turf as 7.5-10 point Dog since 1996
5-29 S/U on grass as 7.5-10 point Dog since 1978
7-2 S/U on grass as 7.5-10 point favorite since 1980
33-9 S/U on Turf as 3.5-7 point favorite since 2008
8-1 S/U on grass as 3.5-7 point favorite since 2001

Dog
17-7 O/U as 10.5 point or more Dog since 1996
8-42 S/U as 10.5 point or more Dog since 1979
6-43 S/U as 7.5-10 point Dog since 1988
3-20 O/U as 7.5-10 point Dog since 2000
4-16 S/U as 3.5-7 point Dog since 2018 {7-13 ATS}

Pointspread Analysis — THU-SAT-SNF-MNF

Playoffs
0-4 S/U on road in Divisional Playoffs since 1978
0-3 S/U @ Philadelphia in Playoffs since 2003
1-5 O/U on road on Saturday in Playoffs since 1992

Favorite
10-2 S/U as 10.5 point or more favorite since 1980
30-9 S/U as 7.5-10 point favorite since 1980
66-16 S/U as 3.5-7 point favorite since 1997
30-4 S/U vs NFC as 3.5-7 point favorite since 2007
1-7 S/U @ home as 3 point or less favorite since 2018 {1-7 ATS}

Atlanta Falcons

Mercedes-Benz Stadium

2023 Schedule + Trends & Angles

NFC South

Coach: Arthur Smith

DATE		OPPONENT	TURF	ATL	OPP	S/U	LINE	ATS	TOT	O/U	Trends & Angles
9/10/2023	vs	CAROLINA	A								6-2 S/U @ home vs Carolina since 2015
9/17/2023	vs	GREEN BAY	A								3-0 S/U @ home vs Green Bay since 2016
9/24/2023	@	Detroit	A								6-1 ATS @ Detroit since 1998
10/1/2023	@	*Jacksonville {London}*	G								Game 1-7 O/U vs Jacksonville since 1996
10/8/2023	vs	*HOUSTON*	A								vs Houston - HOME team 5-0 S/U & ATS s/2003
10/15/2023	vs	WASHINGTON	A								3-1 S/U @ home vs Washington since 2009
10/22/2023	@	Tampa Bay	G								Game 8-2 O/U vs Tampa Bay since 2018
10/29/2023	@	*Tennessee*	G								1-4 S/U @ Tennessee since 1987
11/5/2023	vs	MINNESOTA	A								Game 1-8 O/U @ home vs Minnesota since 1985
11/12/2023	@	Arizona	G								vs Arizona - HOME team 16-1 S/U since 1994
11/19/2023		BYE									
11/26/2023	vs	NEW ORLEANS	A								0-5 S/U @ home vs New Orleans since 2018 {1-4 ATS}
12/3/2023	@	*New York Jets*	A								vs NY Jets - Atlanta leads series 8-5
12/10/2023	vs	TAMPA BAY	A								Game 6-1 O/U @ home vs Tampa Bay since 2016
12/16/2023	@	Carolina	G								4-1 S/U @ Carolina since 2018 {4-1 ATS}
12/24/2023	vs	*INDIANAPOLIS*	A								1-8 S/U @ home vs Indianapolis since 1966
12/31/2023	@	Chicago	G								1-6 S/U @ Chicago since 1985
1/7/2024	@	New Orleans	A								5-12 S/U @ New Orleans since 2006
1/14/2024											NFC Wild Card
1/21/2024											NFC Divisional Playoff
1/28/2024											NFC Championship
2/11/2024											Super Bowl LVIII @ Las Vegas, NV

Pointspread Analysis vs NFC teams		Pointspread Analysis vs NFC teams
8-0 S/U vs NFC teams as 10.5 point or more favorite since 1980		5-1 ATS @ New Orleans as 3 point or less Dog since 1994
30-5 S/U vs NFC as 3.5-7 point favorite since 2007		1-9 S/U @ home vs New Orleans as 3 point or less Dog since 1979
1-9 S/U vs NFC East as 3.5-7 point Dog since 2003		1-8-1 ATS @ home vs New Orleans as 3 point or less Dog since 1979
6-2 S/U vs NFC East as 3.5-7 point favorite since 2001		8-2 S/U @ home vs New Orleans as 3.5-7 point favorite since 1978
0-4 ATS vs Washington as 3.5-7 point favorite since 1978		3-0 S/U vs New Orleans as 7.5-10 point favorite since 1981
3-0 S/U @ home vs Washington as 3.5-7 point favorite since 1978		0-6 S/U vs Tampa Bay as 3.5-7 point Dog since 1999 {1-5 ATS}
6-2 S/U vs Washington since 2006		0-8 S/U vs Tampa Bay as 3 point or less Dog since 1997
0-6 S/U vs NFC North as 7.5-10 point Dog since 1990		12-2 S/U vs Tampa Bay as 3.5-7 point favorite since 1986 {10-4 ATS}
3-9 O/U vs Chicago since 1993		6-0 S/U @ Tampa Bay as 3 point or less favorite since 1992
0-4 S/U vs Chicago as 3.5-7 point Dog since 1986		3-0 S/U vs Tampa Bay as 7.5-10 point favorite since 2010
1-6 S/U & ATS vs Chicago as 3 point or less favorite since 1978		4-0 S/U vs Tampa Bay as 7.5-10 point favorite since 1993
0-4-1 ATS @ Chicago since 1992		0-15 S/U vs NFC West teams as 10.5 point or more Dog since 1990
3-0 S/U @ Detroit since 2011		16-0 O/U vs NFC West teams as 10.5 point or more Dog since 1984
Game 1-6 O/U @ Detroit since 1998		1-8 S/U vs NFC West as 3.5-7 point Dog since 1999
vs Detroit - Lions leads series 24-15		18-0 S/U vs NFC West as 3.5-7 point favorite since 1998
0-3 S/U vs Detroit as 7.5-10 point Dog since 1996		17-6 O/U vs NFC West as 3.5-7 point favorite since 1991
1-5 S/U vs Detroit as 3.5-7 point Dog since 1985		0-4 S/U & ATS @ Arizona as 3 point or less favorite since 1991
0-4 O/U vs Detroit as 3.5-7 point favorite since 1998		5-0 S/U vs Arizona as 7.5-10 point favorite since 1981
4-1 S/U vs Green Bay as 3 point or less favorite since 1988		4-1 O/U vs Arizona as 3.5-7 point favorite since 1995
4-1 S/U & ATS vs Green Bay as 3.5-7 point favorite since 1979		**vs AFC teams**
Game 5-0 O/U vs Green Bay since 2015		0-6 S/U vs AFC teams as 10.5 point or more Dog since 1987
Game 3-0 O/U @ home vs Green Bay since 2016		0-10 S/U vs AFC teams as 7.5-10 point Dog since 1989
0-4 S/U & ATS vs Minnesota as 3 point or less favorite since 1984		0-7 S/U vs AFC South teams as 7.5-10 point Dog since 1989
2-6 S/U @ home vs Minnesota since 1991		0-5 S/U vs AFC South as 3.5-7 point Dog since 1987
1-14 S/U vs NFC South as 7.5-10 point Dog since 1984		5-1 S/U vs AFC South as 3.5-7 point favorite since 1981
33-8 S/U vs NFC South as 3.5-7 point favorite since 1978		6-0 ATS vs Jacksonville since 2003
7-1 S/U vs NFC South as 7.5-10 point favorite since 1995		0-4 ATS @ home vs Indianapolis since 1986
Game 2-8 O/U @ Carolina since 2013		1-5 S/U vs AFC East as 3 point or less Dog since 1986
Game 2-7-1 O/U @ New Orleans since 2013		5-0 S/U vs AFC East as 3.5-7 point favorite since 1992
0-3 S/U & ATS vs Carolina as 7.5-10 point Dog since 1997		
0-7 O/U @ Carolina as 3.5-7 point Dog since 2000		
3-0 S/U & ATS @ home vs Carolina as 3 point or less Dog since 2000		
2-6 O/U vs Carolina as 3 point or less Dog since 1996		
6-0 S/U vs Carolina as 3.5-7 point favorite since 2009		
0-8 S/U vs New Orleans as 7.5-10 point Dog since 1988		
4-0 ATS vs New Orleans as 7.5-10 point Dog since 2003		
0-7 O/U vs New Orleans as 7.5-10 point Dog since 1988		
6-0 O/U @ New Orleans as 3 point or less Dog since 1994	CAROLINA	14-5 S/U in 1st home game of season since 2004

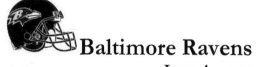

Last 4 seasons + Pointspread Analysis

2022

	Opponent	Day		Surf	Sc	Op	W/L	Spread	ATS	Total	O/U
@	New York Jets			A	24	9	W	-6.5	W	44.0	U
vs	MIAMI			A	38	42	L	-3.0	L	44.0	O
@	New England			A	37	26	W	-2.5	W	44.5	O
vs	BUFFALO			A	20	23	L	3.0	T	50.5	U
vs	CINCINNATI	Su		A	19	17	W	-3.0	L	47.5	U
@	New York Giants			A	20	24	L	-5.5	L	45.5	U
vs	CLEVELAND			A	23	20	W	-6.5	L	47.0	U
@	Tampa Bay	T		G	27	22	W	2.0	W	46.0	O
@	New Orleans	M		A	27	13	W	-1.5	W	46.5	U
	BYE										
vs	CAROLINA			A	13	3	W	-13.0	L	41.5	U
@	Jacksonville			G	27	28	L	-3.0	L	43.0	O
vs	DENVER			A	10	9	W	-8.5	L	40.5	U
@	Pittsburgh			G	16	14	W	1.5	W	36.5	U
@	Cleveland	Sa		G	3	13	L	3.0	L	39.0	U
vs	ATLANTA	Sa		A	17	9	W	-6.5	L	35.5	U
vs	PITTSBURGH	Su		A	13	16	L	-1.5	L	35.5	U
@	Cincinnati			A	16	27	L	12.0	L	39.5	O
@	Cincinnati			A	17	24	L	7.5	W	40.0	O

2021

	Opponent	Day		Surf	Sc	Op	W/L	Spread	ATS	Total	O/U
@	Las Vegas {OT}	M		A	27	33	L	-3.0	L	50.0	O
vs	KANSAS CITY	Su		A	36	35	W	3.5	W	53.5	O
@	Detroit			G	19	17	W	-7.5	L	51.0	U
@	Denver			G	23	7	W	1.0	W	44.0	U
vs	INDIANAPOLIS {OT}	M		A	31	25	W	-7.5	L	46.5	O
vs	L.A. CHARGERS			A	34	6	W	-3.0	W	51.0	U
vs	CINCINNATI			A	17	41	L	-6.5	L	46.0	O
	BYE										
vs	MINNESOTA {OT}			A	34	31	W	-7.0	L	51.0	O
@	Miami	T		A	10	22	L	-8.5	L	46.5	U
@	Chicago			G	22	13	W	-1.0	W	40.0	U
vs	CLEVELAND	Su		A	16	10	W	-3.0	W	47.5	U
@	Pittsburgh			G	19	20	L	-4.0	L	43.5	U
@	Cleveland			G	22	24	L	3.0	W	44.0	U
vs	GREEN BAY			A	30	31	L	8.5	W	45.5	O
@	Cincinnati			A	21	41	L	7.5	L	43.5	O
vs	L.A. RAMS			A	19	20	L	7.0	W	47.0	U
vs	PITTSBURGH {OT}			A	13	16	L	-3.0	L	40.0	U

2020

	Opponent	Day		Surf	Sc	Op	W/L	Spread	ATS	Total	O/U
vs	CLEVELAND			A	38	6	W	-7.0	W	41.5	O
@	Houston			G	33	16	W	-7.0	W	49.5	U
vs	KANSAS CITY	M		A	20	34	L	-3.0	L	54.5	U
@	Washington			G	31	17	W	-14.5	L	45.0	O
vs	CINCINNATI			A	27	3	W	-12.5	W	49.0	U
@	Philadelphia			G	30	28	W	-10.0	L	46.0	O
	BYE										
vs	PITTSBURGH			A	24	28	L	-3.5	L	46.5	O
@	Indianapolis			A	24	10	W	-1.0	W	48.0	U
@	New England	Su		A	17	23	L	-7.0	L	44.0	U
vs	TENNESSEE {OT}			A	24	30	L	-6.0	L	50.5	O
@	Pittsburgh	W		G	14	19	L	10.5	W	41.5	U
vs	DALLAS	Tu		A	34	17	W	-9.0	W	46.0	O
@	Cleveland	M		A	47	42	W	-3.0	W	45.5	O
vs	JACKSONVILLE			A	40	14	W	-12.5	W	49.0	O
vs	N.Y. GIANTS			A	27	13	W	-10.0	W	42.5	U
@	Cincinnati			A	38	3	W	-13.5	W	45.5	U
@	Tennessee			G	20	13	W	-3.5	W	53.5	U
@	Buffalo	Sa		A	3	17	L	2.5	L	50.0	U

2019

	Opponent	Day		Surf	Sc	Op	W/L	Spread	ATS	Total	O/U
@	Miami			G	59	10	W	-7.0	W	40.5	O
vs	ARIZONA			A	23	17	W	-13.0	L	46.0	U
@	Kansas City			G	28	33	L	5.0	T	52.0	O
vs	CLEVELAND			A	25	40	L	-7.0	L	47.0	O
@	Pittsburgh {OT}			G	26	23	W	-3.5	L	44.0	O
vs	CINCINNATI			A	23	17	W	-10.5	L	47.0	O
@	Seattle			A	30	16	W	3.0	W	49.0	U
	BYE										
vs	NEW ENGLAND	Su		A	37	20	W	3.0	W	44.5	O
@	Cincinnati			A	49	13	W	-10.5	W	43.5	O
vs	Houston			A	41	7	W	-4.0	W	51.5	U
@	L.A. Rams	M		G	45	6	W	-3.0	W	46.5	O
vs	SAN FRANCISCO			A	20	17	W	-6.0	T	45.0	U
@	Buffalo			A	24	17	W	-6.0	W	44.0	U
vs	NEW YORK JETS	T		A	42	21	W	-17.0	W	43.5	O
@	Cleveland			G	31	15	W	-10.5	W	48.5	O
vs	PITTSBURGH			A	28	10	W	2.0	W	34.5	O
vs	TENNESSEE	Sa		A	12	28	L	-10.0	L	47.5	U

Pointspread Analysis

THU-SAT-SNF-MNF	Playoffs
7-0 S/U @ home on Thursday since 2011	0-8 O/U @ home in Playoffs since 1994
1-4 S/U on Thursday as 3 point or less dog since 1981	2-9-1 O/U in AFC Wild Card since 1995
5-0 S/U on Thursday as 3 point or less favorite since 1994	6-1 S/U on road in WILD Card since 2002 {7-0 ATS}
0-4 O/U on Thursday as 3.5-7 point favorite since 1983	0-5 O/U @ home in WILD Card since 1995
0-4 S/U on SNF as 7.5 point or more dog since 1996	3-8 S/U on road in Divisional Playoffs since 1972
5-0 O/U on SNF as 3.5-7 point dog since 2002	2-5 S/U in AFC Championship since 1987
1-5-1 ATS on SNF as 3 point or less favorite since 2010	Game 4-1 O/U vs Denver in Playoffs since 1987
5-1 S/U & ATS on road on MNF as 3 point or less favorite since 2001	3-0 ATS vs Miami in Playoffs since 1986
11-4 ATS on road on MNF since 2008	5-0 ATS vs New England in Playoff since 1995
5-1 O/U on road on MNF since 2015	1-4 S/U & ATS @ Pittsburgh in Playoffs since 1995
	Game 4-0-1 O/U @ Pittsburgh in Playoffs since 1995

Baltimore Ravens

M&T Bank Stadium — *2023 Schedule + Trends & Angles*

AFC North

Coach: John Harbaugh

DATE		OPPONENT	TURF	Bal	OPP	S/U	LINE	ATS	TOT	O/U	Trends & Angles
9/10/2023	vs	HOUSTON	A								6-0 S/U @ home vs Houston since 2005
9/17/2023	@	Cincinnati	A								Game 5-1 O/U @ Cincinnati since 2018
9/24/2023	vs	INDIANAPOLIS	A								4-0 S/U @ home vs Indianapolis since 2011
10/1/2023	@	Cleveland	G								11-4 S/U @ Cleveland since 2008 {11-3-1 ATS}
10/8/2023	@	Pittsburgh	G								6-2-1 ATS @ Pittsburgh since 2015
10/15/2023	@	Tennessee {London}	G								Game 4-11 O/U vs Tennessee since 2001
10/22/2023	vs	*DETROIT*	A								4-0 S/U @ home vs Detroit since 1986
10/29/2023	@	Arizona	G								vs Arizona - Ravens leads series 37-12-3
11/5/2023	vs	*SEATTLE*	A								3-1 S/U @ home vs Seattle since 1994
11/12/2023	vs	CLEVELAND	A								17-3 S/U @ home vs Cleveland since 2003
11/16/2023	vs	CINCINNATI	A								2-7 ATS @ home vs Cincinnati since 2014
11/26/2023	@	Los Angeles Chargers	A								vs Los Angeles - Chargers leads series 15-14-1
12/3/2023		BYE									
12/10/2023	vs	*LOS ANGELES RAMS*	A								3-1 S/U @ home vs Los Angeles Rams since 1996
12/17/2023	@	Jacksonville	G								Game 2-5-1 O/U @ Jacksonville since 1998
12/25/2023	@	*San Francisco*	G								0-3 ATS @ San Francisco since 1996
12/31/2023	vs	MIAMI	A								4-1 S/U @ home vs Miami since 2005
1/7/2024	vs	PITTSBURGH	A								1-5 S/U @ home vs Pittsburgh s/2017 {1-5 ATS}
1/14/2024											AFC Wild Card
1/21/2024											AFC Divisional Playoff
1/28/2024											AFC Championship
2/11/2024											Super Bowl LVIII @ Las Vegas, NV

Pointspread Analysis

vs AFC teams		vs NFC teams
3-11 S/U vs AFC East as 3.5-7 point Dog since 1980		16-0 S/U vs NFC teams as 7.5-10 point favorite since 1980
7-2 S/U vs AFC East as 7.5-10 point favorite since 1989		12-0 S/U vs NFC teams as 10.5 point or more favorite since 1987
1-9 S/U @ home vs AFC East as 3 point or less Dog since 1984		11-3 S/U vs NFC teams as 3 point or less favorite since 2008
6-1 S/U @ home vs AFC East as 3 point or less favorite since 1986	DET, SEA, LAR	31-8 S/U @ home vs NFC since 2003
7-0 S/U @ home vs AFC East as 3.5-7 point favorite since 2000		1-8 S/U vs NFC teams as 10.5 point or more Dog since 1986
Game 7-2 O/U @ home vs Miami since 1990		0-10 S/U vs NFC teams as 7.5-10 point Dog since 1984
9-2 ATS vs Miami since 2009		vs Detroit - HOME team 8-2 S/U since 1986
0-8 S/U vs AFC North as 7.5-10 point Dog since 1978		vs Detroit - Lions lead series 16-9
4-21 S/U on road vs AFC North as 3.5-7 point Dog since 1988		0-4 S/U vs NFC North as 3 point or less Dog since 2005
15-3 S/U on road vs AFC North as 3.5-7 point favorite since 1980		6-0 O/U vs NFC North as 3.5-7 point favorite since 1992
17-0 S/U vs AFC North as 10.5 point or more favorite since 1994		4-0 S/U vs NFC North as 7.5-10 point favorite since 1980
1-7 O/U vs AFC North as 10.5 or more favorite since 2011		0-6 S/U vs NFC West as 7.5 point or more Dog since 1984
24-6 S/U vs Cleveland since 2008		9-1 S/U vs NFC West as 3 point or less favorite since 1982
0-5 S/U vs AFC South as 7.5-10 point Dog since 1993		6-0 S/U vs NFC West as 7.5 point or more favorite since 1994
10-1 S/U on road vs AFC South as 3 point or less favorite since 1994		Game 0-3 O/U @ home vs LA Rams since 2007
9-1-1 ATS on road vs AFC South as 3 point or less favorite since 1994		vs San Francisco - HOME team 8-1 S/U since 1987
16-4 S/U vs AFC South as 7.5 point or more favorite since 1979		Game 0-4 O/U vs Seattle since 2007
Game 0-5-1 O/U @ home vs Houston since 2005		**Grass/Turf**
vs Houston - HOME team 7-1 S/U since 2012		0-7 S/U on grass as 10.5 point or more Dog since 1996
vs Indianapolis - Ravens leads series 22-19		8-1 O/U on grass as 7.5-10 point Dog since 1984
2-6 S/U vs AFC West as 3.5-7 point Dog since 2006		4-17 S/U on grass as 3.5-7 point Dog since 2002
2-6 S/U @ home vs AFC West as 3 point or less Dog since 1978		12-3 O/U on grass as 3.5-7 point Dog since 2006
8-0 S/U vs AFC West as 7.5 point or more favorite since 2000		**Dog**
4-0 S/U & ATS on road vs AFC West as 3 point or less Dog since 2006		4-21 S/U as 10.5 or more Dog since 1979
2-6 O/U on road vs AFC West as 3 point or less favorite since 1983		4-27 S/U as 7.5-10 point Dog since 1984
		6-1 ATS as 7.5-10 point Dog since 2013
10-2 S/U after playing @ Cincinnati since 2005	COLTS	11-34 S/U as 3.5-7 point Dog since 2002
14-3 S/U in 1st home game of season since 2006	TEXANS	12-3 O/U on grass as 3.5-7 point Dog since 2006
5-18 S/U prior to BYE week since 2000	Chargers	**Favorite**
16-4 S/U in final home game of season since 2003	STEELERS	44-10 S/U as 7.5-10 point favorite since 1979
18-8 S/U @ home after allowing 30 pts or more last 23		29-4 S/U @ home as 7.5-10 point favorite since 1999
25-8 S/U @ home after a road loss last 33		40-0 S/U as 10.5 or more favorite since 1999
		3-10 O/U as 10.5 or more favorite since 2011
		31-0 S/U @ home as 10.5 point or more favorite since 1999

 **Buffalo Bills**

 **AFC East**

Last 4 seasons + Pointspread Analysis

	2022									
@	Los Angeles Rams	TH	G	31	10	W	-2.0	W	51.5	U
vs	TENNESSEE	M	A	41	7	W	-10.0	W	47.0	O
@	Miami		G	19	21	L	-4.0	L	54.5	U
@	Baltimore		A	23	20	W	-3.0	T	50.5	U
vs	PITTSBURGH		A	38	3	W	-14.0	W	44.5	U
@	Kansas City		G	24	20	W	-2.5	W	54.0	U
	BYE									
vs	GREEN BAY	Su	A	27	17	W	-10.5	L	47.0	U
@	New York Jets		A	17	20	L	-10.5	L	45.5	U
vs	MINNESOTA {OT}		A	30	33	L	-6.5	L	46.5	O
vs	CLEVELAND {@ Detroit}		A	31	23	W	-7.5	W	50.5	O
@	Detroit	T	A	28	25	W	-9.5	L	54.0	U
@	New England	T	A	24	14	W	-4.0	W	44.0	U
vs	NEW YORK JETS		A	20	12	W	-10.0	L	43.5	U
vs	MIAMI	Sa	A	32	29	W	-7.0	L	45.0	O
@	Chicago	Sa	G	35	13	W	-8.0	W	40.5	O
vs	NEW ENGLAND		A	35	23	W	-8.0	W	44.5	O
vs	**MIAMI**		A	34	31	W	-14.0	L	44.5	O
vs	**CINCINNATI**		A	10	27	L	-6.0	L	48.0	U
	2021									
vs	PITTSBURGH		A	16	23	L	-6.5	L	47.0	U
@	Miami		G	35	0	W	-3.5	W	47.5	U
vs	WASHINGTON		A	43	21	W	-7.0	W	45.5	O
vs	HOUSTON TEXANS		A	40	0	W	-18.5	W	47.5	U
@	Kansas City	Su	G	38	20	W	2.5	W	57.5	O
@	Tennessee	M	G	31	34	L	-6.0	L	53.0	O
	BYE									
vs	MIAMI		A	26	11	W	-14.5	W	48.5	U
@	Jacksonville		G	6	9	L	-14.5	L	48.5	U
@	New York Jets		A	45	17	W	-13.0	W	48.5	O
vs	INDIANAPOLIS		A	16	41	L	-7.0	L	49.5	O
@	New Orleans	T	G	31	6	W	-7.0	W	44.5	U
vs	NEW ENGLAND	M	A	10	14	L	-3.0	L	40.0	U
@	Tampa Bay {OT}		G	27	33	L	3.5	W	53.0	O
vs	CAROLINA		A	31	14	W	-14.5	W	43.0	O
@	New England Patriots		A	33	21	W	1.0	W	43.5	O
vs	ATLANTA		A	29	15	W	-14.0	T	46.5	U
vs	NEW YORK JETS		A	27	10	W	-16.0	W	43.0	U
vs	**NEW ENGLAND**	Sa	A	47	17	W	-4.5	W	43.0	O
@	**Kansas City {OT}**		G	36	42	L	2.5	L	54.0	O

	2020									
vs	N.Y. JETS		A	27	17	W	-6.5	W	39.5	O
@	Miami		G	31	28	W	-5.5	L	42.5	O
vs	L.A. RAMS		A	35	32	W	-1.5	W	46.5	O
@	Las Vegas Raiders		G	30	23	W	-3.0	W	52.5	O
@	Tennessee	Tu	G	16	42	L	-3.0	L	52.0	O
vs	KANSAS CITY	M	A	17	26	L	5.5	L	55.0	U
@	New York Jets		A	18	10	W	-10.0	L	46.5	U
vs	New England		A	24	21	W	-4.0	L	40.5	U
vs	SEATTLE		A	44	34	W	3.0	W	55.0	O
@	Arizona		G	30	32	L	3.0	W	55.5	O
	BYE									
vs	L.A. CHARGERS		A	27	17	W	-4.0	W	51.0	O
@	San Francisco	M	G	34	24	W	2.0	W	48.0	O
vs	PITTSBURGH	Su	A	26	15	W	-1.5	W	49.0	U
@	Denver	Sa	G	48	19	W	-6.0	W	47.5	O
@	New England	M	A	38	9	W	-7.0	T	47.0	T
vs	MIAMI		A	56	26	W	3.5	W	42.5	O
vs	**Indianapolis**	Sa	A	27	24	W	-6.5	L	50.5	O
vs	**Baltimore**	Sa	A	17	3	W	-2.5	W	50.0	U
@	**Kansas City**		G	24	38	L	3.0	L	55.0	O
	2019									
vs	New York Jets		A	17	16	W	2.5	W	41.0	U
@	New York Giants		A	28	14	W	-1.5	W	44.5	U
vs	CINCINNATI		A	21	17	W	-6.0	L	43.5	U
vs	NEW ENGLAND		A	10	16	L	7.0	W	41.5	U
@	Tennessee		G	14	7	W	3.0	W	39.5	U
	BYE									
vs	MIAMI		A	31	21	W	-17.0	L	42.5	O
vs	PHILADELPHIA		A	13	31	L	-1.0	L	38.5	U
vs	WASHINGTON		A	24	9	W	-10.5	W	37.0	U
@	Cleveland		G	16	19	L	3.0	T	42.0	U
@	Miami		G	37	20	W	-7.0	W	41.0	O
vs	DENVER		A	20	3	W	-3.5	W	37.5	U
@	Dallas	T	A	26	15	W	6.5	W	46.5	U
vs	Baltimore		A	17	24	L	6.0	L	44.0	U
@	Pittsburgh		G	17	10	W	1.0	W	37.0	U
@	New England		A	17	24	L	7.0	T	39.0	O
vs	N.Y. JETS		A	6	13	L	1.0	L	36.5	U
@	**Houston**		G	19	22	L	2.5	W	43.0	U

Pointspread Analysis Grass/Turf		
0-8 S/U on grass as 10.5 point or more Dog since 1978	GIANTS	
2-17 S/U on grass as 7.5-10 point Dog since 1987	GIANTS	
6-15 S/U on grass as 3 point or less Dog since 2002 {7-14 ATS}	Bengals	
Dog		
2-27 S/U as a 10.5 point or more Dog since 1978	Bengals	
10-49 S/U as 7.5-10 point Dog since 1978	Bengals	
Favorite	Jets	
1-6 ATS on grass as 7.5-10 point favorite since 1988		
33-8 S/U as 7.5-10 point favorite since 1986		
10-3 O/U as 7.5-10 point favorite since 2005		
33-5 S/U as 10.5 point or more favorite since 1982		
13-5-1 ATS as 10.5 point or more favorite since 1993		
5-18 S/U prior to BYE week since 2000	Eagles	

Pointspread Analysis THU-SAT-SNF-MNF
8-1 S/U @ Home on SNF since 1990
1-6 O/U @ Home on SNF since 1992
2-5 S/U on road on SNF since 2001
1-6 O/U on road on SNF since 2001
0-8 S/U on SNF as 5.5 point or more dog since 1995
7-1-1 O/U on road on MNF since 1997
Playoffs
1-6 S/U on road on Saturday in Playoffs since 1981
13-2 S/U @ home in Playoffs since 1989
0-4 S/U in Super Bowls
4-1 S/U in AFC Championship Since 1990
0-7 S/U on road in Playoffs since 1996
1-5 S/U on road in Divisional Playoffs since 1974
7-0 O/U @ home in WILD Card since 1993
4-1 S/U & ATS @ home in Divisional Playoffs since 1989

Buffalo Bills

Ralph Wilson Stadium

AFC East

2023 Schedule + Trends & Angles

Coach: Sean McDermott

DATE		OPPONENT	TURF	Buff	OPP	S/U	LINE	ATS	TOT	O/U	Trends & Angles
9/11/2023	@	New York Jets	A								4-1 S/U @ NY Jets since 2018
9/17/2023	vs	LAS VEGAS RAIDERS	A								Game 11-1 O/U @ home vs Raiders since 1983
9/24/2023	@	*Washington*	G								8-1 S/U & ATS vs Washington since 1993
10/1/2023	vs	MIAMI	A								11-1 S/U @ home vs Miami since 2012
10/8/2023	vs	JACKSONVILLE {London}	A								3-0 S/U @ home vs Jacksonville since 2012
10/15/2023	vs	*NEW YORK GIANTS*	A								0-4 ATS @ home vs New York Giants since 1993
10/22/2023	@	New England	A								5-17 S/U @ New England since 2001
10/26/2023	vs	*TAMPA BAY*	A								vs Tampa Bay - Tampa Bay leads series 8-4
11/5/2023	@	Cincinnati	A								vs Cincinnati - Bills lead series 17-16
11/13/2023	vs	DENVER	A								7-0 ATS vs Denver since 2007
11/19/2023	vs	NEW YORK JETS	A								vs NY Jets - Buffalo leads series 67-57
11/26/2023	@	*Philadelphia*	G								Game 1-4 O/U @ Philadelphia since 1987
12/3/2023		BYE									
12/10/2023	@	Kansas City	G								vs Kansas City - Buffalo leads series 28-24-1
12/17/2023	vs	*DALLAS*	A								4-0 ATS @ home vs Dallas since 1984
12/23/2023	@	Los Angeles Chargers	A								0-6 S/U @ L.A. Chargers s/1985 {1-5 ATS}
12/31/2023	vs	NEW ENGLAND	A								4-16 S/U @ home vs New England since 2004
1/7/2024	@	Miami	G								3-1 S/U @ Miami since 2019
1/14/2024											AFC Wild Card
1/21/2024											AFC Divisional Playoff
1/28/2024											AFC Championship
2/11/2024											Super Bowl LVIII @ Las Vegas, NV

Pointspread Analysis

vs AFC teams		vs AFC teams
0-15 S/U vs AFC East as 10.5 or more Dog since 1978		4-14 O/U vs AFC South as 3 point or less Dog since 1985
1-9 S/U @ home vs AFC East as 7.5-10 point Dog since 1978		14-5 S/U @ home vs AFC South as 3.5-7 point favorite since 1981
2-10 S/U on road vs AFC East as 7.5-10 point Dog since 1984		Game 5-0 O/U @ home vs Jacksonville since 2006
3-18 S/U @ home vs AFC East as 3.5-7 point Dog since 1978		3-0 S/U vs Jacksonville as 3 point or less Dog since 1998
6-1 S/U & ATS vs AFC East as 3 point or less Dog since 2013		3-0 ATS vs Jacksonville as 3 point or less Dog since 1998
13-3 S/U on road vs AFC East as 3.5-7 point favorite since 1980		2-8 S/U vs AFC West as 7.5 point or more Dog since 1979
11-1 S/U vs AFC East as 7.5-10 point favorite since 1989		2-16 S/U vs AFC West as 3.5-7 point Dog since 1987
Game 8-1 O/U @ home vs Miami since 2015		9-2 S/U & ATS vs AFC West as 3 point or less favorite since 1994
11-2 S/U vs Miami since 2017		6-0 S/U vs AFC West as 8 point or more favorite since 1992
5-14-1 ATS @ home vs New England since 2004		1-6 S/U vs Kansas City as 3.5-7 point Dog since 1997
10-35 S/U vs New England since 2001 {4 W} {4-31 S/U as Dog}		7-1 S/U & ATS vs Kansas City as 3 point or less favorite since 1994
0-3 S/U vs Miami as 10.5 point or more Dog since 1978		Game 3-1 O/U @ Kansas City since 2021
1-5 S/U vs Miami as 7.5-10 point Dog since 1978		0-5 S/U vs L.A. Chargers as 3.5-7 point Dog since 1985
1-7 S/U & ATS @ Miami as 3 point or less Dog since 1981		Game 7-0 O/U vs Las Vegas Raiders since 2005
1-7 O/U @ Miami as 3 point or less favorite since 1990		0-3 S/U & ATS vs Las Vegas Raiders as 3 point or less Dog since 2002
1-6 O/U @ home vs Miami as 3 point or less favorite since 2003		3-0 O/U vs Las Vegas Raiders as 3 point or less Dog since 2002
14-3 S/U @ home vs Miami as 3.5-7 point favorite since 1981		3-0 S/U @ home vs Las Vegas Raiders as 3 point or less favorite since 1980
7-0 O/U @ home vs Miami as 3.5-7 point favorite since 2004		0-4 ATS @ home vs Las Vegas Raiders as 3.5-7 point favorite since 1993
5-2 O/U @ Miami as 3.5-7 point favorite since 1989		5-1 O/U @ home vs Las Vegas Raiders as 3.5-7 point favorite since 1988
6-1 S/U @ Miami as 3.5-7 point favorite since 1989		1-4 S/U & ATS vs LA Chargers since 2011
4-34 S/U vs New England since 2001 {3-31 S/U as Dog}		0-3 S/U vs Denver as 7.5-10 point Dog since 2002
3-10-3 ATS as 3.5-7 point Dog vs New England since 2002		**vs NFC teams**
0-12 S/U vs New England as 10.5 point or more Dog since 1978		1-5 S/U vs NFC teams as 10.5 point or more Dog since 1984
1-10 S/U vs New England as 7.5-10 point Dog since 1985		2-8 S/U vs NFC teams as 3 point or less Dog since 2005 {2-7-1 ATS}
0-6 S/U @ New England as 7.5-10 point Dog since 1985		1-7-1 ATS vs NFC as 3 point or less Dog since 2005
0-11 S/U @ home vs New England as 3.5-7 point Dog since 1979		10-1 S/U vs NFC teams as 7.5-10 point favorite since 1991
2-7 O/U @ New England as 3.5-7 point Dog since 2001		9-0 S/U vs NFC teams as 10.5 point or more favorite since 1990
5-0 S/U vs New England as 10.5 point or more favorite since 1990		7-1-1 ATS vs NFC teams as 10.5 point or more favorite since 1990
0-3 S/U vs New York Jets as 7.5-10 point Dog since 1985		Game 3-9 O/U vs Dallas since 1976
5-1 ATS vs New York Jets as 3.5-7 point Dog since 2001		0-4 ATS vs New York Giants as 3.5-7 point favorite since 1991
5-1 S/U & ATS vs NY Jets as 3 point or less Dog since 2013		1-3 S/U vs New York Giants since 2007
0-5 S/U @ New York Jets as 3 point or less favorite since 1994		vs Giants - ROAD team 6-0 ATS since 1999
9-0 S/U vs New York Jets as 7.5-10 point favorite since 1990		Game 5-1 O/U @ Washington since 1972
3-19 S/U vs AFC North as 3.5-10 point Dog since 1978		0-4 S/U vs Tampa Bay as 3 point or less Dog since 1982
24-6 S/U vs AFC North as 3 point or more favorite since 1978		**THU-SAT-SNF-MNF**
Game 0-3 O/U @ Cincinnati since 2011	Buccaneers	0-5 O/U on Thursday since 2019
1-5 S/U vs Cincinnati as 3.5-7 point Dog since 1985	Buccaneers	5-0 S/U on Thursday since 2019 {4-1 ATS}
4-1 S/U vs Cincinnati as 3.5-7 point favorite since 1989	Buccaneers	1-4 ATS @ home on Thursday since 1981
1-7 S/U vs AFC South as 7.5 point or more Dog since 1978	Chargers	8-0 O/U on Saturday as 3.5-7 point favorite since 1991
2-8 S/U vs AFC South as 3.5-7 point Dog since 1997	Chargers	6-0 S/U on Saturday since 2020

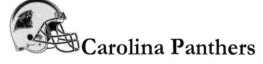 

Last 4 seasons + Pointspread Analysis

	2022									
vs	CLEVELAND		G	24	26	L	-1.5	L	42.0	O
@	New York Giants		A	16	19	L	-1.0	L	43.5	U
vs	NEW ORLEANS		G	22	14	W	2.0	W	41.0	U
vs	ARIZONA		G	16	26	L	-1.0	L	44.0	U
vs	SAN FRANCISCO		G	15	37	L	6.0	L	39.5	U
@	Los Angeles Rams		A	10	24	L	10.0	L	40.5	U
vs	TAMPA BAY		G	21	3	W	13.0	W	38.0	U
@	Atlanta {OT}	T	A	34	37	L	4.0	W	41.5	U
@	Cincinnati		A	21	42	L	7.0	L	42.5	U
vs	ATLANTA		G	25	15	W	2.5	W	41.5	U
@	Baltimore		A	3	13	L	13.0	W	41.5	U
vs	DENVER		G	23	10	W	PK	W	36.5	U
	BYE									
@	Seattle		A	30	24	W	4.0	W	43.5	O
vs	PITTSBURGH		G	16	24	L	-2.5	L	36.5	U
vs	DETROIT	Sa	G	37	23	W	1.5	W	43.5	O
@	Tampa Bay		G	24	30	L	3.0	L	41.0	U
@	New Orleans		A	10	7	W	3.5	W	41.5	U
	2021									
vs	NEW YORK JETS		G	19	14	W	-3.5	W	44.5	U
vs	NEW ORLEANS		G	26	7	W	3.0	W	45.0	U
@	Houston	T	G	24	9	W	-8.5	W	43.5	U
@	Dallas		A	28	36	L	5.0	L	51.5	O
vs	PHILADELPHIA		G	18	21	L	-2.5	L	46.5	U
vs	MINNESOTA {OT}		G	28	34	L	2.0	L	45.0	O
@	New York Giants		A	3	25	L	-3.0	L	43.0	U
@	Atlanta		A	19	13	W	2.5	W	46.5	U
vs	NEW ENGLAND		G	6	24	L	3.0	L	41.5	U
@	Arizona		G	34	10	W	7.0	W	41.0	O
vs	WASHINGTON		G	21	27	L	-3.5	L	43.5	O
@	Miami		G	10	33	L	PK	L	40.5	O
	BYE									
vs	ATLANTA		G	21	29	L	-2.5	L	42.0	O
@	Buffalo		A	14	31	L	14.5	L	43.0	O
vs	TAMPA BAY		G	6	32	L	10.5	L	44.5	U
@	New Orleans		A	10	18	L	7.0	L	37.0	U
@	Tampa Bay		G	17	41	L	10.5	L	43.0	O

	2020									
vs	LAS VEGAS		G	30	34	L	2.5	L	48.0	O
@	Tampa Bay		G	17	31	L	7.5	L	46.5	O
@	L.A. Chargers		G	21	16	W	6.0	W	44.0	U
vs	Arizona		G	31	21	W	3.0	W	52.0	T
@	Atlanta		A	23	16	W	2.5	W	54.0	U
vs	CHICAGO		G	16	23	L	-2.0	L	45.5	U
@	New Orleans		A	24	27	L	6.5	W	50.5	O
vs	ATLANTA	T	G	17	25	L	-1.0	L	52.0	U
@	Kansas City		G	31	33	L	10.0	W	51.5	O
vs	TAMPA BAY		G	23	46	L	6.0	L	49.5	O
vs	DETROIT		G	20	0	W	3.0	W	47.0	U
@	Minnesota		A	27	28	L	2.5	W	50.0	O
	BYE									
vs	DENVER		G	27	32	L	-4.0	L	46.0	O
@	Green Bay	Sa	G	16	24	L	9.5	W	53.0	O
@	Washington		G	20	13	W	-1.0	W	41.5	U
vs	NEW ORLEANS		G	7	33	L	5.5	L	46.5	O
	2019									
vs	L.A. RAMS		G	27	30	L	1.5	L	49.5	O
vs	TAMPA BAY	T	G	14	20	L	-6.5	L	48.0	U
@	Arizona		G	38	20	W	2.0	W	46.0	O
@	Houston		G	16	10	W	5.0	W	48.0	U
vs	JACKSONVILLE		G	34	27	W	-3.0	W	40.5	O
vs	Tampa Bay {London}		G	37	26	W	-2.0	W	48.0	O
	BYE									
@	San Francisco		G	13	51	L	4.5	L	40.5	O
vs	Tennessee		G	30	20	W	-3.5	W	43.0	O
@	Green Bay		G	16	24	L	5.0	L	49.0	U
vs	ATLANTA		G	3	29	L	-3.5	L	48.5	U
@	New Orleans		A	31	34	L	10.0	W	46.5	O
vs	WASHINGTON		G	21	29	L	-10.5	L	39.5	O
@	Atlanta		A	20	40	L	3.5	L	48.0	O
vs	SEATTLE		G	24	30	L	6.0	T	48.5	O
@	Indianapolis		A	6	38	L	7.0	L	46.5	U
vs	NEW ORLEANS		G	10	42	L	13.5	L	45.5	O

Pointspread Analysis Dog	
2-8 ATS as 10.5 point or more Dog since 2010	Bears
1-16 S/U as 10.5 point or more Dog since 2001	FALCONS
10-1 O/U as 7.5-10 point dog since 2011	FALCONS
13-40-1 S/U as 3.5-7 point Dog since 2007	SAINTS
Favorite	
0-7 S/U & ATS as 3 point or less favorite since 2021	
9-3 S/U on Turf as 3.5-7 point favorite since 2003	
15-3-1 ATS as 7.5 or more favorite since 2005	
27-3 S/U as 7.5 point or more favorite since 1996	

Pointspread Analysis THU-SAT-SNF-MNF
4-1 O/U on road on Thursday since 2013
4-0 O/U @ home on Saturday since 2011
0-4 S/U on Saturday as 3.5 point or more dog since 2004
6-2 S/U @ home on MNF since 2005
Playoffs
0-3 S/U on road in Playoffs since 2006
4-0 O/U on road in Playoffs since 2005
3-0 S/U @ home in Playoffs since 2015
3-0 O/U @ home in Playoffs since 2015

Carolina Panthers
NFC South

Bank of America Stadium   *2023 Schedule + Trends & Angles*   **Coach: Frank Reich**

DATE		OPPONENT	TURF	Car	OPP	S/U	LINE	ATS	TOT	O/U	Trends & Angles
9/10/2023	@	Atlanta	A								vs New Orleans - Saints lead series 29-27
9/18/2023	vs	NEW ORLEANS	G								Game 0-3 O/U @ home vs New Orleans since 2020
9/24/2023	@	Seattle	A								2-5 SU @ Seattle since 2004
10/1/2023	vs	MINNESOTA	G								vs Minnesota - Vikings lead series 10-6
10/8/2023	@	Detroit	A								8-2 S/U vs Detroit since 2002
10/15/2023	@	*Miami*	G								0-4 ATS @ Miami since 2001
10/22/2023		BYE									
10/29/2023	vs	*HOUSTON*	G								4-0 S/U & ATS vs Houston since 2011
11/5/2023	vs	*INDIANAPOLIS*	G								vs Indianapolis - Carolina leads series 5-2
11/9/2023	@	Chicago	G								1-5 S/U @ Chicago since 1995 {4-2 ATS}
11/19/2023	vs	DALLAS	G								1-4 S/U @ home vs Dallas since 2005
11/26/2023	@	*Tennessee*	G								Game 0-3 O/U @ Tennessee since 1996
12/3/2023	@	Tampa Bay	G								0-4 S/U & ATS @ Tampa Bay since 2018
12/10/2023	@	New Orleans	A								Game 8-2 O/U @ New Orleans since 2014
12/16/2023	vs	ATLANTA	G								vs Atlanta - Falcons leads series 35-21
12/24/2023	vs	GREEN BAY	G								Game 4-0 O/U @ home vs Green Bay since 2005
12/31/2023	@	*Jacksonville*	G								3-0 S/U vs Jacksonville since 2003 {3-0 ATS}
1/7/2024	vs	TAMPA BAY	G								2-5 ATS @ home vs Tampa Bay since 2016
1/14/2024											NFC Wild Card
1/21/2024											NFC Divisional Playoff
1/28/2024											NFC Championship
2/11/2024											Super Bowl LVIII @ Las Vegas, NV

Pointspread Analysis vs NFC teams	Pointspread Analysis vs NFC teams
0-3 S/U vs Dallas as 3 point or less Dog since 2002	3-0 S/U & ATS @ home vs New Orleans as 3 point or less favorite s/1998
3-0 S/U & ATS vs Dallas as 3 point or less favorite since 2004	0-7 ATS vs New Orleans as 3.5-7 point favorite since 1998
0-3 S/U & ATS vs Dallas as 3.5-7 point favorite since 2000	1-5 O/U @ home vs New Orleans as 3.5-7 point favorite since 1996
2-10 S/U vs Dallas since 1998 (Reg. season)	3-0 S/U vs New Orleans as 7.5-10 point favorite since 2005
vs Dallas - Cowboys lead series 10-5	1-3 O/U vs Tampa Bay as 7.5-10 point Dog since 2002
1-11 S/U vs NFC North as 3.5-7 point Dog since 1996	1-8 O/U @ home vs Tampa Bay as 3.5-7 point favorite since 1996
9-1 O/U vs NFC North as 3 point or less Dog since 2008	4-1 ATS vs Tampa Bay as 3.5-7 point Dog since 1998
10-3 S/U & ATS vs NFC North as 3 point or less Dog since 2000	4-0 S/U vs Tampa Bay as 7.5-10 point favorite since 2006
4-0 S/U vs NFC North as 7.5 point or more favorite since 2003	8-3 ATS vs NFC West as 7.5-10 point Dog since 1996
1-5 S/U vs Chicago since 2010	12-2 S/U vs NFC West as 3.5-7 point favorite since 1996
Game 8-1 O/U vs Green Bay since 2005	0-7 S/U @ home vs NFC West as 3.5-7 point Dog since 1995
4-0 O/U vs Green Bay as 7.5-10 point Dog since 1999	Game 7-0 O/U @ Seattle since 2004
0-6 S/U vs Green Bay as 3.5-7 point Dog since 1997	Game 7-0 O/U vs Seattle since 2015
3-0 S/U & ATS vs Green Bay as 3 point or less Dog since 2000	**vs AFC teams**
3-0 S/U vs Green Bay as 3 point or less Dog since 2000	0-6 S/U vs AFC teams as 10.5 or more Dog since 2007
0-3 O/U vs Minnesota as 3.5-7 point Dog since 1996	11-0 S/U vs AFC teams as 7.5 point or more favorite since 1996
5-0 O/U vs Minnesota as 3 point or less Dog since 2013	1-6 ATS vs Miami since 1998
3-11 S/U vs NFC South as 7.5 point or more Dog since 1995	vs Miami - Dolphins lead series 5-2
4-17 S/U vs NFC South as 3.5-7 point Dog since 2009	Game 0-4 O/U @ Houston since 2003
8-2 O/U on road vs NFC South as 3 point or less favorite since 2005	Game 0-4 O/U vs Houston since 2011
5-2 S/U @ home vs NFC South as 3 point or less favorite since 1998	**Grass/Turf**
5-2 ATS @ home vs NFC South as 3 point or less favorite since 1998	29-9-1 O/U on Turf last 39 times
1-9 ATS vs NFC South as 3.5-7 point favorite since 2013	0-8 S/U on Turf as 10.5 or more Dog since 2001
3-21 O/U @ home vs NFC South as 3.5-7 point favorite since 1996	13-5 O/U on Turf as 7.5-10 point Dog since 1995
6-1 S/U on road vs NFC South as 3.5-7 point favorite since 2006	5-13 O/U on Turf as 7.5-10 point Dog since 1995
8-25 O/U vs NFC South as 3.5-7 point favorite since 1996	4-19-1 S/U on Turf as 3.5-7 point Dog since 2008
9-0 S/U vs NFC South as 7.5-10 point favorite since 2005	20-4 O/U on Turf as 3.5-7 point Dog since 2008
1-10 S/U vs Atlanta as 3.5-7 point Dog since 2001	13-5 ATS on road on grass as 3.5-7 point Dog since 2011
0-3 S/U & ATS @ Atlanta as 3 point or less favorite since 2000	10-3 S/U on road on grass as 3 point or less Dog since 1997
2-6 O/U vs Atlanta as 3 point or less favorite since 1996	7-1 O/U on Turf as 3 point or less favorite since 2006
0-5 O/U vs Atlanta as 3.5-7 point favorite since 2007	
3-0 S/U & ATS vs Atlanta as 7.5-10 point favorite since 1997	
0-3 O/U vs Atlanta as 7.5-10 point favorite since 1997	
5-0 O/U @ New Orleans as 7.5-10 point Dog since 2001	
0-6 S/U @ home vs New Orleans as 3.5-7 point Dog since 2001	

Chicago Bears   NFC North

Last 4 seasons + Pointspread Analysis

2022

	Team	Day		PF	PA	W/L	Spread	ATS	Total	O/U
vs	SAN FRANCISCO		G	19	10	W	6.5	W	38.5	U
@	Green Bay	Su	G	10	27	L	10.0	L	42.0	U
vs	HOUSTON		G	23	20	W	-3.0	T	39.5	O
@	New York Giants		A	12	20	L	3.0	L	39.5	U
@	Minnesota		A	22	29	L	8.5	W	43.5	O
vs	WASHINGTON	T	G	7	12	L	1.0	L	39.0	U
@	New England	M	A	33	14	W	8.5	W	40.0	U
@	Dallas		A	29	49	L	9.5	L	43.0	O
vs	MIAMI		G	32	35	L	3.5	W	46.0	O
vs	DETROIT		G	30	31	L	-3.0	L	48.0	O
@	Atlanta		A	24	27	L	2.0	L	48.0	O
@	New York Jets		A	10	31	L	7.5	L	36.5	U
vs	GREEN BAY		G	19	28	L	3.5	L	44.5	O
	BYE									
vs	PHILADELPHIA		G	20	25	L	8.5	W	47.5	U
vs	BUFFALO	Sa	G	13	35	L	8.0	L	40.5	O
@	Detroit		A	10	41	L	4.0	L	52.0	O
vs	MINNESOTA		G	13	29	L	6.0	L	42.5	U

2021

	Team	Day		PF	PA	W/L	Spread	ATS	Total	O/U
@	Los Angeles Rams	Su	A	14	34	L	9.5	L	46.5	O
vs	CINCINNATI		G	20	17	W	-2.0	W	44.5	U
@	Cleveland		G	6	26	L	7.5	L	45.0	U
vs	DETROIT		G	24	14	W	-3.0	W	41.5	U
@	Las Vegas Raiders		G	20	9	W	5.5	W	45.0	U
vs	GREEN BAY		G	14	24	L	5.5	L	44.0	U
@	Tampa Bay		G	3	38	L	12.0	L	47.0	U
vs	SAN FRANCISCO		G	22	33	L	4.5	L	40.0	O
@	Pittsburgh	M	G	27	29	L	7.0	W	39.5	O
	BYE									
vs	BALTIMORE		G	13	22	L	1.0	L	40.0	U
@	Detroit	T	A	16	14	W	-2.5	L	41.5	U
vs	ARIZONA		G	22	33	L	7.5	L	43.0	O
@	Green Bay	Su	G	30	45	L	12.0	L	43.0	O
vs	MINNESOTA	M	G	9	17	L	7.0	L	47.5	U
@	Seattle		A	25	24	W	7.0	W	41.0	O
vs	N.Y. GIANTS		G	29	3	W	-6.5	W	36.5	O
@	Minnesota		A	17	31	L	3.5	L	45.0	O

2020

	Team	Day		PF	PA	W/L	Spread	ATS	Total	O/U
@	Detroit		A	27	23	W	2.5	W	42.5	O
vs	N.Y. GIANTS		G	17	13	W	-4.5	L	42.5	U
@	Atlanta		A	30	26	W	2.5	W	46.5	O
vs	INDIANAPOLIS		G	11	19	L	3.5	L	43.5	U
vs	TAMPA BAY	T	G	20	19	W	3.5	W	44.0	U
@	Carolina		G	23	16	W	2.0	W	45.5	U
vs	L.A. Rams	M	G	10	24	L	6.5	L	44.0	U
vs	NEW ORLEANS {OT}		G	23	26	L	5.0	W	41.0	O
@	Tennessee		G	17	24	L	6.0	L	47.0	U
vs	MINNESOTA	M	G	13	19	L	3.0	L	44.0	U
	BYE									
@	Green Bay	Su	G	25	41	L	7.5	L	44.5	O
vs	DETROIT		G	30	34	L	-3.0	L	44.0	O
vs	HOUSTON		G	36	7	W	1.0	W	46.0	U
@	Minnesota		A	33	27	W	2.5	W	47.0	O
@	Jacksonville		G	41	17	W	-9.5	W	47.0	O
vs	GREEN BAY		G	16	35	L	5.0	L	48.5	O
@	New Orleans		A	9	21	L	11.0	L	47.5	U

2019

	Team	Day		PF	PA	W/L	Spread	ATS	Total	O/U
vs	GREEN BAY	T	G	3	10	L	-3.0	L	46.5	U
@	Denver		G	16	14	W	-2.5	L	40.0	U
@	Washington	M	G	31	15	W	-5.0	W	41.0	O
vs	MINNESOTA		G	16	6	W	PK	W	38.0	U
vs	Oakland {London}		G	21	24	L	-6.5	L	40.0	O
	BYE									
vs	NEW ORLEANS		G	25	36	L	-4.0	L	37.0	O
vs	L.A. CHARGERS		G	16	17	L	-3.5	L	41.0	U
@	Philadelphia		G	14	22	L	5.0	L	41.0	U
vs	DETROIT		G	20	13	W	-6.5	W	38.0	U
@	L.A. Rams	Su	G	7	17	L	5.5	L	39.5	U
vs	N.Y. GIANTS		G	19	14	W	-6.0	L	40.5	U
@	Detroit	T	A	24	20	W	-5.5	L	37.5	O
vs	DALLAS	T	G	31	24	W	3.0	W	43.0	O
@	Green Bay		G	13	21	L	4.0	L	40.5	U
vs	KANSAS CITY		G	3	23	L	6.5	L	45.5	U
@	Minnesota		A	21	19	W	-5.5	L	35.5	O

Pointspread Analysis

Grass/Turf		THU-SAT-SNF-MNF
1-17 S/U on Turf as 10.5 point or more Dog since 1980	Commanders	3-11 ATS on road on Thursday since 1991
0-7 O/U on Turf as 10.5 point or more Dog since 2007	Commanders	3-8 O/U on road on Thursday since 2009
1-10 S/U on grass as 10.5 point or more Dog since 1995	Commanders	0-5 S/U & ATS on road on Thursday as 3.5-7 point dog since 1994
8-3 ATS on Turf as 7.5-10 point Dog since 2004	Commanders	4-0 S/U on road on Thursday as 3 point or less favorite since 1985
6-30 S/U on Turf as 3.5-7 point Dog since 1998	PANTHERS	8-3-1 S/U @ home on Thursday since 1928
3-24 S/U on road on grass as 3.5-7 point Dog since 2001	Browns	1-6 S/U on road on Saturday since 1965
2-8-1 ATS on Turf as 3 point or less favorite since 1995	Browns	0-4 S/U & ATS on Saturday as 3 point or less dog since 1990
13-1 S/U on Turf as 3.5-7 point favorite since 1989	Chargers	9-1 O/U on road on SNF since 2013
6-21 ATS on road on grass as 3.5-7 point Dog since 2001	Chargers	0-4 S/U & ATS on SNF as 7.5-10 point dog since 2014
Dog	Chargers	2-13 S/U on SNF as 3.5-7 point dog since 1989
2-27 S/U as 10.5 point or more Dog since 1980	Vikings	11-3 ATS on road on MNF since 2006
3-12 O/U as 10.5 point or more Dog since 2002	Vikings	5-16 S/U on MNF as 3.5-7 point dog since 1978
1-13 S/U as 7.5-10 point Dog since 2016		8-1 ATS vs Minnesota on MNF since 1995
13-65 S/U as 3.5-7 point Dog since 2004		4-1 S/U @ Minnesota on MNF since 1991
11-56 S/U on road as 3.5-7 point Dog since 1998		5-0 ATS @ Minnesota on MNF since 1991
Favorite		**Playoffs**
49-13 S/U as 3.5-7 point favorite since 2001		0-3 O/U @ home in WILD Card since 1991
20-2 S/U on road as 3.5-7 point favorite since 2005		5-0 O/U in Divisional Playoffs since 1995
33-5 S/U as 7.5-10 point favorite since 1984		1-4 S/U on road in Divisional Playoffs since 1950
28-2 S/U as 10.5 point or more favorite since 1985		0-3 S/U & ATS vs San Francisco in Playoffs since 1984
		0-3 S/U @ home vs Washington in Playoffs since 1937
20-4 S/U after playing Minnesota last 23	RAIDERS	3-1 S/U & ATS @ Washington in Playoffs since 1940

DATE		OPPONENT	TURF	CHI	OPP	S/U	LINE	ATS	TOT	O/U	Trends & Angles
9/10/2023	vs	**GREEN BAY**	G								1-13 S/U @ home vs Green Bay since 2011
9/17/2023	@	Tampa Bay	G								vs Tampa Bay - Chicago leads series 40-21
9/24/2023	@	*Kansas City*	G								Game 0-7 O/U vs Kansas City since 1996
10/1/2023	vs	*DENVER*	G								5-1 ATS vs Denver since 1996
10/5/2023	@	Washington	G								2-7 S/U @ Washington since 1989
10/15/2023	vs	**MINNESOTA**	G								Game 1-8 O/U @ home vs Minnesota since 2014
10/22/2023	vs	*LAS VEGAS RAIDERS*	G								3-0 S/U & ATS @ home vs Raiders since 1996
10/29/2023	@	*Los Angeles Chargers*	A								6-2 S/U & ATS vs L.A. Chargers since 1993
11/5/2023	@	New Orleans	A								1-5 S/U @ New Orleans since 1992
11/9/2023	vs	**CAROLINA**	G								3-1 S/U @ Minnesota since 2018
11/19/2023	@	Detroit	A								4-1 S/U @ Detroit since 2018
11/27/2023	@	Minnesota	A								vs Minnesota - Vikings lead series 65-57-2
12/3/2023		BYE									
12/10/2023	vs	**DETROIT**	G								vs Detroit - Chicago leads series 103-78-5
12/16/2023	@	*Cleveland*	G								vs Cleveland - Chicago leads series 4-2
12/24/2023	vs	**ARIZONA**	G								vs Arizona - Chicago leads series 59-29-6
12/31/2023	vs	**ATLANTA**	G								vs Atlanta - Bears leads series 15-13
1/7/2024	@	Green Bay	G								2-13 S/U @ Green Bay since 2008
1/14/2024											NFC Wild Card
1/21/2024											NFC Divisional Playoff
1/28/2024											NFC Championship
2/11/2024											Super Bowl LVIII @ Las Vegas, NV

Pointspread Analysis	Pointspread Analysis
vs NFC teams	**vs NFC teams**
0-4 S/U vs NFC East as 10.5 point or more Dog since 1981	6-0 S/U vs Minnesota as 3.5-7 point favorite since 2002
2-11 S/U vs NFC East as 3.5-7 point Dog since 1994	0-8 O/U vs NFC South as 3.5-7 point Dog since 2002
5-1 O/U on road vs NFC East as 3 point or less Dog since 1984	0-9 S/U vs NFC South as 3.5-7 point Dog since 2002
1-7 S/U & ATS vs NFC East as 3 point or less favorite since 2000	15-5 S/U vs NFC South as 3.5-7 point favorite since 1990
2-8 ATS vs NFC East as 3.5-7 point favorite since 1992	12-1 S/U vs NFC South as 7.5 point or more favorite since 1985
5-0 ATS vs Washington as 3.5-7 point Dog since 1978	6-1 S/U @ home vs NFC South as 3 point or less Dog since 1978
0-5 S/U & ATS vs Washington as 3 point or less Dog since 1991	0-3 S/U vs Atlanta as 3.5-7 point Dog since 1980
0-4 S/U & ATS vs Washington as 3 point or less favorite since 1989	6-1 S/U vs Atlanta as 3 point or less Dog since 1978
vs Washington - Commanders lead series 27-24-1	4-0 S/U vs Atlanta as 3.5-7 point favorite since 1992
1-20 S/U on road vs NFC North as 3.5-7 point Dog since 1998	0-7 S/U vs New Orleans since 2011
2-33 S/U vs NFC North as 3.5-7 point Dog since 2001	Game 1-4 O/U vs New Orleans since 2011
5-16 ATS on road vs NFC North as 3.5-7 point Dog since 2006	0-4 S/U & ATS vs New Orleans as 3.5-7 point Dog since 1992
3-10 S/U vs NFC North as 3 point or less Dog since 2012	5-0 S/U vs New Orleans as 3 point or less favorite since 1984
22-2 S/U vs NFC North as 3.5-7 point favorite since 2001	0-3 S/U @ Tampa Bay as 7.5-10 point Dog since 1997
17-0 S/U on road vs NFC North as 3.5-7 point favorite since 1984	2-6 S/U & ATS vs Tampa Bay as 3.5-7 point Dog since 1998
13-1 S/U vs NFC North as 7.5-10 point favorite since 1984	4-0 S/U vs Tampa Bay as 7.5-10 point favorite since 1985
6-0 S/U vs NFC North as 7.5-10 point favorite since 1990	4-0 O/U vs Tampa Bay as 7.5-10 point favorite since 1985
10-0 S/U vs NFC North as 10.5 point or more favorite since 1986	5-1 S/U & ATS vs Tampa Bay as 10.5 point or more favorite s/1986
Game 1-5 O/U @ Detroit since 2016	0-7 S/U vs NFC West as 9.0 point or more Dog since 1985
2-10 ATS @ home vs Green Bay since 2011	1-6 O/U vs NFC West as 9.0 point or more Dog since 1985
3-24 S/U vs Green Bay as Dog since 2008	4-11 S/U vs NFC West as 3 point or less Dog since 1981
3-0 ATS vs Detroit as 7.5-10 point Dog since 2000	8-1 S/U vs NFC West as 7.5 point or more Favorite since 1986
0-12 S/U @ Detroit as 3.5-7 point Dog since 1981	7-2 O/U vs NFC West as 3.5-7 point Dog since 2003
2-6 S/U @ Detroit as 3 point or less Dog since 1983	6-0 S/U vs Arizona as 3.5-7 point favorite since 1979
9-0 S/U @ Detroit as 3.5-7 point favorite since 1984	**vs AFC teams**
1-7 ATS @ home vs Detroit as 3.5-7 point favorite since 1992	11-4 S/U vs AFC teams as 3.5-7 point favorite since 1989
0-7 O/U @ home vs Detroit as 3.5-7 point favorite since 1995	7-0 S/U vs AFC West as 3 point or less favorite since 1987
8-0 S/U vs Detroit as 7.5-10 point favorite since 1985	6-1 ATS vs AFC West as 3 point or less favorite since 1987
4-0 O/U @ home vs Detroit as 7.5-10 point favorite since 1990	6-2-1 ATS vs Las Vegas as Dog since 1981
3-0 S/U vs Detroit as 10.5 point or more favorite since 1986	0-4 O/U vs AFC West as 7.5-10 point Dog since 1996
0-6 S/U vs Green Bay as 10.5 point or more Dog since 1997	0-6 O/U vs AFC West as 3 point or less Dog since 1990
0-17 S/U vs Green Bay as 3.5-7 point Dog since 2001	10-3 S/U & ATS vs AFC West as 3.5-7 point favorite since 1983
1-7 S/U @ home vs Green Bay as 3 point or less Dog since 1984	3-0 O/U vs Las Vegas Raiders as 3.5-7 point Dog since 1999
0-5 S/U & ATS vs Green Bay as 3 point or less favorite since 1995	7-0 S/U vs AFC West as 3 point or less favorite since 1987
4-0 S/U & ATS @ Green Bay as 3.5-7 point favorite since 1988	6-1 ATS vs AFC West as 3 point or less favorite since 1987
4-0 S/U vs Green Bay as 10.5 point or more favorite since 1986	0-3 S/U vs Denver as 3 point or less Dog since 1987
0-4 S/U @ Minnesota as 10.5 point or more Dog since 2004	4-0 S/U vs Denver as 3 point or less favorite since 1983
1-7 S/U @ Minnesota as 3.5-7 point Dog since 2000	3-1 S/U vs Denver as 3 point or less favorite since 1983
1-8 O/U vs Minnesota as 3 point or less Dog since 2001	4-1 ATS vs Kansas City as 7.5-10 point Dog since 1981
7-1 S/U & ATS vs Minnesota as 3 point or less favorite since 1991	1-7 O/U vs Denver since 1990

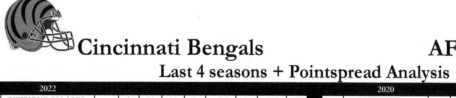
Cincinnati Bengals

AFC North

Last 4 seasons + Pointspread Analysis

	2022									
vs	PITTSBURGH {OT}		A	20	23	L	-7.0	L	45.0	U
@	Dallas		A	17	20	L	-7.0	L	42.0	U
@	New York Jets		A	27	12	W	-6.5	W	45.5	U
vs	MIAMI	T	A	27	15	W	-4.0	W	48.5	U
@	Baltimore Ravens	Su	A	17	19	L	3.0	W	47.5	U
@	New Orleans		A	30	26	W	-3.0	W	43.0	O
vs	ATLANTA		A	35	17	W	-6.5	W	47.5	O
@	Cleveland	M	G	13	32	L	-3.0	L	45.0	T
vs	CAROLINA		A	42	21	W	-7.0	W	42.5	O
	BYE									
@	Pittsburgh {OT}		G	37	30	W	-3.5	W	48.5	U
@	Tennessee		G	20	16	W	PK	W	42.5	U
vs	KANSAS CITY		A	27	24	W	2.5	W	53.5	U
vs	CLEVELAND		A	23	10	W	-4.0	W	47.0	U
@	Tampa Bay		G	34	23	W	-3.0	W	46.5	O
@	New England	Sa	A	22	18	W	-3.0	W	41.5	U
vs	BALTIMORE		A	27	16	W	-12.0	L	39.5	O
vs	**BALTIMORE**		A	24	17	W	-7.5	L	40.0	O
@	**Buffalo**		A	27	10	W	6.0	W	48.0	U
@	**Kansas City**		G	20	23	L	2.5	L	48.0	U

	2021									
vs	MINNESOTA {OT}		A	27	24	W	3.0	W	47.0	O
@	Chicago		G	17	20	L	2.0	L	44.5	U
@	Pittsburgh		G	24	10	W	2.5	W	42.0	U
vs	JACKSONVILLE	T	A	24	21	W	-7.5	W	46.5	U
vs	GREEN BAY {OT}		A	22	25	L	2.0	L	50.0	U
@	Detroit		A	34	11	W	-3.5	W	46.5	U
@	Baltimore		A	41	17	W	6.5	W	46.0	U
@	New York Jets		A	31	34	L	-11.5	L	43.0	O
vs	CLEVELAND		A	16	41	L	-1.0	L	47.5	O
	BYE									
@	Las Vegas Raiders		G	32	13	W	-2.5	W	51.0	O
vs	PITTSBURGH		A	41	10	W	-3.5	W	44.0	O
vs	L.A. CHARGERS		A	22	41	L	-2.5	L	50.0	O
vs	SAN FRANCISCO {OT}		A	23	26	L	1.0	L	49.5	U
@	Denver		G	15	10	W	3.0	W	44.0	U
vs	BALTIMORE		A	41	21	W	-7.5	W	43.5	O
vs	KANSAS CITY		A	34	31	W	3.5	W	51.0	O
@	Cleveland		G	16	21	L	6.5	W	38.5	U
vs	**LAS VEGAS**	Sa	A	26	19	W	-6.0	W	48.5	U
@	**Tennessee Titans**	Sa	A	19	16	W	4.0	W	48.5	U
@	**Kansas City {OT}**		G	27	24	W	7.0	W	54.5	U
vs	Los Angeles Rams		G	20	23	L	4.5	W	49.0	U

	2020									
vs	L.A. CHARGERS		A	13	16	L	2.5	L	41.5	U
@	Cleveland	T	G	30	35	L	6.0	W	44.5	O
@	Philadelphia {OT}		G	23	23	T	5.5	W	47.0	U
vs	JACKSONVILLE		A	33	25	W	-1.0	W	49.5	O
@	Baltimore		A	3	27	L	12.5	L	49.0	U
@	Indianapolis		A	27	31	L	7.0	W	46.5	O
vs	CLEVELAND		A	34	37	L	4.0	W	50.0	O
vs	Tennessee		A	31	20	W	7.0	W	51.0	T
	BYE									
@	Pittsburgh		G	10	36	L	6.5	L	45.5	O
@	Washington		G	9	20	L	1.0	L	48.0	U
vs	N.Y. GIANTS		A	17	19	L	6.5	L	45.0	U
@	Miami		G	7	19	L	10.5	L	43.0	U
vs	DALLAS		A	7	30	L	3.0	L	44.0	U
vs	PITTSBURGH	M	A	27	17	W	14.0	W	44.5	U
@	Houston		G	37	31	W	7.5	W	46.0	O
vs	Baltimore		A	3	38	L	13.5	L	45.5	U

	2019									
@	Seattle		A	20	21	L	9.0	W	44.5	U
vs	SAN FRANCISCO		A	17	41	L	-1.0	L	46.5	O
@	Buffalo		A	17	21	L	6.0	W	43.5	U
@	Pittsburgh	M	G	3	27	L	3.5	L	45.0	U
vs	ARIZONA		A	23	26	L	-3.0	L	46.5	O
@	Baltimore		A	17	23	L	10.5	W	47.0	U
vs	JACKSONVILLE		A	17	27	L	4.0	L	43.5	O
vs	L.A. Rams {London}		G	10	24	L	12.5	L	48.5	U
	BYE									
vs	BALTIMORE		A	13	49	L	10.5	L	43.5	O
@	Oakland		G	10	17	L	13.0	W	48.0	U
vs	PITTSBURGH		A	10	16	L	6.0	T	37.5	U
vs	NEW YORK JETS		A	22	6	W	2.5	W	43.0	U
@	Cleveland		G	19	27	L	6.0	L	43.0	U
vs	NEW ENGLAND		A	13	34	L	10.5	L	42.0	O
@	Miami {OT}		G	35	38	L	PK	L	45.0	O
vs	CLEVELAND		A	33	23	W	2.5	W	44.0	O

Pointspread Analysis vs NFC teams		Pointspread Analysis Dog
0-11 S/U vs NFC teams as 10.5 point or more Dog since 1993		3-47 S/U as 10.5 point or more Dog since 1978
12-3 ATS vs NFC teams as 3.5-7 point Dog since 2004		7-1 ATS as 7.5-10 point Dog since 2010
9-2 S/U vs NFC teams as 7.5-10 point favorite since 1982		11-41-1 S/U as 3.5-7 point Dog since 2009
8-3 S/U vs NFC North as 3 point or less Dog since 1986		7-30-1 S/U on road as 3.5-7 point Dog since 2009
8-2-1 ATS vs NFC North as 3 point or less Dog since 1986		13-1 ATS as 3.5-7 point Dog since 2020
6-2-1 O/U vs NFC North as 3 point or less Dog since 2001		**Favorite**
0-4 O/U vs NFC North as 3 point or less favorite since 1992		10-2 S/U on road as 3.5-7 point favorite since 2009
5-0 S/U vs NFC North as 7.5 point or more favorite since 1986		32-9-1 S/U as 3.5-7 point favorite since 2011
vs Minnesota - HOME team 13-1 S/U since 1973 {13-1 ATS}		32-6 S/U as 7.5-10 point favorite since 1982
0-4 S/U vs NFC West as 10.5 point or more Dog since 1993		13-3 S/U as 10.5 point or more favorite since 1982
1-6 S/U vs NFC West as 3.5-7 point Dog since 1994		**Playoffs**
5-0 S/U & ATS vs NFC West as 3.5-7 point favorite since 1999		1-10 O/U in Playoffs since 2013
1-7 O/U vs NFC West as 3.5-7 point favorite since 1984		2-8 S/U on grass in Playoffs
3-0 S/U & ATS vs Arizona as 3.5-7 point favorite since 1979		**vs NFC teams**
0-3 S/U @ Arizona as 3.5-7 point Dog since 1985		4-1 ATS @ San Francisco since 1984
		Game 1-4 O/U @ San Francisco since 1984
		vs San Francisco - 49ers leads series 13-4

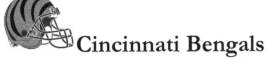

Cincinnati Bengals
Paul Brown Stadium

AFC North
Coach: Zac Taylor

2023 Schedule + Trends & Angles

DATE		OPPONENT	TURF	CIN	OPP	S/U	LINE	ATS	TOT	O/U	Trends & Angles
9/10/2023	@	Cleveland	G								0-5 S/U @ Cleveland since 2018
9/17/2023	vs	BALTIMORE RAVENS	A								vs Baltimore - Series tied 53-53
9/25/2023	vs	LOS ANGELES RAMS	A								Game 0-5 O/U vs Los Angeles Rams since 2003
10/1/2023	@	Tennessee	G								6-0 ATS vs Tennessee since 2011 {5-1 S/U}
10/8/2023	@	Arizona	G								HOME team 9-2 S/U since 1979
10/15/2023	vs	SEATTLE	A								Game 6-2 O/U vs Seattle since 1994
10/22/2023		BYE									
10/29/2023	@	San Francisco	G								1-5 S/U @ San Francisco since 1978
11/5/2023	vs	BUFFALO	A								vs Buffalo - Bills lead series 17-16
11/12/2023	vs	HOUSTON	A								0-4 S/U & ATS @ home vs Houston since 2009
11/16/2023	@	Baltimore Ravens	A								
11/26/2023	vs	PITTSBURGH	A								4-19 S/U @ home vs Pittsburgh since 2002
12/4/2023	@	Jacksonville	G								vs Jacksonville - Jaguars lead series 13-11
12/10/2023	vs	INDIANAPOLIS	A								3-0 S/U @ home vs Indianapolis since 2011
12/16/2023	vs	MINNESOTA	A								7-1 S/U @ home vs Minnesota s/1973 {7-1 ATS}
12/23/2023	@	Pittsburgh	G								2-5 S/U @ Pittsburgh since 2016
12/31/2023	@	Kansas City	G								Game 2-11 O/U @ Kansas City since 1979
1/7/2024	vs	CLEVELAND	A								vs Cleveland - Cincinnati leads series 28-20
1/14/2024											AFC Wild Card
1/21/2024											AFC Divisional Playoff
1/28/2024											AFC Championship
2/11/2024											Super Bowl LVIII @ Las Vegas, NV

Pointspread Analysis
vs AFC teams

0-19 S/U vs AFC East as 7.5 point or more Dog since 1978	8-1 S/U vs AFC South as 7.5-10 point favorite since 1982
1-13 S/U vs AFC East as 3.5-7 point Dog since 1987	1-5 S/U @ home vs AFC South as 3 point or less favorite s/1998 {1-5 ATS}
7-3 O/U vs AFC East as 3.5-7 point Dog since 1994	4-0 S/U on road vs AFC South as 3 point or less favorite since 1995 {4-0 ATS}
14-3 S/U vs AFC East as 3.5-7 point favorite since 1985	Game 1-5 O/U vs Houston since 2013
1-6 S/U @ home vs AFC East as 3 point or less favorite since 1985	Game 5-0 O/U @ home vs Indianapolis since 1996
1-4 S/U & ATS vs Buffalo as 3.5-7 point Dog since 1989	vs Indianapolis - Home team 9-1 S/U since 2006
5-0 S/U vs Buffalo as 3.5-7 point favorite since 1985	0-3 S/U vs Indianapolis as 10.5 point or more Dog since 1999
3-13 S/U vs AFC North as 10.5 point or more Dog since 1978	0-6 S/U vs Indianapolis as 3.5-7 point Dog since 1998
3-22 S/U @ home vs AFC North as 3.5-7 point Dog since 1980	0-4 S/U & ATS vs Indianapolis as 3 point or less Dog since 1992
5-15 O/U vs AFC North as 3 point or less Dog since 2007	0-3 S/U & ATS @ Jacksonville as 3.5-7 point Dog since 1997
9-2 S/U @ home vs AFC North as 3.5-7 point favorite since 2011	0-3 S/U vs Jacksonville as 10.5 point or more Dog since 1998
16-1 S/U vs AFC North as 7.5 or more favorite since 1982	0-4 S/U vs Tennessee as 10.5 point or more Dog since 1991
Game 4-10 O/U @ Pittsburgh since 2009	0-5 S/U vs Tennessee as 7.5-10 point Dog since 1993
Game 2-6 O/U @ home vs Pittsburgh since 2016	6-2-1 O/U vs Tennessee as 3.5-7 point Dog since 1989
Game 2-6-2 O/U @ Cleveland since 2013	4-0 S/U vs Tennessee as 7.5-10 point favorite since 1982
7-2 ATS @ Cleveland since 2014	Game 7-2 O/U @ Tennessee since 1998
0-7 S/U & ATS vs Baltimore as 10.5 point or more Dog since 1994	0-7 S/U vs AFC West as 10.5 or more point Dog since 1992
3-0 ATS @ Baltimore as 7.5-10 point Dog since 2009	5-20 S/U vs AFC West as 3.5-7 point Dog since 1978
4-1 S/U @ home vs Baltimore as 3 point or less Dog since 2009	6-1 S/U & ATS vs AFC West as 3 point or less favorite since 2008
1-6 O/U @ home vs Baltimore as 3 point or less favorite since 1984	1-10 S/U on road vs AFC West as 3.5-7 point Dog since 1983
5-0 S/U @ home vs Baltimore as 3.5-7 point favorite since 1988	Game 3-13 O/U vs Kansas City since 1989
1-5 O/U @ home vs Baltimore as 3.5-7 point favorite since 1986	

Grass/Turf

5-0 S/U @ home vs Baltimore as 7.5-10 point favorite since 1982	0-17 S/U on grass as 10.5 point or more Dog since 1978
5-1 S/U @ home vs Cleveland as 3.5-7 point favorite since 2004	3-13 S/U on grass as 7.5-10 point Dog since 1984
3-0 S/U & ATS vs Cleveland as 7.5-10 point favorite since 2006	2-13-1 S/U on grass as 3.5-7 point Dog since 2013
4-0 S/U vs Cleveland as 10.5 point or more favorite since 2005	15-6-1 ATS on grass as 3 point or less Dog since 2006
0-3 S/U @ Pittsburgh as 10.5 point or more Dog since 2002	1-11-1 O/U on grass as 3 point or less Dog since 2014

THU-SAT-SNF-MNF

5-1 ATS @ Pittsburgh as 10.5 point or more Dog since 1980		
3-0 O/U @ home vs Pittsburgh as 7.5-10 point Dog since 1993	Ravens	1-4 S/U on road on Thursday since 2008
1-5 O/U @ Pittsburgh as 7.5-10 point Dog since 1995		3-0 S/U & ATS vs Baltimore on Thursday since 1986
2-14 S/U @ home vs Pittsburgh as 3.5-7 point Dog since 1992	Steelers	2-8 S/U on road on Saturday since 1969
3-12-1 ATS @ home vs Pittsburgh as 3.5-7 point Dog since 1992	BILLS	1-5 S/U @ home on SNF since 1991
0-4 S/U @ home vs Pittsburgh as 3 point or less Dog since 2006	BILLS	0-6 ATS @ home on SNF since 1991
0-6 S/U & ATS vs Pittsburgh as 3 point or less favorite since 1991	BILLS	1-6 O/U @ home on SNF since 1990
1-4 O/U vs Pittsburgh as 3.5-7 point favorite since 1989		0-11 S/U on SNF as a dog since 1993
3-0 S/U vs Pittsburgh as 7.5-10 point favorite since 1986		0-4 S/U on SNF as 3 point or less favorite since 1991
3-0 O/U vs Pittsburgh as 7.5-10 point favorite since 1986	Jaguars	3-20 S/U on road on MNF since 1970
0-10 S/U vs AFC South as 10.5 point or more Dog since 1991	Jaguars	1-8 ATS on road on MNF since 1991
2-10 S/U vs AFC South as 3.5-7 point Dog since 2002	Jaguars	3-13 S/U on road on MNF as a 6 point or more dog since 1978
0-6 O/U vs AFC South as 3 point or less Dog since 2007		

Cleveland Browns
AFC North
Last 4 seasons + Pointspread Analysis

	2022									
@	Carolina		G	26	24	W	1.5	W	42.0	O
vs	NEW YORK JETS		G	30	31	L	-6.0	L	38.5	O
vs	PITTSBURGH	T	G	29	17	W	-4.0	W	38.0	O
@	Atlanta		A	20	23	L	-1.0	L	49.0	U
vs	L.A. CHARGERS		G	28	30	L	1.0	L	47.0	O
vs	NEW ENGLAND		G	15	38	L	-2.5	L	43.5	O
@	Baltimore Ravens		A	20	23	L	6.5	W	47.0	U
vs	CINCINNATI	M	G	32	13	W	3.0	W	45.0	T
	BYE									
@	Miami		G	17	39	L	3.5	L	49.5	O
@	Buffalo {@ Detroit}		A	23	31	L	7.5	L	50.5	O
vs	TAMPA BAY {OT}		G	23	17	W	3.0	W	42.5	U
@	Houston		G	27	14	W	-7.5	L	46.0	U
@	Cincinnati		A	10	23	L	4.0	L	47.0	U
vs	BALTIMORE	Sa	G	13	3	W	-3.0	W	39.0	U
vs	NEW ORLEANS	Sa	G	10	17	L	-3.5	L	32.0	U
@	Washington		G	24	10	W	1.0	W	41.0	O
@	Pittsburgh		G	14	28	L	2.5	L	40.0	O

	2021									
@	Kansas City		G	29	33	L	5.0	W	55.0	O
vs	HOUSTON		G	31	21	W	-13.5	L	48.5	O
vs	CHICAGO		G	26	6	W	-7.5	W	45.0	U
@	Minnesota		A	14	7	W	PK	W	52.0	U
@	L.A. Chargers		G	42	47	L	2.5	L	47.0	O
vs	ARIZONA		G	14	37	L	-3.0	L	48.0	O
vs	DENVER	T	G	17	14	W	-2.0	W	40.5	U
vs	PITTSBURGH		G	10	15	L	-5.5	L	43.0	U
@	Cincinnati		A	41	16	W	1.0	W	47.5	O
@	New England		A	7	45	L	2.5	L	44.5	O
vs	DETROIT		G	13	10	W	-14.0	L	42.5	U
@	Baltimore	Su	A	10	16	L	3.0	L	47.5	U
	BYE									
vs	BALTIMORE		G	24	22	W	-3.0	W	44.0	U
vs	LAS VEGAS	M	G	14	16	L	2.5	W	41.5	U
@	Green Bay	Sa	G	22	24	L	8.0	W	46.5	U
@	Pittsburgh	M	G	14	26	L	-2.0	L	43.0	U
vs	CINCINNATI		G	21	16	W	-6.5	L	38.5	U

	2020									
@	Baltimore		A	6	38	L	7.0	L	41.5	O
vs	CINCINNATI	T	G	35	30	W	-6.0	L	44.5	O
vs	Washington		G	34	20	W	-7.0	W	45.0	O
@	Dallas		A	49	38	W	3.5	W	56.5	O
vs	Indianapolis		G	32	23	W	PK	W	49.0	O
@	Pittsburgh		G	7	38	L	3.0	L	50.0	U
@	Cincinnati		A	37	34	W	-4.0	L	50.0	O
vs	LAS VEGAS		G	6	16	L	-1.0	L	49.0	U
	BYE									
vs	Houston		G	10	7	W	-4.0	L	46.0	U
vs	PHILADELPHIA		G	22	17	W	-2.5	W	45.5	U
@	Jacksonville		G	27	25	W	-7.5	L	48.5	O
@	Tennessee		G	41	35	W	4.0	W	54.5	O
vs	Baltimore	M	G	42	47	L	3.0	L	45.5	O
@	New York Giants	Su	A	20	6	W	-6.0	W	44.5	U
@	New York Jets		A	16	23	L	-7.0	L	45.0	U
vs	PITTSBURGH		G	24	22	W	-10.5	L	44.5	O
@	Pittsburgh		G	48	37	W	5.0	W	47.0	O
@	Kansas City		G	17	22	L	7.5	W	56.0	U

	2019									
vs	TENNESSEE		G	13	43	L	-5.5	L	44.0	O
@	New York Jets	M	A	23	3	W	-6.5	W	45.0	U
vs	L.A. RAMS	Su	G	13	20	L	4.0	L	47.5	U
@	Baltimore		A	40	25	W	7.0	W	47.0	O
@	San Francisco	M	G	3	31	L	5.0	L	47.5	U
vs	SEATTLE		G	28	32	L	-1.0	L	45.5	O
	BYE									
@	New England		A	13	27	L	9.5	L	43.0	U
@	Denver		G	19	24	L	-4.0	L	39.0	O
vs	BUFFALO		G	19	16	W	-3.0	T	42.0	U
vs	PITTSBURGH	T	G	21	7	W	-3.0	W	41.5	U
vs	MIAMI		G	41	24	W	-11.0	W	46.0	U
@	Pittsburgh		G	13	20	L	-1.0	L	40.0	U
vs	CINCINNATI		G	27	19	W	-6.0	W	43.0	O
@	Arizona		G	24	38	L	-3.0	L	49.0	O
vs	BALTIMORE		G	15	31	L	10.5	L	48.5	U
@	Cincinnati		A	23	33	L	-2.5	L	44.0	O

Pointspread Analysis THU-SAT-SNF-MNF		Pointspread Analysis THU-SAT-SNF-MNF
7-0 S/U @ home on Thursday since 2009 {6-1 ATS}	JETS	0-6 O/U on Thursday as dog since 2009
6-0 S/U on Thursday as favorite since 2013	JETS	
0-4 O/U on Saturday as dog since 2011	BEARS	5-1 ATS on Saturday since 2011
0-6 O/U on Saturday since 2011	BEARS	
2-7 S/U on Monday since 2008	Steelers	

2023 College Football Bible 29.95   **2023 FCS College Football Bible $19.95**

Cleveland Browns

First Energy Stadium

2023 Schedule + Trends & Angles

AFC North

Coach: Kevin Stefanski

DATE		OPPONENT	TURF	CLE	OPP	S/U	LINE	ATS	TOT	O/U	Trends & Angles
9/10/2023	vs	CINCINNATI	G								vs Cincinnati - Bengals leads series 28-20
9/18/2023	@	Pittsburgh	G								1-19 S/U @ Pittsburgh since 2004
9/24/2023	vs	TENNESSEE	G								2-6 S/U @ home vs Tennessee since 1999
10/1/2023	vs	BALTIMORE RAVENS	G								vs Baltimore - Ravens leads series 34-14
10/8/2023		BYE									
10/15/2023	vs	SAN FRANCISCO	G								Game 0-5 O/U vs San Francisco since 2003
10/22/2023	@	Indianapolis	A								2-7 S/U vs Indianapolis since 1999
10/29/2023	@	Seattle	A								6-24 S/U on road vs NFC last 30 times
11/5/2023	vs	ARIZONA	G								vs Arizona - Cardinals leads series 6-1
11/12/2023	@	Baltimore Ravens	A								
11/19/2023	vs	PITTSBURGH	G								6-15-1 S/U @ home vs Pittsburgh since 2001
11/26/2023	@	Denver	G								1-5 S/U @ Denver since 2000
12/3/2023	@	Los Angeles Rams	G								1-5 S/U & ATS vs Los Angeles Rams s/1999
12/10/2023	vs	JACKSONVILLE	G								1-3 S/U vs Jacksonville since 2013 {0-4 ATS}
12/16/2023	vs	CHICAGO	G								vs Chicago - Bears leads series 4-2
12/24/2023	@	Houston	G								1-5 S/U & ATS @ Houston since 2005
12/28/2023	vs	NEW YORK JETS	G								2-7 S/U & ATS vs New York Jets since 2010
1/7/2024	@	Cincinnati	A								
1/14/2024											AFC Wild Card
1/21/2024											AFC Divisional Playoff
1/28/2024											AFC Championship
2/11/2024											Super Bowl LVIII @ Las Vegas, NV

Pointspread Analysis		Pointspread Analysis	
vs AFC teams		**vs AFC teams**	
0-8 S/U & ATS vs AFC East as 3 point or less Dog since 2010		0-4 O/U vs Tennessee as 10.5 point or more Dog since 1999	
0-11 S/U vs AFC East as 7.5 point or more Dog since 1999		0-4 S/U vs Indianapolis as 3 point or less Dog since 2002	
9-3 S/U vs AFC East as 7 point or less favorite since 2005		0-11 S/U vs AFC West as 7.5 point or more Dog since 1999	
0-4 S/U & ATS vs New York Jets as 3 point or less Dog since 2010		vs Denver - Broncos leads series 8-2	
Game 1-4 O/U vs New York Jets since 2017		2-7 S/U vs Denver since 2000	
0-16 S/U on road vs AFC North as 10.5 point or more Dog s/2000		0-3 S/U vs Denver as 10.5 point or more Dog since 2000	
0-19 S/U vs AFC North as 10.5 point or more Dog since 2000		**vs NFC teams**	
0-9 S/U on road vs AFC North as 7.5-10 point Dog since 2005		1-7 S/U vs NFC teams as 10.5 or more Dog since 1999	
0-4 O/U @ home vs AFC North as 7.5-10 point Dog since 2009		0-9 S/U vs NFC teams as 7.5-10 point Dog since 2008	
1-9-1 S/U @ home vs AFC North as 3.5-7 point Dog since 2008		5-21 S/U vs NFC teams as 3.5-7 point Dog since 2003	
9-35-1 S/U vs AFC North as 3.5-7 point Dog since 1999		1-13 S/U vs NFC West as Dog since 2007	
0-10 S/U vs Baltimore as 10.5 point or more Dog since 1999		0-3 S/U vs Arizona as 3.5-7 point Dog since 2000	
4-1 ATS vs Baltimore as 10.5 point or more Dog since 2010		1-5 S/U & ATS vs Los Angeles Rams since 1999	
0-4 S/U vs Cincinnati as 10.5 point or more Dog since 2005		**Grass/Turf**	
9-38-1 S/U vs Pittsburgh		0-28 S/U on grass as 10.5 point or more Dog since 1999	
Game 3-7 O/U @ home vs Pittsburgh since 2013		2-21 S/U on Turf as 10.5 point or more Dog since 1999	
0-6 S/U vs Pittsburgh as 10.5 point or more Dog since 2000		0-17 S/U on grass as 7.5-10 point Dog since 2011	
0-3 S/U & ATS vs Cincinnati as 7.5-10 point Dog since 2006		6-27-1 S/U on grass as 3.5-7 point Dog since 2010	
0-6 S/U @ Pittsburgh as 7.5-10 point Dog since 2003		**Dog**	
0-4 S/U & ATS @ home vs Baltimore as 3.5-7 point Dog s/2010		2-49 S/U as 10.5 point or more Dog since 1999	
1-5 S/U @ Cincinnati as 3.5-7 point Dog since 2004		0-10 S/U @ home as 10.5 point or more Dog since 1999	
1-6 S/U @ Pittsburgh as 3.5-7 point Dog since 2004		0-25 S/U as 7.5-10 point Dog since 2011	
6-1-1 O/U @ Pittsburgh as 3.5-7 point Dog since 2004		7-24 S/U on road as 3.5-7 point Dog since 2011	
0-8-1 S/U @ home vs Pittsburgh as 3.5-7 point Dog since 1999		4-13-1 S/U @ home as 3.5-7 point Dog since 2010	
0-4 S/U & ATS vs Cincinnati as 3 point or less favorite since 2007		**Favorite**	
1-3 O/U vs Cincinnati as 3 point or less favorite since 2007		0-6 S/U & ATS on road as 3 point or less favorite since 2017	
0-6 O/U vs Pittsburgh as 3 point or less favorite since 2003		10-0 S/U as 7.5 point or more favorite since 2007	
0-10 S/U vs AFC South as 10.5 point or more Dog since 1999	BENGALS	1-16-1 S/U in 1st game of season since 2005	
0-6 O/U vs AFC South as 3.5-7 point Dog since 2006	BENGALS	4-13-1 S/U in 1st home game of season since 2005	
1-7 S/U vs AFC South as 3 point or less Dog since 2002	Steelers	3-14 S/U in 1st road game of season since 2006	
1-7 ATS vs Houston since 2008	CARDINALS	2-14 S/U prior to playing @ Baltimore since 2006	
4-1 ATS vs Tennessee since 2015	TITANS	2-9 S/U after playing Monday Night since 2003	
0-3 S/U vs Jacksonville as 10.5 point or more Dog since 1999		9-26 S/U after scoring less than 10 pts last 35 {4W}	
0-4 S/U vs Tennessee as 10.5 point or more Dog since 1999			

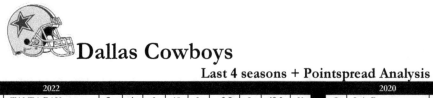

Dallas Cowboys

NFC East

Last 4 seasons + Pointspread Analysis

2022

vs	TAMPA BAY	Su	A	3	19	L	2.5	L	49.0	U
vs	CINCINNATI		A	20	17	W	7.0	W	42.0	U
@	New York Giants	M	A	23	16	W	1.0	W	38.5	O
vs	WASHINGTON		A	25	10	W	-3.0	W	41.0	U
@	Los Angeles Rams		G	22	10	W	5.5	W	41.5	U
@	Philadelphia	Su	G	17	26	L	6.5	L	42.5	O
vs	DETROIT		A	24	6	W	-6.5	W	49.5	U
vs	CHICAGO		A	49	29	W	-9.5	W	43.0	O
@	BYE									
@	Green Bay {OT}		G	28	31	L	-3.5	L	44.5	O
@	Minnesota		A	40	3	W	-2.0	W	48.5	U
vs	N.Y. GIANTS	T	A	28	20	W	-10.0	W	45.5	U
vs	INDIANAPOLIS	Su	A	54	19	W	-11.0	W	44.0	O
vs	HOUSTON		A	27	23	W	-17.0	L	44.5	U
@	Jacksonville {OT}		G	34	40	L	-4.0	L	48.0	O
vs	PHILADELPHIA	Sa	A	40	34	W	-3.5	W	48.0	O
@	Tennessee	T	G	27	13	W	-13.5	W	40.5	U
@	Washington		G	6	26	L	-7.0	L	41.0	U
@	**Tampa Bay**	M	G	31	14	**W**	-2.5	**W**	44.5	**O**
@	**San Francisco**		G	12	19	L	3.5	L	47.0	U

2021

@	Tampa Bay	T	G	29	31	L	9.0	W	52.5	O
@	Los Angeles, Chargers		G	20	17	W	3.0	W	55.0	U
vs	PHILADELPHIA	M	A	41	21	W	-3.5	W	51.5	O
vs	CAROLINA		A	36	28	W	-5.0	W	51.5	U
vs	N.Y. GIANTS		A	44	20	W	-7.0	W	53.0	O
@	New England {OT}		A	35	29	W	-3.0	W	50.0	O
	BYE									
@	Minnesota	Su	A	20	16	W	4.0	W	49.0	U
vs	DENVER		A	16	30	L	-10.0	L	50.0	U
vs	ATLANTA		A	43	3	W	-7.5	W	55.5	U
@	Kansas City		G	9	19	L	2.5	L	56.0	U
vs	LAS VEGAS {OT}	T	A	33	36	L	-7.0	L	51.0	U
@	New Orleans	T	A	27	17	W	-6.5	W	45.5	U
@	Washington		G	27	20	W	-6.5	W	48.0	U
@	New York Giants		A	21	6	W	-12.0	W	43.0	U
vs	WASHINGTON	Su	A	56	14	W	-10.0	W	46.0	O
vs	ARIZONA		A	22	25	L	-6.5	L	53.5	U
@	Philadelphia	Sa	G	51	26	W	-6.0	W	46.0	O
vs	**SAN FRANCISCO**		A	17	23	L	-3.0	L	51.5	U

2020

@	L.A. Rams	Su	G	17	20	L	PK	L	51.5	U
vs	ATLANTA		A	40	39	W	-2.5	L	54.0	O
@	Seattle		A	31	38	L	5.0	L	57.5	O
vs	CLEVELAND		A	38	49	L	-3.5	L	56.5	O
vs	N.Y. GIANTS		A	37	34	W	-7.5	L	52.0	O
vs	ARIZONA	M	A	10	38	L	-1.0	L	56.0	U
@	Washington		G	3	25	L	1.0	L	44.5	U
@	Philadelphia	Su	G	9	23	L	10.0	L	43.5	U
vs	PITTSBURGH		A	19	24	L	14.0	W	43.5	U
	BYE									
@	Minnesota		A	31	28	W	7.0	W	50.0	O
vs	Washington	T	A	16	41	L	-2.5	L	46.0	U
@	Baltimore Ravens	Tu	A	17	34	L	9.0	L	46.0	U
@	Cincinnati		A	30	7	W	-3.0	W	44.0	U
vs	SAN FRANCISCO		A	41	33	W	3.5	W	45.5	U
vs	PHILADELPHIA		A	37	17	W	3.0	W	50.0	O
@	New York Giants		A	19	23	L	-1.5	L	44.0	U

2019

vs	N.Y. GIANTS		A	35	17	W	-7.0	W	44.0	O
@	Washington		G	31	21	W	-6.0	W	46.5	O
vs	MIAMI		A	31	6	W	-21.5	W	46.5	U
@	New Orleans	Su	A	10	12	L	-2.5	L	47.0	U
vs	GREEN BAY		A	24	34	L	-3.5	L	46.5	O
@	New York Jets		A	22	24	L	-7.0	L	43.5	U
vs	PHILADELPHIA	Su	A	37	10	W	-3.0	W	50.0	U
	BYE									
@	New York Giants	M	A	37	18	W	-6.5	W	48.5	O
vs	MINNESOTA	Su	A	24	28	L	-3.0	L	48.0	O
@	Detroit		A	35	27	W	-7.0	W	46.5	O
@	New England		A	9	13	L	5.5	W	44.5	U
vs	BUFFALO	T	A	15	26	L	-6.5	L	46.5	U
@	Chicago	T	G	24	31	L	-3.0	L	43.0	U
vs	L.A. RAMS		A	44	21	W	PK	W	48.5	O
@	Philadelphia		G	9	17	L	-2.0	L	46.5	U
vs	Washington		A	47	16	W	-12.5	W	47.5	O

Pointspread Analysis

vs AFC teams	Dog
0-4 S/U vs AFC teams as 10.5 point or more Dog since 1988	0-9 S/U @ home as 7.5-10 point Dog since 1989
0-8 S/U vs AFC teams as 7.5-10 point Dog since 1989	3-10 S/U @ home as 3.5-7 point Dog since 2002
5-1 S/U vs AFC teams as 7.5-10 point favorite since 2006	**Favorite**
0-5 ATS vs AFC teams as 7.5-10 point favorite since 2007	33-14 S/U as 3.5-7 point favorite since 2014
0-8 S/U vs AFC East as 4 point or more Dog since 1989	13-2 S/U as 7.5-10 point favorite since 2008
11-5 S/U vs AFC East as 3.5-7 point favorite since 1978	2-9 ATS as 7.5-10 point favorite since 2010
0-4 ATS vs AFC East as 7.5-10 point favorite since 1984	71-10 S/U as 10.5 point or more favorite since 1978
5-0 S/U vs AFC East as 10.5 point or more favorite since 1978	**Playoffs**
14-1 S/U vs AFC teams as 10.5 point or more favorite since 1978	0-4 S/U on road on Saturday in Playoffs since 1986
1-4 O/U vs Miami as 3 point or less favorite since 1987	6-1 S/U @ home on Saturday in Playoffs since 1970
3-0 S/U & ATS vs Miami as 3.5-7 point favorite since 1972	0-3 S/U vs L.A. Rams on Saturday in Playoffs since 1970
0-4 S/U vs New England as 3.5-7 point Dog since 2003	1-9 S/U on road in Playoffs since 1994
4-0 S/U vs Miami since 2007	10-3 S/U @ home in Playoffs since 1992
2-8 O/U vs New England since 1984	1-3 S/U on road in WILD Card since 2000
3-1-1 ATS vs New York Jets since 2003	3-1 S/U @ home in WILD Card since 2010
7-0 O/U vs AFC West as 3.5 point or more Dog since 1989	0-7 S/U on road in Divisional Playoffs since 1985
8-2 S/U vs AFC West as 7.5 point or favorite since 1983	1-4 S/U on road in NFC Championship since 1981
3-14 S/U vs AFC West as a Dog since 1980	4-1 S/U @ home vs Green Bay in Playoffs since 1982
vs L.A. Chargers - Dallas leads series 7-5	0-3 S/U @ home vs Los Angeles Rams in Playoffs since 1976
THU-SAT-SNF-MNF	**THU-SAT-SNF-MNF**
6-1 O/U on Saturday as 3.5-7 point favorite since 2006	2-9 S/U @ home on SNF as dog since 1988
4-16 S/U on SNF as a dog since 2010	13-5 S/U @ home on SNF since 2013

EAGLES

Dallas Cowboys
AT&T Stadium

2023 Schedule + Trends & Angles

NFC East
Coach: Mike McCarthy

DATE		OPPONENT	TURF	DAL	OPP	S/U	LINE	ATS	TOT	O/U	Trends & Angles
9/10/2023	@	New York Giants	A								4-1 S/U & ATS @ New York Giants since 2017
9/17/2023	vs	*NEW YORK JETS*	A								0-3 S/U vs New York Jets since 2011
9/24/2023	@	Arizona	G								vs Arizona - Dallas leads series 56-34-1
10/1/2023	vs	*NEW ENGLAND*	A								1-6 S/U vs New England since 1999
10/8/2023	@	San Francisco	G								4-1 S/U @ San Francisco since 2005
10/16/2023	@	*Los Angeles Chargers*	A								4-1 S/U @ Chargers since 1986
10/22/2023		BYE									
10/29/2023	vs	LOS ANGELES RAMS	A								4-1 S/U & ATS @ home vs LA Rams since 2007
11/5/2023	@	Philadelphia	G								Game 2-5 O/U @ Philadelphia since 2015
11/12/2023	vs	NEW YORK GIANTS	A								8-1 S/U @ home vs New York Giants since 2013
11/19/2023	@	Carolina	G								vs Carolina - Dallas leads series 10-5
11/23/2023	vs	WASHINGTON	A								Game 7-0 O/U @ home vs Washington since 2015
11/30/2023	vs	SEATTLE	A								0-4 ATS vs Seattle since 2017
12/10/2023	vs	PHILADELPHIA	A								5-0 S/U @ home vs Philadelphia s/2018 {5-0 ATS}
12/17/2023	@	*Buffalo*	A								Game 3-9 O/U vs Buffalo since 1976
12/24/2023	@	*Miami*	G								3-0 S/U & ATS @ Miami since 1996
12/30/2023	vs	DETROIT	A								12-3 S/U @ home vs Detroit since 1963
1/7/2024	@	Washington	G								7-2 S/U @ Washington since 2013
1/14/2024											NFC Wild Card
1/21/2024											NFC Divisional Playoff
1/28/2024											NFC Championship
2/11/2024											Super Bowl LVIII @ Las Vegas, NV

Pointspread Analysis
vs NFC teams

20-2 S/U vs NFC East as 3.5-7 point favorite since 2013		
17-3 S/U on road vs NFC East as 3.5-7 point favorite since 1986		
6-17-1 O/U on road vs NFC East as 3.5 7 point favorite since 1984		
0-7 ATS on road vs NFC East as 7.5-10 point favorite since 1979		
5-17-1 O/U vs NFC East as 7.5-10 point favorite since 1983		
1-7 ATS vs NFC East as 7.5-10 point favorite since 2007		
34-4 S/U vs NFC East as 10.5 point or more favorite since 1978		
0-4 S/U vs Philadelphia as 10.5 point or more Dog since 1989		
3-0 ATS vs Washington as 10.5 point or more Dog since 1989		
1-4 S/U vs New York Giants as 7.5-10 point Dog since 1989		
3-0 O/U vs New York Giants as 7.5-10 point Dog since 1989		
2-7 S/U @ Philadelphia as 3.5-7 point Dog since 1980		
0-7 S/U @ home vs Philadelphia as 3.5-7 point Dog since 1989		
3-0 ATS vs Washington as 3.5-7 point Dog since 2000		
2-5 S/U @ New York Giants as 3 point or less Dog since 1986		
0-3 S/U @ home vs New York Giants as 3 point or less Dog since 2002		
5-0 S/U vs @ home Washington as 3 point or less Dog since 1992		
6-0 S/U vs @ home Washington as 3 point or less Dog since 1991		
4-1 S/U & ATS @ home vs NY Giants as 3 point or less favorite since 1985		
3-1 S/U @ Philadelphia as 3 point or less favorite since 2007		
6-1 S/U @ New York Giants as 3.5-7 point favorite since 1994		
2-6 O/U @ New York Giants as 3.5-7 point favorite since 1984		
5-0 S/U @ home vs NY Giants as 3.5-7 point favorite since 2014		
9-1 S/U @ Philadelphia as 3.5-7 point favorite since 1978 {8-2 ATS}		
6-0 O/U @ home vs Philadelphia as 3.5-7 point favorite since 2008		
6-0 S/U @ home vs Philadelphia as 3.5-7 point favorite since 2008		
8-2 S/U @ home vs Washington as 3.5-7 point favorite since 1981		
6-1 S/U @ home vs NY Giants as 7.5-10 point favorite since 1979		
2-5 O/U vs NY Giants as 7.5-10 point favorite since 1979		
2-9 ATS vs Philadelphia as 7.5-10 point favorite since 1978		
1-7 O/U vs Philadelphia as 7.5-10 point favorite since 1978		
2-5 ATS vs Washington as 7.5-10 point favorite since 1979		
8-0 S/U @ home vs NY Giants as 10.5 point or more favorite since 1978		
7-0 S/U vs Philadelphia as 10.5 point or more favorite since 1993		
0-5 ATS vs Washington as 10.5 point or more favorite since 1995	WASH, SEA	
6-1 S/U @ home vs Washington since 2016	WASH, SEA	
1-8 ATS vs NFC North as 3 point or less favorite since 2009	WASH, SEA	
13-5 S/U vs NFC North as 3.5-7 point favorite since 1992	WASH, SEA	
11-2 O/U vs NFC North as 3.5-7 point favorite since 2007		
10-0 S/U vs NFC North as 7.5-10 point favorite since 1979		

Pointspread Analysis
vs NFC teams

7-2 S/U vs NFC North as 10.5 point or more favorite since 1981
0-5 S/U & ATS on road vs NFC South as 3 point or less Dog since 1989
4-0 O/U vs Detroit as 3 point or less favorite since 2003
4-0 S/U @ home vs Detroit as 3.5-7 point favorite since 2010
0-3 S/U vs Detroit as 3 point or less Dog since 1991
Game 8-2 O/U vs Detroit since 2006
8-0 S/U vs NFC South as 10.5 point or more favorite since 1978
1-4 O/U vs NFC South as 7.5-10 point Dog since 1990
0-5 S/U & ATS on road vs NFC South as 3 point or less Dog since 1989
14-3 S/U vs NFC South as 3.5-7 point favorite since 1980
2-8 ATS vs NFC South as 7.5-10 point favorite since 1983
3-0 S/U & ATS vs Carolina as 3.5-7 point Dog since 2000
0-3 S/U & ATS vs Carolina as 3 point or less Dog since 2004
8-2 S/U vs NFC West as 3.5-7 point favorite since 1994
0-6 O/U vs NFC West as 10.5 point or more favorite since 1996
0-4 S/U vs Arizona as 3.5-7 point Dog since 1989
1-6 O/U vs Arizona as 3 point or less Dog since 1987
0-3 S/U & ATS @ Arizona as 3.5-7 point favorite since 2008
10-1 S/U vs Arizona as 7.5-10 point favorite since 1980
11-0 S/U vs Arizona as 10.5 point or more favorite since 1978
3-0 ATS vs Los Angeles Rams as 7.5-10 point Dog since 1989
3-0 O/U vs Los Angeles Rams as 7.5-10 point Dog since 1989
4-0 O/U vs San Francisco as 3.5-7 point favorite since 1994
3-0 S/U vs Seattle as 10.5 point or more favorite since 1992
3-1 ATS vs Seattle as 3.5-7 point Dog since 2004
Grass/Turf
12-29 S/U on road on Turf as 3.5-7 point Dog since 1988
5-14 S/U on road on Turf as 3 point or less Dog since 2005
6-15-1 O/U on grass as 3 point or less favorite since 1998
22-7 S/U on road on Turf as 3.5-7 point favorite since 1986
11-3 S/U on grass as 7.5-10 point favorite since 1979
0-6 S/U & ATS on road on Turf as 7.5-10 point favorite since 1995
8-1 S/U on road on Turf as 10.5 point or more favorite since 1978
THU-SAT-SNF-MNF
8-2 O/U on Thursday as 3.5-7 point favorite since 1994
4-0 S/U @ home on Thursday as 7.5-10 point favorite since 1996
1-5 ATS @ home on Thursday as 7.5-10 point favorite since 1986
10-0 S/U on Thursday as 10.5 point or more favorite since 1978 {9-1 ATS}
9-2 S/U @ home vs Washington on Thursday since 1968
Game 6-0 O/U @ home vs Washington on Thursday since 1968

 # Denver Broncos  ## AFC West
Last 4 seasons + Pointspread Analysis

2022

	Opponent	Day	Loc	Tm	Opp	Res	Spr	ATS	Tot	O/U
@	*Seattle*	M	A	16	17	L	-6.0	L	43.5	U
vs	HOUSTON		G	16	9	W	-10.5	L	45.5	U
vs	*SAN FRANCISCO*	Su	G	11	10	W	1.5	W	44.5	U
@	Las Vegas Raiders		G	23	32	L	2.5	L	46.0	O
vs	INDIANAPOLIS {OT}	T	G	9	12	L	2.0	L	42.0	U
@	L.A. Chargers {OT}	M	G	16	19	L	4.0	W	45.5	U
vs	NEW YORK JETS		G	9	16	L	2.0	W	37.0	U
vs	Jacksonville {London}		G	21	17	W	1.0	W	41.0	U
	BYE									
@	Tennessee		G	10	17	L	2.5	L	39.5	U
vs	LAS VEGAS {OT}		G	16	22	L	-2.5	L	41.0	U
@	*Carolina*		G	10	23	L	PK	L	36.5	U
@	Baltimore		A	9	10	L	8.5	W	40.5	U
vs	KANSAS CITY		G	28	34	L	8.5	W	44.0	O
vs	*ARIZONA*		G	24	15	W	-1.0	W	38.0	O
@	*Los Angeles Rams*		A	14	51	L	-3.0	L	36.5	O
@	Kansas City		G	24	27	L	12.5	W	46.5	O
vs	L.A. CHARGERS		G	31	28	W	-6.5	L	39.0	O

2021

	Opponent	Day	Loc	Tm	Opp	Res	Spr	ATS	Tot	O/U
@	*New York Giants*		A	27	13	W	-3.0	W	41.5	U
@	Jacksonville		G	23	13	W	-6.0	W	45.0	U
vs	NEW YORK JETS		G	26	0	W	-10.0	W	41.5	U
vs	BALTIMORE		G	7	23	L	-1.0	W	44.0	U
@	Pittsburgh		G	19	27	L	-1.0	W	40.0	O
vs	LAS VEGAS		G	24	34	L	-5.0	L	44.5	O
@	Cleveland	T	G	14	17	L	2.0	W	40.5	U
vs	*WASHINGTON*		G	17	10	W	-3.5	W	44.5	U
@	Dallas		A	30	16	W	10.0	W	50.0	U
vs	*PHILADELPHIA*		G	13	30	L	PK	L	44.5	U
	BYE									
vs	L.A. CHARGERS		G	28	13	W	2.5	W	47.0	U
@	Kansas City	Su	G	9	22	L	8.5	L	47.0	U
vs	*DETROIT*		G	38	10	W	-12.5	W	42.0	O
vs	CINCINNATI		G	10	15	L	-3.0	L	44.0	U
@	Las Vegas Raiders		G	13	17	L	-1.0	L	41.5	U
@	Los Angeles Chargers		G	13	34	L	9.0	L	45.0	O
vs	KANSAS CITY	Sa	G	24	28	L	11.5	W	44.5	O

2020

	Opponent	Day	Loc	Tm	Opp	Res	Spr	ATS	Tot	O/U
vs	Tennessee	M	G	14	16	L	3.5	W	42.0	U
@	Pittsburgh		G	21	26	L	6.5	W	40.5	O
vs	*TAMPA BAY*		G	10	28	L	6.0	L	42.5	U
@	New York Jets	T	A	37	28	W	1.0	W	41.0	O
	BYE									
@	New England		A	18	12	W	7.0	W	44.5	U
vs	KANSAS CITY		G	16	43	L	7.0	L	46.0	O
vs	L.A. CHARGERS		G	31	30	W	3.0	W	45.0	O
@	*Atlanta*		A	27	34	L	4.5	L	50.0	O
@	Las Vegas Raiders		G	12	37	L	3.0	L	50.5	U
vs	MIAMI		G	20	13	W	3.5	W	49.5	U
vs	*NEW ORLEANS*		G	3	31	L	17.0	L	36.5	U
@	Kansas City	Su	G	16	22	L	13.0	W	51.0	U
@	*Carolina*		G	32	27	W	4.0	W	46.0	O
vs	BUFFALO	Sa	G	19	48	L	6.0	L	47.5	O
@	L.A. Chargers		G	16	19	L	2.0	L	47.5	U
vs	LAS VEGAS		G	31	32	L	2.5	W	50.0	O

2019

	Opponent	Day	Loc	Tm	Opp	Res	Spr	ATS	Tot	O/U
@	Oakland	M	G	16	24	L	-3.0	L	42.5	U
vs	*CHICAGO*		G	14	16	L	2.5	L	40.0	U
@	*Green Bay*		G	16	27	L	7.0	L	41.5	O
vs	JACKSONVILLE		G	24	26	L	-2.5	L	37.0	O
vs	L.A. Chargers		G	20	13	W	5.0	W	45.5	U
vs	TENNESSEE		G	16	0	W	-1.0	W	41.0	U
vs	KANSAS CITY	T	G	6	30	L	3.0	L	49.5	U
@	Indianapolis		A	13	15	L	5.5	W	41.5	U
vs	CLEVELAND		G	24	19	W	4.0	W	39.0	O
	BYE									
@	*Minnesota*		A	23	27	L	10.0	W	40.0	O
@	Buffalo		A	3	20	L	3.5	L	37.5	U
vs	L.A. CHARGERS		G	23	20	W	4.5	W	38.5	O
@	Houston		G	38	24	W	8.0	W	42.5	O
@	Kansas City		G	3	23	L	9.5	L	42.5	U
vs	*DETROIT*		G	27	17	W	-9.0	W	40.5	O
vs	Oakland		G	16	15	W	-5.5	L	41.0	U

Pointspread Analysis

vs NFC teams		vs NFC teams
1-8 S/U vs NFC teams as 7.5-10 point Dog since 1987		6-1 S/U vs NFC North as 3.5-7 point favorite since 1981
12-4 S/U vs NFC teams as 3 point or less favorite since 1996		5-0-1 S/U vs NFC North as 7.5-10 point favorite since 1978
8-2 S/U vs NFC teams as 3.5-7 point favorite since 2011		2-6 O/U vs NFC North as 7.5 point or more favorite s/1987
21-3-1 S/U vs NFC teams as 7.5-10 point favorite since 1978		3-0 S/U vs Chicago as 3 point or less favorite since 1987
14-4 S/U vs NFC teams as 10.5 point of more favorite since 1987		0-4 ATS vs Minnesota as 3.5-7 point favorite since 1981
1-5 S/U vs NFC East as 7.5 point or more Dog since 1987		vs Detroit - Denver leads series 9-5
17-4-1 O/U vs NFC East as 3.5 point or more favorite since 1986		vs Green Bay - HOME team 12-1-1 S/U since 1971
20-4 S/U vs NFC East as 3.5 or more favorite since 1980		**Playoffs**
14-1 S/U vs NFC East as 3.5-7 point favorite since 1980		15-4 S/U @ home in Playoffs since 1986
8-1 O/U vs NFC East as 3.5-7 point favorite since 1992		0-4 S/U on road in Playoffs since 2000
21-4 S/U vs NFC East as 3.5 or more favorite since 1980		5-2 S/U @ home on Saturday in Playoffs since 1977
vs Washington - Denver leads series 8-7		5-0 O/U on road on Saturday in Playoffs since 1994
2-5 ATS @ home vs Washington since 1980		1-11 S/U on Turf in Playoffs
4-0 S/U @ home vs Washington as 3.5-7 point favorite since 1980		7-2 S/U in AFC Championship since 1977
4-1 O/U vs Washington as 3.5-7 point favorite since 1986		0-6 S/U on road in AFC Wild Card since 1979 {0-5 ATS}
6-1 S/U vs NFC North as 3.5-7 point favorite since 1981		1-5 O/U @ home in Divisional Playoffs since 1999
5-0-1 S/U vs NFC North as 7.5-10 point favorite since 1978		0-3 S/U & ATS vs Indianapolis in Playoffs since 2004
1-6 O/U vs NFC North as 7.5 point or more favorite since 1987		4-0 S/U & ATS @ home vs New England in Playoffs s/1987
0-4 S/U & ATS vs Chicago as 3 point or less Dog since 1983		**THU-SAT-SNF-MNF**
0-3 S/U & ATS vs Detroit as 3 point or less Dog since 1990	Chiefs	11-5 S/U & ATS on Thursday since 2008
3-0 O/U vs Detroit as 3 point or less Dog since 1990	Chiefs	6-2 S/U & ATS on road on Thursday since 2008
0-8 ATS vs NFC North as 3.5-7 point favorite since 1978	Lions	5-15-1 S/U on road on Saturday since 1960
1-8 S/U on road vs NFC North as 3 point or less Dog since 1978	Lions	0-6 S/U on Saturday as Dog since 1983
1-7-1 ATS on road vs NFC North as 3 point or less Dog since 1978	Vikings, Patriots	8-2 S/U @ home on SNF vs NFC teams s/1996 {7-3 ATS}
0-4 O/U vs NFC North as 3 point or less favorite since 1993	Bills	3-16 S/U on road on MNF Since 1998

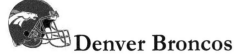

Denver Broncos

Sports Authority Field

2023 Schedule + Trends & Angles

AFC West

Coach: Sean Payton

DATE		OPPONENT	TURF	DEN	OPP	S/U	LINE	ATS	TOT	O/U	Trends & Angles
9/10/2023	vs	LAS VEGAS RAIDERS	G								1-10 ATS vs Raiders last 11 games
9/17/2023	vs	*WASHINGTON*	G								6-1 S/U @ home vs Washington since 1980
9/24/2023	@	Miami	G								1-7 S/U @ Miami since 1967
10/1/2023	@	*Chicago*	G								Game 1-7 O/U vs Chicago since 1990
10/8/2023	vs	NEW YORK JETS	G								8-3 S/U @ home vs New York Jets since 1980
10/12/2023	@	Kansas City	G								0-7 S/U @ Kansas City since 2016
10/22/2023	vs	*GREEN BAY*	G								6-1 S/U @ home vs Green Bay since 1975
10/29/2023	vs	KANSAS CITY	G								2-7 ATS @ home vs Kansas City since 2014
11/5/2023		BYE									
11/13/2023	@	Buffalo	A								0-8 ATS vs Buffalo since 2007
11/19/2023	vs	*MINNESOTA*	G								3-1 S/U vs Minnesota since 2007
11/26/2023	vs	CLEVELAND	G								vs Cleveland - Denver leads series 8-2
12/3/2023	@	Houston	G								4-1 S/U vs Houston since 2013
12/10/2023	@	Los Angeles Chargers	G								Game 1-9 O/U @ LA Chargers since 2013
12/16/2023	@	*Detroit*	A								vs Detroit - Denver leads series 9-5
12/24/2023	vs	NEW ENGLAND	G								18-5 S/U @ Home vs Patriots s/1969 (2 L)
12/31/2023	vs	LOS ANGELES CHARGERS	G								9-1 S/U @ home vs LA Chargers since 2014
1/7/2024	@	Las Vegas Raiders	G								0-7 S/U & ATS @ Las Vegas since 2016
1/14/2024											AFC Wild Card
1/21/2024											AFC Divisional Playoff
1/28/2024											AFC Championship
2/11/2024											Super Bowl LVIII @ Las Vegas, NV

Pointspread Analysis		Pointspread Analysis
vs AFC teams		**vs AFC teams**
0-3 S/U vs AFC East as 10.5 point or more Dog since 1992		Game 7-2 O/U @ home vs LA Chargers since 2014
0-5 S/U & ATS vs AFC East as 3 point or less favorite since 2011		0-7 S/U vs Kansas City as 3.5-7 point Dog since 1995
5-0 O/U vs AFC East as 3 point or less favorite since 2011		0-5 S/U @ Kansas City as 3.5-7 point Dog since 1995
2-8 ATS vs AFC East as 3.5-7 point favorite since 1997		5-1 S/U & ATS vs Kansas City as 3 point or less Dog since 2007
10-1 S/U vs AFC East as 7.5-10 point favorite since 1983		4-0 S/U & ATS @ Kansas City as 3 point or less Dog since 2007
2-8 ATS vs AFC East as 3.5-7 point favorite since 1997		7-1 S/U @ home vs Kansas City as 7.5-10 point favorite since 1978
3-0 S/U vs AFC East as 10.5 point or more favorite since 1999		7-0 S/U vs Kansas City as 10.5 point or more favorite since 1987
3-0 O/U vs AFC East as 10.5 point or more favorite since 1999		1-6 ATS vs Kansas City as 10.5 point or more favorite since 1987
4-0 S/U & ATS vs NY Jets as 7.5-10 point favorite since 1978		0-5 S/U & ATS vs LA Chargers as 7.5-10 point Dog since 2006
Game 1-8 O/U @ home vs NY Jets since 1996		0-5 S/U @ LA Chargers as 3 point or less Dog since 1990
3-0 S/U vs Buffalo as 7.5-10 point favorite since 2002		1-6 O/U @ LA Chargers as 3 point or less Dog since 1983
0-6 ATS vs Miami as 3.5-7 point favorite since 1998		6-0 S/U & ATS @ LA Chargers as 3.5-7 point favorite since 1986
1-5 S/U vs Miami as 3.5-7 point favorite since 1998		0-6 O/U @ LA Chargers as 3.5-7 point favorite since 1986
0-6 ATS vs Miami as 3.5-7 point favorite since 1998		5-0 S/U & ATS vs L.A. Chargers as 10.5 point or more favorite since 1987
5-1 O/U vs Miami as 3.5-7 point favorite since 1998		1-5 O/U & ATS vs L.A. Chargers as 10.5 point or more favorite s/1986
7-0 S/U vs New England as 3.5-7 point favorite since 1984		1-7 O/U @ home vs Las Vegas as 3.5-7 point favorite since 2002
6-1 S/U vs New England as 3.5-7 point favorite since 1984		5-2 S/U & ATS @ Las Vegas as 3 point or less favorite since 2003
3-0 O/U vs New England as 7.5-10 point favorite since 1987		1-4 S/U & ATS @ Raiders as 3.5-7 point favorite since 1997
1-5-1 O/U vs New England as 3 point or less Dog since 1988		4-0 S/U @ Raiders as 7.5-10 point favorite since 1998
5-1 O/U vs New England as 3 point or less favorite since 1986		Game 4-1 O/U @ home vs LA Chargers since 2014
0-5 S/U vs AFC North as 3 point or less favorite since 2017 {0-5 ATS}		1-4 S/U & ATS @ home vs LA Chargers as 3.5-7 point Dog since 2009
14-3 S/U vs AFC North as 3.5-7 point favorite since 1990		10-2 S/U @ home vs LA Chargers as 3.5-7 point favorite since 1978 {9-3 ATS}
0-7 ATS vs AFC North as 7.5-10 point favorite since 1990		10-1 S/U @ home vs LA Chargers as 7.5-10 point favorite since 1984
7-1-1 O/U vs AFC North as 7.5-10 point favorite since 1986		**Grass/Turf**
7-0 S/U vs AFC North as 10.5 point or more favorite since 1996		0-5 S/U on Turf as 10.5 point or more Dog since 1990
1-4 S/U vs AFC South as 7.5-10 point Dog since 1991		2-15 S/U on road on grass as 7.5-10 point Dog since 1982
5-0 O/U vs AFC South as 7.5-10 point Dog since 1991		4-16 S/U vs NFC teams on Turf as 7.5-10 point Dog since 1983
2-7 S/U & ATS vs AFC South as 3 point or less Dog since 2002		7-3 S/U vs NFC teams on Turf as 3.5-7 point favorite since 1996
8-1 S/U vs AFC South as 7.5-10 point favorite since 1985		7-1 S/U on road on grass as 7.5-10 point favorite since 1997
4-1 O/U vs AFC South as 10.5 point or more favorite since 1995		0-4 ATS on Turf as 10.5 point or more favorite since 1987
Game 1-4 O/U vs Houston since 2013		**Dog**
1-10 S/U on road vs AFC West as 7.5-10 point Dog since 1982		1-8 S/U on road as 10.5 point or more Dog since 1992
8-2 ATS @ home vs AFC West as 3 point or less dog since 1981		5-25 S/U as 7.5-10 point Dog since 1987
24-5 S/U @ home vs AFC West as 7.5-10 point favorite since 1978		4-15 S/U on road as 3.5-7 point Dog since 2012
18-2 S/U @ home vs AFC West as 10.5 or more favorite since 1987		**Favorite**
0-8 S/U @ home vs Kansas City since 2015		32-9 S/U as 3.5-7 point favorite since 2011
Game 2-6 O/U @ home vs Las Vegas Raiders since 2015		12-4 S/U on road as 3.5-7 point favorite since 2011
0-15 S/U vs Kansas City last 15 meetings {5-10 ATS}		15-2 S/U as 7.5-10 point favorite since 2012 (reg. season)
Game 4-12 O/U vs Las Vegas Raiders since 2015		34-5 S/U as 10.5 point or more favorite since 1997

Detroit Lions   NFC North

Last 4 seasons + Pointspread Analysis

2022

	Team	Day	Surf				Spread		Total	
vs	PHILADELPHIA		A	35	38	L	6.0	W	49.0	O
vs	WASHINGTON		A	36	27	W	PK	W	48.0	O
@	Minnesota		A	24	28	L	6.5	W	51.5	O
vs	SEATTLE		A	45	48	L	-3.0	L	48.5	O
@	New England		A	0	29	L	3.0	L	47.0	U
	BYE									
@	Dallas		A	6	24	L	6.5	L	49.5	U
vs	MIAMI		A	27	31	L	3.5	L	52.0	O
vs	GREEN BAY		A	15	9	W	3.5	W	49.5	U
@	Chicago		G	31	30	W	3.0	W	48.0	O
@	New York Giants		A	31	18	W	3.0	W	44.0	O
vs	BUFFALO	T	A	25	28	L	9.5	W	54.0	U
vs	JACKSONVILLE		A	40	14	W	-1.5	W	51.5	O
vs	MINNESOTA		A	34	23	W	-2.5	W	51.5	O
@	New York Jets		A	20	17	W	2.0	W	43.5	U
@	Carolina	Sa	G	23	37	L	-1.5	L	43.5	O
vs	CHICAGO		A	41	10	W	-4.0	W	52.0	U
@	Green Bay	Su	G	20	16	W	4.0	W	48.0	U

2021

	Team	Day	Surf				Spread		Total	
vs	SAN FRANCISCO		A	33	41	L	9.5	W	46.0	O
@	Green Bay	M	G	17	35	L	11.5	L	49.5	O
vs	BALTIMORE		A	17	19	L	7.5	W	51.0	U
@	Chicago		G	14	24	L	3.0	L	41.5	U
@	Minnesota		A	17	19	L	10.0	W	50.0	U
vs	CINCINNATI		A	11	34	L	3.5	L	46.5	U
@	Los Angeles Rams		G	19	28	L	16.5	W	50.5	U
vs	PHILADELPHIA		A	6	44	L	3.0	L	48.0	O
	BYE									
@	Pittsburgh {OT}		G	16	16	T	5.5	W	40.5	U
@	Cleveland		G	10	13	L	14.0	W	42.5	U
vs	CHICAGO	T	A	14	16	L	2.5	W	41.5	U
vs	MINNESOTA		A	29	27	W	7.0	L	47.0	O
@	Denver		G	10	38	L	12.5	L	42.0	O
vs	ARIZONA		A	30	12	W	13.0	W	48.5	U
@	Atlanta		A	16	20	L	7.5	W	43.0	U
@	Seattle		A	29	51	L	9.0	L	41.0	O
vs	GREEN BAY		A	37	30	W	4.0	W	45.0	O

2020

	Team	Day	Surf				Spread		Total	
vs	CHICAGO		A	23	27	L	-2.5	L	42.5	O
@	Green Bay		G	21	42	L	6.0	L	51.0	O
@	Arizona		G	26	23	W	5.0	W	55.0	U
vs	NEW ORLEANS		A	29	35	L	3.0	L	51.5	O
	BYE									
@	Jacksonville		G	34	16	W	-3.0	W	52.5	U
@	Atlanta		A	23	22	W	1.0	W	55.0	U
vs	Indianapolis		A	21	41	L	2.5	L	50.0	O
@	Minnesota		A	20	34	L	3.0	L	51.5	O
vs	Washington		A	30	27	W	-2.5	W	45.5	O
@	Carolina		G	0	20	L	-3.0	L	47.0	U
vs	Houston	T	A	25	41	L	3.0	L	52.5	O
@	Chicago		G	34	30	W	3.0	W	44.0	O
vs	GREEN BAY		A	24	31	L	9.5	W	55.5	U
@	Tennessee		G	25	46	L	10.0	L	54.5	O
vs	TAMPA BAY	Sa	A	7	47	L	12.0	L	55.0	U
vs	MINNESOTA		A	35	37	L	3.0	W	53.5	O

2019

	Team	Day	Surf				Spread		Total	
@	Arizona {OT}		G	27	27	T	-3.0	L	45.0	O
vs	L.A. CHARGERS		A	13	10	W	PK	W	47.0	U
@	Philadelphia		G	27	24	W	4.5	W	45.0	O
vs	KANSAS CITY		A	30	34	L	7.5	W	55.0	O
	BYE									
@	Green Bay	M	G	22	23	L	3.5	W	46.0	O
vs	MINNESOTA		A	30	42	L	2.5	L	43.5	O
vs	N.Y. GIANTS		A	31	26	W	-6.5	W	49.5	O
@	Oakland		G	24	31	L	2.5	L	51.5	O
@	Chicago		G	13	20	L	6.5	L	38.0	U
vs	DALLAS		A	27	35	L	7.0	L	46.5	O
@	Washington		G	16	19	L	-4.0	L	39.0	U
vs	CHICAGO	T	A	20	24	L	5.5	W	37.5	O
@	Minnesota		A	7	20	L	12.0	L	44.0	U
vs	TAMPA BAY		A	17	38	L	5.5	W	46.0	O
@	Denver		A	17	27	L	9.0	L	40.5	U
vs	GREEN BAY		A	20	23	L	13.0	W	44.0	U

Pointspread Analysis — Grass/Turf

1-20 S/U on grass as 10.5 point or more Dog since 1984	
1-15 S/U on Turf as 10.5 point or more since 2007	
2-21 S/U on road on grass as 10.5 point or more Dog since 1979	DENVER
1-21 S/U on road on Turf as 7.5-10 point Dog since 1979	Dallas
3-29 S/U on grass as 7.5-10 point Dog since 1985	
0-6 S/U vs AFC teams on grass as 7.5-10 point Dog since 1986	
0-10 S/U vs AFC teams on Turf as 7.5-10 Dog since 1984	
10-38 S/U on grass as 3.5-7 point Dog since 1991	
1-11-1 S/U vs AFC teams on grass as 3.5-7 point Dog since 1978	
3-15 S/U on road on Turf as 3.5-7 point Dog since 2006	
7-19 S/U on grass as 3 point or less Dog since 1994	
5-1 O/U on grass as 3.5-7 point favorite since 1999	LAS VEGAS
1-16 S/U on grass vs NFC West since 1996	
Dog	
1-38 S/U as 7.5-10 point Dog since 2002	
6-49 S/U as 10.5 point or more Dog since 1979	DENVER
10-31 S/U @ home as 3.5-7 point Dog since 2001	Saints
Favorite	
5-0 S/U as 10.5 or more favorite since 1980	
16-3 S/U as 7.5-10 point favorite since 1994	Cowboys
10-2 O/U @ home as 3 point or less favorite since 2015	

Pointspread Analysis — THU-SAT-SNF-MNF

0-16 S/U on Thursday as a Dog since 2004 {3-12-1 ATS}
8-0 S/U @ home on Thursday as a favorite s/1995 {7-1 ATS}
0-5 O/U @ home on Saturday since 1999
1-5 S/U on road on Saturday since 1995 {1-5 ATS}
2-8 S/U on Saturday as Dog since 1983
5-14 S/U on MNF as Dog since 1982
7-2 S/U & ATS @ home on MNF as favorite since 1981
0-6 S/U & ATS vs AFC teams on MNF since 1982
3-16 S/U prior to playing @ Minnesota since 2003
5-17 S/U after playing Thanksgiving day since 2000
8-39 S/U in 2nd of back to back road games since 1998
5-16 S/U in final road game of season since 2001
Playoffs
6-1 S/U @ home in Playoffs since 1935
0-11 S/U on road in Playoffs since 1970
0-9 S/U in Wild Card game since 1983 {1-7-1 ATS}
0-9 S/U in Play-offs on Saturday since 1970
0-3 S/U & ATS @ Washington in Playoffs since 1983

Detroit Lions
Ford Field

NFC North
2023 Schedule + Trends & Angles
Coach: Dan Campbell

DATE		OPPONENT	TURF	DET	OPP	S/U	LINE	ATS	TOT	O/U	Trends & Angles
9/7/2023	@	*Kansas City*	G								0-3 S/U @ Kansas City since 1990
9/17/2023	vs	SEATTLE	A								1-8 S/U vs Seattle since 2003
9/24/2023	vs	ATLANTA	A								vs Atlanta - Detroit leads series 24-15
9/28/2023	@	Green Bay	G								4-28 S/U @ Green Bay since 1992
10/8/2023	vs	CAROLINA	A								vs Carolina - Panthers lead series 8-3
10/15/2023	@	Tampa Bay	G								6-0 ATS @ Tampa Bay since 2000
10/22/2023	@	*Baltimore*	A								vs Baltimore - Detroit leads series 16-9
10/30/2023	vs	*LAS VEGAS RAIDERS*	A								4-1 S/U vs Las Vegas Raiders since 2003
11/5/2023		BYE									
11/12/2023	@	*Los Angeles Chargers*	A								0-5 S/U @ Los Angeles Chargers since 1981
11/19/2023	vs	CHICAGO	A								vs Chicago - Bears leads series 103-78-5
11/23/2023	vs	GREEN BAY	A								10-2 ATS vs Green Bay since 2017 {6-0 @ home}
12/3/2023	@	New Orleans	A								Game 5-1 O/U vs New Orleans since 2012
12/10/2023	@	Chicago	G								vs Chicago - Bears leads series 103-78-5
12/16/2023	vs	*DENVER*	A								vs Denver - Broncos leads series 9-5
12/24/2023	@	Minnesota	A								0-5 S/U @ Minnesota since 2018
12/30/2023	@	Dallas	A								vs Dallas - Cowboys leads series 17-12
1/7/2024	vs	MINNESOTA	A								vs Minnesota - Vikings leads series 80-40-2
1/14/2024											NFC Wild Card
1/21/2024											NFC Divisional Playoff
1/28/2024											NFC Championship
2/11/2024											Super Bowl LVIII @ Las Vegas, NV

Pointspread Analysis	Pointspread Analysis
vs NFC teams	**vs NFC teams**
1-7 S/U vs NFC East as 7.5-10 point Dog since 1978	3-18-1 O/U vs NFC South as 3.5-7 point Dog since 1987
7-0 S/U vs NFC East as 3 point or less favorite since 1999	1-8 O/U @ home vs NFC South as 3.5-7 point Dog since 1988
7-0 S/U @ home vs NFC East as 3 point or less favorite since 1991	1-8-1 ATS vs NFC South as 3 point or less favorite since 1991
0-6 S/U vs Dallas as 3.5-7 point Dog since 1992	6-0 S/U vs NFC South as 7.5-10 point favorite since 1994
4-0 O/U vs Dallas as 3 point or less Dog since 2003	3-0 S/U vs NFC South as 10.5 point or more favorite since 1980
3-0 S/U vs Dallas as 3 point or less favorite since 1991	0-4 O/U vs Atlanta as 3.5-7 point Dog since 1998
3-37 S/U vs NFC North as 7.5 point or more Dog since 1985	3-1 O/U @ Atlanta as 3 point or less Dog since 1984
8-35 S/U vs NFC North as 3.5-7 point Dog since 1999	3-0 S/U @ home vs Atlanta as 7.5-10 point favorite since 1996
5-16 S/U vs NFC North as 3 point or less Dog since 2004	0-3 S/U & ATS vs New Orleans as 7.5-10 point Dog since 1979
14-2 S/U @ home vs NFC North asd 3.5-7 point favorite since 1992	1-6 O/U vs New Orleans as 3.5-7 point Dog since 1988
5-0 S/U vs NFC North as 7.5-10 point favorite since 2011	3-1 S/U & ATS vs New Orleans as 3 point or less Dog since 2000
1-6 ATS vs NFC North as 7.5-10 point favorite since 2000	0-3 S/U vs Tampa Bay as 7.5-10 point Dog since 2001
0-3 S/U vs Chicago as 10.5 point or more Dog since 1986	10-2 ATS vs Tampa Bay as 3.5-7 point Dog since 1979
0-8 S/U vs Chicago as 7.5-10 point Dog since 1985	3-0 S/U vs Tampa Bay as 7.5-10 point favorite since 1994
0-8 S/U @ home vs Chicago as 3.5-7 point Dog since 1988	0-3 S/U & ATS @ Tampa Bay as 3 point or less favorite since 1985
7-1 ATS @ Chicago as 3.5-7 point Dog since 1992	3-0 S/U @ Tampa Bay since 2010
0-7 O/U @ Chicago as 3.5-7 point Dog since 1995	6-29 S/U vs NFC West as 3.5 point or more Dog since 1981
6-2 S/U & ATS @ home vs Chicago as 3 point or less favorite s/1983	2-7 S/U & ATS vs NFC West as 3 point or less Dog since 1984
2-5 O/U @ home vs Chicago as 3 point or less favorite since 1983	0-4 S/U & ATS vs NFC West as 3.5-7 point favorite since 2006
12-0 S/U @ home vs Chicago as 3.5-7 point favorite since 1981	4-0 S/U vs NFC West as 7.5 point or more favorite since 1978
0-3 ATS vs Chicago as 7.5-10 point favorite since 2000	**vs AFC teams**
1-7 S/U vs Green Bay as 10.5 point or more Dog since 1996	0-13 S/U vs AFC teams as 10.5 point or more Dog since 1979
1-6 S/U @ Green Bay as 7.5-10 point Dog since 1997	0-17 S/U vs AFC teams as 7.5-10 point Dog since 1984
1-17 S/U @ Green Bay as 3.5-7 point Dog since 1989	3-17-1 S/U vs AFC teams as 3.5-7 point Dog since 1994
3-13-1 ATS @ Green Bay as 3.5-7 point Dog since 1992	0-10 S/U vs AFC North as 7.5 point or more Dog since 1986
0-3 S/U & ATS @ home vs Green Bay as 3 point or less Dog s/2008	1-6 O/U vs AFC North as 3 point or less Dog since 1983
4-0 S/U & ATS @ Green Bay as 3 point or less favorite since 1986	6-0-1 O/U vs AFC North as 3 point or less favorite since 2001
6-1 S/U & ATS @ home vs Green Bay as 3 point or less favorite since 1986	0-4 ATS vs AFC North as 3.5-7 point favorite since 1983
1-4 S/U @ home vs Green Bay as 3.5-7 point favorite since 1985	1-14 S/U vs AFC West as 3.5 point or more Dog since 1981
1-6 ATS @ home vs Green Bay as 3.5-7 point favorite since 1979	6-1 S/U vs AFC West as 3 point or less favorite since 1981
5-0 O/U @ home vs Green Bay as 3.5-7 point favorite since 1985	3-0 S/U & ATS vs Denver as 3 point or less favorite since 1990
0-8 S/U @ Minnesota as 10.5 point or more Dog since 1988	3-0 O/U vs Denver as 3 point or less favorite since 1990
0-5 S/U vs Minnesota as 7.5-10 point Dog since 2000	Game 8-0 O/U vs Kansas City since 1990
0-5 O/U vs Minnesota as 7.5-10 point Dog since 2000	0-3 S/U vs Kansas City as 3 point or less Dog since 1980
1-8 S/U @ Minnesota as 3.5-7 point Dog since 1994	Game 3-0 O/U vs LA Chargers since 1996
2-7 S/U @ home vs Minnesota as 3.5-7 point Dog since 1994	0-3 ATS @ LA Chargers since 1996
0-5 S/U @ home vs Minnesota as 3 point or less Dog since 2004	0-4 S/U @ L.A. Chargers as 3.5-7 point Dog since 1981
Game 2-8 O/U @ Minnesota since 2013	
0-9 S/U vs NFC South as 8 point or more Dog since 2002	

Last 4 seasons + Pointspread Analysis

2022

@	Minnesota		A	7	23	L	2.0	L	46.0	U
vs	CHICAGO	Su	G	27	10	W	-10.0	W	42.0	U
@	Tampa Bay		G	14	12	W	1.0	W	42.5	U
vs	NEW ENGLAND {OT}		A	27	24	W	-9.5	L	40.0	O
vs	N.Y Giants {London}		G	22	27	L	-9.0	L	42.0	U
vs	NEW YORK JETS		G	10	27	L	-7.5	L	44.0	U
@	Washington		G	21	23	L	-4.0	L	41.0	O
@	Buffalo	Su	A	17	27	L	10.5	W	47.0	U
@	Detroit		A	9	15	L	-3.5	L	49.5	U
vs	DALLAS {OT}		G	31	28	W	3.5	W	44.5	O
vs	TENNESSEE	T	G	17	27	L	-3.0	L	40.5	U
@	Philadelphia	Su	G	33	40	L	6.0	L	46.0	O
@	Chicago		G	28	19	W	-3.5	W	44.5	O
BYE										
vs	LOS ANGELES RAMS	M	G	24	12	W	-7.5	W	39.5	U
@	Miami		G	26	20	W	3.5	W	44.0	O
vs	MINNESOTA		G	41	17	W	-3.5	W	47.5	O
vs	DETROIT	Su	G	16	20	L	-4.0	L	48.0	U

2021

vs	New Orleans {at Jax}		A	3	38	L	-3.5	L	49.0	U
vs	DETROIT	M	G	35	17	W	-11.5	W	49.5	O
@	San Francisco	Su	G	30	28	W	3.0	W	50.5	O
vs	PITTSBURGH		G	27	17	W	-6.0	W	45.0	U
@	Cincinnati {OT}		A	25	22	W	-2.0	W	50.0	U
@	Chicago		G	24	14	W	-5.5	W	44.0	U
vs	WASHINGTON		G	24	10	W	-9.0	W	48.0	U
@	Arizona	T	G	24	21	W	6.5	W	50.5	U
@	Kansas City		G	7	13	L	7.0	W	48.0	U
vs	SEATTLE		G	17	0	W	-3.0	W	49.0	U
@	Minnesota		A	31	34	L	-1.0	L	47.0	O
vs	LOS ANGELES RAMS		G	36	28	W	1.0	W	46.5	O
BYE										
vs	CHICAGO	Su	G	45	30	W	-12.0	W	43.0	O
@	Baltimore Ravens		A	31	30	W	-8.5	W	45.5	O
vs	CLEVELAND	Sa	G	24	22	W	-8.0	L	46.5	U
vs	MINNESOTA	Su	G	37	10	W	-12.5	W	42.5	O
@	Detroit		A	30	37	L	-4.0	L	45.0	O
vs	SAN FRANCISCO	Sa	G	10	13	L	-6.0	L	47.0	U

2020

@	Minnesota		A	43	34	W	1.5	W	44.5	O
vs	DETROIT		G	42	21	W	-6.0	W	51.0	O
@	New Orleans	Su	A	37	30	W	3.0	W	51.5	O
vs	ATLANTA	M	G	30	16	W	-5.0	W	56.5	U
BYE										
@	Tampa Bay		G	10	38	L	-3.0	L	54.0	U
@	Houston		G	35	20	W	-2.5	W	55.5	U
vs	MINNESOTA		G	22	28	L	-6.0	L	50.0	T
@	San Francisco	T	G	34	17	W	-5.5	W	48.5	U
vs	JACKSONVILLE		G	24	20	W	-13.5	L	47.0	U
@	Indianapolis		A	31	34	L	1.0	L	52.0	O
vs	CHICAGO	Su	G	41	25	W	-7.5	W	44.5	O
vs	PHILADELPHIA		G	30	16	W	-8.0	W	50.0	U
@	Detroit		A	31	24	W	-9.5	L	55.5	U
vs	CAROLINA	Sa	G	24	16	W	-9.5	L	53.0	U
vs	Tennessee	Su	G	40	14	W	-3.0	W	52.0	U
@	Chicago		G	35	16	W	-5.0	W	48.5	O
vs	L.A. RAMS	Sa	G	32	18	W	-7.0	W	45.0	O
vs	TAMP BAY		G	26	31	L	-3.0	L	53.0	O

2019

@	Chicago	T	G	10	3	W	3.0	W	46.5	U
vs	MINNESOTA		G	21	16	W	-3.0	W	43.0	U
vs	DENVER		G	27	16	W	-7.0	W	41.5	U
vs	PHILADELPHIA	T	G	27	34	L	-3.5	L	46.5	U
@	Dallas		A	34	24	W	3.5	W	46.5	O
vs	DETROIT	M	G	23	22	W	-3.5	L	46.5	U
vs	OAKLAND		G	42	24	W	-5.5	W	47.5	O
@	Kansas City	Su	G	31	24	W	-5.0	W	48.0	O
@	L.A. Chargers		G	11	26	L	-4.0	L	50.0	U
vs	CAROLINA		G	24	16	W	-5.0	W	49.0	U
BYE										
@	San Francisco	Su	G	8	37	L	3.0	L	47.5	U
@	New York Giants		A	31	13	W	-6.5	W	44.0	T
vs	WASHINGTON		A	20	15	W	-12.5	L	42.0	U
vs	CHICAGO		G	21	13	W	-4.0	W	40.5	U
@	Minnesota	M	A	23	10	W	4.0	W	47.5	U
@	Detroit		A	23	20	W	-13.0	L	45.0	O
vs	SEATTLE		G	28	23	W	-4.5	W	45.5	O
@	San Francisco		G	20	37	L	8.0	L	46.5	O

Pointspread Analysis

Dog
3-18 S/U as 10.5 point or more Dog since 1979
7-26-1 S/U as 7.5-10 point Dog since 1979
16-3 O/U as 3 point or less Dog since 2016

Favorite
59-12-1 S/U as 3.5-7 point favorite since 2005
31-4-1 S/U @ home as 3.5-7 point favorite since 2012
13-3-1 O/U on road as 3.5-7 point favorite since 2011
23-5 S/U as 7.5-10 point favorite since 2010
40-4 S/U @ home as 10.5 point or more favorite since 1993
45-6 S/U as 10.5 point or more favorite since 1993

Playoffs
10-4 S/U on Saturday in Play-offs since 1967
4-0 O/U in Super Bowl since 1968
7-3 S/U @ home in NFC Wild Card since 1983
8-2 S/U @ home in Divisional Playoffs since 1965
7-2 S/U @ home on Saturday in Playoffs since 1967
3-9 S/U on road in Divisional Playoffs since 1972
4-1 O/U on road in Divisional Playoffs since 1994
7-1 O/U in Playoffs since 2017
19-7 S/U @ home in Playoffs since 1961 {2 L}
1-4 S/U @ Dallas in Playoffs since 1982
4-0 O/U @ Dallas in Playoffs since 1994
3-0 O/U vs New York Giants in Playoffs since 2008
4-0 O/U vs Seattle in Playoffs since 2004

Pointspread Analysis

vs AFC teams	
0-5 O/U vs AFC teams as 7.5-10 point Dog since 1987	
13-3 S/U vs AFC teams as 7.5-10 point favorite since 1996	
11-0 S/U @ home vs AFC teams as 10.5 point or more favorite s/1995	
0-3 S/U vs AFC North as 7.5-10 point Dog since 1980	
6-2 O/U vs AFC North as 3 point or less favorite since 1983	
Game 3-0 O/U @ Pittsburgh since 1998	
1-5 S/U vs Pittsburgh since 1998 (Reg season)	
4-0 S/U vs AFC West as 3 point or less Dog since 1993	
8-1 S/U & ATS vs AFC West as 3.5-7 point favorite since 2003	
9-1 O/U vs AFC West as 3.5-7 point favorite since 1999	
5-0 S/U vs AFC West as 7.5-10 point favorite since 1996	
4-0 S/U vs AFC West as 3 point or less Dog since 1993	
8-1 S/U & ATS vs AFC West as 3.5-7 point favorite since 2003	
9-1 O/U vs AFC West as 3.5-7 point favorite since 1999	
0-3 S/U & ATS @ home vs Chiefs as 3 point or less favorite s/1989	
Game 3-0 O/U @ Las Vegas Raiders since 1990	
0-3 S/U vs Las Vegas Raiders as 3.5-7 point Dog since 1984	
THU-SAT-SNF-MNF	
8-2 ATS on SNF since 2020	CHIEFS, Vikings
14-2 S/U @ home on SNF since 2009	CHIEFS
4-11 S/U on road on SNF since 2014	Vikings
3-13 S/U on SNF as a dog since 2007	
25-5 S/U on SNF as favorite since 1996	
3-9 S/U on road on MNF since 2005	Giants

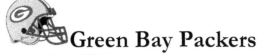

Green Bay Packers

Lambeau Field

NFC North

2023 Schedule + Trends & Angles

Coach: Matt LaFleur

DATE		OPPONENT	TURF	GB	OPP	S/U	LINE	ATS	TOT	O/U	Trends & Angles
9/10/2023	@	Chicago	G								vs Chicago - Green Bay leads series 106-93-6
9/17/2023	@	Atlanta	A								vs Atlanta - Packers lead series 19-16
9/24/2023	vs	NEW ORLEANS	G								9-2 S/U @ home vs New Orleans since 1973
9/28/2023	vs	DETROIT	G								vs Detroit - Green Bay leads series 104-75-7
10/9/2023	@	Las Vegas Raiders	G								3-0 ATS @ Las Vegas Raiders since 1990
10/15/2023		BYE									
10/22/2023	@	Denver	G								HOME team 12-1-1 S/U since 1971
10/29/2023	vs	MINNESOTA	G								12-4-2 S/U @ home vs Minnesota since 2006
11/5/2023	vs	LOS ANGELES RAMS	G								11-1 S/U @ home vs Los Angeles Rams s/1990
11/12/2023	@	Pittsburgh	G								0-5 S/U @ Pittsburgh since 1980
11/19/2023	vs	LOS ANGELES CHARGERS	G								10-2 S/U vs L.A. Chargers since 1970 {9-3 ATS}
11/23/2023	@	Detroit	A								4-1 S/U & ATS @ Detroit on Thursday since 2007
12/3/2023	vs	KANSAS CITY	G								Game 6-2 O/U vs Kansas City since 1993
12/11/2023	@	New York Giants	A								1-3 ATS @ New York Giants since 2011
12/17/2023	vs	TAMPA BAY	G								15-2 S/U @ home vs Tampa Bay since 1990
12/24/2023	@	Carolina	G								vs Carolina - Packers lead series 11-6
12/31/2023	@	Minnesota	A								Game 2-7 O/U @ Minnesota since 2014
1/7/2024	vs	CHICAGO	G								24-6 S/U in final home game of season since 1993
1/14/2024											NFC Wild Card
1/21/2024											NFC Divisional Playoff
1/28/2024											NFC Championship
2/11/2024											Super Bowl LVIII @ Las Vegas, NV

Pointspread Analysis		Pointspread Analysis	
vs NFC teams		**vs NFC teams**	
1-13 S/U vs NFC East as 7.5 point or more Dog since 1979		6-0 S/U @ home vs Minnesota as 10.5 point or more favorite since 1996	
7-2 S/U vs NFC East as 3 point or less favorite since 1981		5-14 S/U vs NFC South as 3 point or less Dog since 1986	
9-3 S/U vs NFC East as 3.5-7 point favorite since 2004		6-13 ATS vs NFC South as 3 point or less Dog since 1986	
3-0 S/U vs New York Giants as 3 point or less favorite since 1981		8-2 O/U vs NFC South as 3 point or less Dog since 2006	
7-1 S/U vs New York Giants as 3.5-7 point favorite since 1961		30-6 S/U vs NFC South as 3.5-7 point favorite since 1983	
1-5 O/U vs NFC North as 10.5 point or more Dog since 1986		15-3 S/U vs NFC South as 7.5 point or more favorite since 1985	
1-5 S/U vs NFC North as 10.5 point or more Dog since 1986		1-4 S/U @ Atlanta as 3 point or less Dog since 1988	
5-1 O/U vs NFC North as 7.5-10 point Dog since 1988		1-4 S/U & ATS vs Atlanta as 3.5-7 point Dog since 1979	
2-7-1 S/U & ATS vs NFC North as 3 point or less Dog since 1990		0-3 S/U & ATS vs Carolina as 3 point or less favorite since 2000	
18-2-1 S/U @ home vs NFC North as 3.5-7 point favorite s/2005		3-0 O/U vs Carolina as 3 point or less favorite since 2000	
15-5-1 O/U vs NFC North as 3.5-7 point favorite since 2013		6-0 S/U vs Carolina as 3.5-7 point favorite since 1997	
24-9 ATS vs NFC North as 3.5-7 point favorite since 2007		3-1 O/U vs Carolina as 7.5-10 point favorite since 1999	
21-7 S/U vs NFC North as 7.5-10 point favorite since 1984		Game 6-1 O/U @ home vs New Orleans since 1985	
19-1 S/U vs NFC North as 10.5 or more favorite since 1996		1-4 S/U & ATS vs New Orleans as 3 point or less Dog since 1986	
0-5 S/U vs Chicago as 10.5 point or more Dog since 1986		3-1 S/U vs New Orleans as 3.5-7 point favorite since 1995	
0-3 S/U vs Chicago as 7.5-10 point Dog since 1985		3-1 O/U vs New Orleans as 3.5-7 point favorite since 1995	
0-4 S/U & ATS @ home vs Chicago as 3.5-7 point Dog since 1988		10-1 S/U @ home vs Tampa Bay as 3.5-7 point favorite since 1983	
5-1 S/U vs Detroit as 3.5-7 point Dog since 1985		3-0 S/U @ home vs Tampa Bay as 7.5-10 point favorite since 1990	
6-1 ATS vs Detroit as 3.5-7 point Dog since 1981		5-0 S/U vs Tampa Bay as 10.5 point or more favorite since 1993	
6-0 O/U vs Detroit as 3.5-7 point Dog since 1985		4-16 S/U vs NFC West as 3.5 point or more Dog since 1978	
4-0 ATS @ home vs Minnesota as 3.5-7 point Dog since 1978		41-8 S/U vs NFC West as a favorite since 1978	
5-0 S/U & ATS @ Chicago as 3 point or less Dog since 1995		4-1 S/U vs NFC West as 10.5 point or more favorite since 1997	
5-2 O/U @ Chicago as 3 point or less Dog since 1989		0-3 S/U vs Los Angeles Rams as 7.5-10 point Dog since 1978	
1-6 S/U & ATS @ Detroit as 3 point or less Dog since 1994		3-0 S/U @ home vs LA Rams as 3 point or less favorite since 1982	
0-4 S/U & ATS @ home vs Detroit as 3 point or less Dog s/1986		6-0 S/U & ATS vs LA Rams as 3.5-7 point favorite since 1992	
4-1 ATS @ Minnesota as 3 point or less Dog since 2004		4-0 S/U & ATS vs L.A. Rams as 7.5-10 point favorite since 1996	
7-1 S/U & ATS @ Chicago as 3 point or less favorite since 1984		10-0 ATS vs LA Rams since 2004	
3-0 S/U @ home vs Chicago as 3 point or less favorite since 1990		**Grass/Turf**	
3-0 S/U & ATS @ Detroit as 3 point or less favorite since 2008		0-12 S/U on Turf as 10.5 point or more Dog since 1980	
6-1 O/U vs Detroit as 3 point or less favorite since 2008		1-13 S/U on road on grass as 7.5-10 point Dog since 1978	
0-4 S/U & ATS @ Minnesota as 3 point or less favorite since 2012		7-0 O/U vs NFC teams on Turf as 7.5-10 point Dog since 1995	
17-0 S/U vs Chicago as 3.5-7 point favorite since 2001		8-2 S/U vs NFC teams on Turf as 3.5-7 point favorite since 2011	
11-0 S/U @ Chicago as 3.5-7 point favorite since 1998		15-3 S/U on road on grass as 3.5-7 point favorite since 2003	
17-1 S/U @ home vs Detroit as 3.5-7 point favorite since 1989		0-3 S/U & ATS vs AFC teams on Turf as 3.5-7 point favorite since 1998	
13-3-1 ATS @ home vs Detroit as 3.5-7 point favorite since 1992		12-2 S/U on Turf as 7.5-10 point favorite since 1984	
5-1-1 S/U @ home vs Minnesota as 3.5-7 point favorite since 2006			
6-1 S/U @ home vs Detroit as 7.5-10 point favorite since 1997	SAINTS	15-1 S/U in 1st home game of season since 2007	
5-0 S/U vs Minnesota as 7.5-10 point favorite since 1984		31-9-1 S/U @ home after road loss since 2007	
6-0 S/U vs Chicago as 10.5 point or more favorite since 1997	VIKINGS	16-6 S/U after playing on Thursday last 22	
7-1 S/U vs Detroit as 10.5 point or more favorite since 1996			

Houston Texans   AFC South
Last 4 seasons + Pointspread Analysis

2022

	Opponent									
vs	INDIANAPOLIS {OT}		G	20	20	T	7.0	W	46.0	U
@	Denver		G	9	16	L	10.5	W	45.5	U
@	Chicago		G	20	23	L	3.0	T	39.5	O
vs	L.A. CHARGERS		G	24	34	L	5.5	L	45.5	O
@	Jacksonville		G	13	6	W	7.0	W	43.5	U
	BYE									
@	Las Vegas		G	20	38	L	7.0	L	46.0	O
vs	TENNESSEE		G	10	17	L	1.0	L	39.5	U
vs	PHILADELPHIA	T	G	17	29	L	14.0	W	45.0	O
@	New York Giants		A	16	24	L	4.5	L	41.5	U
vs	WASHINGTON		G	10	23	L	3.0	L	41.0	U
@	Miami		G	15	30	L	14.0	L	47.5	U
vs	CLEVELAND		G	14	27	L	7.5	L	46.0	U
@	Dallas		A	23	27	L	17.0	W	44.5	O
vs	KANSAS CITY {OT}		G	24	30	L	14.0	W	48.5	O
@	Tennessee Titans	Sa	G	19	14	W	3.0	W	33.5	U
vs	JACKSONVILLE		G	3	31	L	3.5	L	43.0	U
@	Indianapolis Colts		A	32	31	W	3.0	W	38.0	O

2021

	Opponent									
vs	JACKSONVILLE		G	37	21	W	3.5	W	45.5	O
@	Cleveland		G	21	31	L	13.5	W	48.5	O
vs	CAROLINA	T	G	9	24	L	8.5	L	43.5	U
@	Buffalo		A	0	40	L	18.5	L	47.5	U
vs	NEW ENGLAND		G	22	25	L	8.0	W	39.0	O
@	Indianapolis Colts		A	3	31	L	11.5	L	45.0	U
@	Arizona		G	5	31	L	20.5	L	47.5	U
vs	L.A. RAMS		G	22	38	L	16.5	W	47.0	O
@	Miami		G	9	17	L	3.5	L	44.5	U
	BYE									
@	Tennessee Titans		G	22	13	W	10.5	W	44.5	U
vs	NEW YORK JETS		G	14	21	L	-2.5	L	44.5	U
vs	INDIANAPOLIS		G	0	31	L	10.0	L	45.5	U
vs	SEATTLE		G	13	33	L	9.5	L	41.0	O
@	Jacksonville		G	30	16	W	6.0	W	40.5	O
vs	L.A. CHARGERS		G	41	29	W	13.0	W	45.5	O
@	San Francisco		G	7	23	L	13.5	L	44.0	U
vs	TENNESSEE		G	25	28	L	10.5	W	43.0	O

2020

	Opponent									
@	Kansas City	T	G	20	34	L	9.5	L	53.5	O
vs	Baltimore		G	16	33	L	7.0	L	49.5	U
@	Pittsburgh		G	21	28	L	3.5	L	46.5	O
vs	MINNESOTA		G	23	31	L	-3.5	L	53.0	O
vs	JACKSONVILLE		G	30	14	W	-6.5	W	54.5	U
@	Tennessee {OT}		G	36	42	L	3.5	L	52.0	O
vs	GREEN BAY		G	20	35	L	2.5	L	55.5	U
	BYE									
@	Jacksonville		G	27	25	W	-7.0	L	48.5	O
@	Cleveland		G	7	10	L	4.0	W	46.0	U
vs	NEW ENGLAND		G	27	20	W	2.5	W	49.5	U
@	Detroit	T	A	41	25	W	-3.0	W	52.5	O
vs	Indianapolis		G	20	26	L	3.0	L	50.5	U
@	Chicago		G	7	36	L	-1.0	L	46.0	U
@	Indianapolis		A	20	27	L	9.0	L	52.0	U
vs	CINCINNATI		G	31	37	L	-7.5	L	46.0	O
vs	Tennessee		G	38	41	L	7.5	W	55.5	O

2019

	Opponent									
@	New Orleans	M	A	28	30	L	6.5	W	52.0	O
vs	JACKSONVILLE		G	13	12	W	-7.0	L	43.0	U
@	L.A. Chargers		G	27	20	W	3.0	W	49.0	U
vs	CAROLINA		G	10	16	L	-5.0	L	48.0	U
vs	ATLANTA		G	53	32	W	-4.0	W	49.0	O
@	Kansas City		G	31	24	W	3.5	W	54.5	O
@	Indianapolis		A	23	30	L	1.5	L	46.0	O
vs	Oakland		G	27	24	W	-5.5	L	52.0	U
vs	Jacksonville {London}		G	26	3	W	-1.0	W	47.0	U
	BYE									
@	Baltimore		A	7	41	L	4.0	L	51.5	U
vs	Indianapolis	T	G	20	17	W	-3.5	L	46.5	U
vs	New England	Su	G	28	22	W	3.0	W	46.5	O
vs	DENVER		G	24	38	L	-8.0	L	42.5	O
@	Tennessee		G	24	21	W	3.0	W	50.0	U
@	Tampa Bay	Sa	G	23	20	W	-3.0	T	50.0	U
vs	Tennessee		G	14	35	L	10.0	L	42.5	O
vs	BUFFALO {OT}	Sa	G	22	19	W	-2.5	W	43.0	U
@	Kansas City		G	31	51	L	10.0	L	50.5	O

Pointspread Analysis		Pointspread Analysis
Dog		**THU-SAT-SNF-MNF**
2-26 S/U as 10.5 point or more Dog since 2003		
1-17 S/U as 7.5-10 point Dog since 2007		
13-45-1 S/U as 3.5-7 point Dog since 2007		
3-12 S/U @ home as 3 point or less Dog since 2012		
3-11 ATS @ home as 3 point or less Dog since 2013		
Favorite		**Playoffs**
14-6 S/U as 3 point or less favorite since 2014		0-4 S/U on road in Playoffs since 2012
26-7 S/U as 3.5-7 point favorite since 2014		
11-2 S/U on road as 3.5-7 point favorite since 2009		
0-3 ATS on road as 7.5 point or more favorite since 2008		
7-1 O/U as 7.5 point or more favorite since 2013		
6-1 S/U as 10.5 point or more favorite since 2009		

Houston Texans

AFC South

Reliant Stadium

2023 Schedule + Trends & Angles

Coach: DeMeco Ryans

DATE		OPPONENT	TURF	HOU	OPP	S/U	LINE	ATS	TOT	O/U	Trends & Angles
9/10/2023	@	Baltimore	A								HOME team 7-1 S/U since 2012
9/17/2023	vs	INDIANAPOLIS COLTS	G								2-8-1 S/U @ home vs Indianapolis since 2013
9/24/2023	@	Jacksonville	G								7-1 S/U @ Jacksonville since 2014
10/1/2023	vs	PITTSBURGH	G								0-5 S/U & ATS vs Pittsburgh since 2005
10/8/2023	@	Atlanta	A								vs Atlanta - Texans lead series 3-2
10/15/2023	vs	NEW ORLEANS	G								HOME team 5-0 S/U & ATS since 2003
10/22/2023		BYE									
10/29/2023	@	Carolina	G								vs Carolina - Panthers leads series 4-2
11/5/2023	vs	TAMPA BAY	G								4-0 S/U vs Tampa Bay since 2007 {3-0-1 ATS}
11/12/2023	@	Cincinnati	A								vs Cincinnati - Texans leads series 8-5
11/19/2023	vs	ARIZONA	G								vs Arizona - Cardinals lead series 3-2
11/26/2023	vs	JACKSONVILLE	G								13-4 S/U @ home vs Jacksonville since 2006
12/3/2023	vs	DENVER	G								vs Denver - Broncos lead series 6-3
12/10/2023	@	New York Jets	A								3-1 S/U vs New York Jets since 2012
12/17/2023	@	Tennessee Titans	G								Game 1-6 O/U @ Tennessee since 2016
12/24/2023	vs	CLEVELAND	G								vs Cleveland - Houston leads series 7-6
12/31/2023	vs	TENNESSEE TITANS	G								10-3 ATS @ home vs Tennessee since 2010
1/7/2024	@	Indianapolis	A								4-17 S/U @ Indianapolis since 2002
1/14/2024											AFC Wild Card
1/21/2024											AFC Divisional Playoff
1/28/2024											AFC Championship
2/11/2024											Super Bowl LVIII @ Las Vegas, NV

Pointspread Analysis		Pointspread Analysis	
vs AFC teams		**vs AFC teams**	
7-20 S/U vs AFC East as a Dog since 2002		Game 0-7 O/U @ home vs Indianapolis since 2017	
2-11 S/U vs AFC East as 3.5-7 point Dog since 2003		1-9-1 ATS @ home vs Indianapolis since 2013	
10-3 S/U vs AFC East as a favorite since 2007		5-2 O/U @ Jacksonville since 2015	
vs New York Jets - Jets leads series 6-3		1-5 O/U @ home vs Jacksonville since 2017	
0-3 S/U @ New York Jets as 3.5-7 point Dog since 2004		Game 10-2 O/U @ home vs Tennessee since 2011	
1-7 S/U vs AFC North as 7.5-10 point Dog since 2002		0-4 S/U @ home vs Tennessee since 2019	
2-8 O/U vs AFC North as 3.5-7 point Dog since 2009		3-11 ATS vs AFC West as 3.5 point or more Dog since 2002	
5-1 O/U vs AFC North as 3 point or less Dog since 2002		2-12 S/U vs AFC West as 3.5 point or more Dog since 2002	
6-0 S/U & ATS vs AFC North as 3.5-7 point favorite since 2006		2-5 S/U & ATS vs AFC West as 3 point or less Dog since 2010	
Game 0-3 O/U @ home vs Pittsburgh since 2005		5-1 S/U & ATS vs AFC West as 3 point or less favorite since 2007	
0-3 S/U vs Baltimore as 7.5-10 point Dog since 2005		**vs NFC teams**	
3-0 ATS vs Baltimore as 7.5-10 point Dog since 2005		0-10 S/U vs NFC teams as 10.5 point or more Dog since 2002	
1-10 S/U vs AFC South as 10.5 point or more Dog since 2002		0-11 S/U vs NFC teams as 3.5-7 point Dog since 2009	
7-2 ATS vs AFC South as 7.5-10 point Dog since 2006		0-4 ATS vs NFC teams as 7.5 point or more favorite since 2008	
6-17-1 S/U vs AFC South as 3.5-7 point Dog since 2005		vs Carolina - Game 0-4 O/U @ Houston since 2003	
1-8 O/U vs AFC South as 3.5-7 point Dog since 2010		3-0-1 ATS vs Tampa Bay since 2007	
4-0 S/U vs AFC South as 7.5-10 point favorite since 2011		1-12 S/U vs NFC West as a Dog since 2005	
0-8 S/U vs Indianapolis as 10.5 point or more Dog since 2002		vs Arizona - Cardinals lead series 3-2	
0-4 S/U @ Indianapolis as 7.5-10 point Dog since 2004		**Grass/Turf**	
4-1 ATS vs Indianapolis as 7.5-10 point Dog since 2006		13-49 S/U on Turf since 2002	
0-3 O/U vs Jacksonville as 7.5-10 point Dog since 2003		2-15 S/U on Turf vs NFC since 2002	
0-5 S/U vs Tennessee as 7.5-10 point Dog since 2002		0-13 S/U on Turf as 10.5 point or more Dog since 2002	
1-7-1 S/U vs Indianapolis as 3.5-7 point Dog since 2007		1-11 S/U on Turf as 7.5-10 point Dog since 2004	
0-6 O/U vs Indianapolis as 3.5-7 point Dog since 2010		3-22 S/U on Turf as 3.5-7 point Dog since 2003	
1-6 S/U @ Tennessee as 3.5-7 point Dog since 2005		6-19 S/U on road on grass as 3.5-7 point Dog since 2007	
4-0 O/U vs Jacksonville as 3 point or less Dog since 2010		9-0 S/U on road on grass as 3.5-7 point favorite since 2011	
0-3 S/U & ATS vs Tennessee as 3 point or less favorite since 2005			
1-5 S/U vs Indianapolis as 3.5-7 point favorite since 2011			
0-6 ATS vs Indianapolis as 3.5-7 point favorite since 2011			
4-0 S/U @ Jacksonville as 3.5-7 point favorite since 2011			
1-3 O/U @ Jacksonville as 3.5-7 point favorite since 2011			
10-1 S/U vs Jacksonville as 3.5-7 point favorite since 2011			
9-0 S/U vs Tennessee as 3.5-7 point favorite since 2010			
8-1 ATS vs Tennessee as 3.5-7 point favorite since 2010			
Game 3-11 O/U @ Indianapolis since 2009		Colts	5-16 S/U in final road game of season since 2003

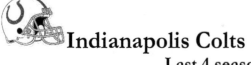
Indianapolis Colts

AFC South

Last 4 seasons + Pointspread Analysis

2022

	Opponent	Day		Colts	Opp	Res	Spread	ATS	Total	O/U
@	Houston Texans		G	20	20	T	-7.0	L	46.0	U
@	Jacksonville		G	0	24	L	-3.0	L	43.5	U
vs	KANSAS CITY		A	20	17	W	4.5	W	51.0	U
vs	TENNESSEE TITANS		A	17	24	L	-4.0	L	43.0	U
@	Denver {OT}	T	G	12	9	W	3.0	W	42.0	U
vs	JACKSONVILLE		A	34	27	W	-2.0	W	41.0	O
@	Tennessee Titans		G	10	19	L	2.5	L	43.0	U
vs	WASHINGTON		A	16	17	L	-3.0	L	40.0	U
@	New England		G	3	26	L	4.5	L	39.5	U
@	Las Vegas		G	25	20	W	3.5	W	41.5	O
vs	PHILADELPHIA		A	16	17	L	6.5	W	45.5	U
vs	PITTSBURGH	M	A	17	24	L	-2.0	L	39.5	O
@	Dallas	Su	A	19	54	L	11.0	L	44.0	O
	BYE									
@	Minnesota {OT}	Sa	A	36	39	L	3.5	W	46.0	U
vs	L.A. CHARGERS	M	A	3	20	L	3.5	L	44.5	U
vs	New York Giants		A	10	38	L	5.5	L	38.5	O
vs	HOUSTON TEXANS		A	31	32	L	-3.0	L	38.0	O

2021

	Opponent	Day		Colts	Opp	Res	Spread	ATS	Total	O/U
vs	SEATTLE		A	16	28	L	3.0	L	49.0	U
vs	L.A. RAMS		A	24	27	L	4.0	W	47.5	O
@	Tennessee Titans		G	16	25	L	4.5	L	47.0	U
@	Miami		G	27	17	W	2.5	W	42.0	O
@	Baltimore Ravens	M	G	25	31	L	7.5	W	46.5	O
vs	HOUSTON TEXANS		A	31	3	W	-11.5	W	45.0	U
@	San Francisco	Su	G	30	18	W	3.5	W	41.5	O
vs	TENNESSEE {OT}		A	31	34	L	-3.0	L	51.0	O
vs	NEW YORK JETS	T	A	45	30	W	-10.0	W	45.0	O
vs	JACKSONVILLE		A	23	17	W	-10.5	L	48.0	U
@	Buffalo		A	41	16	W	7.0	W	49.5	O
vs	TAMPA BAY		A	31	38	L	3.0	L	53.0	O
@	Houston Texans		G	31	0	W	-10.0	W	45.5	U
	BYE									
vs	NEW ENGLAND	Sa	A	27	17	W	-1.0	W	46.5	U
@	Arizona	Sa	G	22	16	W	3.0	W	48.5	U
vs	LAS VEGAS		A	20	23	L	-9.5	L	46.5	U
@	Jacksonville		G	11	26	L	-14.0	L	43.5	U

2020

	Opponent	Day		Colts	Opp	Res	Spread	ATS	Total	O/U
@	Jacksonville		G	20	27	L	-7.5	L	44.0	O
vs	MINNESOTA		A	28	11	W	-3.5	W	49.0	U
vs	N.Y. JETS		A	36	7	W	-12.0	W	44.0	U
@	Chicago		G	19	11	W	-3.5	W	43.5	U
@	Cleveland		G	23	32	L	PK	L	49.0	O
vs	CINCINNATI		A	31	27	W	-7.0	L	46.5	O
	BYE									
@	Detroit		A	41	21	W	-2.5	W	50.0	O
vs	Baltimore		A	10	24	L	1.0	L	48.0	U
@	Tennessee	T	G	34	17	W	-1.0	W	49.0	O
vs	GREEN BAY		A	34	31	W	-1.0	W	52.0	O
vs	Tennessee		A	26	45	L	-3.0	L	51.5	O
@	Houston		G	26	20	W	-3.0	W	50.5	U
@	Las Vegas Raiders		G	44	27	W	-2.5	W	52.0	O
vs	Houston		A	27	20	W	-9.0	L	52.0	U
@	Pittsburgh		G	24	28	L	PK	L	42.5	O
vs	JACKSONVILLE		A	28	14	W	-16.0	L	47.5	O
@	Buffalo	Sa	A	24	27	L	6.5	W	50.5	O

2019

	Opponent	Day		Colts	Opp	Res	Spread	ATS	Total	O/U
@	L.A. Chargers {OT}		G	24	30	L	6.0	T	46.5	O
@	Tennessee		G	19	17	W	3.0	W	43.5	U
vs	ATLANTA		A	27	24	W	-1.0	W	47.0	O
vs	OAKLAND		A	24	31	L	-6.0	L	46.0	O
@	Kansas City	Su	G	19	13	W	10.5	W	55.5	U
	BYE									
vs	HOUSTON		A	30	23	W	-1.5	W	46.0	O
vs	DENVER		A	15	13	W	-5.5	L	41.5	U
@	Pittsburgh		G	24	26	L	1.0	L	39.5	O
vs	MIAMI		A	12	16	L	-10.5	L	44.5	U
vs	JACKSONVILLE		A	33	13	W	-2.5	W	41.5	O
@	Houston	T	G	17	20	L	3.5	L	46.5	O
vs	TENNESSEE		A	17	31	L	PK	L	41.5	O
@	Tampa Bay		G	35	38	L	3.0	T	46.5	O
@	New Orleans	M	A	7	34	L	8.5	L	49.0	U
vs	CAROLINA		A	38	6	W	-7.0	W	46.5	O
@	Jacksonville		G	20	38	L	-5.0	L	41.5	O

Pointspread Analysis

vs NFC teams	Dog
0-6 S/U vs NFC teams as 10.5 point or more Dog since 1998	1-15 S/U as 10.5 point or more Dog since 1997
11-1 S/U vs NFC teams as 7.5-10 point favorite since 1989	1-15 S/U @ home as 7.5-10 point Dog since 1978
7-0 S/U vs NFC teams as 10.5 point or more favorite since 1987	**Favorite**
5-0 O/U vs NFC South as 7.5 point or more Dog since 1986	17-3 S/U on road as 3 point or less favorite since 2009
2-7 S/U vs NFC South as 3.5-7 point Dog since 1986	54-15 S/U as 3.5-7 point favorite since 2004
0-5 S/U & ATS vs NFC South as 3 point or less Dog since 1989	35-10 S/U @ home as 3.5-7 point favorite since 2004
1-4 O/U vs NFC South as 3.5-7 point favorite since 2007	39-9 S/U as 7.5-10 point favorite since 1996
5-0 S/U vs NFC South as 7.5 point or more favorite since 1987	10-1 S/U @ home as 7.5-10 point favorite since 2008
Game 6-1 O/U vs Tampa Bay since 1997	28-2 S/U as 10.5 point or more favorite since 2002
vs Tampa Bay - Colts leads series 8-7	26-1 S/U @ home as 10.5 or more favorite since 1987
0-4 S/U vs NFC West as 10.5 point or more Dog since 1986	**THU-SAT-SNF-MNF**
0-5 O/U vs NFC West as 7.5-10 point Dog since 1986	0-8 O/U on Saturday as a favorite since 1994
1-4 S/U vs NFC West as 3.5-7 point Dog since 1989	**STEELERS** 10-2 S/U @ home on Saturday since 1970
6-0 S/U vs NFC West as 10 point or more favorite since 1996	**Playoffs**
vs L.A. Rams - Colts leads series 23-20-2	1-6 S/U on road in AFC Wild Card since 1996 {2-5 ATS}
Playoffs	5-1 S/U & ATS @ home in AFC Wild Card since 2004
4-1 S/U & ATS vs Kansas City in Playoffs since 1995	1-5 S/U @ home in Divisional Playoffs since 1976
0-4 S/U & ATS @ New England in Playoffs since 2003	1-4 O/U on road in Divisional Playoffs since 2005
3-0 S/U & ATS vs Denver in Playoffs since 2004	1-4-1 O/U on road in AFC Wild Card since 2000
0-5 S/U vs Pittsburgh in Playoffs since 1975	

Indianapolis Colts

Lucas Oil Stadium

2023 Schedule + Trends & Angles

AFC South

Coach: Shane Steichen

DATE		OPPONENT	TURF	IND	OPP	S/U	LINE	ATS	TOT	O/U	Trends & Angles
9/10/2023	vs	JACKSONVILLE	A								9-1 S/U @ home vs Jacksonville since 2013
9/17/2023	@	Houston Texans	G								8-2-1 S/U @ Houston since 2013
9/24/2023	@	Baltimore	A								vs Baltimore - Ravens leads series 21-19
10/1/2023	vs	*LOS ANGELES RAMS*	A								Game 5-0 O/U vs L.A. Rams since 2005
10/8/2023	vs	TENNESSEE TITANS	A								0-4 S/U @ home vs Tennessee since 2019 {0-4 ATS}
10/15/2023	@	Jacksonville	G								0-7 S/U & ATS @ Jacksonville since 2015
10/22/2023	vs	CLEVELAND	A								vs Cleveland - Colts lead series 7-2
10/29/2023	vs	*NEW ORLEANS*	A								Game 0-5 O/U @ home vs New Orleans since 1973
11/5/2023	@	*Carolina*	G								vs Carolina - Panthers lead series 5-2
11/12/2023	@	New England	A								2-16 S/U @ New England Patriots since 1996
11/19/2023		BYE									
11/26/2023	vs	*TAMPA BAY*	A								5-1-1 ATS vs Tampa Bay since 1997
12/3/2023	@	Tennessee Titans	G								8-3 S/U @ Tennessee since 2012
12/10/2023	@	Cincinnati	A								HOME team 9-1 S/U since 2006
12/16/2023	vs	PITTSBURGH	A								2-8 S/U @ home vs Pittsburgh since 1980 {3-7 ATS}
12/24/2023	@	*Atlanta*	A								4-0 ATS @ Atlanta since 1986
12/31/2023	vs	LAS VEGAS RAIDERS	A								1-8 ATS @ home vs Raiders since 1973 {2-7 S/U}
1/7/2024	vs	HOUSTON TEXANS	A								vs Houston - Colts leads series 32-10-1
1/14/2024											AFC Wild Card
1/21/2024											AFC Divisional Playoff
1/28/2024											AFC Championship
2/11/2024											Super Bowl LVIII @ Las Vegas, NV

Pointspread Analysis
vs AFC teams

43-12-1 S/U vs AFC teams as 3.5-7 point favorite since 2004	Game 2-7-1 O/U @ home vs Pittsburgh since 1980
6-1 O/U vs AFC East as 7.5-10 point favorite since 2000	0-6 S/U & ATS vs AFC South as 7.5-10 point Dog since 1990
4-20 S/U vs AFC East as 10.5 point or more Dog since 1979	0-6 O/U vs AFC South as 7.5-10 point Dog since 1990
9-0 O/U vs AFC East as 7.5-10 point Dog since 1991	2-6 S/U vs AFC South as 3 point or less Dog since 2015
4-25 S/U vs AFC East as 7.5-10 point Dog since 1978	25-5 S/U vs AFC South as 3.5-7 point favorite since 2004
1-10 S/U vs AFC East as 3.5-7 point Dog since 1998	27-5 S/U vs AFC South as 7.5 point or more favorite since 2002
9-2-1 O/U vs AFC East as 3.5-7 point Dog since 1998	14-1 S/U vs AFC South as 10.5 point or more favorite since 2002
1-6 ATS vs AFC East as 10.5 point or more favorite since 1978	5-1 S/U & ATS vs Houston as 3.5-7 point Dog since 2011
0-6 S/U vs New England as 10.5 point or more Dog since 1979	7-1-1 S/U vs Houston as 3.5-7 point favorite since 2007
0-8 S/U vs New England as 7.5-10 point Dog since 1978	0-6 O/U vs Houston as 3.5-7 point favorite since 2007
0-9 S/U vs New England as 3.5-7 point Dog s/1996 {0-3 @ home}	6-1 S/U vs Houston as 7.5-10 point favorite since 2003
1-5 O/U vs New England as 3 point or less Dog since 1990	8-0 S/U vs Houston as 10.5 point or more favorite since 2002
0-3 ATS vs New England as 7.5 point or more favorite since 1991	0-4 S/U & ATS vs Jacksonville as 3 point or less Dog since 2011
Game 6-1 O/U @ New England since 2010	3-1 S/U @ Jacksonville as 3 point or less favorite since 2007
Game 9-2 O/U vs New England since 2009	7-2 S/U @ home vs Jacksonville as 3.5-7 point favorite since 2000
vs New England - Patriots leads series 53-30	5-2 S/U vs Jacksonville as 7.5-10 point favorite since 2003
1-9 S/U vs New England since 2010	Game 3-9 O/U @ home vs Jacksonville since 2011
2-18 S/U vs AFC North as 7.5 point or more Dog since 1978	0-3 S/U & ATS vs Tennessee as 7.5-10 point Dog since 1990
11-1 S/U vs AFC North as 3 point or less favorite since 1992	6-1 O/U @ Tennessee as 3.5-7 point Dog since 1984
1-7 O/U vs AFC North as 3 point or less favorite since 2003	7-2 S/U vs Tennessee as 3 point or less favorite since 2003
10-2 ATS vs AFC North as 3 point or less favorite since 1992	12-3 S/U vs Tennessee as 3.5-7 point favorite since 1983
10-1 S/U vs AFC North as 3.5-7 point favorite since 1998	11-4 ATS vs Tennessee as 3.5-7 point favorite since 1983
2-6 O/U vs AFC North as 3.5-7 point favorite since 2006	0-3 O/U vs Tennessee as 7.5-10 point favorite since 2006
5-0 S/U vs AFC North as 10.5 point or more favorite since 1999	3-0 S/U vs Tennessee as 10.5 point or more favorite since 2002
1-4 S/U & ATS @ Baltimore as 3.5-7 point Dog since 1983	10-3-1 O/U vs AFC West as 3.5-7 point Dog since 1993
4-1 O/U @ Baltimore as 3.5-7 point Dog since 1983	2-6-1 O/U vs AFC West as 3.5-7 point favorite since 2005
3-0 S/U & ATS vs Baltimore as 3 point or less favorite since 2005	7-2 S/U vs AFC West as 7.5 point or more favorite since 2004
0-3 O/U vs Baltimore as 3 point or less favorite since 2005	vs Las Vegas - Raiders leads series 11-10
3-0 S/U vs Baltimore as 3.5-7 point favorite since 2002	Game 5-1 O/U vs Las Vegas since 2016
0-3 O/U vs Baltimore as 3.5-7 point favorite since 2002	Game 1-4 O/U @ home vs Las Vegas Raiders since 2001
3-0 S/U vs Baltimore as 7.5-10 point favorite since 1996	**Grass/Turf**
4-0 S/U & ATS vs Cincinnati as 3 point or less favorite since 1992	0-13 S/U on road on Turf as 10.5 point or more Dog since 1993
0-3 O/U vs Cincinnati as 3 point or less favorite since 1992	4-14 S/U on grass as 10.5 or more Dog since 1981
6-0 S/U vs Cincinnati as 3.5-7 point favorite since 1998	5-22 S/U on road on Turf as 7.5-10 point Dog since 1978
3-0 S/U vs Cincinnati as 10.5 point or more favorite since 1999	3-7 S/U on grass vs NFC teams as 3.5-7 point Dog since 1989
4-0 S/U vs Cleveland as 3 point or less favorite since 2002	2-11 S/U on road on Turf as 3 point or less Dog since 2000
0-3 O/U vs Cleveland as 3 point or less favorite since 2003	13-4 O/U on grass as 3 point or less favorite since 2009
0-7 S/U vs Pittsburgh as 10.5 point or more Dog since 1979	14-3 S/U on grass as 3 point or less favorite since 2009
0-6 S/U & ATS vs Pittsburgh as 7.5-10 point Dog since 1978	16-2 S/U on road on Turf as 3 point or less favorite since 1992
1-4 ATS vs Pittsburgh as 3.5-7 point Dog since 1983	16-5 S/U on grass as 3.5-7 point favorite since 2005
0-8 S/U vs Pittsburgh since 2011 {1-7 ATS}	

Jacksonville Jaguars — AFC South
Last 4 seasons + Pointspread Analysis

2022
	Opponent		G/A			W/L	Spread	ATS	Total	O/U
@	Washington		G	22	28	L	3.0	L	43.0	O
vs	INDIANAPOLIS		G	24	0	W	3.0	W	43.5	U
@	Los Angeles Chargers		G	38	10	W	6.5	W	45.5	O
@	Philadelphia		G	21	29	L	6.5	L	43.5	O
vs	HOUSTON TEXANS		G	6	13	L	-7.0	L	43.5	U
@	Indianapolis Colts		A	27	34	L	2.0	L	41.0	O
vs	NEW YORK GIANTS		G	17	23	L	-3.5	L	44.0	U
vs	Denver {London}		G	17	21	L	-1.0	L	41.0	U
vs	LAS VEGAS		G	27	20	W	2.5	W	48.0	O
@	Kansas City		G	17	27	L	9.5	L	51.5	U
	BYE									
vs	BALTIMORE		G	28	27	W	3.0	W	43.0	O
@	Detroit		A	14	40	L	1.5	L	51.5	O
@	Tennessee Titans		G	36	22	W	3.0	W	42.0	O
vs	DALLAS {OT}		G	40	34	W	4.0	W	48.0	O
@	New York Jets	T	A	19	3	W	2.5	W	36.5	U
@	Houston Texans		G	31	3	W	-3.5	W	43.0	U
vs	TENNESSEE	Sa	G	20	16	W	-6.0	L	47.0	
vs	L.A. CHARGERS	Sa	G	31	30	W	2.0	W	46.5	O
@	Kansas City	Sa	G	20	27	L	9.5	W	52.0	U

2021
	Opponent		G/A			W/L	Spread	ATS	Total	O/U
@	Houston Texans		G	21	37	L	-3.5	L	45.5	O
vs	DENVER		G	13	23	L	6.0	L	45.0	U
vs	ARIZONA		G	19	31	L	8.0	L	51.5	U
@	Cincinnati	T	A	21	24	L	7.5	W	46.5	U
vs	TENNESSEE		G	19	37	L	4.5	L	48.5	O
vs	MIAMI {London}		G	23	20	W	1.5	W	47.0	U
	BYE									
@	Seattle		A	7	31	L	4.0	L	44.5	U
vs	BUFFALO		G	9	6	W	14.5	W	48.5	U
@	Indianapolis Colts		A	17	23	L	10.5	W	48.0	U
vs	SAN FRANCISCO		G	10	30	L	6.5	L	45.5	U
vs	ATLANTA		G	14	21	L	1.5	L	45.5	U
@	Los Angeles Rams		G	7	37	L	14.0	L	48.0	U
@	Tennessee Titans		G	0	20	L	9.0	L	44.5	U
vs	HOUSTON TEXANS		G	16	30	L	-6.0	L	40.5	O
@	New York Jets		A	21	26	L	2.5	L	43.5	O
@	New England Patriots		A	10	50	L	17.0	L	42.0	O
vs	INDIANAPOLIS		G	26	11	W	14.0	W	43.5	U

2020
	Opponent		G/A			W/L	Spread	ATS	Total	O/U
vs	Indianapolis		G	27	20	W	7.5	W	44.0	O
@	Tennessee		G	30	33	L	7.0	W	44.5	O
vs	MIAMI	T	G	13	31	L	-2.5	L	49.5	U
@	Cincinnati		A	25	33	L	1.0	L	49.5	O
@	Houston		G	14	30	L	6.5	L	54.5	U
vs	DETROIT		G	16	34	L	3.0	L	52.5	U
	BYE									
vs	L.A. Chargers		G	29	39	L	7.5	L	48.5	O
vs	Houston		G	25	27	L	7.0	W	48.5	O
@	Green Bay		G	20	24	L	13.5	W	47.0	U
vs	PITTSBURGH		G	3	27	L	10.5	L	47.0	U
vs	CLEVELAND		G	25	27	L	7.5	W	48.5	O
@	Minnesota {OT}		G	24	27	L	10.5	W	52.0	U
vs	Tennessee		G	10	31	L	9.0	L	53.0	U
@	Baltimore		A	14	40	L	12.5	L	49.0	O
vs	CHICAGO		G	17	41	L	9.5	L	47.0	O
@	Indianapolis		A	14	28	L	16.0	W	47.5	U

2019
	Opponent		G/A			W/L	Spread	ATS	Total	O/U
vs	KANSAS CITY		G	25	40	L	3.5	L	48.5	O
@	Houston		G	12	13	L	7.0	W	43.0	U
vs	TENNESSEE	T	G	20	7	W	1.5	W	38.0	U
@	Denver		G	26	24	W	2.5	W	37.0	O
@	Carolina		G	27	34	L	3.0	L	40.5	O
vs	NEW ORLEANS		G	6	13	L	-2.5	L	42.5	U
@	Cincinnati		A	27	17	W	-4.0	W	43.5	O
vs	N.Y. JETS		G	29	15	W	-7.0	W	40.0	U
vs	HOUSTON {London}		G	3	26	L	1.0	L	47.0	U
	BYE									
@	Indianapolis		A	13	33	L	2.5	L	41.5	O
@	Tennessee		G	20	42	L	4.0	L	41.5	O
vs	TAMPA BAY		G	11	28	L	3.0	L	46.5	O
vs	L.A. CHARGERS		G	10	45	L	3.0	L	42.0	O
@	Oakland		G	20	16	W	7.0	W	46.5	U
@	Atlanta		A	12	24	L	7.5	L	48.0	U
vs	INDIANAPOLIS		G	38	20	W	5.0	W	41.5	O

Pointspread Analysis

Dog	
5-28 S/U as 10.5 point or more Dog since 1995	
5-1 ATS @ home as 10.5 point or more Dog since 1995	
3-27 S/U as 7.5-10 point Dog since 2009	
12-43 S/U as 3.5-7 point Dog since 2010	
Favorite	
7-2 S/U @ home as 7.5-10 point favorite since 2007	
15-1 S/U as 10.5 point or more favorite since 1998	

Playoffs	
5-1 O/U in Divisional Playoffs since 1997	
0-4 S/U @ New England in Playoffs since 1996	
4-1 S/U @ home in Playoffs since 1999	
0-3 S/U in AFC Championship since 1997	
THU-SAT-SNF-MNF	
0-5 O/U on Thursday as favorite since 2001	
0-5 O/U on road on Thursday since 2011	
Saints — 1-4 S/U on road on Thursday since 2011	
2-7 O/U on MNF as a Dog since 2000	
6-0 S/U on MNF as favorite since 1997 {5-1 ATS}	
BENGALS — 1-6 O/U on MNF since 2006	

Jacksonville Jaguars   AFC South

EverBank Field   *2023 Schedule + Trends & Angles*   Coach: Doug Pederson

DATE		OPPONENT	TURF	JAX	OPP	S/U	LINE	ATS	TOT	O/U	Trends & Angles
9/10/2023	@	Indianapolis Colts	A								1-9 S/U @ Indianapolis since 2013
9/17/2023	vs	KANSAS CITY	G								vs Kansas City - Chiefs lead series 9-6
9/24/2023	vs	HOUSTON TEXANS	G								vs Houston - Texans lead series 28-14
10/1/2023	vs	*ATLANTA*	G								0-6 ATS vs Atlanta since 2003
10/8/2023	@	Buffalo	A								vs Buffalo - Series tied 9-9
10/15/2023	vs	INDIANAPOLIS COLTS	G								vs Indianapolis - Colts leads series 27-17
10/19/2023	@	*New Orleans*	A								0-3 ATS @ New Orleans since 1996
10/29/2023	@	Pittsburgh	G								5-1 S/U & ATS @ Pittsburgh since 2005
11/5/2023		BYE									
11/12/2023	vs	*SAN FRANCISCO*	G								0-5 ATS vs San Francisco since 2005
11/19/2023	vs	TENNESSEE TITANS	G								Game 4-12 O/U @ home vs Tennessee since 2007
11/26/2023	@	Houston Texans	G								Game 1-5 O/U @ Houston since 2017
12/4/2023	vs	CINCINNATI	G								vs Cincinnati - Jaguars leads series 13-11
12/10/2023	@	Cleveland	G								vs Cleveland - Jaguars lead series 10-6
12/17/2023	vs	BALTIMORE	G								vs Baltimore - Jaguars lead series 15-10
12/24/2023	@	*Tampa Bay*	G								Game 3-1 O/U vs Tampa Bay since 2007
12/31/2023	vs	*CAROLINA*	G								vs Carolina - Panthers leads series 4-3
1/7/2024	@	Tennessee Titans	G								1-8 S/U @ Tennessee since 2014
1/14/2024											AFC Wild Card
1/21/2024											AFC Divisional Playoff
1/28/2024											AFC Championship
2/11/2024											Super Bowl LVIII @ Las Vegas, NV

Pointspread Analysis		Pointspread Analysis
vs AFC teams		**vs AFC teams**
1-12 S/U vs AFC East as 7.5 point or more Dog since 1996		8-3 O/U vs AFC West as 7.5 point or more Dog since 1995
2-7 S/U vs AFC East as 3.5-7 point Dog since 1995		2-7 S/U vs AFC West as 3.5-7 point Dog since 2010
7-1 S/U vs AFC East as 7.5-10 point favorite since 1996		0-3 S/U vs Kansas City as 3 point or less Dog since 2006
0-3 S/U & ATS @ Buffalo as 3 point or less favorite since 1998		Game 1-6 O/U vs Kansas City since 2010
3-0 S/U vs Buffalo as 7.5-10 point favorite since 2007		0-7 S/U vs Kansas City since 2010
0-5 S/U vs AFC North as 10.5 point or more Dog since 1996		**vs NFC teams**
9-4 S/U & ATS vs AFC North as 3.5-7 point Dog since 1995		0-11 S/U vs NFC teams as 10.5 point or more Dog s/1995
10-3 S/U vs AFC North as 3 point or less favorite since 1996		1-10 ATS vs NFC teams as 3.5-7 point Dog since 2012
12-3 S/U vs AFC North as 3.5-7 point favorite since 1996		1-12 S/U vs NFC team as 3.5-7 point Dog since 2011
8-0 S/U vs AFC North as 10.5 point or more favorite since 1998		1-10 S/U & ATS vs NFC teams as 3 point or less Dog since 2015
4-0 S/U & ATS vs Cincinnati as 3.5-7 point favorite since 1998		0-7 ATS vs NFC teams as 7.5-10 point favorite since 1996
5-0 S/U vs Baltimore as 3.5-7 point favorite since 1996		4-0 S/U vs NFC teams as 10.5 point or favorite since 1999
3-0 S/U vs Cincinnati as 10.5 point or more favorite since 1998		6-1 O/U vs NFC East as 3.5-7 point Dog since 2000
3-0 S/U vs Cleveland as 10.5 point or more favorite since 1999		7-0 S/U vs NFC South as 3.5 point or more favorite s/1996
4-0 ATS vs Pittsburgh as 3 point or less Dog since 2002		0-5 ATS vs New Orleans since 2003
4-0 S/U vs Pittsburgh as 3 point or less favorite since 1998		0-4 S/U vs New Orleans since 2007
vs Pittsburgh - ROAD team 5-0 S/U & ATS since 2014		0-8 S/U & ATS vs NFC West as a Dog since 1995
2-11 S/U vs AFC South as 7.5-10 point Dog since 2002		0-4 S/U vs San Francisco since 2009
4-21 S/U vs AFC South as 3.5-7 point Dog since 2010		vs San Francisco - 49ers lead series 4-2
7-2 S/U & ATS vs AFC South as 3 point or less favorite since 2010		**Grass/Turf**
1-6 O/U vs AFC South as 7.5-10 point favorite since 1999		0-17 S/U on Turf as 10.5 point or more Dog since 1995
2-9 S/U vs Tennessee since 2017		5-12 ATS on Turf as 10.5 point or more Dog since 1995
Game 9-3 O/U @ Tennessee since 2011		10-2 ATS on road on grass as 10.5 or more Dog since 1995
2-5 S/U vs Indianapolis as 7.5-10 point Dog since 2002		1-12 S/U on road on grass as 7.5-10 point Dog since 1997
1-7 S/U @ Indianapolis as 3.5-7 point Dog since 2000		0-10 S/U on Turf as 7.5-10 point Dog since 2009
1-3 S/U & ATS @ home vs Indianapolis as 3 point or less Dog since 2007		4-16 S/U on Turf as 3.5-7 point Dog since 2000
4-0 S/U & ATS vs Indianapolis as 3 point or less favorite since 2011		6-14 S/U on road on grass as 3 point or less Dog since 2002
1-10 S/U vs Houston as 3.5-7 point Dog since 2011		6-13-1 ATS on road on grass as 3 point or less Dog s/2002
2-8 O/U vs Houston as 3.5-7 point Dog since 2011		9-2 O/U on Turf as 3.5-7 point favorite since 1997
4-0 O/U vs Houston as 3 point or less favorite since 2003	Ind, Buff, N.O.	3-20 S/U on Turf last 23 times
1-5 ATS vs Houston as 3.5-7 point favorite since 2008	Colts	2-13 S/U in 1st road game of season since 2008
0-5 S/U @ Tennessee as 3.5-7 point Dog since 2012	CHIEFS	3-8 S/U in 1st home game of season since 2012
2-5 S/U @ Tennessee as 3 point or less Dog since 2001	Steelers	2-11 S/U after playing on Thursday since 2001
0-3 S/U & ATS @ Tennessee as 3 point or less favorite since 1999		7-36 S/U on road after home loss last 43 times
3-0 S/U & ATS @ home vs Tennessee as 3 point or less favorite since 2001	Titans	1-16 S/U in final road game of season since 2006
0-3 O/U @ home vs Tennessee as 3 point or less favorite since 2001	Buccaneers	10-1 S/U after playing Sunday Night since 1995
0-5 S/U & ATS vs AFC West as 7.5-10 point Dog since 2006		5-15 S/U after winning by 20 pts or more last 20 times

2022

@	Arizona		G	44	21	W	-6.5	W	54.0	O
vs	L.A. CHARGERS	T	G	27	24	W	-4.0	L	51.5	U
@	Indianapolis		A	17	20	L	-4.5	L	51.0	U
@	Tampa Bay	Su	G	41	31	W	2.0	W	47.5	O
vs	LAS VEGAS	M	G	30	29	W	-7.0	L	51.5	O
vs	BUFFALO		G	20	24	L	2.5	L	54.0	U
@	San Francisco		G	44	23	W	PK	W	48.0	O
	BYE									
vs	TENNESSEE {OT}	Su	G	20	17	W	-14.0	L	45.0	U
vs	JACKSONVILLE		G	27	17	W	-9.5	L	51.0	U
@	L.A. Chargers	Su	A	30	27	W	-4.5	L	52.5	O
vs	L.A. RAMS		G	26	10	W	-15.5	L	42.0	U
@	Cincinnati		A	24	27	L	-2.5	L	53.5	U
@	Denver		G	34	28	W	-8.5	W	44.0	O
@	Houston {OT}		G	30	24	W	-14.0	L	48.5	O
vs	SEATTLE	Sa	G	24	10	W	-10.5	L	51.0	U
vs	DENVER		G	27	24	W	-12.5	L	46.5	O
@	Las Vegas Raiders	Sa	G	31	13	W	-8.0	L	51.5	U
vs	JACKSONVILLE	Sa	G	27	20	W	-9.5	L	52.0	U
vs	CINCINNATI		G	23	20	W	-2.5	W	48.0	U
vs	Philadelphia		G	38	35	W	1.0	W	51.5	O

2021

vs	CLEVELAND		G	33	29	W	-5.0	L	55.0	O
@	Baltimore Ravens	Su	A	35	36	L	-3.5	L	53.5	O
vs	L.A. CHARGERS		G	24	30	L	-7.0	L	55.0	U
@	Philadelphia		A	42	30	W	-7.0	W	53.0	O
vs	BUFFALO	Su	G	20	38	L	-2.5	L	57.5	O
@	Washington		G	31	13	W	-6.5	L	54.0	U
@	Tennessee		G	3	27	L	-4.0	L	59.0	U
vs	N.Y GIANTS	M	G	20	17	W	-11.0	L	53.0	U
vs	GREEN BAY		G	13	7	W	-7.0	L	48.0	U
@	Las Vegas Raiders	Su	G	41	14	W	-2.5	L	53.5	O
vs	DALLAS		G	19	9	W	-2.5	L	56.0	U
	BYE									
vs	DENVER		G	22	9	W	-8.5	W	47.0	U
vs	LAS VEGAS		G	48	9	W	-10.0	W	48.0	O
@	L.A. Chargers {OT}	T	G	34	28	W	-3.0	L	53.5	O
vs	PITTSBURGH		G	36	10	W	-10.0	W	44.0	O
@	Cincinnati		A	31	34	L	-3.5	L	51.0	O
@	Denver	Sa	G	28	24	W	-11.5	L	44.5	O
vs	PITTSBURGH	Su	G	42	21	W	-12.0	W	46.5	O
vs	BUFFALO {OT}		G	42	36	W	-2.5	W	54.0	O
vs	CINCINNATI {OT}		G	24	27	L	-7.0	L	54.5	U

2020

vs	Houston	T	G	34	20	W	-9.5	W	53.5	O
@	L.A. Chargers {OT}		G	23	20	W	-9.0	L	46.5	U
@	Baltimore	M	A	34	20	W	3.0	W	54.5	O
vs	New England	M	G	26	10	W	-11.5	W	48.5	U
vs	LAS VEGAS		G	32	40	L	-11.0	L	55.0	O
@	Buffalo	M	A	26	17	W	-5.5	W	55.0	U
@	Denver		G	43	16	W	-7.0	W	46.0	O
vs	NEW YORK JETS		G	35	9	W	-19.5	W	49.0	U
vs	CAROLINA		G	33	31	W	-10.0	L	51.5	O
	BYE									
@	Las Vegas Raiders	Su	G	35	31	W	-7.5	W	56.5	O
@	Tampa Bay		G	27	24	W	-3.0	T	56.0	U
vs	DENVER	Su	G	22	16	W	-13.0	L	51.0	U
@	Miami		G	33	27	W	-7.0	W	51.0	O
@	New Orleans		A	32	29	W	-2.5	W	53.5	O
vs	ATLANTA		G	17	14	W	-10.5	L	54.0	U
vs	L.A. CHARGERS		G	21	38	L	7.0	L	43.0	O
vs	CLEVELAND		G	22	17	W	-7.5	L	56.0	U
vs	BUFFALO		G	38	24	W	-3.0	W	55.0	O
vs	Tampa Bay		G	9	31	L	-3.0	L	55.5	U

2019

@	Jacksonville		G	40	25	W	-3.5	W	48.5	U
@	Oakland		G	28	10	W	-7.0	W	53.5	U
vs	Baltimore		G	33	28	W	-5.0	T	52.0	O
@	Detroit		A	34	30	W	-7.5	W	55.0	O
vs	Indianapolis	Su	G	13	19	L	-10.5	L	55.5	U
vs	HOUSTON		G	24	31	L	-3.5	L	54.5	O
@	Denver	T	G	30	6	W	-3.0	W	49.5	U
vs	GREEN BAY	Su	G	24	31	L	5.0	L	48.0	U
vs	MINNESOTA		G	26	23	W	5.0	W	45.0	U
@	Tennessee		G	32	35	L	-5.5	L	48.5	O
vs	L.A. Chargers {Mex City}	M	G	24	17	W	-5.5	W	52.5	U
	BYE									
vs	Oakland		G	40	9	W	-10.5	W	49.5	U
@	New England		A	23	16	W	2.5	W	49.0	U
vs	DENVER		G	23	3	W	-9.5	W	42.5	U
@	Chicago	Su	G	23	3	W	-6.5	W	45.5	U
vs	L.A. CHARGERS		G	31	21	W	-9.5	W	45.5	U
vs	Houston		G	51	31	W	-10.0	W	50.5	O
vs	Tennessee		G	35	24	W	-7.0	W	51.0	O
vs	San Francisco		G	31	20	W	-1.5	W	52.5	U

Pointspread Analysis
vs NFC teams

11-1 S/U @ home vs NFC teams as 3.5-7 point favorite since 2005	Jets, Packers
2-6 S/U vs NFC East as 3 point or less Dog since 1998	EAGLES
7-1 S/U vs NFC East as 3 point or less favorite since 1983	PHIL, NE
8-0 S/U vs NFC East as 3.5-7 point favorite since 1995	
7-0 ATS vs NFC East as 3.5-7 point favorite since 2001	
Game 8-2 O/U vs Philadelphia since 1972	
7-0 S/U & ATS vs NFC North as 3 point or less Dog since 1981	EAGLES
9-1 S/U @ home vs NFC teams as 3.5-7 point favorite since 2005	PHIL, NE
0-3 O/U @ home vs Chicago as 7.5-10 point favorite since 1996	
3-0 S/U vs Detroit as 3 point or less favorite since 1980	
4-0 S/U & ATS vs Green Bay as 3 point or less Dog since 1989	
3-0 S/U vs Minnesota as 3 point or less Dog since 1981	
Game 1-3 O/U vs Minnesota since 2007	

Favorite

13-3 S/U on road as 3 point or less favorite since 2014 {12-3-1 ATS}
25-8 S/U @ home as 3.5-7 point favorite since 2013
18-0 S/U as 7.5-10 point or more favorite since 2018
23-2 S/U as 10.5 point or more favorite since 1998

Pointspread Analysis
THU-SAT-SNF-MNF

10-1 O/U on road on Sunday Night since 2016
8-0 S/U home on MNF since 2010 {6-2 ATS}
7-2-1 ATS on MNF since 2017 {9-1 S/U}
16-3 S/U as favorite on MNF since 1991
8-2 S/U on road as favorite on SNF since 1994
7-1 O/U on road as favorite on SNF since 2005
8-2 S/U vs NFC on MNF since 1971
1-5 O/U on MNF since 2019

Dog

2-27 S/U as 10.5 point or more Dog since 1978
16-5 ATS as 10.5 point or more Dog since 1998

Playoffs

2-9 S/U on road in Playoffs since 1986
2-7 ATS on road in Playoff since 1992
8-1 S/U @ home in Playoffs since 2019 {6-3 ATS}
6-2 O/U @ home in Playoff since 2018
2-5 S/U in Wild Card since 1994
2-8 ATS in Wild Card since 1991

Kansas City Chiefs   AFC West

Arrowhead Stadium   *2023 Schedule + Trends & Angles*   **Coach: Andy Reid**

DATE		OPPONENT	TURF	KC	OPP	S/U	LINE	ATS	TOT	O/U	Trends & Angles
9/7/2023	vs	*DETROIT*	G								Game 8-0 O/U vs Detroit since 1990
9/17/2023	@	Jacksonville	G								vs Jacksonville - Chiefs lead series 9-6
9/24/2023	vs	*CHICAGO*	G								20-4 S/U @ home vs NFC teams since 2010
10/1/2023	@	New York Jets	A								0-4 S/U @ New York Jets since 2007
10/8/2023	@	*Minnesota*	A								HOME team 6-0 S/U since 1999
10/12/2023	vs	DENVER	G								vs Denver - Denver leads series 70-56-1
10/22/2023	vs	LOS ANGELES CHARGERS	G								vs L.A. Chargers - Chiefs leads series 67-58-1
10/29/2023	@	Denver	G								
11/5/2023	vs	MIAMI	G								vs Miami - Dolphins lead series 16-15
11/12/2023		BYE									
11/20/2023	vs	*PHILADELPHIA*	G								4-0 S/U vs Philadelphia since 2013 {4-0 ATS}
11/26/2023	@	Las Vegas Raiders	G								16-4 S/U @ Las Vegas Raiders since 2003
12/3/2023	@	*Green Bay*	G								vs Green Bay - Chiefs leads series 8-5-1
12/10/2023	vs	BUFFALO	G								vs Buffalo - Bills leads series 28-24-1
12/18/2023	@	New England	A								2-7 S/U @ New England since 1998
12/25/2023	vs	LAS VEGAS RAIDERS	G								9-1 S/U @ home vs Las Vegas Raiders s/2013
12/31/2023	vs	CINCINNATI	G								vs Cincinnati - Bengals leads series 18-15
1/7/2024	@	Los Angeles Chargers	A								8-0 S/U @ LA Chargers since 2014
1/14/2024											AFC Wild Card
1/21/2024											AFC Divisional Playoff
1/28/2024											AFC Championship
2/11/2024											Super Bowl LVIII @ Las Vegas, NV

Pointspread Analysis	Pointspread Analysis
vs AFC teams	**vs AFC teams**
1-8 S/U vs AFC East as 7.5 or more Dog since 1983	1-8 S/U @ L.A. Chargers as 3.5-7 point Dog since 1980
1-7 S/U vs AFC East as 3.5-7 point Dog since 1994	3-0 S/U & ATS vs Denver as 3 point or less Dog since 2005
5-13 S/U vs AFC East as 3 point or less Dog since 1994	3-0 O/U @ home vs Denver as 3 point or less Dog since 2002
6-2 S/U & ATS vs AFC East as 3 point or less favorite since 2002	9-1 S/U @ Las Vegas Raiders as 3 point or less Dog since 1970
1-7 S/U & ATS vs Buffalo as 3 point or less Dog since 1994	8-2 ATS @ Las Vegas Raiders as 3 point or less Dog since 1970
3-0 O/U @ home vs Buffalo as 3 point or less favorite since 2020	1-5 S/U & ATS vs Denver as 3 point or less favorite since 2007
6-1 S/U vs Buffalo as 3.5-7 point favorite since 1997	5-0 S/U & ATS vs L.A. Chargers as 3 point or less favorite s/2014
0-3 S/U @ New England as 3.5-7 point Dog since 1981	1-4 O/U vs L.A. Chargers as 3 point or less favorite since 2014
Game 5-2 O/U vs New England since 2014	7-0 S/U vs Denver as 3.5-7 point favorite since 1995
vs New England - HOME team 13-4 S/U since 1992	6-1 S/U & ATS @ Las Vegas Raiders as 3.5-7 point favorite since 1980
0-3 S/U @ New York Jets as 3.5-7 point Dog since 1988	1-5 O/U @ home vs Las Vegas as 3.5-7 point favorite since 2008
3-0 O/U vs Miami as 3.5-7 point Dog since 1994	5-1 S/U @ L.A. Chargers as 3.5-7 point favorite since 1991
4-0 S/U & ATS vs New York Jets as 3 point or less favorite since 1988	1-6 ATS @ L.A. Chargers as 3.5-7 point favorite since 1985
Game 3-0 O/U @ New York Jets since 2008	0-4 ATS @ home vs L.A. Chargers as 3.5-7 point favorite s/2013
vs NY Jets - HOME team 8-0 S/U since 2005	0-4 O/U @ home vs L.A. Chargers as 3.5-7 point favorite s/2013
0-5 S/U vs AFC North as 10.5 point or more Dog since 1978	7-0 S/U @ home vs Las Vegas as 7.5-10 point favorite since 1993
1-5 S/U vs AFC North as 3.5-7 point Dog since 2006	2-5 O/U @ home vs Las Vegas as 7.5-10 point favorite since 1993
0-6 O/U vs AFC North as 3 point or less Dog since 2008	5-0 S/U vs L.A. Chargers as 7.5-10 point favorite since 1991
8-0 S/U vs AFC North as 7.5 point or more favorite since 1993	6-0 S/U vs Las Vegas as 10.5 point or more favorite since 2003
4-1 ATS vs Cincinnati as 3.5-7 point Dog since 1984	Game 7-3 O/U @ Las Vegas since 2013
4-1 O/U vs Cincinnati as 3.5-7 point Dog since 1984	Game 3-8 O/U @ home vs Las Vegas Raiders since 2008
1-4 O/U vs Cincinnati as 3 point or less Dog since 1983	7-2 ATS @ LA Chargers since 2013
3-17 S/U vs AFC South as 3.5 point or more Dog since 1978	15-3 S/U vs Los Angeles Chargers since 2014
3-0 S/U & ATS vs Jacksonville as 3 point or less favorite since 2006	**Grass/Turf**
1-13 S/U vs AFC West as 10.5 point or more Dog since 1978	1-14 S/U on road on grass as 10.5 or more Dog since 1978
10-2 ATS vs AFC West as 10.5 or more Dog since 1987	13-2 ATS on road on grass as 10.5 or more Dog since 1987
2-16 S/U vs AFC West as 7.5-10 point Dog since 1978	0-11 S/U on Turf as 10.5 point or more Dog since 1978
13-2 S/U vs AFC West as 3.5-7 point favorite since 2016	2-9 S/U on Turf as 7.5-10 point Dog since 1983
27-0 S/U vs AFC West as 7.5 point or more favorite since 1991	2-20 S/U on road on grass as 7.5-10 point Dog since 1978
0-7 S/U vs Denver as 10.5 point or more Dog since 1987	2-10 O/U on road on grass as 7.5-10 point Dog since 1988
6-1 ATS vs Denver as 10.5 point or more Dog since 1987	2-12 S/U on Turf as 3.5-7 point Dog since 1996
0-4 S/U @ L. A. Chargers as 10.5 point or more Dog since 2008	7-17 S/U on road on grass as 3.5-7 point Dog since 2002
4-1 ATS @ L. A. Chargers as 10.5 point or more Dog since 2007	10-3 S/U on road on grass as 3 point or less Dog since 2007
1-7 S/U @ Denver as 7.5-10 point Dog since 1978	10-2-1 ATS on road on grass as 3 point or less Dog since 2007
1-4 O/U @ Denver as 7.5-10 point Dog since 1988	3-14-1 O/U on Turf as 3 point or less Dog since 1997
0-6 S/U @ Las Vegas Raiders as 7.5-10 point Dog since 1979	14-2 S/U on road on grass as 3 point or less favorite since 2013 {13-2-1 ATS}
0-3 S/U @ L. A. Chargers as 7.5-10 point Dog since 1978	15-6 S/U on Turf as 3 point or less favorite since 1988
6-1-1 O/U vs Denver as 3.5-7 point Dog since 2000	20-8 S/U on road on grass as 3.5-7 point favorite since 1993
0-4 S/U @ home vs Las Vegas Raiders as 3.5-7 point Dog since 1978	
5-1 S/U & ATS @ Las Vegas Raiders as 3.5-7 point Dog since 1990	5-16 S/U after scoring less than 10 pts last 21 times

Last 4 seasons + Pointspread Analysis

2022									
@ Los Angeles Chargers		A	19	24	L	3.5	L	52.0	U
vs ARIZONA {OT}		G	23	29	L	-5.5	L	52.5	U
@ Tennessee		G	22	24	L	-2.0	L	45.5	O
vs DENVER		G	32	23	W	-2.5	W	46.0	O
@ Kansas City	M	G	29	30	L	7.0	W	51.5	O
BYE									
vs HOUSTON		G	38	20	W	-7.0	W	46.0	O
@ New Orleans		A	0	24	L	-1.0	L	48.0	U
@ Jacksonville		G	20	27	L	-2.5	L	48.0	U
vs INDIANAPOLIS		G	20	25	L	-3.5	L	41.5	O
@ Denver {OT}		G	22	16	W	2.5	W	41.0	U
@ Seattle {OT}		A	40	34	W	4.0	W	48.0	U
vs L.A. CHARGERS		G	27	24	W	-2.5	W	49.5	O
@ Los Angeles Rams	T	A	16	17	L	-6.0	L	42.5	U
vs NEW ENGLAND		G	30	24	W	-2.5	W	45.0	O
@ Pittsburgh	Sa	G	10	13	L	2.5	L	37.5	U
vs SAN FRANCISCO {OT}		G	34	37	L	10.0	W	41.5	O
vs KANSAS CITY	Sa	G	13	31	L	8.0	L	51.5	U

2021									
vs BALTIMORE {OT}	M	G	33	27	W	3.0	W	50.0	O
@ Pittsburgh		G	26	17	W	5.5	W	46.5	U
vs MIAMI {OT}		G	31	28	W	-3.5	L	44.5	O
@ L.A. Chargers	M	G	14	28	L	3.0	L	51.5	U
vs CHICAGO		G	9	20	L	-5.5	L	45.0	U
@ Denver		G	34	24	W	5.0	W	44.5	O
vs PHILADELPHIA		G	33	22	W	-1.0	W	48.5	O
BYE									
@ New York Giants		A	16	23	L	-3.0	L	46.5	U
vs KANSAS CITY	Su	G	14	41	L	2.5	L	53.5	O
vs CINCINNATI		G	13	32	L	2.5	L	51.0	U
@ Dallas {OT}	T	A	36	33	W	7.0	W	51.0	O
vs WASHINGTON		G	15	17	L	-1.0	L	47.5	U
@ Kansas City		G	9	48	L	10.0	L	48.0	O
@ Cleveland	M	G	16	14	W	-2.5	W	41.5	U
vs DENVER		G	17	13	W	1.0	W	41.5	U
@ Indianapolis Colts		A	23	20	W	9.5	W	46.5	U
vs L.A. CHARGERS {OT}	Su	G	35	32	W	3.0	W	50.0	U
@ Cincinnati	Sa	A	19	26	L	6.0	L	48.5	U

2020									
@ Carolina		G	34	30	W	-2.5	W	48.0	O
vs NEW ORLEANS	M	G	34	24	W	4.0	W	47.5	O
@ New England		A	20	36	L	7.0	L	47.0	O
vs BUFFALO		G	23	30	L	3.0	L	52.5	O
@ Kansas City		G	40	32	W	11.0	W	55.0	O
BYE									
vs TAMPA BAY		G	20	45	L	4.0	L	51.5	O
@ Cleveland		G	16	6	W	1.0	W	49.0	U
@ L.A. Chargers		G	31	26	W	-1.0	W	52.5	O
vs DENVER		G	37	12	W	-3.0	W	50.5	U
vs KANSAS CITY	Su	A	31	35	L	7.5	L	56.5	O
@ Atlanta		A	6	43	L	-3.5	L	53.0	U
@ New York Jets		A	31	28	W	-7.5	L	48.5	O
vs Indianapolis		G	27	44	L	2.5	L	52.0	O
vs L.A. CHARGERS {OT}	T	G	27	30	L	-3.0	L	52.0	O
vs MIAMI	Sa	G	25	26	L	2.0	W	51.0	T
@ Denver		G	32	31	W	-2.5	L	50.0	O

2019									
vs DENVER	M	G	24	16	W	3.0	W	42.5	U
vs KANSAS CITY		G	10	28	L	7.0	L	53.5	U
@ Minnesota		A	14	34	L	9.0	L	43.0	O
@ Indianapolis		A	31	24	W	6.0	W	46.0	O
vs Chicago {London}		G	24	21	W	6.5	W	40.0	O
BYE									
@ Green Bay		G	24	42	L	5.5	L	47.5	O
@ Houston		G	24	27	L	5.5	L	52.0	U
vs DETROIT		G	31	24	W	-2.5	W	51.5	O
vs L.A. CHARGERS	T	G	26	24	W	1.0	W	48.5	O
vs CINCINNATI		G	17	10	W	-13.0	L	48.0	U
@ New York Jets		A	3	34	L	-3.0	L	44.5	U
@ Kansas City		G	9	40	L	10.5	L	49.5	U
vs Tennessee		G	21	42	L	3.0	L	47.0	O
vs JACKSONVILLE		G	16	20	L	-7.0	L	46.5	U
@ L.A. Chargers		G	24	17	W	7.5	W	45.0	U
@ Denver		G	15	16	L	5.5	L	41.0	U

Pointspread Analysis vs NFC teams

Pointspread Analysis vs NFC teams	
8-27 S/U on road vs NFC since 2006	Bears, Lions
1-12 S/U vs NFC teams as 7.5-10 point Dog since 1999	
5-14 S/U vs NFC teams as 3.5-7 point Dog since 2006	
5-13 S/U vs NFC teams as 3 point or less favorite since 2002	
5-13 ATS vs NFC teams as 3 point or less favorite since 2002	
14-3 S/U vs NFC teams as 7.5-10 point favorite since 1984	
0-4 S/U vs NFC East as 7.5-10 point Dog since 2005	
1-5 ATS vs NFC East as 3 point or less favorite since 1998	
1-5 O/U vs NFC East as 3 point or less favorite since 1998	
4-0 O/U vs NFC East as 10.5 point or more favorite since 1986	
3-0 S/U vs New York Giants as 7.5-10 point favorite since 1980	
3-9 S/U vs NFC North as 3.5 point or more Dog since 1987	
1-5 S/U & ATS vs NFC North as 3 point or less favorite since 2003	
3-0 S/U vs NFC North as 7.5 point or more favorite since 1978	
3-1 O/U vs Chicago as 3.5-7 point favorite since 1999	
0-3 S/U & ATS vs Green Bay as 10.5 point or more Dog since 1968	
3-0 O/U vs Green Bay as 10.5 point or more Dog since 1968	
3-0 S/U & ATS vs Minnesota as 3 point or less Dog since 1981	
1-3 S/U & ATS vs Detroit as 3 point or less favorite since 2003	
THU-SAT-SNF-MNF	
11-3 S/U on SNF as favorite since 1991	
2-9 S/U on MNF as a Dog since 1997	
3-9 S/U on road on MNF since 1997	Lions, Chiefs
1-6 S/U vs NFC on MNF since 1991	Packers, Lions

Pointspread Analysis Grass/Turf

Pointspread Analysis Grass/Turf
12-4 O/U on road on grass as 10.5 point or more Dog s/2007
0-9 S/U on Turf as 10.5 point or more Dog since 2006
5-20 S/U on road on grass as 7.5-10 point Dog since 1981
1-15 S/U on Turf as 7.5-10 point Dog since 1993
14-6 ATS on Turf as 3.5-7 point Dog since 1993
3-9 S/U on Turf as 3.5-7 point Dog since 2006
12-5 S/U on Turf as 3.5-7 point favorite since 1978
Dog
1-12 S/U as 10.5 point or more Dog since 2011
11-48 S/U as 7.5-10 point Dog since 1993
6-33 S/U on road as 7.5-10 point Dog since 1993
7-2-1 O/U @ home as 3 point or less Dog since 2019
Favorite
23-7 S/U @ home as 3.5-7 point favorite since 2002
16-1 S/U @ home as 7.5-10 point favorite since 1989
36-6 S/U as 7.5-10 point favorite since 1980
9-2 S/U & ATS on road as 7.5-10 point favorite since 1978
Playoffs
0-7 S/U on road in Playoffs since 1984
8-2 S/U @ home in Playoffs since 1984
0-6 S/U on road on Saturday in Playoffs since 1984
4-0 S/U @ home in WILD Card since 1980 {3-0 ATS}
0-4 S/U on road in WILD Card since 1984
11-2 S/U @ home in Divisional Playoffs since 1968

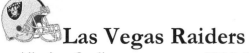

Las Vegas Raiders
Allegiant Stadium
2023 Schedule + Trends & Angles
AFC West
Coach: Josh McDaniel

DATE		OPPONENT	TURF	LV	OPP	S/U	LINE	ATS	TOT	O/U	Trends & Angles
9/10/2023	@	Denver	G								Game 2-6 O/U @ Denver since 2015
9/17/2023	@	Buffalo	A								8-40 S/U on TURF last 48 times
9/24/2023	vs	PITTSBURGH	G								4-0 S/U & ATS @ home vs Pittsburgh s/2006
10/1/2023	@	Los Angeles Chargers	G								Game 4-19 O/U @ LA Chargers since 2000
10/9/2023	vs	*GREEN BAY*	G								vs Green Bay - Packers lead series 8-6
10/15/2023	vs	NEW ENGLAND	G								2-5 ATS vs New England since 2005
10/22/2023	@	*Chicago*	G								vs Chicago - Bears lead series 8-7
10/30/2023	@	*Detroit*	A								8-27 S/U on road vs NFC since 2006
11/5/2023	vs	*NEW YORK GIANTS*	G								vs NY Giants - Raiders leads series 8-6
11/12/2023	vs	NEW YORK JETS	G								17-4-1 S/U @ home vs NY Jets since 1963
11/19/2023	@	Miami	G								Game 4-0 O/U @ Miami since 2011
11/26/2023	vs	KANSAS CITY	G								Game 7-3 O/U @ home vs Kansas City s/2013
12/3/2023		BYE									
12/10/2023	vs	*MINNESOTA*	G								vs Minnesota - Raiders lead series 9-7
12/14/2023	vs	LOS ANGELES CHARGERS	G								Game 4-0 O/U @ home vs LA Chargers s/2019
12/25/2023	@	Kansas City	G								1-9 S/U @ Kansas City since 2013
12/31/2023	@	Indianapolis	A								vs Indianapolis - Raiders lead series 11-10
1/7/2024	vs	DENVER	G								vs Denver - Raiders leads series 70-55-2
1/14/2024											AFC Wild Card
1/21/2024											AFC Divisional Playoff
1/28/2024											AFC Championship
2/11/2024											Super Bowl LVIII @ Las Vegas, NV

Pointspread Analysis		Pointspread Analysis
vs AFC teams		**vs AFC teams**
0-6 S/U vs AFC East as 7.5 point or more Dog since 1998		3-13 O/U on road vs AFC West as 3.5-7 point Dog since 2008
1-8 S/U vs AFC East as 3.5-7 point Dog since 2008		5-12 S/U & ATS @ home vs AFC West as 3 point or less Dog since 2003
0-8 S/U on road vs AFC East as 3 point or less Dog since 1997		13-0 S/U @ home vs AFC West as 7.5-10 point favorite since 1982
6-0-1 O/U vs AFC East as 3 point or less Dog since 2011		1-5 S/U vs Denver as 10.5 point or more Dog since 2005
7-1-1 O/U vs AFC East as 3 point or less favorite since 2002		1-5 S/U vs Denver as 10.5 point or more Dog since 2005
5-1-1 O/U on road vs AFC East as 3 point or less favorite s/1983		0-4 S/U @ home vs Denver as 7.5-10 point Dog since 1998
12-2 S/U vs AFC East as 3.5-7 point favorite since 1987		2-5 S/U @ Denver as 3.5-7 point Dog since 2003
7-1 S/U vs AFC East as 7.5 point or more favorite since 1980		1-7 O/U @ Denver as 3.5-7 point Dog since 2002
5-0 ATS vs Buffalo as 3.5-7 point Dog since 1993		2-5 S/U & ATS @ home vs Denver as 3 point or less Dog since 1999
6-1 O/U vs Buffalo as 3.5-7 point Dog since 1988		4-1 S/U @ home vs Denver as 3.5-7 point favorite since 2001
0-4 S/U & ATS vs Buffalo as 3 point or less Dog since 1980		1-5 S/U vs Kansas City as 10.5 point or more Dog since 2003
3-0 S/U & ATS vs Buffalo as 3 point or less favorite since 2002		0-7 S/U @ Kansas City as 7.5-10 point Dog since 1993
4-0 O/U vs Buffalo as 3 point or less favorite since 1991		2-5 O/U @ Kansas City as 7.5-10 point Dog since 1993
0-7 S/U vs Miami as 3 point or less Dog since 1997 {1-6 ATS}		0-4 S/U @ Kansas City as 3.5-7 point Dog since 2015
vs Miami - Raiders leads series 21-19-1		3-10 O/U @ Kansas City as 3.5-7 point Dog since 1991
Game 7-0-1 O/U vs Miami since 2010		4-0 S/U & ATS @ Kansas City as 3 point or less Dog since 2000
0-5 S/U vs New England as 3.5-7 point Dog since 1987		1-5 S/U & ATS @ home vs Kansas City as 3 point or less Dog since 2004
0-4 ATS vs New England as 3.5-7 point Dog since 2008		1-4 S/U & ATS vs Kansas City as 3 point or less favorite since 2002
3-0 S/U & ATS @ home vs NY Jets as 3 point or less Dog s/2008		1-4 O/U vs Kansas City as 3 point or less favorite since 2002
6-1 S/U vs New York Jets as 3.5-7 point favorite since 1996		1-6 S/U & ATS @ home vs Kansas City as 3.5-7 point favorite since 1990
vs NY Jets - Las Vegas Raiders leads series 26-20-2		5-0 S/U @ home vs Kansas City as 7.5-10 point favorite since 1983
vs NY Jets - HOME team 9-2 S/U since 2005		0-4 O/U vs L.A. Chargers as 10.5 point or more Dog since 2005
8-2 ATS vs AFC North as 3.5-7 point Dog since 2003		3-0 ATS vs L.A. Chargers as 10.5 point or more Dog since 2006
4-11 O/U vs AFC North as 3 point or less Dog since 1983		0-5 S/U @ home vs L.A. Chargers as 7.5-10 point Dog since 2007
3-9 S/U vs AFC North as 3 point or less Dog since 1996		4-1 O/U @ home vs L.A. Chargers as 7.5-10 point Dog since 2007
2-10 ATS vs AFC North as 3 point or less favorite since 1985		1-7 S/U @ L.A. Chargers as 7.5-10 point Dog since 1981
3-0 S/U on road vs AFC North as 3.5-7 point favorite since 1978		1-6 O/U @ L.A. Chargers as 7.5-10 point Dog since 2007
0-4 O/U vs AFC North as 3.5-7 point favorite since 1994		1-5 S/U & ATS @ home vs Chargers as 3 point or less favorite s/1996
0-3 O/U vs Pittsburgh as 7.5-10 point Dog since 2006		6-0 S/U @ L.A. Chargers as 3.5-7 point favorite since 1978
1-3 S/U @ Pittsburgh as 3.5-7 point Dog since 2003		0-4 O/U @ L.A. Chargers as 3.5-7 point favorite since 1991
4-0 ATS vs Pittsburgh as 3.5-7 point Dog since 2004		6-1 S/U @ home vs L.A. Chargers as 3.5-7 point favorite since 1998
3-1 O/U vs Pittsburgh as 3.5-7 point Dog since 2004		0-5 ATS @ home vs L.A. Chargers as 3.5-7 point favorite since 1998
Game 1-6-1 O/U @ home vs Pittsburgh since 1984		3-0 S/U @ home vs L.A. Chargers as 7.5-10 point favorite since 1983
8-2 ATS vs Pittsburgh since 2004		**THU-SAT-SNF-MNF**
vs Pittsburgh - Raiders leads series 17-14	CHARGERS	4-1 S/U @ home on Thursday as a Dog since 1979
vs Pittsburgh - HOME team 9-2 S/U since 2003	CHARGERS	4-1 S/U @ home on Thursday since 2014
0-8 S/U & ATS @ home vs AFC South as 7 point or less Dog since 1997	VIKINGS	4-15 S/U after playing @ home vs KC since 2003
5-1 S/U @ home vs AFC South as 3.5-7 point favorite since 2002	Bills	3-17 S/U in 2nd road game of season since 2003
7-25 S/U vs AFC South as a Dog since 1979	VIKINGS	4-16 S/U after BYE week since 2003
0-10 S/U @ home vs AFC West as 7.5 point or more Dog since 1988		14-31 S/U after scoring less than 10 pts since 2003

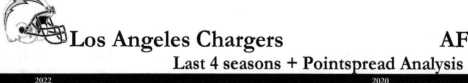

Los Angeles Chargers   AFC West
Last 4 seasons + Pointspread Analysis

2022

Loc	Opponent	Day	Surf	Sc	Opp	W/L	Spread	ATS	Total	O/U
vs	LAS VEGAS		G	24	19	W	-3.5	W	52.0	U
@	Kansas City	T	G	24	27	L	4.0	W	51.5	U
vs	JACKSONVILLE		G	10	38	L	-6.5	L	45.5	O
@	Houston		G	34	24	W	-5.5	W	45.5	U
@	Cleveland		G	30	28	W	-1.0	W	47.0	U
vs	DENVER	M	G	19	16	W	-4.0	L	45.5	U
vs	SEATTLE		G	23	37	L	-4.5	L	51.0	O
	BYE									
@	Atlanta		A	20	17	W	-2.5	W	49.0	U
@	San Francisco	Su	G	16	22	L	8.0	W	45.5	U
vs	KANSAS CITY	Su	G	27	30	L	4.5	W	52.5	O
@	Arizona		G	25	24	W	-2.5	L	49.0	T
@	Las Vegas Raiders		G	24	27	L	2.5	L	49.5	O
vs	MIAMI	Su	G	23	17	W	3.0	W	55.0	U
vs	TENNESSEE		G	17	14	W	-3.0	T	48.5	U
@	Indianapolis	M	A	20	3	W	-3.5	W	44.5	U
vs	L.A. RAMS		G	31	10	W	-6.5	W	41.0	T
@	Denver		G	28	31	L	6.5	W	39.0	O
@	Jacksonville	Sa	G	30	31	L	-2.0	L	46.5	O

2021

Loc	Opponent	Day	Surf	Sc	Opp	W/L	Spread	ATS	Total	O/U
@	Washington		G	20	16	W	1.0	W	45.5	U
vs	DALLAS		G	17	20	L	-3.0	L	55.0	U
@	Kansas City		G	30	24	W	7.0	W	55.0	U
vs	LAS VEGAS	M	G	28	14	W	-3.0	W	51.5	U
vs	CLEVELAND		G	47	42	W	-2.5	W	47.0	O
@	Baltimore Ravens		A	6	34	L	3.0	L	51.0	U
	BYE									
vs	NEW ENGLAND		G	24	27	L	-3.5	L	50.5	O
@	Philadelphia		G	27	24	W	PK	W	49.5	O
@	MINNESOTA		G	20	27	L	-3.5	L	53.5	U
vs	PITTSBURGH	Su	G	41	37	W	-6.0	L	47.5	O
@	Denver		G	13	28	L	-2.5	L	47.0	U
@	Cincinnati		A	41	22	W	2.5	W	50.0	O
vs	N.Y. GIANTS		G	37	21	W	-9.0	W	43.5	O
vs	KANSAS CITY {OT}	T	G	28	34	L	3.0	L	53.5	O
@	Houston		G	29	41	L	-13.0	L	45.5	O
vs	DENVER		G	34	13	W	-9.0	W	45.0	O
@	Las Vegas {OT}	Su	G	32	35	L	-3.0	L	50.0	O

2020

Loc	Opponent	Day	Surf	Sc	Opp	W/L	Spread	ATS	Total	O/U
@	Cincinnati		A	16	13	W	-2.5	W	41.5	U
vs	KANSAS CITY {OT}		G	20	23	L	9.0	W	46.5	U
vs	CAROLINA		G	16	21	L	-6.0	L	44.0	U
@	Tampa Bay		G	31	38	L	7.5	W	42.0	O
@	New Orleans {OT}	M	A	27	30	L	7.0	W	49.0	O
	BYE									
vs	JACKSONVILLE		G	39	29	W	-7.5	W	48.5	O
@	Denver		G	30	31	L	-3.0	L	45.0	O
vs	LAS VEGAS		G	26	31	L	1.0	L	52.5	O
@	Miami		G	21	29	L	2.0	L	48.5	O
vs	NEW YORK JETS		G	34	28	W	-10.0	L	47.0	O
@	Buffalo		A	17	27	L	4.0	L	51.0	U
vs	New England		G	0	45	L	-1.5	L	46.5	U
vs	ATLANTA		G	20	17	W	-1.5	W	48.5	U
@	Las Vegas {OT}	T	G	30	27	W	3.0	W	52.0	U
vs	DENVER		G	19	16	W	-2.0	L	47.5	U
@	Kansas City		G	38	21	W	-7.0	W	43.0	O

2019

Loc	Opponent	Day	Surf	Sc	Opp	W/L	Spread	ATS	Total	O/U
vs	Indianapolis {OT}		G	30	24	W	-6.0	T	46.5	O
@	Detroit		A	10	13	L	PK	L	47.0	U
vs	Houston		G	20	27	L	-3.0	L	49.0	U
@	Miami		G	30	10	W	-15.0	W	43.5	U
vs	DENVER		G	13	20	L	-5.0	L	45.5	U
vs	PITTSBURGH	Su	G	17	24	L	-6.0	L	42.5	U
@	Tennessee		G	20	23	L	2.5	L	42.0	O
@	Chicago		G	17	16	W	3.5	W	41.0	U
vs	GREEN BAY		G	26	11	W	4.0	W	50.0	U
@	Oakland	T	G	24	26	L	-1.0	L	48.5	O
vs	Kansas City {Mex City}	M	G	17	24	L	5.5	L	52.5	O
	BYE									
@	Denver		G	20	23	L	-4.5	L	38.5	O
@	Jacksonville		G	45	10	W	-3.0	W	42.0	O
vs	MINNESOTA		G	10	39	L	PK	L	44.5	O
vs	Oakland		G	17	24	L	-7.5	L	45.0	U
@	Kansas City		G	21	31	L	9.5	L	45.5	O

Pointspread Analysis — Grass/Turf

0-6 S/U on road on grass as 10.5 point or more Dog since 1991	
0-8 S/U on Turf as 10.5 point or more Dog since 1985	
0-5 O/U on road on grass as 10.5 point or more Dog since 1997	
9-0 ATS on Turf as 7.5-10 point Dog since 1988	
2-25 S/U on road on grass as 7.5-10 point Dog since 1983	
11-25 S/U on road on grass as 3.5-7 point Dog since 1995	
16-6 O/U on road on grass as 3.5-7 point Dog since 2003	
5-12 O/U on Turf as 3 point or less Dog since 1997	BEARS
8-0 S/U on road on grass as 7.5-10 point favorite since 2004	COWBOYS

Dog

0-15 S/U as 10.5 point or more Dog since 1988	Jets
6-27 S/U as 7.5-10 point Dog since 1990	
17-4-1 ATS as 7.5-10 point Dog since 1997	
6-20 S/U as 3.5-7 point Dog since 2014	

Favorite

45-8 S/U as 7.5-10 point favorite since 1981	
27-6 S/U as 10.5 point or more favorite since 1979	
5-13 ATS as 10.5 point or more favorite since 2006	

Pointspread Analysis — Playoffs

1-7 O/U @ home in Playoffs since 1993
4-1 S/U & ATS in WILD CARD since 2008
1-5 O/U in WILD CARD since 2005
0-4 S/U in Divisional Playoffs since 2009
0-3 S/U vs New England in Playoff since 2007
2-7 S/U in AFC/AFL Championship since 1960

THU-SAT-SNF-MNF

1-6 S/U vs NFC teams on Sunday Night since 1980 {2-5 ATS}
0-5 O/U @ home on MNF since 2013
1-8 S/U on road on MNF as Dog since 1982
0-5 O/U @ home on MNF as favorite since 2010
6-2 S/U on road on MNF as favorite since 1983

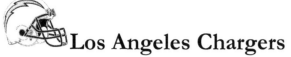 **Los Angeles Chargers**   **AFC West**  **Coach: Brandon Staley**

SoFi Stadium   *2023 Schedule + Trends & Angles*

DATE		OPPONENT	TURF	LAC	OPP	S/U	LINE	ATS	TOT	O/U	Trends & Angles
9/10/2023	vs	MIAMI	G								Game 1-10 O/U @ home vs Miami since 1995
9/17/2023	@	Tennessee	G								12-2 S/U vs Tennessee since 1993
9/24/2023	@	*Minnesota*	A								0-5 ATS vs Minnesota since 2007
10/1/2023	vs	LAS VEGAS RAIDERS	G								Game 4-19 O/U @ home vs Raiders since 2005
10/8/2023		BYE									
10/16/2023	vs	*DALLAS*	G								vs Dallas - Cowboys lead series 7-5
10/22/2023	@	Kansas City	G								3-15 S/U vs Kansas City since 2014
10/29/2023	vs	*CHICAGO*	G								vs Chicago - Bears lead series 7-5
11/5/2023	@	New York Jets	G								4-0 S/U vs NY Jets since 2012
11/12/2023	vs	*DETROIT*	G								3-0 ATS @ home vs Detroit since 1996
11/19/2023	@	*Green Bay*	G								1-7 S/U vs Green Bay since 1993
11/26/2023	vs	BALTIMORE	G								vs Baltimore - L.A. Chargers leads series 15-14-1
12/3/2023	@	New England	A								3-20 S/U vs New England since 1973
12/10/2023	vs	DENVER	G								Game 1-8 O/U @ home vs Denver since 2013
12/14/2023	@	Las Vegas Raiders	G								vs Las Vegas - Raiders leads series 67-57-2
12/23/2023	vs	BUFFALO	G								4-0 S/U & ATS vs Buffalo since 2011
12/31/2023	@	Denver	G								Game 6-2 O/U @ Denver since 2014
1/7/2024	vs	KANSAS CITY	G								0-8 S/U @ home vs Kansas City since 2014
1/14/2024											AFC Wild Card
1/21/2024											AFC Divisional Playoff
1/28/2024											AFC Championship
2/11/2024											Super Bowl LVIII @ Las Vegas, NV

Pointspread Analysis vs AFC teams			Pointspread Analysis vs AFC teams
3-16 S/U vs AFC East as 3.5 point or more Dog since 1978			0-6 S/U & ATS @ home vs Denver as 3.5-7 point Dog since 1986
2-8 ATS vs AFC East as 3 point or less favorite since 1995			0-6 O/U @ home vs Denver as 3.5-7 point Dog since 1986
3-9 O/U vs AFC East as 3.5-7 point Dog since 2007			5-0 S/U @ home vs Denver as 3 point or less favorite since 1990
5-0 S/U vs Buffalo as 3.5-7 point favorite since 1985			1-6 O/U @ home vs Denver as 3 point or less favorite since 1983
3-0 S/U vs Buffalo as 7.5-10 point favorite since 1979			4-1 S/U @ Denver as 3.5-7 point favorite since 2009
0-3 S/U & ATS vs Miami as 3.5-7 point Dog since 2000			5-1 S/U @ home vs Denver as 7.5-10 point favorite since 2006
0-3 O/U vs Miami as 3.5-7 point Dog since 2000			0-5 S/U vs Kansas City as 7.5-10 point Dog since 1989
0-4 O/U vs Miami as 3 point or less favorite since 1995			0-5 S/U & ATS vs Kansas City as 3 point or less Dog since 2014
0-5 S/U & ATS vs New England as 3.5-7 point Dog since 2007			1-4 O/U vs Kansas City as 3 point or less Dog since 2014
0-5 S/U & ATS vs New England as 3 point or less favorite s/1994			8-1 S/U @ home vs Kansas City as 3.5-7 point favorite since 1980
3-0 S/U vs New York Jets as 3.5-7 point favorite since 2005			3-0 S/U vs Kansas City as 7.5-10 point favorite since 1978
vs New England - Patriots leads series 27-15-2			4-0 S/U vs Kansas City as 10.5 point or more favorite since 2008
0-3 S/U & ATS vs AFC North as 10.5 point or more Dog s/1988			1-5 ATS vs Kansas City as 10.5 point or more favorite since 1979
0-4 O/U vs AFC North as 9 point or more Dog since 1988			0-3 S/U vs Las Vegas Raiders as 7.5-10 point Dog since 1983
0-7 ATS vs AFC North as 3.5-7 point favorite since 2009			0-6 S/U @ home vs Las Vegas Raiders as 3.5-7 point Dog s/1978
8-1 S/U vs AFC North as 7.5 point or more favorite since 1992			0-4 O/U @ home vs Las Vegas Raiders as 3.5-7 point Dog s/1991
4-0 O/U vs Baltimore as 3.5-7 point Dog since 1986			10-2 ATS @ Las Vegas Raiders as 3.5-7 point Dog since 1991
3-1 S/U & ATS @ Baltimore as 3 point or less Dog since 1981			5-1 S/U & ATS @ Las Vegas as 3 point or less Dog since 1996
1-4 S/U & ATS vs Baltimore as 3.5-7 point favorite since 1983			3-1 S/U & ATS @ Raiders as 3 point or less favorite since 1992
11-0 ATS vs AFC South as 3.5-10 point Dog since 1989			11-2 S/U vs Raiders as 7.5-10 point favorite since 1981 {5-0 on road}
1-4 O/U vs AFC South as 3 point or less Dog since 2010			0-3 ATS vs Raiders as 10.5 point or more favorite since 2006
9-3 S/U vs AFC South as 3 point or less favorite since 1993			0-4 O/U vs Raiders as 10.5 point or more favorite since 2005
7-3-1 ATS vs AFC South as 3 point or less favorite since 1993			**vs NFC teams**
20-4 S/U vs AFC South as 3.5 point or more favorite since 1984			0-5 S/U vs NFC teams as 10.5 point or more Dog since 1991
19-4-1 ATS vs AFC South as 3.5 point or more favorite since 1984			7-0 ATS vs NFC teams as 7.5-10 point Dog since 1998
9-2 O/U vs AFC South as 3.5-7 point favorite since 1995			14-2 S/U vs NFC teams as 7.5-10 point favorite since 1985
9-2-2 ATS vs Tennessee since 1998			2-8 O/U vs NFC East as 3.5-7 point Dog since 1983
4-0 S/U vs Tennessee as 3.5-7 point favorite since 2010			6-2 O/U vs NFC East as 3 point or less Dog since 1995
0-7 S/U vs AFC West as 10.5 point or more Dog since 1987			12-2 S/U vs NFC East as 3.5 point or more favorite since 1980
1-7 O/U vs AFC West as 10.5 or more Dog since 1986			0-4 O/U vs NFC North as 3 point or less Dog since 2003
1-6 ATS vs AFC West as 10.5 point or more Dog since 1987			4-0 S/U @ home vs Detroit as 3.5-7 point favorite since 1981
2-19 S/U vs AFC West as 7.5-10 point Dog since 1983			0-4 O/U vs NFC North as 3 point or less Dog since 2003
5-23 S/U vs AFC West as 3.5-7 point Dog since 2000			**THU-SAT-SNF-MNF**
5-11 O/U vs AFC West as 3 point or less favorite since 1993	Raiders		6-2 ATS on Thursday since 2015
18-3 S/U vs AFC West as 7.5-10 point favorite since 1981	Raiders		4-0 ATS on road on Thursday as Dog since 2015
1-8 ATS vs AFC West as 10.5 point or more favorite since 2005			1-6 S/U vs Las Vegas Raiders on Thursday since 1979
0-5 S/U & ATS vs Denver as 10.5 point or more Dog since 1987	BILLS		16-5 S/U @ home on Saturday since 1960
0-5 O/U @ Denver as 10.5 point or more Dog since 1986	BILLS		2-8 O/U on Saturday since 2005
1-11 S/U vs Denver as 7.5-10 point Dog since 1984			
2-15 S/U vs Denver as 3.5-7 point Dog since 1978 {4-11 ATS}			

 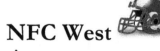

Last 4 seasons + Pointspread Analysis

2022

	Opponent	Day	Surf							
vs	BUFFALO	T	A	10	31	L	2.0	L	51.5	U
vs	ATLANTA		A	31	27	W	-10.0	L	46.0	O
@	Arizona		G	20	12	W	-3.0	W	49.0	U
@	San Francisco	M	G	9	24	L	2.0	L	42.0	U
vs	DALLAS		A	10	22	L	-5.5	L	41.5	U
vs	CAROLINA		A	24	10	W	-10.0	W	40.5	U
	BYE									
vs	SAN FRANCISCO		A	14	31	L	-1.0	L	42.5	O
@	Tampa Bay		G	13	16	L	3.0	T	43.0	U
vs	ARIZONA		A	17	27	L	-3.0	L	37.5	O
@	New Orleans		A	20	27	L	2.0	L	39.5	O
@	Kansas City		G	10	26	L	15.5	L	42.0	U
vs	SEATTLE		A	23	27	L	6.5	W	41.0	U
vs	LAS VEGAS	T	A	17	16	W	6.0	W	42.5	U
@	Green Bay	M	G	12	24	L	7.5	L	39.5	U
vs	DENVER		A	51	14	W	3.0	W	36.5	O
@	Los Angeles Chargers		A	10	31	L	6.5	L	41.0	T
@	Seattle {OT}		A	16	19	L	4.0	W	43.0	U

2021

	Opponent	Day	Surf							
vs	CHICAGO	Su	A	34	14	W	-9.5	W	46.5	O
@	Indianapolis		A	27	24	W	-4.0	L	47.5	O
vs	TAMPA BAY		A	34	24	W	-1.0	W	55.0	O
vs	ARIZONA		A	20	37	L	-3.5	L	54.0	O
@	Seattle	T	A	26	17	W	-2.5	W	53.5	U
@	New York Giants		A	38	11	W	-7.5	W	49.0	T
vs	DETROIT		A	28	19	W	-16.5	L	50.5	U
@	Houston		G	38	22	W	-16.5	L	47.0	O
vs	TENNESSEE	Su	A	16	28	L	-7.0	L	53.0	U
@	San Francisco	M	G	10	31	L	-3.5	L	50.0	U
	BYE									
@	Green Bay		G	28	36	L	-1.0	L	46.5	O
vs	JACKSONVILLE		A	37	7	W	-14.0	W	48.0	U
@	Arizona	M	G	30	23	W	3.0	W	51.0	O
vs	SEATTLE	Tu	A	20	10	W	-7.0	W	47.5	U
@	Minnesota		A	30	23	W	-3.0	W	49.0	O
@	Baltimore		A	20	19	W	-7.0	L	47.0	U
vs	SAN FRANCISCO {OT}		A	24	27	L	-3.5	L	46.0	O
vs	ARIZONA	M	A	34	11	W	-3.0	W	49.0	U
@	Tampa Bay		G	30	27	W	3.0	W	48.0	O
vs	SAN FRANCISCO		A	20	17	W	-3.5	L	46.0	U
vs	Cincinnati		A	23	20	W	-4.5	L	49.0	U

2020

	Opponent	Day	Surf							
vs	DALLAS	Su	G	20	17	W	PK	W	51.5	U
@	Philadelphia		G	37	19	W	1.5	W	45.5	O
@	Buffalo		A	32	35	L	1.5	L	46.5	O
vs	N.Y. GIANTS		G	17	9	W	-13.5	L	50.0	U
@	Washington		G	30	10	W	-7.0	W	44.5	U
@	San Francisco	Su	G	16	24	L	-2.0	L	51.0	U
vs	CHICAGO	M	G	24	10	W	-6.5	W	44.0	U
@	Miami		G	17	28	L	-3.5	L	45.5	U
	BYE		G							
vs	SEATTLE		G	23	16	W	-2.5	W	55.0	U
@	Tampa Bay	M	G	27	24	W	4.0	W	47.5	O
vs	SAN FRANCISCO		G	20	23	L	-5.0	L	44.5	U
@	Arizona		G	38	28	W	-2.5	W	49.0	O
vs	New England	T	G	24	3	W	-4.5	W	43.5	U
vs	N.Y. JETS		G	20	23	L	-17.0	L	44.5	U
@	Seattle		A	9	20	L	1.5	L	48.0	U
vs	Arizona		G	18	7	W	-1.0	W	42.0	U
@	**Seattle**	Sa	A	30	20	W	3.0	W	42.0	O
@	**Green Bay**	Sa	G	18	32	L	7.0	L	45.0	O

2019

	Opponent	Day	Surf							
@	Carolina		G	30	27	W	-1.5	W	49.5	O
vs	NEW ORLEANS		G	27	9	W	-2.0	W	52.5	U
@	Cleveland	Su	G	20	13	W	-4.0	W	47.5	U
vs	TAMPA BAY		G	40	55	L	-9.0	L	48.0	O
@	Seattle	T	A	29	30	L	1.5	L	49.0	U
vs	SAN FRANCISCO		G	7	20	L	-3.0	L	50.0	U
@	Atlanta		A	37	10	W	-3.0	W	54.5	U
vs	Cincinnati {London}		G	24	10	W	-12.5	L	48.5	U
	BYE									
@	Pittsburgh		G	12	17	L	-4.0	L	43.5	U
vs	CHICAGO	Su	G	17	7	W	-5.5	W	39.5	U
vs	Baltimore	M	G	6	45	L	3.0	L	46.5	U
@	Arizona		G	34	7	W	-2.5	W	47.5	U
vs	SEATTLE	Su	G	28	12	W	-1.0	W	48.5	U
@	Dallas		A	21	44	L	PK	L	48.5	O
@	San Francisco	Sa	G	31	34	L	7.0	W	45.5	O
vs	Arizona		G	31	24	W	-7.0	T	46.0	O

Pointspread Analysis vs AFC teams		Pointspread Analysis Grass/Turf
0-8 S/U vs AFC teams as 10.5 point or more Dog since 1996		1-7 S/U on road on Turf as 10.5 point or more Dog since 2008
1-5 S/U & ATS @ home vs AFC teams as 3 point or less Dog since 2007		0-7 O/U on road on Turf as 10.5 point or more Dog since 2011
5-1 O/U @ home vs AFC teams as 3 point or less Dog since 2007		3-15-1 S/U on road on grass as 10.5 point or more Dog since 1992
2-7 S/U vs AFC teams as 3 point or less favorite since 1999		4-14 S/U on road on grass as 7.5-10 point Dog since 1987
1-7-1 ATS vs AFC team as 3 point or less favorite since 1999		0-12 S/U on road on Turf as 7.5-10 point Dog since 2007
23-6 S/U vs AFC teams as 3.5-7 point favorite since 1990		4-1-1 O/U on road on Turf as 3.5-7 point Dog since 2013
3-0 S/U vs AFC teams as 7.5-10 point favorite since 1980		7-29 S/U on road on grass as 3.5-7 point Dog since 1990
0-7 S/U vs AFC North as 7.5 point or more Dog since 1980		3-13 S/U on road on Turf as 3 point or less Dog since 2003
7-1 S/U & ATS vs AFC North as 3.5-7 point favorite since 1990		5-13-1 ATS on road on Turf as 3 point or less Dog since 1998
0-7 S/U vs AFC North as 7.5 point or more favorite since 1980		10-2-1 ATS on road on grass as 3 point or less Dog since 2003
9-1 S/U vs AFC North as 3.5-7 point favorite since 1990 {7-3 ATS}		9-2 S/U on road on Turf as 3.5-7 point favorite since 1999
0-4 S/U vs Baltimore as 3.5-7 point Dog since 1955		12-2 O/U on road on Turf as 3.5-7 point favorite since 1987
0-4 S/U vs AFC South as 10.5 point or more Dog since 2005		**THU-SAT-SNF-MNF**
13-1 S/U vs AFC South as 3.5 point or more favorite since 1984	Bengals	2-14 S/U on road on MNF as Dog since 1989 {4-12 ATS}
Dog		**Favorite**
6-30-1 S/U as 10.5 point or more Dog since 1994		13-5 S/U & ATS as 3 point or less favorite since 2019
0-9 O/U as a 10.5 point or more Dog since 2012		12-24 S/U as 3 point or less favorite since 2003
5-28 S/U as 7.5-10 point Dog since 2006		8-21 O/U on road as 3 point or less favorite since 2001
0-6 O/U @ home as 7.5-10 point Dog since 2008		11-3 S/U on road as 3.5-7 point favorite since 2005
15-3 O/U as 3.5-7 point Dog since 2014		14-2 S/U on road as 7.5-10 point favorite since 1978
Playoffs		13-2 S/U @ home as 10.5 point or more favorite since 2002
8-2 S/U @ home in Playoffs since 1985	STEELERS	3-10 S/U after playing @ home vs Arizona since 2006
8-2 S/U @ home in Divisional Playoffs since 1950 {4-1 ATS}	Seahawks	6-0 S/U in 1st road game of season since 2017

 **Los Angeles Rams**
SoFi Stadium

2023 Schedule + Trends & Angles

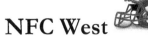 **NFC West**
Coach: Sean McVay

DATE		OPPONENT	TURF	LAR	OPP	S/U	LINE	ATS	TOT	O/U	Trends & Angles
9/10/2023	@	Seattle	A								5-14 S/U @ Seattle since 2005
9/17/2023	vs	SAN FRANCISCO	A								1-6 S/U @ home vs 49ERS since 2016 {1-6 ATS}
9/25/2023	@	Cincinnati	A								vs Cincinnati - Bengals lead series 8-7
10/1/2023	@	Indianapolis	A								vs Indianapolis - Colts leads series 23-20-2
10/8/2023	vs	PHILADELPHIA	A								1-6 ATS @ home vs Philadelphia since 1990
10/15/2023	vs	ARIZONA	A								vs Arizona - Rams leads series 50-40-2
10/22/2023	vs	PITTSBURGH	A								10-2 S/U @ home vs Pittsburgh since 1942
10/29/2023	@	Dallas	A								vs Dallas - Rams lead series 19-18
11/5/2023	@	Green Bay	G								vs Green Bay - Packers leads series 50-44-2
11/12/2023		BYE									
11/19/2023	vs	SEATTLE	A								7-2 S/U @ home vs Seattle since 2014
11/26/2023	@	Arizona Cardinals	G								8-0 S/U & ATS @ Arizona since 2015
12/3/2023	vs	CLEVELAND	A								vs Cleveland - Rams lead series 5-1
12/10/2023	@	Baltimore	A								Game 0-3 O/U @ Baltimore since 2007
12/17/2023	vs	WASHINGTON	A								4-12-1 S/U @ home vs Washington since 1963
12/21/2023	vs	NEW ORLEANS	A								6-0 ATS @ home vs New Orleans since 2005
12/31/2023	@	New York Giants	A								2-9 ATS vs New York Giants since 2002
1/7/2024	@	San Francisco	G								Game 2-8 O/U @ San Francisco since 2013
1/14/2024											NFC Wild Card
1/21/2024											NFC Divisional Playoff
1/28/2024											NFC Championship
2/11/2024											Super Bowl LVIII @ Las Vegas, NV

Pointspread Analysis vs NFC teams		Pointspread Analysis vs NFC teams
0-4 O/U vs NFC East as 10.5 point or more Dog since 2006		1-10 S/U on road vs NFC West as 3.5-7 point Dog since 2006
1-8 S/U & ATS vs NFC East as 3 point or less Dog since 1998		10-0 S/U vs NFC West as 10.5 point or more favorite since 1978
2-7 O/U vs NFC East as 3 point or less favorite since 2001		1-7 S/U vs Arizona as 3.5-7 point Dog since 2007
2-9 S/U & ATS vs NFC East as 3.5-7 point favorite since 1988		1-6 ATS vs Arizona as 3.5-7 point Dog since 2007
5-0-1 O/U vs NFC East as 7.5-10 point favorite since 1985		2-7 S/U @ home vs Arizona as 3.5-7 point favorite since 1988
0-3 O/U @ Dallas as 10.5 point or more Dog since 2006		0-8-1 ATS @ home vs Arizona as 3.5-7 point favorite since 1988
Game 4-1 O/U @ home vs Washington since 2006		3-0 S/U @ home vs Arizona as 10.5 point or more favorite since 2002
0-3 S/U & ATS @ home vs Washington as 3 point or less Dog since 1981		1-8-1 S/U @ San Francisco as 10.5 point or more Dog since 1992
0-4 S/U & ATS vs Philadelphia as 3.5-7 point Dog since 1949		0-4 S/U @ home vs San Francisco as 10.5 point or more Dog since 1993
0-4 O/U vs Philadelphia as 3 point or less favorite since 2001		0-5 S/U & ATS vs San Francisco as 7.5-10 point Dog since 1987
1-3 S/U & ATS vs Washington as 3.5-7 point favorite since 1994		0-4 O/U vs San Francisco as 7.5-10 point Dog since 1991
3-0 S/U @ NY Giants as 3.5-7 point favorite since 1978		0-6 S/U @ San Francisco as 3.5-7 point Dog since 1990
Game 3-0-1 O/U @ New York Giants since 2005		1-8 S/U @ home vs San Francisco as 3.5-7 point Dog since 1983 {2-7 ATS}
vs NY Giants - Rams leads series 29-17		1-6 S/U & ATS @ home vs San Francisco as 3 point or less Dog since 1982
0-11 S/U vs NFC North as 7.5 point or more Dog since 1996		3-0 O/U @ home vs San Francisco as 3 point or less Dog since 1982
4-24 S/U vs NFC North as 7 point or less Dog since 1979		0-4 ATS @ San Francisco as 3 point or less favorite since 2016
5-22-1 ATS vs NFC North as 7 point or less Dog since 1979		1-5 O/U @ San Francisco as 3 point or less favorite since 2006
7-2 O/U vs NFC North as 3.5-7 point favorite since 1999		0-7 ATS vs San Francisco as 3.5-7 point favorite since 2005
30-7 S/U vs NFC North as 3.5 point or more favorite since 1978		4-0 S/U @ San Francisco as 7.5-10 point favorite since 1978
0-4 S/U & ATS vs Green Bay as 7.5-10 point Dog since 1996		4-0 S/U @ home vs San Francisco as 10.5 point or more favorite since 1978
0-6 S/U & ATS vs Green Bay as 3.5-7 point Dog since 1992		1-5 S/U vs Seattle as 10.5 point or more Dog since 2012
6-0 O/U vs Green Bay as 3.5-7 point Dog since 1992		0-6 O/U vs Seattle as 10.5 point or more Dog since 2012
0-3 S/U vs Green Bay as 3 point or less Dog since 1982		0-3 S/U & ATS @ Seattle as 7.5-10 point Dog since 2007
3-0 S/U vs Green Bay as 7.5-10 point favorite since 1978		4-1 O/U @ Seattle as 7.5-10 point Dog since 2007
5-0 O/U vs NFC South as 10.5 point or more Dog since 1993		1-5 O/U @ Seattle as 3.5-7 point Dog since 1991
5-0 ATS vs NFC South as 10.5 point or more Dog since 1993		0-4 S/U @ Seattle as 3.5-7 point Dog since 2005
0-4 S/U vs NFC South as 7.5-10 point Dog since 1992		3-1 S/U @ home vs Seattle as 3.5-7 point Dog since 2014 {4-0 ATS}
6-22 S/U vs NFC South as 3.5-7 point Dog since 1987		5-1 ATS vs Seattle as 3 point or less Dog since 2010
9-1 S/U & ATS vs NFC South as 3 point or less favorite since 2007		5-1 ATS vs Seattle as 3 point or less Dog since 2010
17-4 O/U vs NFC South as 3.5-7 point favorite since 1989		0-6 O/U vs Seattle as 3 point or less favorite since 2005
2-8 O/U vs NFC South as 7.5-10 point favorite since 1987		4-0 S/U @ home vs Seattle as 3.5-7 point favorite since 1988
11-3 S/U vs NFC South as 7.5-10 point favorite since 1978		3-0 S/U vs Seattle as 7.5-10 point favorite since 2000
4-0 ATS vs New Orleans as 10.5 point or more Dog since 1993		0-3 ATS vs Seattle as 7.5-10 point favorite since 2000
4-0 O/U vs New Orleans as 10.5 point or more Dog since 1993		3-0 O/U vs Seattle as 7.5-10 point favorite since 2000
0-3 S/U vs New Orleans as 7.5-10 point Dog since 1992		9-2 ATS @ home vs Seattle since 2012
1-7 S/U vs New Orleans as 3.5-7 point Dog since 1987		Playoffs
4-1 O/U vs New Orleans as 3.5-7 point Dog since 1991		2-5 S/U on road on Saturday in Playoffs since 1967
3-0 S/U vs New Orleans as 7.5-10 point favorite since 1978		7-0 O/U in Divisional Playoffs since 2000
2-19-1 S/U vs NFC West as 10.5 point or more Dog since 1992		1-5 ATS in NFC Championship since 1986
0-7 O/U vs NFC West as 10.5 point or more Dog since 2012		3-0 S/U & ATS vs Dallas in Playoffs since 1983
2-9 S/U vs NFC West as 7.5-10 point Dog since 1987		0-4 S/U @ Minnesota in Playoffs since 1969

Miami Dolphins   AFC East
Last 4 seasons + Pointspread Analysis

2022

	Opponent			S1	S2	W/L	Spread	W/L	Total	O/U
vs	NEW ENGLAND		G	20	7	W	-3.0	W	46.0	U
@	Baltimore		A	42	38	W	3.0	W	44.0	O
vs	BUFFALO		G	21	19	W	4.0	W	54.5	U
@	Cincinnati	T	A	15	27	L	4.0	L	48.5	U
@	New York Jets		A	17	40	L	-3.0	L	46.0	O
vs	MINNESOTA		G	16	24	L	3.0	L	45.0	U
vs	PITTSBURGH	Su	G	16	13	W	-7.5	L	44.0	U
@	Detroit		A	31	27	W	-3.5	W	52.0	O
@	Chicago		G	35	32	W	-3.5	W	46.0	O
vs	CLEVELAND		G	39	17	W	-3.5	W	49.5	O
	BYE									
vs	HOUSTON		G	30	15	W	-14.0	W	47.5	U
@	San Francisco		G	17	33	L	5.0	L	46.0	O
@	L.A. Chargers	Su	G	17	23	L	-3.0	L	55.0	U
@	Buffalo	Sa	A	29	32	L	7.0	W	45.0	O
vs	GREEN BAY		G	20	26	L	-3.5	L	44.0	O
@	New England		A	21	23	L	2.5	W	41.5	O
vs	N.Y. JETS		G	11	6	W	-3.5	W	37.0	U
@	Buffalo		A	31	34	L	14.0	W	44.5	O

2021

	Opponent			S1	S2	W/L	Spread	W/L	Total	O/U
@	New England		A	17	16	W	3.5	W	43.0	U
vs	BUFFALO		G	0	35	L	3.5	L	47.5	U
@	Las Vegas {OT}		G	28	31	L	3.5	W	44.5	O
vs	INDIANAPOLIS		G	14	24	L	-2.5	L	42.0	U
@	Tampa Bay		G	17	45	L	11.0	L	48.0	O
vs	Jacksonville {London}		G	20	23	L	-1.5	L	47.0	U
vs	ATLANTA		G	28	30	L	1.5	L	48.0	O
@	Buffalo		A	11	26	L	14.5	L	43.5	U
vs	HOUSTON		G	17	9	W	-3.5	W	44.5	U
vs	BALTIMORE	T	G	22	10	W	8.5	W	46.5	U
@	New York Jets		A	24	17	W	-3.5	W	44.5	U
vs	CAROLINA		G	33	10	W	PK	W	40.5	O
vs	N.Y. GIANTS		G	20	9	W	-6.5	W	40.0	U
	BYE									
vs	N.Y. JETS		G	31	24	W	-9.5	L	42.0	O
@	New Orleans	M	A	20	3	W	-3.5	W	37.0	U
@	Tennessee Titans		G	3	34	L	3.0	L	41.0	U
vs	NEW ENGLAND		G	33	24	W	5.5	W	41.0	O

2020

	Opponent			S1	S2	W/L	Spread	W/L	Total	O/U
@	New England		A	11	21	L	7.5	L	44.5	U
vs	BUFFALO		G	28	31	L	5.5	W	42.5	O
@	Jacksonville	T	G	31	13	W	2.5	W	49.5	U
vs	SEATTLE		G	23	31	L	4.5	L	55.0	U
@	San Francisco		G	43	17	W	8.5	W	50.5	O
vs	N.Y. JETS		G	24	0	W	-8.5	W	46.5	U
	BYE									
vs	L.A. RAMS		G	28	17	W	3.5	W	45.5	U
@	Arizona		G	34	31	W	6.0	W	49.0	O
vs	L.A. CHARGERS		G	29	21	W	-2.0	W	48.5	U
@	Denver		G	13	20	L	-3.5	L	46.0	U
@	New York Jets		A	20	3	W	-7.5	W	46.0	U
vs	CINCINNATI		G	19	7	W	-10.5	L	43.0	U
vs	KANSAS CITY		G	27	33	L	7.0	W	51.0	O
vs	New England		G	22	12	W	PK	W	40.0	U
@	Las Vegas	Sa	G	26	25	W	-2.0	L	51.0	T
@	Buffalo		A	26	56	L	-3.5	L	42.5	O

2019

	Opponent			S1	S2	W/L	Spread	W/L	Total	O/U
vs	Baltimore		G	10	59	L	7.0	L	40.5	O
vs	NEW ENGLAND		G	0	43	L	18.0	L	48.5	U
@	Dallas		A	6	31	L	21.5	L	46.5	U
vs	L.A. CHARGERS		G	10	30	L	15.0	L	43.5	U
	BYE									
vs	WASHINGTON		G	16	17	L	5.5	W	42.0	U
@	Buffalo		A	21	31	L	17.0	W	42.5	O
@	Pittsburgh	M	G	14	27	L	14.0	W	43.0	U
vs	N.Y. JETS		G	26	18	W	3.0	W	42.5	O
@	Indianapolis		A	16	12	W	10.5	W	44.5	U
vs	BUFFALO		G	20	37	L	7.0	L	41.0	U
vs	Cleveland		G	24	41	L	11.0	L	46.0	O
vs	PHILADELPHIA		G	37	31	W	10.5	W	45.0	O
@	New York Jets		A	21	22	L	5.0	L	46.5	U
@	New York Giants		A	20	36	L	3.5	L	46.0	O
vs	CINCINNATI {OT}		G	38	35	W	PK	W	45.0	O
@	New England		A	27	24	W	17.0	W	45.0	O

Pointspread Analysis — vs NFC teams

Analysis	Note
1-7 S/U on road vs NFC teams as 7.5-10 point Dog since 2004	Patriots, Eagles
4-12 S/U vs NFC teams as 3.5-7 point Dog since 2005	
3-10 S/U on road vs NFC teams as 3.5-7 point Dog since 2001	Eagles
9-1 S/U vs NFC teams as 3.5-7 point favorite since 2011	Eagles
9-0 S/U vs NFC teams as 7.5-10 point favorite since 1998	TITANS
3-0 S/U vs NFC teams as 10.5 point or more favorite since 1979	
0-4 S/U vs NFC East as 7.5-10 point Dog since 2007	
0-5 O/U vs NFC East as 7.5-10 point Dog since 1993	
2-8 S/U vs NFC East as 3 point or less Dog since 1990	
2-6 O/U vs NFC East as 3 point or less Dog since 1996	
14-2 S/U vs NFC East as 3.5 point or more favorite since 1981	
1-9 O/U vs NFC East as 3.5 point or more favorite since 1989	
0-3 S/U vs Dallas as 3.5-7 point Dog since 1972	
0-3 S/U vs Washington as 3 point or less Dog since 2007	
5-0 S/U vs Washington as 3.5-7 point favorite since 1981	
2-8 S/U vs NFC East as 3 point or less Dog since 1990	
2-6 O/U vs NFC East as 3 point or less Dog since 1996	
13-2 S/U vs NFC East as 3.5 point or more favorite since 1981	
1-9 O/U vs NFC East as 3.5 point or more favorite since 1989	
1-3 S/U & ATS @ home vs New York Giants since 1993	
0-8 S/U vs NFC South as 3.5-7 point Dog since 1992	
0-5-1 ATS vs NFC South as 3.5-7 point favorite since 1980	
11-2 S/U vs NFC South as 3.5 point or more favorite since 1980	

Pointspread Analysis — THU-SAT-SNF-MNF

Analysis
7-3 ATS on road on Sunday Night since 1987
0-6 ATS on SNF as favorite since 2003
7-1 S/U vs NFC teams on SNF since 1987
6-0 O/U vs NFC teams on SNF since 1990
7-1 O/U @ home on MNF as Dog since 1998
0-5 S/U & ATS on MNF as 3 point or less favorite since 1996
6-1 S/U on MNF as 7.5 point or more favorite since 1978
11-3 O/U @ home on MNF since 1998

Playoffs

Analysis
0-6 S/U on road on Saturday in Playoffs since 1974
6-0 S/U @ home on Saturday in Playoff since 1984
0-5 ATS on road on Saturday in Playoffs since 1991
1-10 S/U on road in Playoffs since 1974
0-4 O/U @ home in Playoffs since 1998
0-7 O/U in WILD Card since 1997
3-0 S/U @ home in Divisional Playoffs since 1984
0-7 S/U on road in Divisional Playoffs since 1974
0-3 S/U @ Raiders in Playoffs since 1970
3-0 vs Kansas City in Playoffs since 1971

Miami Dolphins

Hard Rock Stadium

2023 Schedule + Trends & Angles

AFC East

Coach: Mike McDaniel

DATE		OPPONENT	TURF	MIA	OPP	S/U	LINE	ATS	TOT	O/U	Trends & Angles
9/10/2023	@	Los Angeles Chargers	A								Game 2-16 O/U vs LA Chargers since 1995
9/17/2023	@	New England	A								4-18 S/U @ New England since 2001
9/24/2023	vs	DENVER	G								vs Denver - Dolphins lead series 12-7-1
10/1/2023	@	Buffalo	A								1-11 S/U @ Buffalo since 2012
10/8/2023	vs	*NEW YORK GIANTS*	G								vs New York Giants - Giants lead series 7-3
10/15/2023	vs	*CAROLINA*	G								vs Carolina - Miami leads series 5-2
10/22/2023	@	*Philadelphia*	G								Game 1-5 O/U @ Philadelphia since 1978
10/29/2023	vs	NEW ENGLAND	G								8-2 S/U & ATS @ home vs New England since 2013
11/5/2023	@	Kansas City	G								vs Kansas City - Dolphins lead series 16-15
11/12/2023		BYE									
11/19/2023	vs	LAS VEGAS	G								8-2 S/U @ home vs Las Vegas Raiders since 1992
11/24/2023	@	New York Jets	A								Game 3-10 O/U @ New York Jets since 2010
12/3/2023	@	*Washington*	G								Game 0-3 O/U @ Washington since 2000
12/11/2023	vs	TENNESSEE	G								vs Tennessee - Miami leads series 21-18
12/17/2023	vs	NEW YORK JETS	G								6-0 S/U @ home vs NY Jets since 2016 {4-1-1 ATS}
12/24/2023	vs	*DALLAS*	G								0-4 S/U vs Dallas since 2007
12/31/2023	@	Baltimore	A								vs Baltimore - Series tied 15-15
1/7/2024	vs	BUFFALO	G								vs Buffalo - Miami leads series 63-54-1
1/14/2024											AFC Wild Card
1/21/2024											AFC Divisional Playoff
1/28/2024											AFC Championship
2/11/2024											Super Bowl LVIII @ Las Vegas, NV

Pointspread Analysis		Pointspread Analysis
vs AFC teams		**vs AFC teams**
2-7 S/U vs AFC East as 7.5-10 point Dog since 2006		9-1 S/U @ home vs AFC South as 3.5-7 point favorite since 1992
5-15 S/U vs AFC East as 3.5-7 point Dog since 2011		16-4 S/U vs AFC South as 7.5 point or more favorite since 1983
7-1 O/U vs AFC East as 3.5-7 point Dog since 2014		0-6 O/U vs AFC West as 7.5 point or more Dog since 1999
9-3 S/U vs AFC East as 3 point or less favorite since 2009		13-2 ATS vs AFC West as 3.5-7 point Dog since 1998
18-5 S/U vs AFC East as 7.5-10 point favorite since 1981		7-2-1 ATS vs AFC West as 3 point or less Dog since 1995
10-0 S/U vs AFC East as 10.5 point or more favorite since 1978		15-3 S/U vs AFC West as 3 point or less favorite since 1993
3-8 ATS @ New England since 2012		13-4-1 ATS vs AFC West as 3 point or less favorite since 1993
vs New England - HOME team 17-4 S/U last 21 meetings		13-4 S/U vs AFC West as 3.5 point or more favorite since 1985
8-2 ATS vs New York Jets since 2018		Game 1-10 O/U @ Los Angeles Chargers since 1995
5-1-1 ATS @ home vs New York Jets since 2016		3-0 S/U vs Los Angeles Chargers as 3.5-7 point favorite since 2000
2-5 S/U @ New England as 10.5 point or more Dog since 2004		0-3 O/U vs Los Angeles Chargers as 3.5-7 point favorite since 2000
0-6 S/U @ New England as 7.5-10 point Dog since 1980		0-3 ATS vs Los Angeles Chargers as 7.5-10 point favorite since 1984
3-13 S/U @ Buffalo as 3.5-7 point Dog since 1981		Game 4-0 O/U @ home vs Las Vegas Raiders since 2011
7-0 O/U @ Buffalo as 3.5-7 point Dog since 2004		vs Las Vegas - Raiders leads series 21-19-1
2-5 ATS @ Buffalo as 3.5-7 point Dog since 2004		Game 7-0-1 O/U vs Las Vegas Raiders since 2010
1-6 S/U @ home vs Buffalo as 3.5-7 point Dog since 1989		5-1 S/U vs Denver as 3.5-7 point Dog since 1998
5-2 O/U @ home vs Buffalo as 3.5-7 point Dog since 1989		6-0 S/U vs Denver as 3.5-7 point Dog since 1998
3-12 S/U @ New England as 3.5-7 point Dog since 1978		5-1 O/U vs Denver as 3.5-7 point Dog since 1998
4-11 ATS @ New England as 3.5-7 point Dog since 1978		7-0 S/U vs Las Vegas as 3 point or less favorite s/1997 {6-1 ATS}
1-6 O/U @ Buffalo as 3 point or less Dog since 2003		**Grass/Turf**
1-6 O/U @ home vs Buffalo as 3 point or less Dog since 1990		4-10 O/U on road on grass as 10.5 point or more Dog since 1997
0-5 S/U vs New England as 3 point or less Dog s/2001 {1-4 ATS}		0-9 S/U on road on grass as 10.5 point or more Dog since 2007
4-0 S/U & ATS @ New York Jets as 3 point or less Dog since 2008		0-15 S/U on Turf as 7.5-10 point Dog since 2004
0-4 O/U @ New York Jets as 3 point or less Dog since 2008		3-16 S/U on Turf as 3.5-7 point Dog since 2011
7-1 S/U & ATS @ home vs Buffalo as 3 point or less favorite since 1981		5-14 ATS on Turf as 3.5-7 point Dog since 2011
3-0 S/U @ home vs New York Jets as 3 point or less favorite since 2012		8-2 ATS on road on grass as 3.5-7 point Dog since 2011
7-1 S/U vs New England as 3.5-7 point favorite since 1989		10-3 S/U on road on grass as 3 point or less Dog since 2009
1-4 ATS @ New York Jets as 3.5-7 point favorite since 1992		11-2 ATS on road on grass as 3 point or less Dog since 2009
4-0 O/U @ home vs New York Jets as 3.5-7 point favorite since 2003		15-3 S/U on road on grass as 3.5-7 point favorite since 1979
3-0 S/U @ Buffalo as 7.5-10 point favorite since 1978		9-2 S/U on Turf as 7.5-10 point favorite since 1978
5-1 S/U vs New England as 7.5-10 point favorite since 1983		3-0 S/U on Turf as 10.5 point or more favorite since 1983
3-0 S/U vs Buffalo as 10.5 point or more favorite since 1978		**Dog**
3-0 S/U vs New York Jets as 10.5 point or more favorite since 1978		3-16 S/U on road as 10.5 point or more Dog since 2009
0-3 ATS vs New York Jets as 10.5 point or more favorite since 1978		1-19 S/U on road as 7.5-10 point Dog since 2000
7-1 ATS vs AFC North as 3 point or less Dog since 2010		**Favorite**
0-6 ATS vs AFC North as 3 point or less favorite since 2002		22-1 S/U as 7.5-10 point favorite since 1998
19-3 S/U vs AFC North as 3.5 point or more favorite since 1978		3-10 ATS as 7.5-10 point favorite since 2004
0-4 S/U & ATS vs Baltimore as 3.5-7 point Dog since 2009		0-7 O/U on road as 7.5-10 point favorite since 1985
3-0 S/U vs Baltimore as 3.5-7 point favorite since 1990		25-2 S/U as 10.5 point or more favorite since 1978
1-11 S/U & ATS vs AFC South as 3 point or less favorite since 1999		2-7 ATS as 10.5 point or more favorite since 1992

Last 4 seasons + Pointspread Analysis

2022

	Team	Day		F	A	W/L	Spread	ATS	Total	O/U
vs	GREEN BAY		A	23	7	W	-2.0	W	46.0	U
@	Philadelphia	M	G	7	24	L	3.0	L	49.5	U
vs	DETROIT		A	28	24	W	-6.5	L	51.5	O
vs	New Orleans {London}		G	28	25	W	-4.0	L	42.0	U
vs	CHICAGO		A	29	22	W	-8.5	L	43.5	O
@	Miami		G	24	16	W	-3.0	W	45.0	U
	BYE									
vs	ARIZONA		A	34	26	W	-4.0	W	48.5	O
@	Washington		G	20	17	W	-3.0	T	43.0	
@	Buffalo {OT}		A	33	30	W	6.5	W	46.5	O
vs	DALLAS		A	3	40	L	2.0	L	48.5	U
vs	NEW ENGLAND	T	A	33	26	W	-2.5	W	41.5	O
vs	N.Y. JETS		A	27	22	W	-2.5	W	43.0	O
@	Detroit		A	23	34	L	2.5	L	51.5	O
vs	INDIANAPOLIS {OT}	Sa	A	39	36	W	-3.5	L	46.0	O
vs	N.Y. GIANTS	Sa	A	27	24	W	-4.5	L	48.5	O
@	Green Bay		G	17	41	L	3.5	L	47.5	O
@	Chicago		G	29	13	W	-6.0	W	42.5	U
vs	**N.Y. GIANTS**		A	24	31	L	-2.5	L	48.0	O

2021

	Team	Day		F	A	W/L	Spread	ATS	Total	O/U
@	Cincinnati		A	24	27	L	-3.0	L	47.0	O
@	Arizona		G	33	34	L	3.5	W	51.0	O
vs	SEATTLE		A	30	17	W	2.0	W	53.0	U
vs	CLEVELAND		A	7	14	L	PK	L	52.0	U
vs	DETROIT		A	19	17	W	-10.0	L	50.0	U
@	Carolina {OT}		G	34	28	W	-2.0	W	45.0	O
	BYE									
vs	DALLAS	Su	A	16	20	L	-4.0	L	49.0	U
@	Baltimore {OT}		A	31	34	L	7.0	W	51.0	O
@	Los Angeles Chargers		A	27	20	W	3.5	W	53.5	U
vs	GREEN BAY		A	34	31	W	1.0	W	47.0	O
@	San Francisco		G	26	34	L	4.0	L	48.5	O
@	Detroit		A	27	29	L	-7.0	L	47.0	O
vs	PITTSBURGH	T	A	36	28	W	-3.5	W	45.0	O
@	Chicago	M	G	17	9	W	-7.0	W	47.5	U
vs	L.A. RAMS		A	23	30	L	3.0	L	49.0	O
@	Green Bay	Su	G	10	37	L	12.5	L	42.5	O
vs	CHICAGO		A	31	17	W	-3.5	W	45.0	O

2020

	Team	Day		F	A	W/L	Spread	ATS	Total	O/U
vs	GREEN BAY		A	34	43	L	-1.5	L	44.5	O
@	Indianapolis		A	11	28	L	3.5	L	49.0	U
vs	Tennessee		A	30	31	L	3.0	W	49.5	O
@	Houston		G	31	23	W	3.5	W	53.0	O
@	Seattle	Su	A	26	27	L	6.5	W	53.5	U
vs	ATLANTA		A	23	40	L	-4.0	L	53.0	O
	BYE									
@	Green Bay		G	28	22	W	6.0	W	50.0	T
vs	DETROIT		A	34	20	W	-3.0	W	51.5	O
@	Chicago	M	G	19	13	W	-3.0	W	44.0	U
vs	DALLAS		A	28	31	L	-7.0	L	50.0	O
vs	CAROLINA		A	28	27	W	-2.5	W	50.0	O
vs	JACKSONVILLE {OT}		A	27	24	W	-10.5	L	52.0	U
@	Tampa Bay		G	14	26	L	6.5	L	52.0	U
vs	CHICAGO		A	27	33	L	-2.5	L	47.0	O
@	New Orleans	Fr	A	33	52	L	6.5	L	49.0	O
@	Detroit		A	37	35	W	-3.0	L	53.5	O

2019

	Team	Day		F	A	W/L	Spread	ATS	Total	O/U
vs	ATLANTA		A	28	12	W	-3.5	W	46.5	U
@	Green Bay		G	16	21	L	3.0	L	43.0	U
vs	Oakland		A	34	14	W	-9.0	W	43.0	O
@	Chicago		G	6	16	L	PK	L	38.0	U
@	New York Giants		A	28	10	W	-5.5	W	44.0	U
vs	PHILADELPHIA		A	38	20	W	-3.5	W	45.0	O
@	Detroit		A	42	30	W	-2.5	W	43.5	O
vs	WASHINGTON	T	A	19	9	W	-16.5	W	42.0	U
@	Kansas City		G	23	26	L	-5.0	L	45.0	O
@	Dallas	Su	A	28	24	W	3.0	W	48.0	O
vs	DENVER		A	27	23	W	-10.0	L	40.0	O
	BYE									
@	Seattle	M	A	30	37	L	3.0	L	48.5	O
vs	DETROIT		A	20	7	W	-12.0	W	44.0	U
@	L.A. Chargers		G	39	10	W	PK	W	44.5	O
vs	GREEN BAY	M	A	10	23	L	-4.0	L	47.5	O
vs	CHICAGO		A	19	21	L	5.5	L	35.5	U
@	New Orleans {OT}		A	26	20	W	7.0	W	50.0	U
@	**San Francisco**	Sa	G	10	27	L	7.0	L	44.5	U

Pointspread Analysis

Grass/Turf		THU-SAT-SNF-MNF
0-8 S/U on road on grass as 10.5 point or more Dog since 1995		1-6 S/U on road on Thursday since 2006
8-1 O/U on road on grass as 10.5 point or more Dog since 194	Eagles	1-11 S/U on Thursday as a Dog since 1982
1-11 S/U on road on Turf as 7.5-10 point Dog since 1980		3-9 S/U & ATS on road on Saturday as Dog since 1981
1-14 S/U on road on Grass as 7.5-10 point Dog since 1984	Broncos	2-8 S/U on road on SNF since 2005
4-16 S/U on road on Turf as 3.5-7 point Dog since 2010	PACKERS	0-4 O/U @ home on SNF since 2016
6-1 S/U on road on Turf as 3.5-7 point favorite since 2002		3-11 S/U on SNF as Dog since 1999
1-7 O/U on road on Grass as 7.5-10 point favorite since 1986	49ers, BEARS	8-3 S/U @ home on MNF since 1999
5-0 S/U on road on Turf as 7.5-10 point favorite since 1998		0-8 S/U & ATS on MNF as Dog since 2010
Dog		8-1 S/U @ home on MNF as favorite since 1999
1-10 S/U as 10.5 point or more Dog since 1995		1-7 ATS vs Chicago on MNF since 1995
2-24 S/U as 7.5-10 point Dog since 1990		**Playoffs**
1-7 O/U as 7.5-10 point Dog since 2012		3-13 S/U on road in Playoffs since 1988
9-27-1 S/U as 3.5-7 point Dog since 2012		1-5 S/U @ home in WILD Card since 1993
11-5 ATS @ home as 3 point or less Dog since 2012		Game 1-3 O/U @ home in WILD Card since 2000
Favorite		5-0 S/U @ home in Divisional Playoff since 1976
29-10 S/U @ home as 3.5-7 point favorite since 2008		1-9 S/U on road in Divisional Playoffs since 1978
1-8 O/U on road as 7.5-10 point favorite since 2000		0-6 ATS on road in Divisional Playoffs since 1989
20-3 S/U @ home as 7.5-10 point favorite since 1991		4-1 S/U @ home on Saturday in Playoffs since 1973
18-1 S/U as 10.5 or more favorite since 1999		2-7 S/U on road on Saturday in Playoffs since 1981
32-4 S/U @ home ss 10.5 point or more favorite since 1982		4-0 S/U @ home vs L.A. Rams in Playoffs since 1969
		0-4 S/U vs Philadelphia in Playoffs since 1981
		4-1 vs New Orleans in Playoffs since 1988
		0-6 S/U in NFC Championship since 1977
		0-4 S/U & ATS in Super Bowl

Minnesota Vikings
U.S. Bank Stadium
2023 Schedule + Trends & Angles

NFC North
Coach: Kevin O'Connell

DATE		OPPONENT	TURF	MN	OPP	S/U	LINE	ATS	TOT	O/U	Trends & Angles
9/10/2023	vs	TAMPA BAY	A								Game 3-0 O/U @ home vs Tampa Bay since 2011
9/14/2023	@	Philadelphia	G								2-9 S/U & ATS @ Philadelphia since 1989
9/24/2023	vs	*LOS ANGELES CHARGERS*	A								3-0 S/U @ home vs Los Angeles Chargers s/1999
10/1/2023	@	Carolina	G								vs Carolina - Vikings lead series 10-6
10/8/2023	vs	*KANSAS CITY*	A								vs Kansas City - Chiefs lead series 8-5
10/15/2023	@	Chicago	G								vs Chicago - Vikings leads series 65-57-2
10/23/2023	vs	SAN FRANCISCO	A								6-0 S/U @ home vs San Francisco since 1994
10/29/2023	@	Green Bay	G								4-12-2 S/U @ Green Bay since 2006
11/5/2023	@	Atlanta	A								6-2 S/U @ Atlanta since 1991
11/12/2023	vs	NEW ORLEANS	A								14-4 S/U @ home vs New Orleans since 1970
11/19/2023	@	*Denver*	G								13-31 S/U on road vs AFC last 44 times
11/27/2023	vs	CHICAGO	A								0-6 ATS @ home vs Chicago on MNF since 1988
12/3/2023		BYE									
12/10/2023	@	*Las Vegas Raiders*	G								vs Las Vegas - Raiders lead series 9-7
12/16/2023	@	*Cincinnati*	A								vs Cincinnati - Series tied 7-7
12/24/2023	vs	DETROIT	A								Game 2-8 O/U @ home vs Detroit since 2013
12/31/2023	vs	GREEN BAY	A								Game 2-7 O/U @ home vs Green Bay since 2014
1/7/2024	@	Detroit	A								vs Detroit - Vikings leads series 80-40-2
1/14/2024											NFC Wild Card
1/21/2024											NFC Divisional Playoff
1/28/2024											NFC Championship
2/11/2024											Super Bowl LVIII @ Las Vegas, NV

Pointspread Analysis		Pointspread Analysis	
vs NFC teams		**vs NFC teams**	
0-9 O/U @ home vs NFC teams as 10.5 point or more favorite since 2007		0-3 O/U vs Carolina as 3.5-7 point favorite since 1996	
3-12 S/U vs NFC East as 3 point or less Dog since 1986		Game 7-1-1 O/U @ home vs New Orleans since 1994	
4-0 S/U vs NFC East as 7.5 point or more favorite since 1993		9-0 S/U vs New Orleans as favorite since 1994	
0-3 S/U & ATS @ Philadelphia as 3 point or less favorite since 1989		1-4 S/U vs New Orleans as 3.5-7 point Dog since 2010	
5-1 O/U vs Philadelphia as 3.5-7 point Dog since 1985		7-0 S/U vs New Orleans as 3.5-7 point favorite since 1988 {5-2 ATS}	
Game 1-6 O/U @ Philadelphia since 2004		7-1 O/U vs New Orleans as 3.5-7 point favorite since 1985	
1-16 S/U vs NFC North as 7.5 or more Dog since 1984		3-0 S/U vs New Orleans as 7.5-10 point favorite since 1981	
1-8-1 S/U vs NFC North as 3.5-7 point Dog since 2012		6-0 O/U vs NFC West as 10.5 point or more Dog since 1984	
7-0-1 O/U vs NFC North as 3.5-7 point Dog since 2013		0-4 S/U vs NFC West as 7.5-10 point Dog since 1990	
7-0 S/U & ATS @ home vs NFC North as 3 point or less Dog since 2012		10-2 O/U on road vs NFC West as 3.5-7 point Dog since 1990	
20-6 S/U vs NFC North as 3.5-7 point favorite since 1998		6-0 S/U & ATS @ home vs NFC West as 3 point or less favorite s/2003	
2-7 O/U vs NFC North as 7.5-10 point favorite since 2003		1-6 O/U vs NFC West as 3 point or less favorite since 2003	
3-10 ATS vs NFC North as 7.5-10 point favorite since 1988		10-1 S/U & ATS @ home vs NFC West as 3.5-7 point favorite since 1988	
10-0 S/U vs NFC North as 10.5 point or more favorite since 2001		7-0 S/U @ home vs NFC West as 7.5 point or more favorite since 1979	
0-7 O/U vs NFC North as 10.5 point or more favorite since 2007		10-1 S/U vs NFC West as 7.5 point or more favorite since 1979	
0-6 S/U @ Green Bay as 10.5 point or more Dog since 1996		9-1 ATS @ home vs San Francisco since 1985	
0-5 S/U vs Green Bay as 7.5-10 point Dog since 1984		vs San Francisco - HOME team 13-1 S/U since 1993	
0-3 S/U @ home vs Chicago as 3.5-7 point Dog since 1984		vs San Francisco - 49ers lead series 25-22-1	
2-6 S/U & ATS @ Detroit as 3.5-7 point Dog since 1980		5-0 O/U vs San Francisco as 10.5 point or more Dog since 1984	
1-5-1 S/U @ Green Bay as 3.5-7 point Dog since3 2006		0-3 S/U vs San Francisco as 7.5-10 point Dog since 1990	
0-8 S/U & ATS @ Chicago as 3 point or less Dog since 1990		3-0 O/U vs San Francisco as 7.5-10 point Dog since 1990	
5-1 S/U & ATS vs Green Bay as 3 point or less Dog since 2012		1-6 O/U vs San Francisco as 3.5-7 point Dog snice 1989	
1-8 O/U vs Chicago as 3 point or less favorite since 2001		3-0 S/U @ home vs San Francisco as 3.5-7 point favorite since 1999	
5-0 S/U @ Detroit as 3 point or less favorite since 2004		3-0 S/U vs San Francisco as 7.5-10 point favorite since 1979	
2-8 O/U @ home vs Detroit as 3 point or less favorite since 1983		**vs AFC teams**	
1-5 ATS vs Green Bay as 3 point or less favorite since 2004		1-8 S/U vs AFC teams as 7.5-10 point Dog since 1980	
0-6 O/U @ Chicago as 3.5-7 point favorite since 2000		3-12 S/U vs AFC teams as 3.5-7 point Dog since 2009	
7-1 S/U @ home vs Chicago as 3.5-7 point favorite since 2000		18-5 S/U vs AFC teams as 3.5-7 point favorite since 2004	
7-2 S/U @ Detroit as 3.5-7 point favorite since 1987		9-2 S/U vs AFC teams as 10.5 point or more favorite since 1982	
8-1 S/U @ home vs Detroit as 3.5-7 point favorite since 1994		0-4 S/U vs AFC North as 7.5 point or more Dog since 1980	
5-0 S/U vs Detroit as 7.5-10 point favorite since 2000		0-5 S/U vs AFC North as 3.5-7 point Dog since 2005	
0-5 O/U vs Detroit as 7.5-10 point favorite since 2000		3-0 S/U & ATS vs AFC North as 10.5 point or more favorite since 1982	
4-0 S/U @ home vs Chicago as 10.5 point or more favorite since 2004		0-3 S/U vs AFC West as 7.5 point or more Dog since 1984	
7-0 S/U @ home vs Detroit as 10.5 point or more favorite since 1988		7-0 ATS vs AFC West as 3.5-7 point Dog since 1981	
0-4 S/U & ATS vs NFC South as 7.5-10 point Dog since 2002		3-8 S/U & ATS vs AFC West as 3 point or less favorite since 1981	
4-1 S/U & ATS vs NFC South as 3 point or less Dog since 2008		0-3 S/U vs Kansas City as 3 point or less favorite since 1981	
7-0 O/U vs NFC South as 3 point or less favorite since 2011		5-0 ATS vs Los Angeles Chargers since 2007	
11-3 S/U on road vs NFC South as 3.5-7 point favorite since 1988		vs L.A. Chargers - Vikings leads series 8-6	
8-1-1 O/U on road vs NFC South as 3.5-7 point favorite since 1988			
4-0 S/U & ATS vs Atlanta as 3 point or less Dog since 1984			

New England Patriots   AFC East

Last 4 seasons + Pointspread Analysis

	2022												2020									
@	Miami		G	7	20	L	3.0	L	46.0	U		vs	MIAMI		A	21	11	W	-7.5	W	44.5	U
@	Pittsburgh		G	17	14	W	-3.0	T	40.0	U		@	Seattle	Su	A	30	35	L	4.5	L	45.0	O
vs	BALTIMORE		A	26	37	L	2.5	L	44.5	O		vs	LAS VEGAS		A	36	20	W	-7.0	W	47.0	O
@	Green Bay {OT}		G	24	27	L	9.5	W	40.0	O		@	Kansas City	M	G	10	26	L	11.5	L	48.5	U
vs	DETROIT		A	29	0	W	-3.0	W	47.0	U			BYE									
@	Cleveland		G	38	15	W	2.5	W	43.5	O		vs	DENVER		A	12	18	L	-7.0	L	44.5	U
vs	CHICAGO	M	A	14	33	L	-8.5	L	40.0	O		vs	SAN FRANCISCO		A	6	33	L	-3.0	L	44.5	U
@	New York Jets		A	22	17	W	-3.0	W	40.0	U		@	Buffalo		A	21	24	L	4.0	W	40.5	O
vs	INDIANAPOLIS		A	26	3	W	-4.5	W	39.5	U		@	New York Jets	M	A	30	27	W	-9.0	L	42.0	U
	BYE											vs	Baltimore	Su	A	23	17	W	7.0	W	44.0	U
vs	N.Y. JETS		A	10	3	W	-3.0	W	38.5	U		@	Houston		G	20	27	L	-2.5	L	49.5	U
@	Minnesota	T	A	26	33	L	2.5	L	41.5	O		vs	Arizona		A	20	17	W	PK	W	50.5	U
vs	BUFFALO	T	A	10	24	L	4.0	L	44.0	U		@	L.A. Chargers		G	45	0	W	1.5	W	46.5	U
@	Arizona	M	G	27	13	W	-2.0	W	44.0	U		@	L.A. Rams	T	G	3	24	L	4.5	L	43.5	U
@	Las Vegas		G	24	30	L	2.5	L	45.0	O		@	Miami		G	12	20	L	PK	L	40.0	U
vs	CINCINNATI	Sa	A	18	22	L	3.0	L	41.5	U		vs	BUFFALO	M	A	9	38	L	7.0	L	47.0	T
vs	MIAMI		A	23	21	W	-2.5	L	41.5	O		vs	N.Y. JETS		A	28	14	W	-3.0	W	41.0	O
@	Buffalo		A	23	35	L	8.0	L	44.5	U												

	2021												2019									
vs	MIAMI		A	16	17	L	-3.5	L	43.0	U		vs	PITTSBURGH	Su	A	33	3	W	-5.5	W	49.0	U
@	New York Jets		A	25	6	W	-5.5	W	43.0	U		@	Miami		G	43	0	W	-18.0	W	48.5	U
vs	NEW ORLEANS		A	13	28	L	-3.0	L	43.5	U		vs	N.Y. JETS		A	30	14	W	-20.5	L	43.0	O
vs	TAMPA BAY	Su	A	17	19	L	6.5	W	49.0	U		@	Buffalo		A	16	10	W	-7.0	L	41.5	U
@	Houston		G	25	22	W	-8.0	L	39.0	O		@	Washington		G	33	7	W	-16.5	W	41.5	U
vs	DALLAS {OT}		G	29	35	L	3.0	L	50.0	O		vs	N.Y. GIANTS	T	A	35	14	W	-16.5	W	43.0	O
vs	N.Y. JETS		A	54	13	W	-7.0	W	42.5	O		@	New York Jets	M	A	33	0	W	-10.0	W	43.0	U
@	L.A. Chargers		A	27	24	W	3.5	W	50.5	U		vs	CLEVELAND		A	27	13	W	-9.5	W	43.0	U
@	Carolina		G	24	6	W	-3.0	W	41.5	U		@	Baltimore	Su	A	20	37	L	-3.0	L	44.5	U
vs	CLEVELAND		A	45	7	W	-2.5	W	44.5	O			BYE									
@	Atlanta	T	A	25	0	W	-7.0	W	47.0	U		@	Philadelphia		G	17	10	W	-4.5	W	44.5	U
vs	TENNESSEE		A	36	13	W	-7.0	W	43.5	O		vs	DALLAS		A	13	9	W	-5.5	L	44.5	U
@	Buffalo	M	A	14	10	W	3.0	W	40.0	U		@	Houston	Su	G	22	28	L	-3.0	L	46.5	U
	BYE											vs	KANSAS CITY		A	16	23	L	-2.5	L	49.0	U
@	Indianapolis	Sa	A	17	27	L	1.0	L	46.5	U		@	Cincinnati		A	34	13	W	-10.5	W	42.0	O
vs	BUFFALO		A	21	33	L	-1.0	L	43.5	O		vs	BUFFALO	Sa	A	24	17	W	-7.0	T	39.0	O
vs	JACKSONVILLE		A	50	10	W	-17.0	W	42.0	O		vs	MIAMI		A	24	27	L	-17.0	L	45.0	U
@	Miami		G	24	33	L	-5.5	L	41.0	O		vs	Tennessee	Sa	A	13	20	L	-4.5	L	45.0	U
@	Buffalo	Sa	A	17	47	L	4.5	L	43.0	O												

Pointspread Analysis vs NFC teams		Pointspread Analysis Grass/Turf
32-10 S/U @ home vs NFC last 42 times	PHL, NYG, N.O.	0-7 S/U on road on Turf as 10.5 point or more Dog since 1990
14-2 S/U vs NFC teams as 10.5 point or more favorite since 1978		4-1 ATS on road on Turf as 7.5-10 point Dog since 1998
28-3 S/U vs NFC teams as 3.5-7 point favorite since 2003		11-3 O/U on Turf as 7.5-10 point Dog since 1983
5-17 ATS vs NFC teams as 7.5-10 point favorite since 1978		12-3 ATS on grass as 7.5-10 point Dog since 1990
0-6 S/U vs NFC East as 3 point or less Dog since 1981		12-3 O/U on Turf as 7.5-10 point Dog since 1983
2-8 S/U vs NFC East as 3.5 point or more Dog since 1987		7-3 ATS on road on Turf as 3.5-7 point Dog since 2000
3-12 ATS vs NFC East as 3.5-7 point favorite since 1981		13-5-1 ATS on road on Turf as 3 point or less Dog since 1996
Game 3-0 O/U @ home vs Philadelphia since 1987		10-3 O/U on Turf as 3 point or less Dog since 2011
Game 1-4 O/U @ home vs New York Giants since 1990		11-3 S/U on grass as 3.5-7 point favorite since 2011
3-9 ATS vs Philadelphia since 1981		51-9 S/U on Turf as 3.5-7 point favorite since 2010
4-0 S/U vs Dallas as 3.5-7 point favorite since 2003		22-4 S/U on road on Turf as 3.5-7 point favorite since 2001
8-0 S/U vs NFC South as 3.5-7 point favorite since 2002		12-3 S/U on grass as 7.5-10 point favorite since 1996
6-0 ATS vs NFC South as 3.5-7 point favorite since 2005		18-1 S/U on road on Turf as 7.5-10 point favorite since 1978
0-5 ATS vs NFC South as 7.5-10 point favorite since 1986		4-11 O/U on road on Turf as 7.5-10 point favorite since 1986
3-1 S/U @ home vs New Orleans since 2013		12-2 S/U on grass as 10.5 point or more favorite since 1996
vs New Orleans - Patriots leads series 10-5		0-7 O/U on grass as 10.5 point or more favorite since 2008
Favorite		7-0 S/U on road on Turf as 10.5 point or more favorite since 1986
60-14 S/U as 3.5-7 point favorite since 2010		**Dog**
12-3 S/U on road as 3.5-7 point favorite since 2014		4-18 S/U as 10.5 point Dog or more since 1989
15-2 S/U on road as 7.5-10 point favorite since 2011		9-1 ATS as 7.5-10 point Dog since 1999
51-12 S/U as 7.5-10 point favorite since 1996		11-3 ATS on grass as 7.5-10 point Dog since 1990
71-7 S/U as 10.5 point or more favorite since 1978		8-2 ATS on road as 3.5-7 point Dog since 2003
30-2 S/U @ home as 10.5 point or more favorite since 2009		2-8 S/U as 3.5-7 point dog since 2014
14-4 ATS @ home as 10.5 point or more favorite since 2015		9-1 O/U @ home as 3 point or less Dog since 2001

 **New England Patriots**

Gillette Stadium

2023 Schedule + Trends & Angles

 **AFC East**

Coach: Bill Bellicheck

DATE		OPPONENT	TURF	NE	OPP	S/U	LINE	ATS	TOT	O/U	Trends & Angles
9/10/2023	vs	*PHILADLEPHIA*	A								0-3 ATS @ home vs Philadelphia since 1987
9/17/2023	vs	MIAMI	A								9-2 ATS @ home vs Miami since 2012
9/24/2023	@	New York Jets	A								14-0 S/U vs New York Jets since 2016
10/1/2023	@	*Dallas*	A								Game 2-8 O/U vs Dallas since 1984
10/8/2023	vs	*NEW ORLEANS*	A								Game 5-1 O/U @ home vs New Orleans s/1989
10/15/2023	@	Las Vegas	G								6-1 S/U vs Raiders since 2005 {5-2 ATS}
10/22/2023	vs	BUFFALO	A								vs Buffalo - Patriots leads series 76-45-1
10/29/2023	@	Miami	G								vs Miami - Patriots leads series 58-57
11/5/2023	vs	*WASHINGTON*	A								4-0 S/U vs Washington since 2007
11/12/2023	vs	INDIANAPOLIS {Frankfurt}	A								9-1 S/U vs Indianapolis since 2010
11/19/2023		BYE									
11/26/2023	@	*New York Giants*	A								1-5 ATS vs New York Giants since 2007
12/3/2023	vs	LOS ANGELES CHARGERS	A								12-1 S/U @ home vs LA Chargers since 1973
12/7/2023	@	Pittsburgh	G								7-1 S/U vs Pittsburgh since 2013
12/18/2023	vs	KANSAS CITY	A								vs Kansas City - HOME team 13-4 S/U since 1992
12/24/2023	@	Denver	G								0-4 S/U & ATS on road on SNF since 2018
12/31/2023	@	Buffalo	A								35-10 S/U vs Buffalo since 2001
1/7/2024	vs	NEW YORK JETS	A								12-0 S/U @ home vs NY Jets since 2011
1/14/2024											AFC Wild Card
1/21/2024											AFC Divisional Playoff
1/28/2024											AFC Championship
2/11/2024											Super Bowl LVIII @ Las Vegas, NV

Pointspread Analysis vs AFC teams		Pointspread Analysis vs AFC teams
0-7 S/U vs AFC East as 10.5 point or more Dog since 1990		Game 0-5 O/U @ Pittsburgh since 2011
14-1 S/U vs AFC East as 7.5-10 point favorite since 2011		3-0 O/U vs Pittsburgh as 3 point or less Dog since 1989
14-1 S/U @ home vs AFC East as 7.5-10 point favorite since 1997		0-4 O/U @ Pittsburgh as 3 point or less favorite s/2011
30-5 S/U vs AFC East as 10.5 point or more favorite since 1978		3-0 S/U vs Pittsburgh as 3.5-7 point favorite since 2013
Game 1-6 O/U @ New York Jets since 2016		11-2 ATS vs AFC South as 3.5-7 point Dog since 1988
0-5 S/U vs Buffalo as 10.5 point or more Dog since 1990		5-1 O/U vs AFC South as 3 point or less Dog since 2006
1-5 S/U vs Miami as 7.5-10 point Dog since 1983		2-8 O/U vs AFC South as 3 point or less favorite s/1990
1-5 S/U @ Miami as 3.5-7 point Dog since 1989		20-1 S/U vs AFC South as 3.5-7 point or more favorite since 1996
1-7 S/U vs Miami as 3.5-7 point Dog since 1989		14-0 S/U vs AFC South as 7.5-10 point favorite since 1984
0-3 O/U @ home vs New York Jets as 3.5-7 point Dog since 1983		41-1 S/U vs AFC South as 3.5 point or more favorite since 1996
1-7 O/U @ Miami as 3 point or less Dog since 1979		14-0 S/U vs AFC South as 10.5 point or more favorite since 1986
7-1 S/U & ATS @ NY Jets as 3 point or less Dog since 1986		10-0 O/U @ home vs AFC South as 10.5 point or more favorite s/2006
5-0 S/U vs Miami as 3 point or less favorite since 2001 {4-1 ATS}		1-5 O/U vs Indianapolis as 3 point or less favorite since 1990
11-0 S/U @ Buffalo as 3.5-7 point favorite since 1979		4-1 O/U @ home vs Indianapolis as 3.5-7 point favorite since 1999
6-1-1 ATS @ Buffalo as 3.5-7 point favorite since 2004		9-0 S/U vs Indianapolis as 3.5-7 point favorite since 1996
9-2 S/U @ home vs Buffalo as 3.5-7 point favorite since 1980		8-0 S/U vs Indianapolis as 7.-10 point favorite since 1978
2-7 S/U @ home vs Buffalo as 3.5-7 point favorite since 2001		6-0 O/U vs Indianapolis as 10.5 point or more favorite since 1979
12-3 S/U @ home vs Miami as 3.5-7 point favorite since 1978		5-0 O/U vs AFC West as 7.5 or more Dog since 1987
11-4 ATS @ home vs Miami as 3.5-7 point favorite since 1978		2-10 S/U vs AFC West as 3.5-7 point Dog since 1987
5-2 O/U @ New York Jets as 3.5-7 point favorite since 2005		5-0 S/U & ATS @ home vs AFC West as 3 point or less Dog since 1994
5-1 S/U @ home vs NY Jets as 3.5-7 point favorite since 2003		5-0 O/U @ home vs AFC West as 3 point or less Dog since 1994
8-1 O/U @ home vs New York Jets as 3.5-7 point favorite since 1999		5-0 O/U vs AFC West as 7.5-10 point favorite since 1997
9-1 S/U vs Buffalo as 7.5-10 point favorite since 1986		5-0 S/U vs AFC West as 10.5 point or more favorite since 2008
1-8 O/U vs Buffalo as 7.5-10 point favorite since 1986		11-1 S/U & ATS vs AFC West as 3.5-7 point favorite since 2011
6-0 S/U @ home vs Miami as 7.5-10 point favorite since 1980		0-7 S/U vs Denver as 3.5-7 point Dog since 1984
10-1 S/U vs NY Jets as 7.5-10 point favorite since 1997		1-6 ATS vs Denver as 3.5-7 point Dog since 1984
1-5 ATS vs NY Jets as 7.5-10 point favorite since 2014		5-1 O/U vs Denver as 3 point or less Dog since 1986
7-1 O/U vs NY Jets as 7.5-10 point favorite since 1986		1-5 O/U vs Denver as 3 point or less favorite since 1988
12-0 S/U vs Buffalo as 10.5 point or more favorite since 1978		3-0 S/U vs Kansas City as 3.5-7 point favorite since 1981
7-1 O/U vs Buffalo as 10.5 point or more favorite since 2007		5-0 S/U vs Las Vegas as 3.5-7 point favorite since 1987
5-2 S/U @ home vs Miami as 10.5 point or more favorite since 2004		Game 8-2 O/U @ home vs L.A. Chargers since 1983
9-0 S/U vs New York Jets as 10.5 point or more favorite since 2007		20-3 S/U vs Los Angeles Chargers since 1973
4-1 ATS vs New York Jets as 10.5 point or more favorite since 2016		vs L.A. Chargers - Patriots leads series 27-15-1
1-5 O/U vs New York Jets as 10.5 point or more favorite since 2013		4-0 S/U & ATS @ home vs L.A. Chargers as 3.5-7 point favorite s/2007
0-3 S/U vs AFC North as 10.5 point or more Dog since 1990		5-0 S/U & ATS vs L.A. Chargers as 3 point or less Dog since 1994
5-0 S/U & ATS vs AFC North as 3.5-7 point Dog since 1993	Jets, Bills	28-5 S/U after playing Sunday Night last 33 times
6-2 ATS vs AFC North as 3 point or less Dog since 2000	JETS	16-2 S/U after playing @ Buffalo since 2001
6-1 O/U vs AFC North as 3 point or less Dog since 2002	Cowboys, Bills	28-9 S/U in 2nd of back to back road games since 2000
15-0 S/U vs AFC North as 7.5 point or more favorite since 1978		13-2 S/U after 2 straight S/U loss since 2006
8-0 S/U on road vs AFC North as 7.5 point or more favorite since 1978		17-4 S/U after scoring less than 10 points since 1996

New Orleans Saints   NFC South

Last 4 seasons + Pointspread Analysis

2022

	Team	Day	Surf							
@	Atlanta		A	27	26	W	-5.5	L	44.0	O
vs	TAMPA BAY		A	10	20	L	2.5	L	43.5	U
@	Carolina		G	14	22	L	-2.0	L	41.0	U
vs	Minnesota {London}		G	25	28	L	4.0	W	42.0	O
vs	SEATTLE		A	39	32	W	-5.5	W	45.0	O
vs	CINCINNATI		A	26	30	L	3.0	L	43.0	O
@	Arizona	T	G	34	42	L	2.5	L	44.0	O
vs	LAS VEGAS		A	24	0	W	1.0	W	48.0	U
vs	BALTIMORE	M	A	13	27	L	1.5	L	46.5	U
@	Pittsburgh		G	10	20	L	1.5	L	39.0	U
vs	L.A. RAMS		A	27	20	W	-2.0	W	39.5	O
@	San Francisco		G	0	13	L	8.5	L	43.5	U
@	Tampa Bay	M	G	16	17	L	3.0	L	41.0	U
BYE										
vs	ATLANTA		A	21	18	W	-5.5	L	43.5	U
@	Cleveland	Sa	G	17	10	W	3.5	W	32.0	U
@	Philadelphia		G	20	10	W	4.5	W	42.0	U
vs	CAROLINA		A	7	10	L	-3.5	L	41.5	U

2021

	Team	Day	Surf							
vs	GREEN BAY {@Jax}		A	38	3	W	3.5	W	49.0	U
@	Carolina		G	7	26	L	-3.0	L	45.0	U
@	New England		A	28	13	W	3.0	W	43.5	U
vs	N.Y. GIANTS {OT}		A	21	27	L	-7.5	L	42.5	O
@	Washington		G	33	22	W	-2.5	W	43.5	U
BYE										
@	Seattle	M	A	13	10	W	-6.0	L	42.0	U
vs	TAMPA BAY		A	36	27	W	3.5	W	43.5	O
vs	ATLANTA		A	25	27	L	-7.0	L	43.5	O
@	Tennessee		G	23	25	L	3.0	L	42.5	O
@	Philadelphia		G	29	40	L	3.0	L	42.5	O
vs	BUFFALO	T	A	6	31	L	7.0	L	44.5	U
vs	DALLAS	T	A	17	27	L	6.5	L	45.5	U
@	New York Jets		A	30	9	W	-4.5	W	41.5	U
@	Tampa Bay	Su	G	9	0	W	11.5	W	46.0	U
vs	MIAMI	M	A	3	20	L	3.5	L	37.0	U
vs	CAROLINA		A	18	10	W	-7.0	W	37.0	U
@	Atlanta		A	30	20	W	-4.5	W	40.0	O

2020

	Team	Day	Surf							
vs	TAMPA BAY		A	34	23	W	-4.0	W	48.0	O
@	Las Vegas	M	G	24	34	L	-4.0	L	47.5	O
vs	GREEN BAY	Su	A	30	37	L	-3.0	L	51.5	O
@	Detroit		A	35	29	W	-3.0	W	51.5	O
vs	L.A. CHARGERS {OT}	M	A	30	27	W	-7.0	L	49.0	O
BYE										
vs	CAROLINA		A	27	24	W	-6.5	L	50.5	O
@	Chicago {OT}		G	26	23	W	-5.0	L	41.0	O
@	Tampa Bay	Su	G	38	3	W	3.0	W	51.0	U
vs	SAN FRANCISCO		A	27	13	W	-10.0	W	49.0	U
vs	ATLANTA		A	24	9	W	-3.5	W	49.5	U
@	Denver		G	31	3	W	-17.0	W	36.5	U
@	Atlanta		A	21	16	W	-2.0	W	46.0	U
@	Philadelphia		G	21	24	L	-7.5	L	42.5	O
vs	KANSAS CITY		A	29	32	L	2.5	L	53.5	O
vs	MINNESOTA	Fr	A	52	33	W	-6.5	W	49.0	O
@	Carolina		G	33	7	W	-5.5	W	46.5	U
vs	CHICAGO		A	21	9	W	-11.0	W	47.5	U
vs	TAMPA BAY		G	20	30	L	-2.5	L	53.0	U

2019

	Team	Day	Surf							
vs	HOUSTON	M	A	30	28	W	-6.5	L	52.0	O
@	L.A. Rams		G	9	27	L	2.0	L	52.5	U
@	Seattle		A	33	27	W	5.0	W	44.0	O
vs	DALLAS	Su	A	12	10	W	2.5	W	47.0	U
vs	TAMPA BAY		A	31	24	W	-3.0	W	46.5	O
@	Jacksonville		G	13	6	W	2.5	W	42.5	U
@	Chicago		G	36	25	W	4.0	W	37.0	O
vs	ARIZONA		A	31	9	W	-12.5	W	48.0	U
BYE										
vs	ATLANTA		A	9	26	L	-14.0	L	51.5	U
@	Tampa Bay		G	34	17	W	-5.0	W	50.5	O
vs	CAROLINA		A	34	31	W	-10.0	L	46.5	O
@	Atlanta	T	A	26	18	W	-7.0	W	48.0	U
vs	SAN FRANCISCO		A	46	48	L	-1.5	L	45.0	O
vs	Indianapolis	M	A	34	7	W	-8.5	W	49.0	U
@	Tennessee		G	38	28	W	-3.5	W	49.0	O
@	Carolina		G	42	10	W	-13.5	W	45.5	O
vs	MINNESOTA {OT}		A	20	26	L	-7.0	L	50.0	U

Pointspread Analysis — Grass/Turf

Grass/Turf	
4-1 O/U on grass as 10.5 point or more Dog since 1997	
5-0 O/U on road on Turf as 10.5 point or more Dog since 1998	
1-5 S/U on grass as 10.5 point or more Dog since 1996	
2-10 S/U on road on Turf as 7.5-10 point Dog since 1978	
1-6 O/U on grass as 7.5-10 point Dog since 2003	
8-21 S/U on road on Turf as 3.5-7 point Dog since 1995	
5-11-1 ATS on grass as 3 point or less Dog since 2007	
4-14 S/U on grass as 3 point or less Dog since 2007	
11-2 S/U on road on Turf as 3 point or less favorite since 2000	
8-3 O/U on road on Turf as 3 point or less favorite since 2002	
21-6 S/U on grass as 3.5-7 point favorite since 2000	
0-4 ATS on road on Turf as 7.5-10 point favorite since 2002	
6-1 S/U on grass as 7.5 point or more favorite since 1988	

Dog

Dog	
9-1 O/U on road as 10.5 point or more Dog since 1997	
0-4 S/U & ATS @ home as 10.5 point or more Dog since 1980	
9-2 ATS on road as 7.5-10 point Dog since 2003	
1-11 S/U @ home as 7.5-10 point Dog since 1978	
15-4-1 ATS as 3.5-7 point Dog since 2015	

THU-SAT-SNF-MNF

THU-SAT-SNF-MNF	
2-9-1 O/U on Thursday since 2012	
1-7 O/U on road on Thursday since 2013	JAX, LA Rams
1-7 O/U on Thursday as favorite since 1992	LA Rams
5-1 S/U on road on MNF as favorite since 2007	
1-5 ATS on MNF since 2020	Carolina

Pointspread Analysis — vs AFC teams

vs AFC teams
18-4 S/U vs AFC teams as 3.5-7 point favorite since 2007
1-9 S/U vs AFC teams as 7.5-10 point Dog since 1978
10-2 O/U vs AFC East as 7 point or less Dog since 1983
4-0 S/U & ATS vs AFC East as 7.5-10 point favorite since 1992
0-5 O/U vs AFC South as 3.5-7 point Dog since 2003
1-6 S/U vs AFC South as 3 point or less Dog since 1978
11-2 S/U vs AFC South as 7 point or less favorite since 1984
10-3 ATS vs AFC South as 7 point or less favorite since 1984
4-0 S/U & ATS vs AFC South as 7.5 or more favorite since 1987
0-3 S/U vs Tennessee as 3.5-7 point Dog since 1990
Game 4-0-1 O/U @ home vs Tennessee since 1993
0-3-1 ATS @ home vs Tennessee since 1996
vs Tennessee leads - Titans series 9-6-1
0-3 O/U vs Indianapolis as 3.5-7 point Dog since 2007

Playoffs

Playoffs
8-3 S/U @ home in Playoffs since 2000
0-5 O/U @ home in Playoffs since 2019
1-7 S/U on road in Playoffs since 1990
6-2 O/U @ home in WILD Card since 1988
3-1 S/U @ home in Divisional Playoff since 2007
0-4 S/U on road in Divisional Playoffs since 2001
4-0 S/U @ home on Saturday in Play-offs since 2000
5-0 O/U @ home on Saturday in Playoffs since 1991
1-4 S/U on road on Saturday in Playoffs since 2001
3-0 S/U vs Philadelphia in Playoffs since 2007

 **New Orleans Saints**

 **NFC South**

Mercedes-Benz Superdome *2023 Schedule + Trends & Angles* **Coach: Dennis Allen**

DATE		OPPONENT	TURF	NO	OPP	S/U	LINE	ATS	TOT	O/U	Trends & Angles
9/10/2023	vs	*TENNESSEE*	A								0-4 S/U @ home vs Tennessee since 1996
9/18/2023	@	Carolina	G								vs Carolina - Saints leads series 29-27
9/24/2023	@	Green Bay	G								vs Green Bay - Packers leads series 17-10
10/1/2023	vs	TAMPA BAY	A								9-4 S/U @ home vs Tampa Bay since 2011
10/8/2023	@	*New England*	G								vs New England - Patriots leads series 10-5
10/15/2023	@	*Houston*	G								HOME team 5-0 S/U & ATS since 2003
10/19/2023	vs	*JACKSONVILLE*	A								4-0 S/U vs Jacksonville since 2007
10/29/2023	@	*Indianapolis*	G								vs Indianapolis - Saints lead series 9-5
11/5/2023	vs	CHICAGO	A								7-0 S/U vs Chicago since 2011
11/12/2023	@	Minnesota	G								Game 7-1-1 O/U @ Minnesota since 1994
11/19/2023		BYE									
11/26/2023	@	Atlanta	A								vs Atlanta - Falcons leads series 55-54
12/3/2023	vs	DETROIT	A								vs Detroit - Saints lead series 14-12-1
12/10/2023	vs	CAROLINA	A								Game 8-2 O/U @ home vs Carolina since 2014
12/17/2023	vs	NEW YORK GIANTS	A								5-1 S/U @ home vs New York Giants since 1994
12/21/2023	@	Los Angeles Rams	G								0-5 S/U & ATS @ Los Angeles Rams since 2005
12/31/2023	@	Tampa Bay	G								11-4 S/U @ Tampa Bay since 2009
1/7/2024	vs	ATLANTA	A								
1/14/2024											NFC Wild Card
1/21/2024											NFC Divisional Playoff
1/28/2024											NFC Championship
2/11/2024											Super Bowl LVIII @ Las Vegas, NV

Pointspread Analysis	Pointspread Analysis
vs NFC teams	**vs NFC teams**
6-1 ATS vs NFC East as 7.5-10 point Dog since 1983	0-3 S/U vs Atlanta as 7.5-10 point Dog since 1981
4-13 S/U vs NFC East as 3.5-7 point Dog since 1981	0-3 S/U vs Carolina as 7.5-10 point Dog since 2005
7-1 S/U & ATS vs NFC East as 3 point or less Dog since 2003	2-8 S/U @ Atlanta as 3.5-7 point Dog since 1978
8-3 O/U vs NFC East as 3 point or less favorite since 2002	7-0 ATS vs Carolina as 3.5-7 point Dog since 1998
15-4 S/U vs NFC East as 3.5-7 point favorite since 1979	2-7 O/U vs Carolina as 3.5-7 point Dog since 1996
7-1 O/U vs NFC East as 3.5-7 point favorite since 2001	1-3 O/U vs Tampa Bay as 3.5-7 point Dog since 2005
1-9 ATS vs NFC East as 7.5-10 point favorite since 1994	5-1 S/U & ATS vs Atlanta as 3 point or less Dog since 2010
0-4 S/U @ New York Giants as 3.5-7 point Dog since 1997	0-3 S/U & ATS @ Carolina as 3 point or less Dog since 1998
1-5 O/U @ New York Giants as 3.5-7 point Dog since 1985	3-0 O/U @ home vs Carolina as 3 point or less Dog since 2006
5-1 S/U vs New York Giants as 3 point or less favorite since 1978	9-1 S/U @ Atlanta as 3 point or less favorite since 1979
vs New York Giants - Giants leads series 16-14	8-1-1 ATS @ Atlanta as 3 point or less favorite since 1979
4-1-1 ATS @ home vs New York Giants since 1994	1-4 S/U & ATS @ home vs Atlanta as 3 point or less favorite since 1995
Game 7-0 O/U @ home vs NY Giants since 1993	6-0 O/U @ home vs Atlanta as 3 point or less favorite since 1994
0-6 S/U vs NFC North as 8 point or more Dog since 1980	1-6 O/U vs Carolina as 3 point or less favorite since 2007
2-6 S/U vs NFC North as 3.5-7 point Dog since 2004	5-1 S/U vs Tampa Bay as 3 point or less favorite since 2008
12-1 O/U vs NFC North since 1995	6-0 S/U vs Carolina as 3.5-7 point favorite since 2001
0-6 S/U vs NFC North as 3 point or less Dog since 2005	8-0 S/U vs Atlanta as 7.5-10 point favorite since 1988
7-0 O/U vs NFC North as 3 point or less Dog since 2002	0-4 ATS vs Atlanta as 7.5-10 point favorite since 2003
8-2 O/U vs NFC North as 3 point or less favorite since 2006	0-7 O/U vs Atlanta as 7.5-10 point favorite since 1988
11-2 S/U vs NFC North as 3.5-7 point favorite since 2003	5-0 O/U vs Carolina as 7.5-10 point favorite since 2001
1-7 ATS vs NFC North as 3.5-7 point favorite since 2002	6-1 S/U vs Tampa Bay as 10.5 point or more favorite since 1988
7-1 S/U vs NFC North as 7.5 or more favorite since 1979	Game 3-12 O/U @ Tampa Bay since 2008
0-5 S/U vs Chicago as 3 point or less Dog since 1984	5-0 O/U on road vs NFC West as 10.5 point or more Dog s/1997
5-0 S/U vs Chicago as 3.5-7 point favorite since 1992 {4-1 ATS}	2-11 S/U vs NFC West as 7.5-10 point Dog since 1978
1-3 O/U vs Chicago as 3.5-7 point favorite since 1992	4-1 ATS vs NFC West as 7.5-10 point Dog since 1995
1-3 S/U & ATS vs Detroit as 3 point or less favorite since 2000	2-10 S/U & ATS vs NFC West as 3 point or less Dog since 2001
1-6 O/U vs Detroit as 3.5-7 point favorite since 1988	20-3 S/U vs NFC West as 3.5-7 point favorite since 1987
1-3 S/U vs Green Bay as 3.5-7 point Dog since 1995	5-1 O/U vs NFC West as 10.5 point or more favorite since 1993
4-1 S/U & ATS vs Green Bay as 3 point or less favorite since 1986	Game 6-2 O/U @ home vs LA Rams since 2000
0-5 S/U @ Minnesota as 3.5-7 point Dog since 1988	0-3 S/U vs Los Angeles Rams as 7.5-10 point Dog since 1978
0-3 S/U vs Minnesota as 7.5-10 point Dog since 1981	5-1 O/U @ Los Angeles Rams as 3.5-7 point Dog since 1989
7-1 O/U vs Minnesota as 3.5-7 point Dog since 1985	1-5 S/U @ Los Angeles Rams as 3 point or less Dog since 1983
1-3 S/U & ATS vs NFC South as 10.5 or more Dog since 1980	7-1 S/U vs Los Angeles Rams as 3.5-7 point favorite since 1987
0-4 S/U vs NFC South as 7.5-10 point Dog since 2005	3-0 S/U vs Los Angeles Rams as 7.5-10 point favorite since 1992
13-2 ATS vs NFC South as 3.5-7 point Dog since 2002	vs Los Angeles Rams - HOME team 8-1 S/U & ATS since 2010
4-10 O/U vs NFC South as 3.5-7 point Dog since 2003	
0-7 O/U on road vs NFC South as 3 point or less Dog since 2010	**Favorite**
15-3 S/U vs NFC South as 7.5-10 point favorite since 1987	8-3 S/U on road as 7.5-10 point favorite since 1988
4-9 ATS vs NFC South as 10.5 point or more favorite since 1988	
12-3 S/U vs NFC South as 10.5 point or more favorite since 1988	27-7 S/U @ home after road loss since 2008

Last 4 seasons + Pointspread Analysis

	2022										
@	Tennessee		G	21	20	W	5.5	W	44.0	U	
vs	CAROLINA		A	19	13	W	1.0	W	43.5	U	
vs	DALLAS		A	16	23	L	-1.0	L	38.5	O	
vs	CHICAGO		A	20	12	W	-3.0	W	39.5	U	
vs	Green Bay {London}		G	27	22	W	9.0	W	42.0	O	
vs	BALTIMORE		A	24	20	W	5.5	W	45.5	U	
@	Jacksonville		G	23	17	W	3.5	W	44.0	U	
@	Seattle		A	13	27	L	3.0	L	44.5	U	
	BYE										
vs	HOUSTON		A	24	16	W	-4.5	W	41.5	U	
vs	DETROIT		A	18	31	L	-3.0	L	44.0	O	
@	Dallas		A	20	28	L	10.0	W	45.5	O	
vs	WASHINGTON		A	20	20	T	2.5	W	40.0	T	
vs	PHILADELPHIA		A	22	48	L	7.0	L	44.5	O	
@	Washington		G	20	12	W	4.0	W	40.0	U	
@	Minnesota		A	24	27	L	4.5	W	48.5	O	
vs	INDIANAPOLIS		A	38	10	W	-5.5	W	38.5	O	
@	Philadelphia		G	16	22	L	17.0	W	42.5	U	
@	**Minnesota**		A	**31**	**24**	**W**	**2.5**	**W**	**48.0**	**O**	
@	**Philadelphia**		G	**7**	**38**	**L**	**8.0**	**L**	**47.5**	**U**	

	2021										
vs	DENVER		A	13	27	L	3.0	L	41.5	U	
@	Washington	T	G	29	30	L	4.0	W	41.0	O	
vs	ATLANTA		A	14	17	L	-2.5	L	48.0	U	
@	New Orleans {OT}		A	27	21	W	7.5	W	42.5	O	
@	Dallas		A	20	44	L	7.0	L	53.0	O	
vs	L.A. RAMS		A	11	38	L	7.5	L	49.0	T	
vs	CAROLINA		A	25	3	W	3.0	W	43.0	U	
@	Kansas City	M	G	17	20	L	11.0	W	53.0	U	
vs	LAS VEGAS		A	23	16	W	3.0	W	46.5	U	
	BYE		A								
@	Tampa Bay	M	G	10	30	L	10.5	L	50.0	U	
vs	PHILADELPHIA		A	13	7	W	4.0	W	45.0	U	
@	Miami		G	9	20	L	6.5	L	40.0	U	
@	Los Angeles Chargers		A	21	37	L	9.0	L	43.5	O	
vs	DALLAS		A	6	21	L	12.0	L	43.0	U	
@	Philadelphia		G	10	34	L	11.0	L	40.5	O	
@	Chicago		G	3	29	L	6.5	L	36.5	U	
vs	WASHINGTON		A	7	22	L	6.0	L	35.5	U	

	2020										
vs	PITTSBURGH	M	A	16	26	L	6.0	L	43.5	U	
@	Chicago		G	13	17	L	4.5	W	42.5	U	
vs	SAN FRANCISCO		A	9	36	L	3.0	L	43.5	O	
@	L.A. Rams		G	9	17	L	13.5	W	50.0	U	
@	Dallas		A	34	37	L	7.5	W	52.0	O	
vs	Washington		A	20	19	W	-2.0	L	42.0	U	
@	Philadelphia	T	G	21	22	L	4.5	W	44.5	U	
vs	TAMPA BAY	M	A	23	25	L	10.0	W	47.0	O	
@	Washington		G	23	20	W	3.0	W	43.0	T	
vs	PHILADELPHIA		A	27	17	W	5.0	W	46.0	U	
	BYE		A								
@	Cincinnati		A	19	17	W	-6.5	L	45.0	U	
@	Seattle		A	17	12	W	10.0	W	48.0	U	
vs	Arizona		A	7	26	L	3.0	L	47.0	U	
vs	CLEVELAND	Su	A	6	20	L	6.0	L	44.5	U	
@	Baltimore		A	13	27	L	10.0	L	42.5	U	
vs	DALLAS		A	23	19	W	1.5	W	44.0	U	

	2019										
@	Dallas		A	17	35	L	7.0	L	44.0	O	
vs	BUFFALO		A	14	28	L	1.5	L	44.5	U	
@	Tampa Bay		G	32	31	W	4.5	W	47.5	O	
vs	Washington		A	24	3	W	-3.0	W	48.0	U	
@	MINNESOTA		A	10	28	L	5.5	L	44.0	U	
vs	New England	T	A	14	35	L	16.5	L	43.0	U	
vs	Arizona		A	21	27	L	-3.5	L	49.5	U	
@	Detroit		A	26	31	L	6.5	W	49.5	O	
vs	DALLAS	M	A	18	37	L	6.5	L	48.5	O	
@	New York Jets		A	27	34	L	-3.0	L	43.0	O	
	BYE										
@	Chicago		G	14	19	L	6.0	W	40.5	U	
vs	GREEN BAY		A	13	31	L	6.5	L	44.0	T	
@	Philadelphia {OT}	M	G	17	23	L	9.0	W	45.0	U	
vs	MIAMI		A	36	20	W	-3.5	W	46.0	O	
@	Washington {OT}		G	41	35	W	-1.0	W	42.5	O	
vs	PHILADELPHIA		A	17	34	L	4.0	L	44.5	O	

Pointspread Analysis vs AFC teams	
4-20 S/U vs AFC teams as 3.5-7 point Dog since 1995	
1-14 O/U vs AFC teams as 3 point or less Dog since 2001	
12-1 S/U vs AFC teams as 7.5-10 point favorite since 1985	
7-0 S/U vs AFC teams as 10.5 point or more favorite since 1989	
14-2 ATS vs AFC East as 3.5 point or more Dog since 1991	
0-5 O/U vs AFC East as 3 point or less Dog since 2003	
4-0 S/U vs AFC East as 8 point or more favorite since 1987	
0-4 O/U vs AFC East as 8 point or more favorite since 1987	
18-4 S/U vs AFC West as favorite since 1978	
1-3 O/U vs AFC West as 7.5-10 point Dog since 1983	
0-8 S/U vs AFC West as 3.5-7 point Dog since 1995	
0-6 ATS vs AFC West as 3.5-7 point Dog since 1995	
7-2-1 O/U vs AFC West as 3.5-7 point Dog since 1992	
4-0 S/U & ATS vs AFC West as 7.5-10 point favorite since 1987	
vs Las Vegas - Raiders leads series 8-6	
THU-SAT-SNF-MNF	
8-2 O/U on Thursday since 2013	49ers
0-7 S/U on Thursday since 2016	49ers
0-4 S/U on Thursday as 3.5-7 point dog since 2002	
4-11 S/U on road on SNF since 2010	Bills
2-11-1 S/U on road on SNF as 3.5-7 point dog since 1996	
2-8 S/U vs AFC teams on SNF since 1992	Bills
0-4 S/U @ Dallas on SNF since 2013	
5-16 S/U on MNF as 3.5-7 point dog since 1979	SEA, GB

Pointspread Analysis Dog	
6-24 S/U as 10.5 point or more Dog since 1978	
6-22 S/U @ home as 3.5-7 point Dog since 1998	
7-26 S/U on road as 3.5-7 point Dog since 2013	
9-20-1 S/U as 3 point or less Dog since 2012	
Favorite	
17-4 S/U as 3.5-7 point favorite since 2012	
2-15-1 O/U on road as 3.5-7 point favorite since 1993	
34-7 S/U as 7.5-10 point favorite since 1987	
11-2 S/U on road as 7.5-10 point favorite since 1988	
Playoffs	
6-2 S/U on road in Playoffs since 2007	
8-2 ATS on road in Playoffs since 2003	
1-9 O/U @ home in Playoffs since 1987	
0-3 S/U on Saturday in Playoffs since 1984	
6-1 ATS on road in WILD Card since 1984	
0-5 O/U @ home in Divisional Playoffs since 1990	
5-0 S/U in NFC Championship since 1986	
3-0 S/U @ Green Bay in Playoffs since 2008	
5-1 ATS vs San Francisco in Playoffs since 1985	
THU-SAT-SNF-MNF	
2-9 S/U on road on MNF since 2011	
0-6 S/U @ Philadelphia on MNF since 1980	
1-6 ATS @ Philadelphia on MNF since 1980	
0-5 S/U @ home on MNF since 2017	

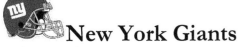 
2023 Schedule + Trends & Angles

DATE		OPPONENT	TURF	NYG	OPP	S/U	LINE	ATS	TOT	O/U	Trends & Angles
9/10/2023	vs	DALLAS	A								vs Dallas - Cowboys leads series 73-47-2
9/17/2023	@	Arizona	G								vs Arizona - Giants lead series 80-45-2
9/21/2023	@	San Francisco	G								Game 4-0 O/U vs San Francisco since 2015
10/2/2023	vs	SEATTLE	A								0-3 S/U & ATS @ home vs Seattle since 2011
10/8/2023	@	*Miami*	G								7-2 S/U vs Miami since 1990
10/15/2023	@	*Buffalo*	A								ROAD team 6-0 ATS since 1999
10/22/2023	vs	WASHINGTON	A								10-4-1 S/U @ home vs Washington since 2008
10/29/2023	vs	*NEW YORK JETS*	A								5-2 S/U & ATS vs New York Jets since 1996
11/5/2023	@	*Las Vegas Raiders*	G								2-5 S/U @ Raiders since 1973
11/12/2023	@	Dallas	A								vs Dallas - Cowboys lead series 71-47-2
11/19/2023	@	Washington	G								4-1 S/U @ Washington since 2018 {5-0 ATS}
11/26/2023	vs	*NEW ENGLAND*	A								5-1 ATS vs New England since 2007
12/3/2023		BYE									
12/11/2023	vs	GREEN BAY	A								vs Green Bay - Packers lead series 34-27-2
12/17/2023	@	New Orleans	A								vs New Orleans - Giants leads series 16-14
12/25/2023	@	Philadelphia	G								0-10 S/U @ Philadelphia since 2014
12/31/2023	vs	LOS ANGELES RAMS	A								8-3 S/U vs Los Angeles Rams since 2002 {9-2 ATS}
1/7/2024	vs	PHILADELPHIA	A								4-12 S/U @ home vs Philadelphia since 2008 {2 W}
1/14/2024											NFC Wild Card
1/21/2024											NFC Divisional Playoff
1/28/2024											NFC Championship
2/11/2024											Super Bowl LVIII @ Las Vegas, NV

Pointspread Analysis vs NFC teams		Pointspread Analysis vs NFC teams
Game 9-2 O/U @ home vs Philadelphia since 2012		14-2 S/U vs NFC South as 3.5-7 point favorite since 1978
Game 3-11 O/U @ Philadelphia since 2010		1-5 S/U vs New Orleans as 3 point or less Dog since 1978
Game 2-10-1 O/U @ home vs Washington since 2010		6-1 S/U vs New Orleans as 3.5-7 point favorite since 1981
2-13 S/U vs NFC East as 10.5 point or more Dog since 1978		1-5 O/U vs New Orleans as 3.5-7 point favorite since 1985
7-1 ATS vs NFC East as 7.5-10 point Dog since 2008		2-8 S/U vs NFC West as 7.5 point or more Dog since 1994
4-10 O/U vs NFC East as 7.5-10 point Dog since 1992		2-7 S/U vs NFC West as 3.5-7 point Dog since 2002
2-12 S/U on road vs NFC East as 3.5-7 point Dog since 2014		0-9 S/U @ home vs NFC West as 3.5-7 point Dog since 1978
3-8-1 S/U vs NFC East as 3 point or less Dog since 2009		4-0 S/U & ATS on road vs NFC West as 3.5-7 point favorite since 1990
0-6 O/U on road vs NFC East as 3.5-7 point favorite since 1993		3-10 S/U on road vs NFC West as 3 point or less Dog since 1984
11-2 S/U on road vs NFC East as 3.5-7 point favorite since 1985		5-0 S/U @ home vs NFC West as 3 point or less favorite since 1991
13-2 S/U vs NFC East as 7.5-10 point favorite since 1989		9-3 S/U vs NFC West as 7.5-10 point favorite since 1993
5-1 O/U vs NFC East as 7.5-10 point favorite since 2001		3-0 S/U vs Seattle as 3.5-7 point favorite since 2002
0-8 S/U @ Dallas as 10.5 point or more Dog since 1978		3-0 S/U & ATS @ Arizona as 3.5-7 point Dog since 1994
1-6 S/U @ Dallas as 7.5-10 point Dog since 1979		3-0 O/U @ Arizona as 3.5-7 point Dog since 1994
0-5 S/U @ Dallas as 3.5-7 point Dog since 2014		0-3 S/U & ATS @ Arizona as 3 point or less Dog since 1996
8-1 O/U @ Dallas as 3.5-7 point Dog since 2006		6-0 S/U @ Arizona as 3.5-7 point favorite since 1985
1-6 S/U @ home vs Dallas as 3.5-7 point Dog since 1994		13-3 S/U vs Arizona as 3.5-7 point favorite since 1985
2-6 O/U @ home vs Dallas as 3.5-7 point Dog since 1984		6-0 S/U vs Arizona as 7.5-10 point favorite since 1986
1-4 S/U & ATS @ Dallas as 3 point or less Dog since 1985		5-0 ATS vs Arizona as 7.5-10 point favorite since 1986
7-2 S/U vs Dallas as 3 point or less favorite since 2002		1-5 O/U vs Arizona as 7.5-10 point favorite since 1986
4-1 S/U vs Dallas as 7.5-10 point favorite since 1989		Game 3-0-1 O/U @ home vs L.A. Rams since 2005
5-1 O/U vs Dallas as 7.5-10 point favorite since 1987		vs Los Angeles Rams - Rams leads series 29-17
1-9 S/U @ Philadelphia as 3.5-7 point Dog since 2001		0-3 S/U @ San Francisco as 10.5 point or more Dog since 1984
1-6 O/U @ Philadelphia as 3.5-7 point Dog since 2007		2-10 S/U vs San Francisco as 3.5-7 point Dog since 1981
0-3 S/U & ATS @ Philadelphia as 3 point or less Dog since 2012		vs Seattle - Series tied 10-10
0-5 S/U & ATS vs Philadelphia as 3 point or less Dog since 2009		Grass/Turf
1-6 S/U & ATS vs Philadelphia as 3 point or less favorite since 2001		2-10 S/U on road on Turf as 10.5 point or more Dog since 1978
4-1 S/U @ Philadelphia as 3.5-7 point favorite since 1985		1-10 O/U on grass as 10.5 point or more Dog since 1984
3-0 S/U vs Philadelphia as 7.5-10 point favorite since 1993		7-1 ATS on grass as 7.5-10 point Dog since 2008
1-4-1 S/U @ home vs Washington as 3 point or less Dog since 1980		6-22 S/U on road on Turf as 3.5-7 point Dog since 2004
12-3 S/U vs Washington as 3.5-7 point favorite since 1986		4-15 S/U on grass as 3.5-7 point Dog since 2013
2-9 O/U vs Washington as 3.5-7 point favorite since 2006		3-10 S/U vs AFC on grass as 3.5-7 point Dog since 1997
3-0 S/U vs Washington as 7.5-10 point favorite since 1990		9-2 ATS on grass as 3 point or less Dog since 2008
1-14 S/U vs NFC North as 3.5-7 point Dog since 2008		2-9-1 S/U on road on Turf as 3 point or less Dog since 2012
1-5 O/U vs NFC North as 3 point or less favorite since 2007		9-3 S/U on road on Turf as 3 point or less favorite since 1999
6-0 S/U vs NFC North as 3.5-7 point favorite since 2010		8-3-1 ATS on road on Turf as 3 point or less favorite since 1999
0-6 O/U vs NFC North as 3.5-7 point favorite since 2010		1-8 O/U on road on Turf as 3.5-7 point favorite since 1993
1-7 S/U vs Green Bay as 3.5-7 point Dog since 1961		0-6 O/U on grass as 3.5-7 point Dog since 2007
0-3 S/U vs Green Bay as 3 point or less Dog since 1981		5-0 S/U on road on Turf as 7.5-10 point favorite since 1989
1-6 S/U vs NFC South as 3.5-7 point Dog since 2003		8-2 S/U on grass as 7.5 or more favorite since 1987
3-8 O/U vs NFC South as 3 point or less favorite since 2000	JETS	12-4 S/U after playing @ home vs Washington since 2004

2022

vs	BALTIMORE		A	9	24	L	6.5	L	44.0	U
@	Cleveland		G	31	30	W	6.0	W	38.5	O
vs	CINCINNATI		A	12	27	L	6.5	L	45.5	U
@	Pittsburgh		G	24	20	W	3.0	W	41.0	O
vs	MIAMI		A	40	17	W	3.0	W	46.0	O
@	Green Bay		G	27	10	W	7.5	W	44.0	O
@	Denver		G	16	9	W	-2.0	W	37.0	U
vs	NEW ENGLAND		A	17	22	L	3.0	L	40.0	U
vs	BUFFALO		A	20	17	W	10.5	W	45.5	U
	BYE									
@	New England		A	3	10	L	3.0	L	38.5	U
vs	CHICAGO		A	31	10	W	-7.5	W	36.5	O
@	Minnesota		A	22	27	L	2.5	L	43.0	O
@	Buffalo		A	12	20	L	10.0	W	43.5	U
vs	DETROIT		A	17	20	L	-2.0	L	43.5	U
vs	JACKSONVILLE	T	A	3	19	L	-2.5	L	36.5	U
@	Seattle		A	6	23	L	-1.0	L	43.0	U
@	Miami		G	6	11	L	3.5	L	37.0	U

2021

@	Carolina		G	14	19	L	3.5	L	44.5	U
vs	NEW ENGLAND		A	6	25	L	5.5	L	43.0	U
@	Denver		G	0	26	L	10.0	L	41.5	U
vs	TENNESSEE {OT}		A	27	24	W	5.5	W	44.5	O
vs	Atlanta {London}		A	20	27	L	2.5	L	45.5	O
	BYE									
@	New England		A	13	54	L	7.0	L	42.5	O
vs	CINCINNATI		A	34	31	W	11.5	W	43.0	O
@	Indianapolis	T	A	30	45	L	10.0	L	45.0	O
vs	BUFFALO		A	17	45	L	13.0	L	48.5	O
vs	MIAMI		A	17	24	L	3.5	L	44.5	U
@	Houston		G	21	14	W	2.5	W	44.5	U
vs	PHILADELPHIA		A	18	33	L	4.5	L	44.0	O
vs	NEW ORLEANS		A	9	30	L	4.5	L	41.5	U
@	Miami		G	24	31	L	9.5	W	42.0	O
vs	JACKSONVILLE		A	26	21	W	-2.5	W	43.5	O
vs	TAMPA BAY		A	24	28	L	14.5	W	48.0	O
@	Buffalo		A	10	27	L	16.0	L	43.0	U

2020

@	Buffalo		A	17	27	L	6.5	L	39.5	O
vs	SAN FRANCISCO		A	13	31	L	7.0	L	41.5	O
@	Indianapolis		A	7	36	L	12.0	L	44.0	U
vs	DENVER	T	A	28	37	L	-1.0	L	41.0	O
vs	ARIZONA		A	10	30	L	7.0	L	48.5	U
@	Miami		G	0	24	L	8.5	L	46.5	U
vs	BUFFALO		A	10	18	L	10.0	W	46.5	U
@	Kansas City		G	9	35	L	19.5	L	49.0	U
vs	New England	M	A	27	30	L	9.0	W	42.0	O
	BYE									
@	L.A. Chargers		G	28	34	L	10.0	W	47.0	O
vs	MIAMI		A	3	20	L	7.5	L	46.0	U
vs	LAS VEGAS		A	28	31	L	7.5	W	48.5	O
@	Seattle		A	3	40	L	16.5	L	49.5	U
@	L.A. Rams		G	23	20	W	17.0	W	44.5	U
vs	CLEVELAND		A	23	16	W	7.0	W	45.0	U
@	New England		A	14	28	L	3.0	L	41.0	O

2019

vs	BUFFALO		A	16	17	L	-2.5	L	41.0	U
vs	CLEVELAND	M	A	3	23	L	6.5	L	45.0	U
@	New England		A	14	30	L	20.5	W	43.0	O
	BYE									
@	Philadelphia		G	6	31	L	14.0	L	43.0	U
vs	DALLAS		A	24	22	W	7.0	W	43.5	O
vs	New England	M	A	0	33	L	10.0	L	43.0	U
@	Jacksonville		G	15	29	L	7.0	L	40.0	U
@	Miami		G	18	26	L	-3.0	L	42.5	U
vs	N.Y. GIANTS		A	34	27	W	3.0	W	43.0	O
@	Washington		G	34	17	W	1.5	W	38.0	O
vs	OAKLAND		A	34	3	W	3.0	W	44.5	U
@	Cincinnati		A	6	22	L	-2.5	L	43.0	U
vs	MIAMI		A	22	21	W	-5.0	L	46.5	U
@	Baltimore	T	A	21	42	L	17.0	L	43.5	O
vs	PITTSBURGH		A	16	10	W	3.0	W	36.5	U
@	Buffalo		A	13	6	W	-1.0	W	36.5	U

Pointspread Analysis — THU-SAT-SNF-MNF

0-5 S/U on Thursday since 2018 {0-5 ATS}	Browns
1-6 S/U on road on Thursday since 2011 {2-5 ATS}	Browns
2-7 S/U on road on Thursday as Dog since 2003	Chiefs, Raiders
7-0 O/U on SNF since 2002	Raiders
4-0 O/U on road on SNF since 2001	CHIEFS
4-0 O/U @ home on SNF since 2005	BUFF, LAC
0-7 S/U @ home on MNF since 2012	
1-9 S/U @ home on MNF as Dog since 1990	
1-8 S/U on MNF as favorite since 1986	
0-3 S/U @ home vs Buffalo on MNF since 1988	

Playoffs

3-0 S/U & ATS @ home in Playoffs since 1986
7-2 ATS in Playoffs on Saturday since 1983
6-1 ATS on road on Saturday in Playoffs since 1983
5-1 ATS on road in Divisional Playoffs since 1983
0-4 S/U & ATS in AFC Championship since 1982

Pointspread Analysis — Grass/Turf

1-14 S/U on road on Turf as 10.5 point or more Dog s/2007
1-10 S/U on grass as 10.5 point or more Dog since 1978
6-29 S/U on grass as 7.5-10 point Dog since 1980
2-12 S/U on road on Turf as 7.5-10 point Dog since 1995
11-3-1 O/U on road on Turf as 7.5-10 point Dog since 1994
4-12 S/U on road on Turf as 3.5-7 point Dog since 2010
10-4 O/U on grass as 3.5-7 point Dog since 2006
17-5 S/U on grass as 3 point or less favorite since 2002
15-5-2 ATS on grass as 3 point or less favorite since 2002
3-8-1 O/U on grass as 3.5-7 point favorite since 1983
3-0 S/U on road on Turf as 7.5 point or more favorite s/1985

Dog

5-29 S/U as 10.5 point or more Dog since 1978
7-45 S/U as 7.5-10 point Dog since 1996
11-3 ATS @ home as 7.5-10 point Dog since 1995
2-18 S/U @ home as 7.5-10 point Dog since 1989
6-19 S/U on road as 3.5-7 point Dog since 2011

Favorite

3-11 S/U & ATS @ home as 3 point or less favorite since 2014
9-0 S/U as 7.5-10 point favorite since 2010
7-2 S/U as 10.5 point or more favorite since 1981

 **New York Jets**
MetLife Stadium

2023 Schedule + Trends & Angles

AFC East

Coach: Robert Saleh

DATE		OPPONENT	TURF	NYJ	OPP	S/U	LINE	ATS	TOT	O/U	Trends & Angles
9/11/2023	vs	BUFFALO	A								vs Buffalo - Bills leads series 67-57
9/17/2023	@	*Dallas*	A								vs Dallas - Cowboys lead series 7-5
9/24/2023	vs	NEW ENGLAND	A								7-35 S/U vs New England since 2003
10/1/2023	vs	KANSAS CITY	A								HOME team 8-0 S/U since 2005
10/8/2023	@	Denver	G								vs Denver - Broncos leads series 22-16-1
10/15/2023	vs	*PHILADELPHIA*	A								0-12 S/U vs Philadelphia since 1973
10/22/2023		BYE									
10/29/2023	@	*New York Giants*	A								vs New York Giants - Giants lead series 8-6
11/6/2023	vs	L.A. CHARGERS	A								1-4 S/U @ home vs Los Angeles Chargers since 1994
11/12/2023	@	Las Vegas Raiders	G								4-17-1 S/U @ Las Vegas Raiders since 1963
11/19/2023	@	Buffalo	A								0-9 S/U vs Buffalo as 7.5-10 point Dog since 1989
11/24/2023	vs	MIAMI	A								Game 3-10 O/U @ home vs Miami since 2010
12/3/2023	vs	*ATLANTA*	A								vs Atlanta - Falcons leads series 8-5
12/10/2023	vs	HOUSTON	A								vs Houston - Jets lead series 6-3
12/17/2023	@	Miami	G								vs Miami - Jets lead series 57-56-1
12/24/2023	vs	*WASHINGTON*	A								1-4 S/U @ home vs Washington since 1972
12/28/2023	@	Cleveland	G								Game 1-4 O/U vs Cleveland since 2017
1/7/2024	@	New England Patriots	A								0-12 S/U @ New England since 2011
1/14/2024											AFC Wild Card
1/21/2024											AFC Divisional Playoff
1/28/2024											AFC Championship
2/11/2024											Super Bowl LVIII @ Las Vegas, NV

Pointspread Analysis vs AFC teams		Pointspread Analysis vs AFC teams
3-17 S/U vs AFC East as 10.5 point or more Dog since 1984		0-4 ATS vs AFC South as 10.5 point or more favorite s/1986
4-24 S/U vs AFC East as 7.5-10 point Dog since 1989		3-0 S/U vs Houston as 3.5-7 point favorite since 2004
10-4 O/U on road vs AFC East as 7.5-10 point Dog since 1995		2-12 S/U vs AFC West as 7.5 point or more Dog since 1985
7-2 O/U @ home vs AFC East as 3 point or less Dog since 2006		0-4 S/U on road vs AFC West as 3 point or less Dog s/1988
2-9 S/U & ATS vs AFC East as 3 point or less favorite since 2013		8-2 O/U vs AFC West as 3 point or less favorite since 2000
12-4 S/U vs AFC East as 7.5 point or more favorite since 1978		8-1 S/U vs AFC West as 3.5-7 point favorite since 1991
1-5 S/U @ home vs Buffalo as 3.5-7 point Dog since 1980		0-4 S/U & ATS vs AFC West as 7.5-10 point favorite s/1981
3-0 ATS @ home vs Buffalo as 3.5-7 point Dog since 1995		3-0 S/U vs AFC West as 10.5 point or more favorite since 2006
5-0 S/U & ATS @ home vs Buffalo as 3 point or less Dog since 1994		0-4 S/U & ATS vs Denver as 7.5-10 point Dog since 1996
1-5 S/U & ATS vs Buffalo as 3 point or less favorite since 2013		Game 4-0 O/U @ Las Vegas Raiders since 2009
1-5 ATS vs Buffalo as 3.5-7 point favorite since 2001		0-3 ATS @ Las Vegas Raiders since 2011
0-4 ATS @ home vs Buffalo as 7.5-10 point favorite since 1986		0-4 S/U vs LA Chargers since 2012 {1-3 ATS}
0-3 S/U @ Miami as 10.5 point or more Dog since 1984		vs Raiders - HOME TEAM 9-2 S/U since 2005
3-0 ATS @ Miami as 10.5 point or more Dog since 1984		1-5 S/U @ Las Vegas Raiders as 3.5-7 point Dog since 1999
3-1 O/U @ Miami as 3.5-7 point Dog since 2003		0-3 S/U & ATS @ Las Vegas Raiders as 3 point or less favorite s/2008
1-4 S/U vs Miami as 3 point or less Dog since 2012		0-3 S/U vs Los Angeles Chargers as 3.5-7 point Dog s/2005
0-5 S/U & ATS @ home vs Miami as 3 point or less favorite since 2008		0-4 S/U vs Kansas City as 3 point or less Dog since 1988
0-9 S/U vs New England as 10.5 point or more Dog since 2007		0-3 O/U vs Kansas City as 3.5-7 point favorite since 1988
1-4 ATS vs New England as 10.5 point or more Dog since 2016		**vs NFC teams**
1-5 O/U vs New England as 10.5 point or more Dog since 2013		1-6 S/U vs NFC teams as 10.5 point or more Dog since 1989
2-12 S/U vs New England as 7.5-10 point Dog since 1978		3-14 S/U vs NFC teams as 7.5-10 point Dog since 1980
1-5 S/U @ New England as 3.5-7 point Dog since 2003		4-11 S/U vs NFC teams as 3 point or less Dog since 2003
12-3 O/U vs New England as 3.5-7 point Dog since 1999		6-0 S/U vs NFC teams as 7.5-10 point favorite since 1998
5-2 O/U vs New England as 3 point or less Dog since 2000		0-5 S/U vs NFC East as 7.5 point or more Dog since 1987
1-8 S/U & ATS @ home vs New England as 3 point or less favorite s/1984		2-6 S/U @ home vs NFC East as 3.5-7 point Dog since 1978
3-0 S/U vs New England as 3.5-7 point favorite since 1993		2-5 S/U vs NFC East as 3 point or less Dog since 1999
2-7 S/U vs AFC North as 7.5 point or more Dog since 1978		5-0 S/U vs NFC East as 4.5 point or more favorite since 1978
7-2 ATS vs AFC North as 7.5 point or more Dog since 1978		0-5 S/U vs NFC East as 7.5 point or more Dog since 1987
4-14 S/U & ATS vs AFC North as 3.5-7 point Dog since 2000		2-7 S/U @ home vs NFC East as 3.5-7 point Dog since 1978
3-14 S/U on road vs AFC North as 3.5-7 point Dog since 1986		2-5 S/U vs NFC East as 3 point or less Dog since 1999
5-1 S/U & ATS vs AFC North as 3 point or less favorite since 2010		5-0 S/U vs NFC East as 4.5 point or more favorite since 1978
6-1 S/U vs AFC North as 3.5-7 point favorite since 1987		1-10 ATS vs Philadelphia since 1973
6-1 S/U vs AFC North as 7.5 point or more favorite since 1985		1-5 ATS @ home vs Philadelphia since 1987
1-5 O/U vs AFC North as 7.5 point or more favorite since 1993		Game 3-0 O/U @ home vs Washington since 1999
0-9 S/U vs AFC South as 7.5-10 point Dog since 1991		4-0 ATS vs Washington since 2007
7-3 ATS vs AFC South as 7.5-10 point Dog since 1990		0-3 S/U vs Washington as 3.5-7 point Dog since 1978
4-0-1 ATS @ home vs AFC South as 3.5-7 point Dog since 1979		1-6 S/U vs NFC South as 7.5 point or more Dog since 2005
6-2-1 ATS vs AFC South as 3.5-7 point Dog since 2008		
7-2 S/U vs AFC South as 3.5-7 point favorite since 1995	Bills	4-16 S/U prior to playing @ home vs Miami since 2003
4-0 S/U vs AFC South as 7.5-10 point favorite since 1999	Cowboys	16-6 S/U prior to playing @ home vs New England since 1998

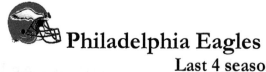

Philadelphia Eagles

NFC East

Last 4 seasons + Pointspread Analysis

2022

	Team	Day	Loc	PF	PA	W/L	Spread	ATS	Total	O/U
@	Detroit		A	38	35	W	-6.0	L	49.0	O
vs	MINNESOTA	M	G	24	7	W	-3.0	W	49.5	U
@	Washington		G	24	8	W	-5.5	W	47.5	U
vs	JACKSONVILLE		G	29	21	W	-6.5	W	43.5	O
@	Arizona		G	20	17	W	-5.5	L	47.5	U
vs	DALLAS	Su	G	26	17	W	-6.5	W	42.5	O
	BYE									
vs	PITTSBURGH		G	35	13	W	-11.5	W	43.0	O
@	Houston	T	G	29	17	W	-14.0	L	45.0	O
vs	WASHINGTON	M	G	21	32	L	-10.5	L	43.0	O
@	Indianapolis		A	17	16	W	-6.5	L	45.5	U
vs	GREEN BAY	Su	G	40	33	W	-6.0	W	46.0	O
vs	TENNESSEE		G	35	10	W	-4.5	W	44.5	O
@	New York Giants		A	48	22	W	-7.0	W	44.5	O
@	Chicago		G	25	20	W	-8.5	L	47.5	U
@	Dallas	Sa	A	34	40	L	3.5	L	48.0	O
vs	NEW ORLEANS		G	10	20	L	-4.5	L	42.0	U
vs	N.Y. GIANTS		G	22	16	W	-17.0	L	42.5	U
vs	N.Y. GIANTS	Sa	G	38	7	W	-8.0	W	47.5	U
vs	San Francisco		G	31	7	W	-2.5	W	44.5	U
vs	Kansas City		G	35	38	L	-1.0	L	51.5	O

2021

	Team	Day	Loc	PF	PA	W/L	Spread	ATS	Total	O/U
@	Atlanta		A	32	6	W	3.5	W	49.0	U
vs	SAN FRANCISCO		G	11	17	L	3.0	L	49.0	U
@	Dallas	M	A	21	41	L	3.5	L	51.5	O
vs	KANSAS CITY		G	30	42	L	7.0	L	53.0	O
@	Carolina		G	21	18	W	2.5	W	46.5	U
vs	TAMPA BAY	T	G	22	28	L	7.0	W	52.0	U
@	Las Vegas		G	22	33	L	1.0	L	48.5	O
@	Detroit		A	44	6	W	-3.0	W	48.0	O
vs	L.A. CHARGERS		G	24	27	L	PK	L	49.5	O
@	Denver		G	30	13	W	PK	W	44.5	O
vs	NEW ORLEANS		G	40	29	W	-3.0	W	42.5	O
@	New York Giants		A	7	13	L	-4.0	L	45.0	U
@	New York Jets		A	33	18	W	-4.5	W	44.0	O
	BYE									
vs	WASHINGTON	Tu	G	27	17	W	-10.0	T	39.5	O
vs	N.Y. GIANTS		G	34	10	W	-11.0	W	40.5	O
@	Washington		G	20	16	W	-6.0	L	44.5	U
vs	DALLAS	Sa	G	26	51	L	6.0	L	46.0	O
@	Tampa Bay		G	15	31	L	7.0	L	47.5	U

2020

	Team	Day	Loc	PF	PA	W/L	Spread	ATS	Total	O/U
@	Washington		G	17	27	L	-5.5	L	41.5	O
vs	L.A. RAMS		G	19	37	L	-1.5	L	45.5	O
vs	CINCINNATI {OT}		G	23	23	T	-5.5	L	47.0	O
@	San Francisco	Su	G	25	20	W	7.5	W	45.5	U
@	Pittsburgh		G	29	38	L	7.5	L	44.0	O
vs	Baltimore		G	28	30	L	10.0	W	46.0	O
vs	N.Y. GIANTS	T	G	22	21	W	-4.5	L	44.5	U
vs	DALLAS	Su	G	23	9	W	-10.0	W	43.5	U
	BYE									
@	New York Giants		A	17	27	L	-5.0	L	46.0	U
@	Cleveland		G	17	22	L	2.5	L	45.5	U
vs	SEATTLE	M	G	17	23	L	6.5	W	50.5	O
@	Green Bay		G	16	30	L	8.0	L	50.0	U
vs	NEW ORLEANS		G	24	21	W	7.5	W	42.5	O
@	Arizona		G	26	33	L	7.0	T	49.5	O
@	Dallas		A	17	37	L	-3.0	L	50.0	O
vs	WASHINGTON	Su	G	14	20	L	6.5	W	43.5	U

2019

	Team	Day	Loc	PF	PA	W/L	Spread	ATS	Total	O/U
vs	WASHINGTON		G	32	27	W	-10.0	L	44.0	O
@	Atlanta	Su	A	20	24	L	-1.0	L	53.0	U
vs	DETROIT		G	27	24	L	-4.5	L	45.0	O
@	Green Bay	T	G	34	27	W	3.5	W	46.5	O
vs	N.Y. JETS		G	31	6	W	-14.0	W	43.0	U
@	Minnesota		A	20	38	L	3.5	L	45.0	O
@	Dallas	Su	A	10	37	L	3.0	L	50.0	U
@	Buffalo		A	31	13	W	1.0	W	35.5	O
vs	CHICAGO		G	22	14	W	-5.0	W	41.0	U
	BYE									
vs	New England		G	10	17	L	4.5	L	44.5	U
vs	SEATTLE		G	9	17	L	1.5	L	46.0	U
@	Miami		G	31	37	L	-10.5	L	45.0	O
vs	N.Y. GIANTS {OT}	M	G	23	17	W	-9.0	L	45.0	U
@	Washington		G	37	27	W	-6.5	W	38.5	O
vs	DALLAS		G	17	9	W	2.0	W	46.5	U
@	New York Giants		A	34	17	W	-4.0	W	44.5	O
vs	SEATTLE		G	9	17	L	1.0	L	44.5	U

Pointspread Analysis vs AFC teams		Pointspread Analysis Dog
0-4 S/U vs AFC teams as 10.5 or more Dog since 1998		1-12 S/U as 10.5 point or more Dog since 1995
3-14 S/U vs AFC teams as 3.5-7 point Dog since 1993		16-5 ATS as 7.5-10 point Dog since 1996
11-3 O/U vs AFC teams as 3 point or less Dog since 2003		4-22 S/U @ home as 3.5-7 point Dog since 1993
14-1-1 S/U vs AFC teams as 3.5-7 point favorite since 1997		7-16 ATS @ home as 3.5-7 point Dog since 1994
13-3-1 S/U vs AFC teams as 7.5-10 point favorite since 1985		3-11 S/U @ home as 3 point or less Dog since 2007 (reg. season)
0-3 S/U vs AFC East as 10.5 point or more Dog since 1984		**Favorite**
4-1 ATS vs AFC East as 3.5-7 point Dog since 1993		11-0-1 S/U or road as 7.5-10 point favorite since 1992
5-0 S/U & ATS on road vs AFC East as 3 point or less Dog s/2003		56-11-1 S/U as 7.5-10 point favorite since 1979
6-0 S/U vs AFC East as 7.5 point or more favorite since 1981		**Playoffs**
5-0 S/U & ATS @ home vs AFC East as 3 point or less favorite since 1987		4-0 ATS on road in Divisional Playoffs since 2002
0-4 S/U & ATS @ home vs AFC East as 3.5-7 point favorite s/1983		6-0 S/U @ home in Divisional Playoffs since 1980
4-1 ATS vs New England as 3.5-7 point Dog since 1987		0-5 O/U @ home in Divisional Playoffs since 2003
3-0 O/U vs New England as 3 point or less Dog since 1983		1-11 O/U @ home in Playoffs since 2003
0-9 S/U vs AFC West 10 point or less Dog since 1980		0-5 O/U in WILD CARD since 2011
7-1 O/U vs AFC West as 3 point or less Dog since 1986		0-4 ATS @ home in WILD Card since 2007
1-5 O/U vs AFC West as 3 point or less favorite since 1995		0-4 O/U @ home in WILD Card since 2007
14-2 S/U vs AFC West as 3.5-10 point favorite since 1980		5-1 S/U @ home on Saturday in Playoffs since 1995
THU-SAT-SNF-MNF		1-4 S/U on road on Saturday in Playoffs since 1979
2-9 O/U as 3 point or less favorite on MNF since 1981		3-0 S/U & ATS @ home vs Atlanta in Playoffs since 2003
4-1 ATS vs AFC teams on MNF since 1991	Chiefs	0-3 O/U @ home vs Atlanta in Playoffs since 2003
5-0 S/U vs AFC teams on MNF since 1991	Chiefs	0-3 S/U & ATS @ Dallas in Playoffs since 1992
		4-0 S/U vs Minnesota in Playoffs since 1980 {3-0 ATS}

Philadelphia Eagles
Lincoln Financial Field

NFC East
2023 Schedule + Trends & Angles

Coach: Nick Sirianni

DATE		OPPONENT	TURF	PHL	OPP	S/U	LINE	ATS	TOT	O/U	Trends & Angles
9/10/2023	@	*New England Patriots*	A								Game 3-0 O/U @ New England since 1987
9/14/2023	vs	MINNESOTA	G								9-2 S/U & ATS @ home vs Minnesota since 1989
9/25/2023	@	Tampa Bay	G								0-3 S/U vs Tampa Bay since 2015
10/1/2023	vs	WASHINGTON	G								Game 7-2 O/U @ home vs Washington since 2014
10/8/2023	@	Los Angeles Rams	A								6-1 S/U & ATS vs LA Rams since 2005
10/15/2023	@	*New York Jets*	A								11-1 ATS vs New York Jets since 1973
10/22/2023	vs	*MIAMI*	G								
10/29/2023	@	Washington	G								5-1 S/U @ Washington since 2017
11/5/2023	vs	DALLAS	G								vs Dallas - Cowboys leads series 73-55
11/12/2023		BYE									
11/20/2023	@	*Kansas City*	G								vs Kansas City - Chiefs lead series 5-4
11/26/2023	vs	*BUFFALO*	G								14-1-1 S/U vs AFC teams as 3.5-7 point favorite since 1997
12/3/2023	vs	SAN FRANCISCO	G								Game 0-5 O/U vs San Francisco since 2014
12/10/2023	@	Dallas	A								vs Dallas - Cowboys lead series 72-54
12/17/2023	@	Seattle	A								0-7 S/U vs Seattle since 2011 {1-6 ATS}
12/25/2023	vs	NEW YORK GIANTS	G								Game 3-11 O/U @ home vs NY Giants since 2010
12/31/2023	vs	ARIZONA	G								vs Arizona - Eagles lead series 60-57-5
1/7/2024	@	New York Giants	A								Game 9-1 O/U @ New York Giants since 2012
1/14/2024											NFC Wild Card
1/21/2024											NFC Divisional Playoff
1/28/2024											NFC Championship
2/11/2024											Super Bowl LVIII @ Las Vegas, NV

Pointspread Analysis vs NFC teams		Pointspread Analysis vs NFC teams
0-8 S/U vs NFC East as 10.5 point or more Dog since 1987		0-6 O/U vs NFC North as 9 point or more Favorite since 1990
2-8 S/U on road vs NFC East as 7.5-10 point Dog since 1984		3-0 S/U & ATS @ home vs Minnesota as 3 point or less Dog since 1989
5-18 S/U @ home vs NFC East as 3.5-7 point Dog since 1978		4-0 S/U & ATS vs Minnesota as 3 point or less favorite since 2004
2-8 S/U @ home vs NFC East as 3 point or less Dog since 1998		5-1 O/U vs Minnesota as 3.5-7 point favorite since 1985
14-5 S/U on road vs NFC East as 3.5-7 point favorite since 2001		5-1 O/U on road vs NFC South as 3 point or less favorite since 2006
31-6 S/U vs NFC East as 7.5 point or more favorite since 1980		0-4 O/U vs NFC South as 7.5-10 point favorite since 2003
6-0 S/U on road vs NFC East as 7.5-10 point favorite since 1990		6-0 S/U vs NFC South as 7.5 point or more favorite since 1981
0-7 S/U vs Dallas as 10.5 point or more Dog since 1987		0-4 O/U vs Tampa Bay as 3.5-7 point Dog since 1999
3-0 ATS vs Washington as 10.5 point or more Dog since 1983		3-0 O/U vs Tampa Bay as 3.5-7 point favorite since 2002
9-2 ATS vs Dallas as 7.5-10 point Dog since 1978		2-9 S/U @ home vs NFC West as 3.5-7 point Dog since 1991
1-7 O/U vs Dallas as 7.5-10 point Dog since 1978		0-6 S/U @ home vs NFC West as 3.5-7 point Dog since 1991 {1-5 ATS}
0-3 S/U vs New York Giants as 7.5-10 point Dog since 1993		2-11 O/U vs NFC West as 3 point or less Dog since 1997
0-3 S/U vs Washington as 7.5-10 point Dog since 1984		1-7 S/U vs Arizona as 3.5-7 point Dog since 1983
0-6 S/U @ Dallas as 3.5-7 point Dog since 2008		0-4 S/U vs Arizona as 3 point or less Dog since 1993
13-2 O/U vs Dallas as 3.5-7 point Dog since 1983		6-0 S/U vs Arizona as 7.5-10 point favorite since 1980
1-9 S/U @ home vs Dallas as 3.5-7 point Dog since 1978		4-0 S/U @ home vs Arizona as 3.5-7 point favorite since 1993
5-1 S/U & ATS @ New York Giants as 3.5-7 point Dog since 2006		4-1 ATS vs Los Angeles Rams as 3.5-7 point Dog since 1978
1-4 S/U @ home vs NY Giants as 3.5-7 point Dog since 1985		4-0 S/U & ATS vs LA Rams as 3.5-10 point favorite since 1995
1-4 O/U @ home vs NY Giants as 3.5-7 point Dog since 1985		0-3 S/U & ATS @ home vs San Francisco as 3.5-7 point Dog since 1984
2-9 S/U @ Washington as 3.5-7 point Dog since 1978		0-3 O/U @ home vs San Francisco as 3.5-7 point Dog since 1984
3-1 O/U @ home vs Washington as 3.5-7 point Dog since 1987		3-0 O/U vs San Francisco as 3.5-7 point favorite since 2003
1-3 S/U @ home vs Dallas as 3 point or less Dog since 2007		0-5 S/U vs Seattle as 3.5-7 point Dog since 1986
6-1 S/U @ New York Giants as 3 point or less Dog since 1995		3-0 O/U vs Seattle as 3 point or less favorite since 2002
10-2 ATS @ New York Giants as 3 point or less Dog since 1983		0-3 O/U vs Seattle as 3.5-7 point favorite since 1989
4-0 O/U @ New York Giants as 3 point or less Dog since 1995		Game 0-6 O/U vs Seattle since 2014
3-0 O/U @ home vs NY Giants as 3 point or less Dog since 1990		6-1 ATS @ Los Angeles Rams since 1990
1-4 O/U @ Washington as 3 point or less Dog since 1992		**Grass/Turf**
5-0 S/U & ATS vs NY Giants as 3 point or less favorite since 2009		0-11 S/U on Turf as 10.5 point or more Dog since 1986
1-7 O/U @ Washington as 3 point or less favorite since 1995		1-5 S/U on road on grass as 10.5 point or more Dog since 1996
7-0 S/U @ Dallas as 3.5-7 point favorite since 1989		2-9 S/U on road on grass as 7.5-10 point Dog since 1984
14-2 S/U vs Dallas as 3.5-7 point favorite since 1980		13-5-1 O/U on road on grass as 3 point or less Dog since 2002
12-3 S/U vs New York Giants as 3.5-7 point favorite since 2001		8-1 O/U on road on Turf as 3 point or less favorite since 2009
3-9 O/U vs New York Giants as 3.5-7 point favorite since 2004		18-6 S/U on road on Turf as 3.5-7 point favorite since 2002
4-1 S/U @ home vs Washington as 3.5-7 point favorite since 2013		5-11 ATS on road on Turf as 3.5-7 point on favorite since 2010
3-1 O/U vs Dallas as 7.5-10 point favorite since 2001		7-0 S/U on road on grass as 7.5-10 point favorite since 2003
9-0 S/U vs Washington as 7.5-10 point favorite since 2002		6-0-1 S/U on road on Turf as 7.5-10 point favorite since 1980
3-0 S/U vs Dallas as 10.5 point or more favorite since 1989	Chiefs	18-6 S/U after BYE week since 1999
0-4 S/U vs NFC North as 8.5 point or more Dog since 1986		**THU-SAT-SNF-MNF**
6-1 ATS vs NFC North as 3.5-7 point Dog since 1993	VIKINGS	7-1 S/U on Thursday since 2016 (6-2 ATS)
0-5-1 O/U @ home vs NFC North as 3 point or less favorite s/1991	DOLPHINS	8-2 S/U as home favorite on SNF since 2010 {8-2 ATS}
2-9 ATS vs NFC North as 3.5-7 point favorite since 2007	Bucs, Chiefs	7-3 ATS on road on MNF since 2006

Last 4 seasons + Pointspread Analysis

2022

	Opponent	Day	Site	PF	PA	W/L	Spread	ATS	Total	O/U
@	Cincinnati {OT}		A	23	20	W	7.0	W	45.0	U
vs	NEW ENGLAND		G	14	17	L	3.0	T	40.0	U
@	Cleveland	T	G	17	29	L	4.0	L	38.0	O
vs	N.Y. JETS		G	20	24	L	-3.0	L	41.0	O
@	Buffalo		A	3	38	L	14.0	L	44.5	U
vs	TAMPA BAY		G	20	18	W	9.5	W	46.5	U
@	Miami	Su	G	13	16	L	7.5	W	44.0	U
@	Philadelphia		G	13	35	L	11.5	L	43.0	O
	BYE									
vs	NEW ORLEANS		G	20	10	W	-1.5	W	39.0	U
vs	CINCINNATI		G	30	37	L	3.5	L	39.5	O
@	Indianapolis	M	A	24	17	W	2.0	W	39.5	O
@	Atlanta		A	19	16	W	-1.0	W	43.0	U
vs	BALTIMORE		G	14	16	L	-1.5	L	36.5	U
@	Carolina		G	24	16	W	2.5	W	36.5	O
vs	LAS VEGAS	Sa	G	13	10	W	-2.5	W	37.5	U
@	Baltimore	Su	A	16	13	W	1.5	W	35.5	U
vs	CLEVELAND		G	28	14	W	-2.5	W	40.0	O

2021

	Opponent	Day	Site	PF	PA	W/L	Spread	ATS	Total	O/U
@	Buffalo		A	23	16	W	6.5	W	47.0	U
vs	LAS VEGAS		G	17	26	L	-5.5	L	46.5	U
vs	CINCINNATI		G	10	24	L	-2.5	L	42.0	U
@	Green Bay		G	17	27	L	6.0	L	45.0	U
vs	DENVER		G	27	19	W	1.0	W	40.0	O
vs	SEATTLE {OT}	Su	G	23	20	W	-5.5	L	43.0	T
	BYE									
@	Cleveland		G	15	10	W	5.5	W	43.0	U
vs	CHICAGO	M	G	29	27	W	-7.0	W	39.5	O
vs	DETROIT {OT}		G	16	16	T	-5.5	L	40.5	U
@	Los Angeles Chargers	Su	G	37	41	L	6.0	W	47.5	O
@	Cincinnati		A	10	41	L	3.5	L	44.0	O
vs	BALTIMORE		G	20	19	W	4.0	W	43.5	U
@	Minnesota	T	A	28	36	L	3.5	L	45.0	O
vs	TENNESSEE		G	19	13	W	-1.0	W	44.0	U
@	Kansas City		G	10	36	L	10.0	L	44.0	O
vs	CLEVELAND	M	G	26	14	W	2.0	W	43.0	U
@	Baltimore {OT}		A	16	13	W	3.0	W	40.0	U
@	**Kansas City**	Su	G	21	42	L	12.0	L	46.5	O

2020

	Opponent	Day	Site	PF	PA	W/L	Spread	ATS	Total	O/U
@	New York Giants	M	A	26	16	W	-6.0	W	43.5	U
vs	DENVER		G	26	21	W	-6.5	L	40.5	O
vs	Houston		G	28	21	W	-3.5	W	46.5	O
	BYE									
vs	PHILADELPHIA		G	38	29	W	-7.5	W	44.0	O
vs	CLEVELAND		G	38	7	W	-3.0	W	50.0	U
@	Tennessee		G	27	24	W	1.0	W	51.0	T
@	Baltimore		A	28	24	W	3.5	W	46.5	U
@	Dallas		A	24	19	W	-14.0	L	43.5	U
vs	CINCINNATI		G	36	10	W	-6.5	W	45.5	O
@	Jacksonville		G	27	3	W	-10.5	W	47.0	U
vs	BALTIMORE	W	G	19	14	W	-10.5	L	41.5	U
@	Washington	M	G	17	23	L	-5.5	L	43.5	U
vs	Buffalo	Su	A	15	26	L	1.5	L	49.0	U
@	Cincinnati	M	A	17	27	L	-14.0	L	44.5	U
vs	Indianapolis		G	28	24	W	PK	W	42.5	O
@	Cleveland		G	22	24	L	10.5	L	44.5	O
vs	**CLEVELAND**		G	37	48	L	-5.0	L	47.0	O

2019

	Opponent	Day	Site	PF	PA	W/L	Spread	ATS	Total	O/U
@	New England	Su	A	3	33	L	5.5	L	49.0	U
vs	SEATTLE		G	26	28	L	-4.0	L	47.0	O
@	San Francisco		G	20	24	L	6.5	W	44.5	U
vs	CINCINNATI	M	G	27	3	W	-3.5	W	45.0	U
vs	BALTIMORE {OT}		G	23	26	L	3.5	W	44.0	O
@	L.A. Chargers	Su	G	24	17	W	6.0	W	42.5	U
	BYE									
vs	MIAMI	M	G	27	14	W	-14.0	L	43.0	U
vs	Indianapolis		G	26	24	W	-1.0	W	39.5	O
vs	L.A. RAMS		G	17	12	W	4.0	W	43.5	U
@	Cleveland	T	G	7	21	L	3.0	L	41.5	U
@	Cincinnati		A	16	10	W	-6.0	T	37.5	U
vs	CLEVELAND		G	20	13	W	1.0	W	40.0	U
@	Arizona		G	23	17	W	-2.5	W	43.5	U
vs	BUFFALO	Su	G	10	17	L	-1.0	L	37.0	U
vs	New York Jets		A	10	16	L	-3.0	L	36.5	U
@	Baltimore		A	10	28	L	-2.0	L	34.5	O

Pointspread Analysis vs NFC teams

14-0 S/U vs NFC teams as 7.5-10 point favorite since 1978
15-0 S/U vs NFC teams as 10.5 point or more favorite since 1978
5-2 ATS vs NFC teams as 3.5-7 point Dog since 2012
3-9 O/U vs NFC teams as 3.5-7 point Dog since 2001
5-0 O/U vs NFC North as 3 point or less Dog since 1995
1-6 ATS vs NFC North as 3 point or less favorite since 1983
1-5-1 O/U vs NFC North as 3.5-7 point favorite since 2005
10-0 S/U vs NFC North as 7.5 point or more favorite since 1980
3-0 O/U vs Green Bay as 3 point or less Dog since 1983
5-1 S/U @ home vs NFC West as 3.5-7 point favorite since 1981
8-0 S/U vs NFC West as 7.5 point or more favorite since 1978
7-0 ATS vs NFC West as 7.5 point or more favorite since 1980
6-1 S/U vs Arizona as 3.5-7 point favorite since 1979
4-1 O/U vs Arizona as 3.5-7 point favorite since 2003
3-0 S/U vs Seattle as 10.5 point or more favorite since 1978
2-8 O/U on road vs NFC West as Dog since 1984
4-0 S/U & ATS vs Los Angeles Rams since 2007
vs Seattle - Series tied 10-10
vs Seattle -HOME team 10-2 S/U since 1992 {8-3-1 ATS}

THU-SAT-SNF-MNF

8-1 S/U @ home on Thursday since 2006
10-2 S/U on Thursday as favorite since 2006
0-11 S/U on Thursday as a Dog since 1980 {1-8-2 ATS}
vs Tennessee - HOME team 4-0 S/U on Thursday since 1980
11-1 S/U on Saturday as favorite since 1993

Pointspread Analysis Dog

0-7 S/U as 10.5 point or more Dog since 1996

Favorite

8-3 S/U on road as 3 point or less favorite since 2014
20-3-1 S/U @ home as 3.5-7 point favorite since 2015
23-6-1 O/U @ home as 3.5-7 point favorite since 2014
2-9 O/U as 7.5-10 point favorite since 2016
20-1 S/U @ home as 7.5-10 point favorite since 2002
3-8 O/U @ home as 7.5-10 point favorite since 2010
15-2 ATS @ home as 7.5-10 point favorite since 2005
56-8 S/U as 10.5 point or more favorite since 1978

Playoffs

1-4 S/U on road on Saturday in Playoffs since 1973
6-1 O/U on road in WILD Card since 1983
12-2 S/U @ home in Divisional Play-offs since 1972
5-0 O/U @ home in Divisional Play-offs since 2002
5-1-1 ATS on road in Divisional Playoffs since 1984
5-0 S/U vs Indianapolis in Playoffs since 1975
7-0 O/U in AFC Championship since 1998
21-4 S/U prior to playing @ Baltimore since 1995 — *Seahawks*
18-2 S/U prior to playing @ home vs Baltimore since 2000 — *BENGALS*
30-7 S/U in 2nd of back to back home games last 37 (9-1 after loss in 1st game) — *TENN, NE*
12-1 S/U after scoring less than 10 pts last 12 times

THU-SAT-SNF-MNF

7-1 O/U on road on Saturday since 1994
5-1 ATS on Saturday as Dog since 1994

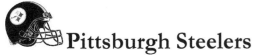 
DATE		OPPONENT	TURF	PIT	OPP	S/U	LINE	ATS	TOT	O/U	Trends & Angles
9/10/2023	vs	*SAN FRANCISCO*	G								Game 5-0 O/U @ home vs San Francisco s/1987
9/18/2023	vs	CLEVELAND	G								20-0 S/U @ home on MNF since 1992
9/24/2023	@	Las Vegas Raiders	G								Game 1-6-1 O/U @ Las Vegas Raiders since 1984
10/1/2023	@	Houston	G								Game 0-3 O/U @ Houston since 2005
10/8/2023	vs	BALTIMORE RAVENS	G								vs Baltimore - Ravens leads series 77-74
10/15/2023		BYE									
10/22/2023	@	*Los Angeles Rams*	A								2-10 S/U @ Los Angeles Rams since 1941
10/29/2023	vs	JACKSONVILLE	G								ROAD team 5-0 S/U & ATS since 2014
11/2/2023	vs	TENNESSEE	G								5-1 S/U @ home vs Tennessee since 2005
11/12/2023	vs	*GREEN BAY*	G								vs Green Bay - Packers leads series 19-17
11/19/2023	@	Cleveland	G								vs Cleveland - Steelers leads series 39-10-1
11/26/2023	@	Cincinnati	A								19-4 S/U @ Cincinnati since 2002
12/3/2023	vs	*ARIZONA*	G								vs Arizona - Pittsburgh leads series 35-23-3
12/7/2023	vs	NEW ENGLAND	G								Game 0-5 O/U @ home vs Patriots since 2011
12/16/2023	@	Indianapolis	A								8-0 S/U vs Indianapolis since 2011 {7-1 ATS}
12/23/2023	vs	CINCINNATI	G								16-4 S/U @ home on Saturday since 1958
12/31/2023	@	*Seattle*	A								0-5 S/U & ATS @ Seattle since 1986
1/7/2024	@	Batlimore Ravens	A								Game 2-7 O/U @ Baltimore since 2014
1/14/2024											AFC Wild Card
1/21/2024											AFC Divisional Playoff
1/28/2024											AFC Championship
2/11/2024											Super Bowl LVIII @ Las Vegas, NV

Pointspread Analysis

vs AFC teams		vs AFC teams
2-10 S/U vs AFC East as 3.5-7 point Dog since 1987		1-4 ATS vs AFC South as 10.5 point or more favorite s/2002
2-8 O/U on road vs AFC East as 3 point or less Dog since 1986		3-0 ATS @ home vs AFC South as 3.5-7 point Dog since 1991
0-4 O/U vs AFC East as 3.5-7 point favorite since 1984		3-0 O/U @ home vs AFC South as 3.5-7 point Dog since 1991
0-4 O/U vs AFC East as 3.5-7 point favorite since 1984		13-4 O/U @ home vs AFC South as 3.5-7 point favorite s/1993
0-4 O/U vs AFC East as 7.5-10 point favorite since 2007		5-0 S/U & ATS vs Indianapolis as 7.5-10 point favorite s/1985
15-0 S/U vs AFC East as 10.5 point or more favorite since 1978		7-0 S/U vs Indianapolis as 10.5 point or more favorite s/1979
3-0 O/U vs New England as 3 point or less favorite since 1989		0-4 ATS vs Indianapolis as 10.5 point or more favorite s/1996
3-0 S/U vs New England as 10.5 point or more favorite since 1990		0-4 S/U vs Jacksonville as 3 point or less Dog since 1998
0-3 O/U vs New England as 10.5 point or more favorite since 1990		6-1 ATS vs Tennessee as 3.5-7 point Dog since 1991
1-6 S/U vs AFC North as 7.5-10 point Dog since 1986		3-0 O/U vs Tennessee as 3 point or less Dog s/1989
24-6 S/U vs AFC North as 3.5-7 point favorite since 2007		7-2 O/U @ home vs Tennessee as 3.5-7 point favorite s/1992
4-10 ATS vs AFC North as 3.5-7 point favorite since 2012		vs Tennessee - Steelers leads series 48-32
1-6 O/U vs AFC North as 7.5-10 point favorite since 2009		Game 13-5 O/U @ home vs Tennessee since 1994
12-1 S/U vs AFC North as 7.5-10 point favorite since 2002		4-14 O/U vs AFC West as 3.5-7 point Dog since 1986
10-0 S/U @ home vs AFC North as 7.5-10 point favorite since 2000		12-2 O/U vs AFC West as 3.5-7 point favorite since 2003
11-1 S/U vs AFC North as 10.5 point or more favorite since 2000		1-7 S/U vs AFC West as 7.5-10 point favorite since 1981
0-3 S/U vs Cincinnati as 7.5-10 point Dog since 1986		1-9 ATS vs AFC West as 7.5-10 point favorite since 1980
3-0 O/U vs Cincinnati as 7.5-10 point Dog since 1986		6-1 S/U vs AFC West as 10.5 point or more favorite since 1978
0-5 S/U @ home vs Baltimore as 3 point or less Dog since 1986		1-6 ATS vs AFC West as 10.5 point or more favorite since 1978
0-3 O/U vs Baltimore as 3 point or less Dog since 2000		0-7 S/U & ATS on road vs AFC West as 3.5-7 point favorite since 1979
6-0 S/U & ATS vs Cincinnati as 3 point or less Dog since 1991		1-6 ATS vs Las Vegas as 3.5-7 point favorite since 1981
6-1 O/U @ Baltimore as 3 point or less favorite since 1997		0-3 O/U vs Las Vegas Raiders as 7.5-10 point favorite s/2006
4-0 S/U @ Cincinnati as 3 point or less favorite since 2006		vs Las Vegas - Raiders leads series 18-13
0-7 O/U vs Cincinnati as 3 point or less favorite since 2012		
1-4 ATS @ Baltimore as 3.5-7 point favorite since 1982		**Grass/Turf**
21-2 S/U @ home vs Baltimore as 3.5-7 point favorite since 1980		7-1 ATS on road on Turf as 7.5-10 point Dog since 1992
7-0 O/U @ home vs Baltimore as 3.5-7 point favorite since 2006		4-14 S/U on road on grass as 7.5 point or more Dog since 1985
14-2 S/U @ Cincinnati as 3.5-7 point favorite since 1992 {12-3-1 ATS}		2-9 O/U on road on grass as 3.5-7 point Dog since 2010
2-5 O/U @ home vs Cincinnati as 3.5-7 point favorite since 2007		8-21-2 O/U on road on grass as 3 point or less Dog since 1996
16-2-1 S/U vs Cleveland as 3.5-7 point favorite since 1999		8-1 S/U on road on Turf as 3 point or less favorite since 2013
3-0 S/U @ home vs Baltimore as 7.5-10 point favorite since 1978		15-4 S/U on road on Turf as 3.5-7 point favorite since 1997
1-5 O/U @ home vs Cincinnati as 7.5-10 point favorite since 1995		4-13-1 O/U on road on Turf as 3.5-7 point favorite since 1997
3-0 O/U @ Cincinnati as 7.5-10 point favorite since 1993		2-7 ATS on road on grass as 3.5-7 point favorite since 2012
1-6 ATS vs Cincinnati as 10.5 point or more favorite since 1980		14-4 S/U on road on Turf as 3.5-7 point favorite since 1997
0-5 O/U vs AFC South as 7.5-10 point Dog since 1989		4-13-1 O/U on road on Turf as 3.5-7 point favorite since 1997
4-11 S/U vs AFC South as 3 point or less Dog since 1980		1-6 ATS on road on grass as 3.5-7 point favorite since 2012
0-7-1 ATS on road vs AFC South as 3 point or less favorite s/1990		5-2 S/U on road on Turf as 10.5 point or more favorite s/1978
8-2 S/U on road vs AFC South as 3.5-7 point favorite since 1982		0-6 ATS on road on Turf as 10.5 point or more favorite s/1978
1-5 O/U vs AFC South as 7.5-10 point favorite since 1995	49ERS	15-5 S/U in 1st home game of season since 2003
6-1 S/U & ATS vs AFC South as 7.5-10 point favorite since 1994	BENGALS	20-3 S/U in final home game of season since 2000
8-2 S/U vs AFC South as 10.5 point or more favorite since 1983		26-8 S/U @ home after a road loss last 34 times

Copyright © 2023 by Steve's Football Bible, LLC

San Francisco 49ers   NFC West
Last 4 seasons + Pointspread Analysis

	2022										
@	Chicago		G	10	19	L	-6.5	L	38.5	U	
vs	SEATTLE		G	27	7	W	-8.0	W	39.5	U	
@	Denver	Su	G	10	11	L	-1.5	L	44.5	U	
vs	L.A. RAMS	M	G	24	9	W	-2.0	W	42.0	U	
@	Carolina		G	37	15	W	-6.0	W	39.5	O	
@	Atlanta		A	14	28	L	-3.0	L	45.0	U	
vs	KANSAS CITY		G	23	44	L	PK	L	48.0	O	
@	Los Angeles Rams		G	31	14	W	1.0	W	42.5	O	
	BYE										
vs	L.A. CHARGERS	Su	G	22	16	W	-8.0	L	45.5	U	
vs	Arizona {Mexico City}	M	G	38	10	W	-9.5	W	43.0	O	
vs	NEW ORLEANS		G	13	0	W	-8.5	W	43.5	U	
vs	MIAMI		G	33	17	W	-5.0	W	46.0	U	
vs	TAMPA BAY		G	35	7	W	-3.5	W	38.5	U	
@	Seattle	T	A	21	13	W	-3.0	W	42.5	U	
vs	WASHINGTON	Sa	G	37	20	W	-6.0	W	37.0	O	
@	Las Vegas {OT}		G	37	34	W	-10.0	L	41.5	O	
vs	ARIZONA		G	38	13	W	-14.5	W	40.0	O	
vs	**SEATTLE**	Sa	G	41	23	W	-9.0	W	42.0	O	
vs	**DALLAS**		G	19	12	W	-3.5	W	47.0	U	
@	**Philadelphia**		G	7	31	L	2.5	L	44.5	U	
	2021										
@	Detroit		A	41	33	W	-9.5	L	46.0	O	
@	Philadelphia		G	17	11	W	-3.0	W	49.0	U	
vs	GREEN BAY	Su	G	28	30	L	-3.0	L	50.5	O	
vs	SEATTLE		G	21	28	L	-2.5	L	52.0	U	
@	Arizona		G	10	17	L	6.0	L	48.5	U	
	BYE										
vs	INDIANAPOLIS	Su	G	18	30	L	-3.5	L	41.5	O	
@	Chicago		G	33	22	W	-4.5	W	40.0	O	
vs	ARIZONA		G	17	31	L	-5.5	L	44.5	O	
vs	L.A. RAMS	M	G	31	10	W	3.5	W	50.0	U	
@	Jacksonville		G	30	10	W	-6.5	W	45.5	U	
vs	MINNESOTA		G	34	26	W	-4.0	W	48.5	O	
@	Seattle		A	23	30	L	-2.5	L	44.5	O	
@	Cincinnati {OT}		A	26	23	W	-1.0	W	49.5	U	
vs	ATLANTA		G	31	13	W	-9.0	W	48.0	U	
@	Tennessee Titans	T	G	17	20	L	-3.5	L	45.0	U	
vs	HOUSTON		G	23	7	W	-13.5	W	44.0	U	
@	Los Angeles Rams {OT}		A	27	24	W	3.5	W	46.0	O	
@	**Dallas**		A	23	17	W	3.0	W	51.5	U	
@	**Green Bay**	Sa	G	13	10	W	6.0	W	47.0	U	
@	**Los Angeles Rams**		A	17	20	L	3.5	W	46.0	U	

	2020										
vs	Arizona		G	20	24	L	-6.5	L	49.0	U	
@	New York Jets		A	31	13	W	-7.0	W	41.5	O	
@	New York Giants		A	36	9	W	-3.0	W	43.5	O	
vs	PHILADELPHIA	Su	G	20	25	L	-7.5	L	45.5	U	
vs	MIAMI		G	17	43	L	-8.5	L	50.5	O	
vs	L.A. RAMS	Su	G	24	16	W	2.0	W	51.0	U	
@	New England		A	33	6	W	3.0	W	44.5	U	
@	Seattle		A	27	37	L	1.0	L	54.5	O	
vs	GREEN BAY	T	G	17	34	L	5.5	L	48.5	O	
@	New Orleans		A	13	27	L	10.0	L	49.0	U	
	BYE										
@	L.A. Rams		G	23	20	W	5.0	W	44.5	U	
vs	BUFFALO	M	G	24	34	L	-2.0	L	48.0	O	
vs	Washington		G	15	23	L	-3.0	L	43.5	U	
@	Dallas		A	33	41	L	-3.5	L	45.5	O	
@	Arizona	Sa	G	20	12	W	5.5	W	49.5	U	
vs	SEATTLE		G	23	26	L	7.5	L	45.5	O	
	2019										
@	Tampa Bay		G	31	17	W	1.0	W	51.0	U	
@	Cincinnati		A	41	17	W	1.0	W	46.5	O	
vs	PITTSBURGH		G	24	20	W	-6.5	W	44.5	U	
	BYE										
vs	CLEVELAND	M	G	31	3	W	-5.0	W	47.5	U	
@	L.A. Rams		G	20	7	W	3.0	W	50.0	U	
@	Washington		G	9	0	W	-10.0	W	38.5	U	
vs	CAROLINA		G	51	13	W	-4.5	W	40.5	O	
@	Arizona	T	G	28	25	W	-10.0	L	43.5	O	
vs	SEATTLE {OT}	M	G	24	27	L	-6.5	L	48.0	O	
vs	Arizona		G	30	26	W	-10.0	L	43.5	O	
vs	GREEN BAY	Su	G	37	8	W	-3.0	W	47.5	U	
@	Baltimore		A	17	20	L	6.0	W	45.0	U	
@	New Orleans		A	48	46	W	1.5	W	45.0	O	
vs	ATLANTA		G	22	29	L	-10.0	L	50.0	O	
vs	L.A. RAMS	Sa	G	34	31	W	-7.0	L	45.5	O	
@	Seattle	Su	A	26	21	W	-3.5	W	47.0	T
vs	**MINNESOTA**	Sa	G	27	10	W	-7.0	W	44.5	U	
vs	**GREEN BAY**		G	37	20	W	-8.0	W	46.5	O	
vs	*Kansas City*		G	20	31	L	1.5	L	52.5	U	

Pointspread Analysis Dog		Pointspread Analysis Playoffs
3-43 S/U as 10.5 point or more Dog since 1978		23-6 S/U @ home in Playoffs since 1981
1-15 S/U on road as 7.5-10 point Dog since 2007		0-4 O/U on road in WILD Card since 1985
7-40 S/U as 7.5-10 point Dog since 1978		5-0 S/U @ home in NFC WILD Card since 1983
13-4 S/U as 3 point or less Dog since 2017 {12-5 ATS}		6-1 S/U in WILD Card since 1996
Favorite		10-2 ATS @ home in Divisional Playoffs since 1988
13-3 S/U & ATS on road as 3.5-7 point favorite since 2013		11-1 S/U @ home in Divisional Playoffs since 1988
26-5 S/U @ home as 7.5-10 point favorite since 1996		2-5 S/U on road in Divisional Playoffs since 1983
35-1-1 S/U as 10.5 or more favorite since 1995		0-4 O/U on road in Divisional Playoffs since 1999
7-0 S/U on road as 10.5 point or more favorite since 1995		12-2 S/U @ home on Saturday in Playoffs since 1983
8-2 O/U as 10.5 point or more favorite since 2012		5-2 S/U in Super Bowl
THU-SAT-SNF-MNF		3-1 O/U in Super Bowl since 1990
1-5 S/U @ home on Thursday since 2014	GIANTS	0-7 O/U on road in Playoffs since 2014
10-3-1 S/U on road on Thursday since 1947	Seahawks	3-0 S/U vs Chicago in Playoffs since 1984
0-5 O/U vs Seattle on Thursday since 2006		4-0 S/U & ATS @ home vs Minnesota in Playoffs since 1989
0-5 ATS on SNF as favorite since 2020		1-5 ATS vs New York Giants in Playoffs since 1985
11-4 S/U on Monday Night Football since 2011	Minn, BALT	4-0 S/U vs Green Bay in Playoffs since 2013
16-4 ATS on MNF since 2008	Minn, BALT	29-8-2 ATS on Monday Night since 1996
6-0 ATS on road on MNF since 2008	Minnesota	2-8 S/U on road on MNF as Dog since 1986
7-0 ATS on MNF as Dog since 2008	Rams	3-14 S/U in 2nd road game of season since 2003
10-0 S/U & ATS on road on MNF as favorite since 1996	RAMS	12-1 S/U in final home game of season since 2007

    Copyright © 2023 by Steve's Football Bible, LLC

San Francisco 49ers

Levi's Stadium

2023 Schedule + Trends & Angles

Coach: Kyle Shanahan

NFC West

DATE		OPPONENT	TURF	SF	OPP	S/U	LINE	ATS	TOT	O/U	Trends & Angles
9/10/2023	@	Pittsburgh	G								vs Pittsburgh - 49ers lead series 12-10
9/17/2023	@	Los Angeles Rams	G								8-1 S/U vs Los Angeles Rams since 2019 {8-1 ATS}
9/21/2023	vs	NEW YORK GIANTS	G								vs New York Giants - Series tied 20-20
10/1/2023	vs	ARIZONA CARDINALS	G								vs Arizona - 49ers leads series 33-29
10/8/2023	vs	DALLAS	G								vs Dallas - 49ers lead series 19-18-1
10/15/2023	@	Cleveland	G								vs Cleveland - Browns lead series 3-2
10/23/2023	@	Minnesota	A								vs Vikings - HOME team 13-1 S/U since 1993
10/29/2023	vs	CINCINNATI	G								vs Cincinnati - 49ers leads series 13-4
11/5/2023		BYE									
11/12/2023	@	Jacksonville	G								vs Jacksonville - 49ers leads series 4-2
11/19/2023	vs	TAMPA BAY	G								13-3 S/U @ home vs Tampa Bay since 1977
11/23/2023	@	Seattle	A								2-10 S/U @ Seattle since 2012
12/3/2023	@	Philadelphia	G								vs Philadelphia - 49ers leads series 20-15-1
12/10/2023	vs	SEATTLE	G								3-7 S/U @ home vs Seattle since 2014
12/17/2023	@	Arizona Cardinals	G								
12/25/2023	vs	BALTIMORE	G								vs Ravens - HOME team 8-1 S/U since 1987
12/31/2023	@	Washington	G								vs Washington - 49eres lead series 21-12-1
1/7/2024	vs	LOS ANGELES RAMS	G								11-3-1 S/U @ home vs Los Angeles Rams s/2008
1/14/2024											NFC Wild Card
1/21/2024											NFC Divisional Playoff
1/28/2024											NFC Championship
2/11/2024											Super Bowl LVIII @ Las Vegas, NV

Pointspread Analysis

vs NFC teams (left)

0-10 S/U vs NFC teams as 10.5 point or more Dog since 2008
2-18 S/U vs NFC teams as 7.5-10 point Dog since 2007
0-7 O/U @ home vs NFC teams as 7.5-10 point Dog since 1999
2-9 S/U @ home vs NFC teams as 3.5-7 point Dog since 2010
10-2 S/U & ATS on road vs NFC teams as 3.5-7 point favorite since 2013
26-2 S/U @ home vs NFC teams as 7.5-10 point favorite since 1996
0-4 S/U vs Washington as 10.5 point or more Dog since 1978
8-0 S/U vs Washington as 3.5-7 point favorite since 1985
7-1 ATS vs Washington as 3.5-7 point favorite since 1985
5-0 S/U vs Washington as 7.5-10 point favorite since 1991
0-5 O/U vs Washington as 7.5-10 point favorite since 1991
1-4 S/U vs Dallas as 3.5-7 point Dog since 1993
4-0 O/U vs Dallas as 3.5-7 point Dog since 1994
1-4 ATS vs New York Giants as 3 point or less favorite since 1985
3-0 S/U vs New York Giants as 10.5 point or more favorite s/1984
0-3 O/U vs New York Giants as 10.5 point or more favorite s/1984
0-3 S/U & ATS vs Philadelphia as 10.5 point or more Dog s/1985
3-0 S/U & ATS @ Philadelphia as 3.5-7 point favorite since 1984
0-3 O/U @ Philadelphia as 3.5-7 point favorite since 1984
0-3 S/U @ Minnesota as 3.5-7 point Dog since 1999
1-6 O/U vs Minnesota as 3.5-7 point favorite since 1989
3-0 S/U & ATS vs Minnesota as 7.5-10 point favorite since 1990
4-0 O/U Minnesota as 7.5-10 point favorite since 1986
vs Minnesota - 49ers leads series 25-22-1
3-0 S/U & ATS @ home vs Tampa Bay as 3.5-7 point Dog s/1979
6-0 S/U vs Tampa Bay as 10.5 point or more favorite since 1983
6-0 S/U vs Tampa Bay as 10.5 point or more favorite since 1983
3-12 ATS @ Seattle since 2009
Game 7-3-1 O/U vs Seattle since 2018
0-3 S/U vs Arizona as 7.5-10 point Dog since 2006
3-0 ATS vs Arizona as 7.5-10 point Dog since 2006
0-3 S/U & ATS @ home vs Arizona as 3 point or less Dog s/2005
0-3 O/U @ home vs Arizona as 3 point or less Dog since 2005
0-4 O/U @ Arizona as 3 point or less favorite since 1999
5-0 S/U & ATS vs Arizona as 7.5-10 point favorite since 2002
7-0 S/U @ home vs Arizona as 10.5 point or more favorite s/1986
0-4 S/U vs Los Angeles Rams as 10.5 point or more Dog s/1978
0-4 S/U @ home vs Los Angeles Rams as 7.5-10 point Dog s/1978
4-0 ATS @ home vs L.A. Rams as 3 point or less Dog since 2016
1-5 O/U @ home vs L.A. Rams as 3 point or less Dog since 2006
7-1 S/U @ Los Angeles Rams as 3 point or less favorite since 1982

vs NFC teams (right)

7-1 S/U @ L.A. Rams as 3.5-7 point favorite since 1987
6-2 ATS @ L.A. Rams as 3.5-7 point favorite since 1987
6-0 S/U @ home vs L.A. Rams as 3.5-7 point favorite since 1987
5-0 S/U & ATS vs L.A. Rams as 7.5-10 point favorite since 1987
0-4 O/U vs L.A. Rams as 7.5-10 point favorite since 1991
4-0 S/U @ Los Angeles Rams as 10.5 point or more favorite since 1994
8-1-1 S/U @ home vs L.A. Rams as 10.5 point or more favorite s/1992
0-6 S/U vs Seattle as 10.5 point or more Dog since 2005
5-1 O/U vs Seattle as 10.5 point or more Dog since 2005
0-3 S/U & ATS @ Seattle as 7.5-10 point Dog since 2007
1-4 O/U @ Seattle as 7.5-10 point Dog since 2007
0-5 S/U & ATS vs Seattle as 3 point or less Dog since 1997
1-7 ATS vs Seattle as 3 point or less favorite since 2009
1-8-1 O/U vs Seattle as 3 point or less favorite since 2003
4-0-1 O/U vs Seattle as 3.5-7 point favorite since 1991
5-0 S/U @ home vs Seattle as 7.5-10 point favorite since 1985

vs AFC teams

0-10 S/U vs AFC teams as 10.5 or more Dog since 1979
6-1 O/U vs AFC teams as 3.5-7 point Dog since 2012
19-0 S/U vs AFC teams as 10.5 or more favorite since 1984
0-3 ATS vs Cincinnati as 3.5-7 point favorite since 1989
0-3 O/U vs Cincinnati as 3.5-7 point favorite since 1989

Grass/Turf

0-12 S/U on Turf as 10.5 point or more Dog since 2000
1-15 S/U on road on grass as 10.5 point or more Dog since 1978
2-10 ATS on Turf as 7.5-10 point or more Dog since 2005
4-22 S/U on Turf as 7.5-10 point Dog since 1978
1-12 S/U on road on grass as 7.5-10 point Dog since 1979
2-8 ATS on Turf as 7.5-10 point or more Dog since 2005
8-0 O/U on road on grass as 7.5-10 point Dog since 2005
6-16 O/U on Turf as 3.5-7 point Dog since 2000
9-22 S/U on road on grass as 3.5-7 point Dog since 1978
12-3 S/U as 3 point or less Dog since 2017 {11-4 ATS}
0-7 O/U on road on grass as 3 point or less favorite since 2010
20-7 S/U on Turf as 3 point or less favorite since 1978
12-4 S/U on road on grass as 3.5-7 point favorite since 2001
8-2 ATS on road on grass as 3.5-7 point favorite since 2012
26-6 S/U on Turf as 3.5-7 point favorite since 1987
5-0 S/U on Turf as 10.5 point or more favorite since 1996
6-0 S/U & ATS on road on grass as 10.5 point or more favorite s/1993

Last 4 seasons + Pointspread Analysis

2022

	Team	Day	Net			R	Spread	ATS	Total	O/U
vs	DENVER	M	A	17	16	W	6.0	W	43.5	U
@	San Francisco		G	7	27	L	8.0	L	39.5	U
vs	ATLANTA		A	23	27	L	-1.0	L	43.5	O
@	Detroit		A	48	45	W	3.0	W	48.5	O
@	New Orleans		A	32	39	L	5.5	L	45.0	O
vs	ARIZONA		A	19	9	W	2.5	W	50.5	U
@	Los Angeles Chargers		G	37	23	W	4.5	W	51.0	O
vs	N.Y. GIANTS		A	27	13	W	-3.0	W	44.5	U
@	Arizona		G	31	21	W	2.0	W	49.0	O
vs	Tampa Bay {Munich}		G	16	21	L	2.5	L	45.0	U
	BYE									
vs	LAS VEGAS {OT}		A	34	40	L	-4.0	L	48.0	O
@	Los Angeles Rams		G	27	23	W	-6.5	L	41.0	O
vs	CAROLINA		A	24	30	L	-4.0	L	43.5	O
vs	SAN FRANCISCO	T	A	13	21	L	3.0	L	42.5	U
@	Kansas City	Sa	G	10	24	L	10.5	L	51.0	U
vs	N.Y. JETS		A	23	6	W	1.0	W	43.0	U
vs	L.A. RAMS {OT}		A	19	16	W	-4.0	L	43.0	U
@	**San Francisco**	Sa	G	**23**	**41**	**L**	9.0	**L**	42.0	**O**

2021

	Team	Day	Net			R	Spread	ATS	Total	O/U
@	Indianapolis		A	28	16	W	-3.0	W	49.0	U
vs	TENNESSEE {OT}		A	30	33	L	-6.0	L	53.5	O
@	Minnesota		A	17	30	L	-2.0	L	53.0	U
@	San Francisco		G	28	21	W	2.5	W	52.0	U
vs	L.A. RAMS	T	A	17	26	L	2.5	L	53.5	U
@	Pittsburgh {OT}	Su	G	20	23	L	5.5	W	43.0	T
vs	NEW ORLEANS	M	A	10	13	L	6.0	W	42.0	U
vs	JACKSONVILLE		A	31	7	W	-4.0	W	44.5	U
	BYE									
@	Green Bay		G	0	17	L	3.0	L	49.0	U
vs	ARIZONA		A	13	23	L	-5.0	L	45.0	U
@	Washington	M	G	15	17	L	-1.5	L	46.5	U
vs	SAN FRANCISCO		A	30	23	W	2.5	W	44.5	O
@	Houston		G	33	13	W	-9.5	W	41.0	O
@	Los Angeles Rams	Tu	G	10	20	L	7.0	L	47.5	U
vs	CHICAGO		A	24	25	L	-7.0	L	41.0	O
vs	DETROIT		A	51	29	W	-9.0	W	41.0	O
@	Arizona		G	38	30	W	5.5	W	49.0	O

2020

	Team	Day	Net			R	Spread	ATS	Total	O/U
@	Atlanta		A	38	25	W	1.0	W	49.5	O
vs	New England	Su	A	35	30	W	-4.5	W	45.0	O
vs	DALLAS		A	38	31	W	-5.0	W	57.5	O
@	Miami		G	31	23	W	-4.5	W	55.0	U
vs	MINNESOTA	Su	A	27	26	W	-6.5	L	53.5	U
	BYE									
@	Arizona {OT}	Su	G	34	37	L	-3.5	L	55.5	O
vs	SAN FRANCISCO		A	37	27	W	-1.0	W	54.5	O
@	Buffalo		A	34	44	L	-3.0	L	55.0	O
@	L.A. Rams		G	16	23	L	2.5	L	55.0	U
vs	Arizona	T	A	28	21	W	-3.0	W	56.5	U
@	Philadelphia	M	G	23	17	W	-6.5	L	50.5	U
vs	N.Y. GIANTS		A	12	17	L	-10.0	L	48.0	U
vs	N.Y. JETS		A	40	3	W	-16.5	W	49.5	U
@	Washington		G	20	15	W	-6.0	L	44.0	U
vs	L.A. RAMS		A	20	9	W	-1.5	W	48.0	U
@	San Francisco		G	26	23	W	-7.5	L	45.5	O
vs	**L.A. RAMS**	Sa	A	**20**	**30**	**L**	-3.0	**L**	42.0	**O**

2019

	Team	Day	Net			R	Spread	ATS	Total	O/U
vs	CINCINNATI		A	21	20	W	-9.0	L	44.5	U
@	Pittsburgh		G	28	26	W	4.0	W	47.0	O
vs	NEW ORLEANS		A	27	33	L	-5.0	L	44.0	O
@	Arizona		G	27	10	W	-5.5	W	48.0	U
vs	L.A. RAMS	T	A	30	29	W	-1.5	L	49.0	U
@	Cleveland		G	32	28	W	1.0	W	45.5	O
vs	BALTIMORE		A	16	30	L	-3.0	L	49.0	U
@	Atlanta		A	27	20	W	-7.5	L	48.5	U
vs	TAMPA BAY {OT}		A	40	34	W	-4.0	W	51.0	O
vs	San Francisco {OT}	M	A	27	24	W	6.5	W	48.0	O
	BYE									
@	Philadelphia		G	17	9	W	-1.5	W	46.0	U
vs	MINNESOTA	M	A	37	30	W	-3.0	W	48.5	O
@	L.A. Rams	Su	G	12	28	L	1.0	L	48.5	U
@	Carolina		G	30	24	W	-6.0	T	48.5	O
vs	ARIZONA		A	13	27	L	-8.0	L	50.5	U
vs	SAN FRANCISCO	Su	A	21	26	L	3.5	L	47.0	T
@	**Philadelphia**		G	17	9	**W**	-1.0	**W**	44.5	**U**
@	**Green Bay**		G	23	28	**L**	4.5	**L**	45.5	**O**

Pointspread Analysis — vs AFC teams

vs AFC teams		vs AFC teams
4-11 S/U vs AFC teams as 3 point or less Dog since 2003		9-0 S/U vs AFC South as 5 point or more favorite since 1980
16-2 O/U vs AFC teams as 3 point or less Dog since 2001		0-3 S/U vs Tennessee as 3.5-7 point Dog since 1981
8-3 O/U vs AFC teams as 3 point or less favorite since 2012		vs Tennessee - Seahawks leads series 10-8
17-3 S/U vs AFC teams 3.5-7 point favorite since 2000		**Grass/Turf**
12-0 S/U vs AFC teams as 10.5 point or more favorite since 1984		0-8 S/U on road on Turf as 10.5 point or more Dog since 1978
0-4 S/U vs AFC North as 10.5 point or more Dog since 1978		0-11 S/U on grass as 10.5 point or more Dog since 1994
4-0 S/U & ATS vs AFC North as 10.5 point or more favorite s/1999		2-23 S/U on grass as 7.5-10 point Dog since 1984
2-9-1 O/U vs AFC North as 3.5-7 point Dog since 1983		8-0 O/U on road on Turf as 7.5-10 point Dog since 1993
1-5 S/U vs AFC North as 3 point or less Dog since 1998		12-3 O/U on grass as 7.5-10 point Dog since 1996
5-0 O/U vs AFC North as 3 point or less Dog since 2003		2-11 S/U on road on Turf as 3.5-7 point Dog since 1993
1-5 S/U on road vs AFC North as 3 point or less Dog since 1986		10-22 S/U on grass as 3.5-7 point Dog since 2000
0-5 S/U on road vs AFC North as 3 point or less Dog since 1986		8-2 O/U on road on Turf as 3 point or less Dog since 2005
6-0 S/U vs AFC North as 3.5-7 point favorite since 1993		3-12 O/U on grass as 3.5-7 point favorite since 2014
1-8 O/U vs AFC North as 3.5-7 point favorite since 1986		10-2 S/U on road on Turf as 3.5-7 point favorite since 1998
4-0 S/U & ATS vs Baltimore as 3.5-7 point Dog since 1979		1-7 ATS on grass 7.5 point or more favorite since 1978
0-3 O/U & vs Baltimore as 3.5-7 point Dog since 1983		**THU-SAT-SNF-MNF**
0-3 S/U vs Baltimore as 3 point or less Dog since 1982		8-0 S/U on Thursday as favorite since 2013
3-0 O/U vs Cincinnati as 3 point or less Dog since 1990		9-2 S/U on Thursday since 2013
0-3 O/U vs Pittsburgh as 3.5-7 point favorite since 1986	Cowboys	4-0 S/U on road on Thursday since 2013
2-7 S/U vs AFC South as 3.5-10 point Dog since 1981	Giants	16-4 S/U on MNF since 2005
0-3 S/U & ATS vs AFC South as 3 point or less Dog since 2005	Lions	3-12 S/U in 1st road game of season since 2007
3-0 O/U vs AFC South as 3 point or less Dog since 2005	RAMS	17-2 S/U in 1st home game of season since 2003
6-2 S/U @ home on Thursday since 2011	49ERS	15-4 S/U after playing @ Los Angeles Rams since 1998

Seattle Seahawks
Century Link Field

NFC West
Coach: Pete Carroll

2023 Schedule + Trends & Angles

DATE		OPPONENT	TURF	SEA	OPP	S/U	LINE	ATS	TOT	O/U	Trends & Angles
9/10/2023	vs	LOS ANGELES RAMS	A								vs L.A. Rams - Seahawks lead series 26-25
9/17/2023	@	Detroit	A								8-1 S/U vs Detroit since 2003
9/24/2023	vs	CAROLINA	A								Game 7-0 O/U vs Carolina since 2015
10/2/2023	@	New York Giants	A								5-0 S/U & ATS vs New York Giants since 2011
10/8/2023		BYE									
10/15/2023	@	Cincinnati	A								Game 6-2 O/U vs Bengals since 1994
10/22/2023	vs	ARIZONA	A								vs Arizona - Seahawks leads series 25-22-1
10/29/2023	vs	CLEVELAND	A								vs Cleveland - Seahawks lead series 4-2
11/5/2023	@	Baltimore	A								Game 0-4 O/U vs Ravens since 20074
11/12/2023	vs	WASHINGTON	A								0-3 S/U @ home vs Washington since 2008
11/19/2023	@	Los Angeles Rams	G								vs Los Angeles Rams - Seahawks lead series 26-25
11/23/2023	vs	SAN FRANCISCO	A								11-3 ATS @ home vs San Francisco since 2009
11/30/2023	@	Dallas	A								Game 3-8 O/U vs Dallas since 2005
12/10/2023	@	San Francisco	G								vs San Francisco - Seahawks leads series 29-21
12/17/2023	vs	PHILADELPHIA	A								7-0 S/U vs Philadelphia since 2011 {6-1 ATS}
12/24/2023	@	Tennessee	G								1-6 ATS vs Tennessee since 1997
12/31/2023	vs	PITTSBURGH	A								vs Pittsburgh - HOME team 10-2 S/U since 1992 {8-3-1 ATS}
1/7/2024	@	Arizona	G								8-0-1 S/U @ Arizona since 2013
1/14/2024											NFC Wild Card
1/21/2024											NFC Divisional Playoff
1/28/2024											NFC Championship
2/11/2024											Super Bowl LVIII @ Las Vegas, NV

Pointspread Analysis vs NFC teams		Pointspread Analysis vs NFC teams
0-5 S/U vs NFC East as 10.5 point or more Dog since 1992		5-1 ATS @ home vs Arizona as 3.5-7 point favorite since 2005
3-10 S/U vs NFC East as 3.5-7 point Dog since 1980		5-2 O/U vs Arizona as 7.5-10 point favorite since 1998
4-0 ATS vs NFC East as 3 point or less Dog since 2007		0-3 S/U vs Los Angeles Rams as 7.5-10 point Dog since 2000
0-9 O/U vs NFC East as 3 point or less favorite since 2002		3-0 ATS vs Los Angeles Rams as 7.5-10 point Dog since 2000
12-1 S/U vs NFC East as 3.5-7 point favorite since 2005		0-3 S/U & ATS @ L.A. Rams as 3.5-7 point favorite since 2014
1-4 S/U @ home vs NFC East as 3.5-7 point Dog since 1983		3-0 S/U @ home vs L.A. Rams as 3.5-7 point favorite since 2005
7-0 S/U on road vs NFC East as 3.5-10 point favorite since 2005		1-4 O/U @ home vs L.A. Rams as 3.5-7 point favorite since 1991
0-6 O/U on road vs NFC East as 3.5-10 point favorite since 2013		3-0 S/U & ATS @ home vs L.A. Rams as 7.5-10 point favorite s/2007
0-3 S/U @ Dallas as 10.5 point or more Dog since 1992		4-1 O/U @ home vs L.A. Rams as 7.5-10 point favorite since 1985
0-3 O/U @ Dallas as 10.5 point or more Dog since 1992		4-0-1 O/U vs San Francisco as 3.5-7 point Dog since 1991
0-3 S/U vs New York Giants as 3.5-7 point Dog since 2002		7-1 ATS vs San Francisco as 3 point or less Dog since 2009
4-0 S/U & ATS vs NY Giants as 3 point or less favorite since 1983		1-8-1 O/U vs San Francisco as 3 point or less Dog since 2003
3-0 S/U vs New York Giants as 3.5-7 point favorite since 2005		0-6 O/U @ San Francisco as 3 point or less Dog since 2003
vs Philadelphia - Seahawks lead series 12-7		5-0 S/U & ATS vs San Francisco as 3 point or less favorite since 1997
0-3 O/U vs Philadelphia as 3.5-7 point Dog since 1989		3-0 S/U & ATS @ home vs San Francisco as 7.5-10 point favorite since 2007
3-0 O/U vs Philadelphia as 3 point or less Dog since 2002		1-4 O/U @ home vs San Francisco as 7.5-10 point favorite since 2007
5-0 S/U vs Philadelphia as 3.5-7 point favorite since 1986		6-0 S/U vs San Francisco as 10.5 point or more favorite since 2005
3-1 ATS vs Philadelphia as 3.5-7 point favorite since 1988		5-1 O/U vs San Francisco as 10.5 point or more favorite since 2005
0-3 S/U vs Washington as 7.5-10 point favorite since 1998		5-1 S/U vs L.A. Rams as 10.5 point or more favorite since 2012
Game 2-7 O/U @ home vs Washington since 1989		0-6 O/U vs L.A. Rams as 10.5 point or more favorite since 2012
vs Washington - Road team 6-1 S/U since 2008		**Dog**
0-7 S/U vs NFC North as 7.5 point or more Dog since 1996		0-21 S/U as 10.5 point or more Dog since 1978
6-0 S/U vs NFC North as 7.5-10 point favorite since 2006		6-34 S/U as 7.5-10 point Dog since 1990
6-0 S/U vs NFC North as 10.5 point or more favorite since 1984		20-3 O/U as 7.5-10 point Dog since 1996
0-6 S/U vs NFC South as 3.5-7 point Dog since 2010		7-1 ATS @ home as 3.5-7 point Dog since 2011
7-1 O/U vs NFC South as 3.5-10 point Dog since 2002		**Favorite**
2-7 O/U vs NFC South as 3 point or less favorite since 1996		16-3 S/U @ home as 3.5-7 point favorite since 2012
0-4-1 ATS vs NFC South as 3.5-7 point favorite since 2014		2-5 ATS as 7.5-10 point favorite since 2019
5-0 S/U @ home vs NFC South as 7.5 point or more favorite s/2004		34-1 S/U as 10.5 point or more favorite since 1984
vs Carolina - Seahawks lead sereis 10-5		**Playoffs**
0-9 S/U vs NFC West as 7.5-10 point Dog since 1991		3-14 S/U on road in Playoffs since 1984
5-13 S/U on road vs NFC West as 3.5-10 point Dog since 1988		10-1 S/U @ home in Playoffs since 2005 {7-4 ATS}
13-4 ATS vs NFC West as 3 point or less Dog since 2009		0-9 S/U on road in Divisional Playoffs since 1984
3-15-1 O/U vs NFC West as 3 point or less Dog since 2008		7-0 O/U on road in Divisional Playoffs since 2007
12-3 S/U @ home vs NFC West as 3.5-7 point favorite since 2003		3-0 S/U @ home in Divisional Playoffs since 2006
0-6 O/U @ home vs NFC West as 3.5-7 point favorite since 2009		3-0 S/U @ home in NFC Championship since 2006
14-1 S/U vs NFC West as 10.5 point or more favorite since 1985		7-1 S/U @ home on Saturday in Playoff since 2006
7-1-1 ATS @ Arizona since 2013		0-6 S/U on road on Saturday in Playoffs since 1984
1-6 S/U & ATS vs Arizona as 3 point or less favorite since 1993		3-0 O/U vs Carolina in Playoffs since 2006
5-1 S/U @ Arizona as 3.5-7 point favorite since 2005		4-0 O/U vs Green Bay in Playoffs since 2004
6-1 S/U @ home vs Arizona as 3.5-7 point favorite since 2004		3-0 S/U vs Washington in Playoffs since 2006

	2022									
@	Dallas	Su	A	19	3	W	-2.5	W	49.0	U
@	New Orleans		A	20	10	W	-2.5	W	43.5	U
vs	GREEN BAY		G	12	14	L	-1.0	L	42.5	U
vs	KANSAS CITY	Su	G	31	41	L	-2.0	L	47.5	O
vs	ATLANTA		G	21	15	W	-10.0	L	46.0	U
@	Pittsburgh		G	18	20	L	-9.5	L	46.5	U
@	Carolina		G	3	21	L	-13.0	L	38.0	U
vs	BALTIMORE	T	G	22	27	L	-2.0	L	46.0	O
vs	L.A. RAMS		G	16	13	W	-3.0	T	43.0	U
vs	Seattle {Munich}		G	21	16	W	-2.5	W	45.0	U
	BYE									
@	Cleveland {OT}		G	17	23	L	-3.0	L	42.5	U
vs	NEW ORLEANS	M	G	17	16	W	-3.0	L	41.0	U
@	San Francisco		G	7	35	L	3.5	L	38.5	O
vs	CINCINNATI		G	23	34	L	3.0	L	46.5	O
@	Arizona {OT}	Su	G	19	16	W	-7.5	L	41.5	U
vs	CAROLINA		G	30	24	W	-3.0	W	41.0	U
@	Atlanta		A	17	30	L	6.0	L	40.5	O
vs	DALLAS	M	G	14	31	L	2.5	L	44.5	O
	2021									
vs	DALLAS	T	G	31	29	W	-9.0	L	52.5	O
vs	ATLANTA		G	48	25	W	-13.0	W	51.5	O
@	Los Angeles Rams		A	24	34	L	1.0	L	55.0	O
@	New England	Su	A	19	17	W	-6.5	L	49.0	U
vs	MIAMI		G	45	17	W	-11.0	W	48.0	O
@	Philadelphia	T	G	28	22	W	-7.0	L	52.0	U
vs	CHICAGO		G	38	3	W	-12.0	W	47.0	U
@	New Orleans		A	27	36	L	-3.5	L	43.5	O
	BYE									
@	Washington		G	19	29	L	-9.5	L	51.0	U
vs	N.Y. GIANTS	M	G	30	10	W	-10.5	W	50.0	U
@	Indianapolis		A	38	31	W	-3.0	W	53.0	O
@	Atlanta		A	30	17	W	-11.0	W	51.0	U
vs	BUFFALO {OT}		G	33	27	W	-3.5	W	53.0	O
vs	NEW ORLEANS	Su	G	0	9	L	-11.5	L	46.0	U
@	Carolina		G	32	6	W	-10.5	W	44.5	U
@	New York Jets		A	28	24	W	-14.5	L	48.0	O
vs	CAROLINA		G	41	17	W	-10.5	W	43.0	O
vs	PHILADELPHIA		G	31	15	W	-7.0	W	47.5	U
vs	L.A. RAMS		G	27	30	L	-3.0	L	48.0	O

	2020									
@	New Orleans		A	23	34	L	4.0	L	48.0	O
vs	CAROLINA		G	31	17	W	-7.5	W	46.5	O
@	Denver		G	28	10	W	-6.0	W	42.5	U
vs	L.A. CHARGERS		G	38	31	W	-7.5	L	42.0	O
@	Chicago	T	G	19	20	L	-3.5	L	44.0	U
vs	GREEN BAY		G	38	10	W	3.0	W	54.0	U
@	Las Vegas	Su	G	45	20	W	-4.0	W	51.5	O
@	New York Giants	M	A	25	23	W	-1.0	L	47.0	O
vs	NEW ORLEANS	Su	G	3	38	L	-3.0	L	51.0	O
vs	Carolina		G	46	23	W	-6.0	W	49.5	O
vs	L.A. RAMS	M	G	24	27	L	-4.0	L	47.5	O
vs	KANSAS CITY		G	24	27	L	3.0	T	56.0	U
	BYE									
vs	MINNESOTA		G	26	14	W	-6.5	W	52.0	U
@	Atlanta		A	31	27	W	-6.0	L	49.5	O
@	Detroit	Sa	A	47	7	W	-12.0	W	55.0	U
vs	ATLANTA		G	44	27	W	-7.0	W	51.0	O
@	Washington	Sa	G	31	23	W	-10.5	L	45.0	O
@	New Orleans		A	30	20	W	2.5	W	53.0	U
@	Green Bay		G	31	26	W	3.0	W	53.0	O
vs	Kansas City		G	31	9	W	3.0	W	55.5	O
	2019									
vs	SAN FRANCISCO		G	17	31	L	-1.0	L	51.0	U
@	Carolina	T	G	20	14	W	6.5	W	48.0	U
vs	N.Y. GIANTS		G	31	32	L	-4.5	L	47.5	O
@	L.A. Rams		G	55	40	W	9.0	W	48.0	O
@	New Orleans		A	24	31	L	3.0	L	46.5	O
vs	Carolina {London}		G	26	37	L	2.0	L	48.0	O
	BYE									
@	Tennessee		G	23	27	L	2.0	L	45.5	U
@	Seattle {OT}		A	34	40	L	4.0	L	51.0	O
vs	ARIZONA		G	30	27	W	-5.5	L	51.5	O
vs	NEW ORLEANS		G	17	34	L	5.0	L	50.5	O
@	Atlanta		A	35	22	W	3.5	W	52.0	O
@	Jacksonville		G	28	11	W	-3.0	W	46.5	U
vs	INDIANAPOLIS		G	38	35	W	-3.0	T	46.5	O
@	Detroit		A	38	17	W	-5.5	W	46.0	O
vs	HOUSTON	Sa	G	20	23	L	3.0	T	50.0	U
vs	ATLANTA {OT}		G	22	28	L	PK	L	48.0	O

Pointspread Analysis vs AFC teams	
0-13 S/U vs AFC teams as 7.5-10 point Dog since 1998	Buffalo
1-6-1 O/U vs AFC teams as 3.5-7 point Dog since 2014	Buffalo
0-5 ATS vs AFC teams as 7.5-10 point favorite since 1992	EAGLES
0-6 S/U on road vs AFC East as 7.5 point or more Dog since 1985	
0-8 S/U vs AFC East as 3.5-7 point Dog since 1982	
0-5 ATS vs AFC East as 3.5-7 point Dog since 2005	
7-2 O/U vs AFC East as 3.5-7 point favorite since 1997	
4-0 S/U vs Buffalo as 3 point or less favorite since 1982	
0-8-1 ATS vs Tennessee since 1995	
0-6 ATS vs AFC South as 7 point or less Dog since 2003	
0-12 S/U vs AFC South as a Dog since 1980	
7-1 O/U vs AFC South as 3 point or less favorite since 1983	
0-4 ATS vs AFC South as 3.5-10 point favorite since 1995	
0-6 ATS vs AFC South as 7 point or less Dog since 2003	
0-12 S/U vs AFC South as a Dog since 1980	
8-1 O/U vs AFC South as 3 point or less favorite since 1983	
0-4 ATS vs AFC South as 3.5-10 point favorite since 1995	

Pointspread Analysis THU-SAT-SNF-MNF
1-9 ATS on Thursday since 2013
1-5 S/U & ATS on Thursday as Dog since 2012
2-8 ATS on MNF as favorite since 1998
Playoffs
2-6 O/U @ home in Playoffs since 1997
1-3 S/U on road NFC Wild Card since 1982 {0-4 ATS}
3-1 S/U @ home in Divisional Playoffs since 1979

Tampa Bay Buccaneers　　NFC South

Raymond James Stadium　　*2023 Schedule + Trends & Angles*　　**Coach: Todd Bowles**

DATE		OPPONENT	TURF	TB	OPP	S/U	LINE	ATS	TOT	O/U	Trends & Angles
9/10/2023	@	Minnesota	A								vs Minnesota - Vikings lead series 33-23
9/17/2023	vs	CHICAGO	G								vs Chicago - Bears leads series 40-21
9/25/2023	vs.	PHILADELPHIA	G								vs Philadelphia - Eagles leads series 10-9
10/1/2023	@	New Orleans	A								3-9 S/U @ New Orleans since 2011
10/8/2023		BYE									
10/15/2023	vs	DETROIT	G								vs Detroit - Lions leads series 31-29
10/22/2023	vs	ATLANTA	G								vs Atlanta leads - Tampa Bay leads series 30-29
10/26/2023	@	*Buffalo*	A								vs Buffalo - Tampa Bay leads series 8-4
11/5/2023	@	*Houston*	G								vs Houston - Texans lead series 4-1
11/12/2023	vs	*TENNESSEE*	G								1-9 S/U vs Tennessee since 1989
11/19/2023	@	San Francisco	G								vs San Francisco - 49ers leads series 19-7
11/26/2023	@	*Indianapolis*	A								vs Indianapolis - Colts lead series 8-7
12/3/2023	vs	CAROLINA	G								vs Carolina - Panthers leads series 25-20
12/10/2023	@	Atlanta	A								Game 8-2 O/U @ Atlanta since 2013
12/17/2023	@	Green Bay	G								vs Green Bay - Packers lead series 34-23-1
12/24/2023	vs	*JACKSONVILLE*	G								vs Jacksonville - Jaguars lead series 4-3
12/31/2023	vs	NEW ORLEANS	G								4-10 S/U @ home vs New Orleans since 2009
1/7/2024	@	Carolina	G								
1/14/2024											NFC Wild Card
1/21/2024											NFC Divisional Playoff
1/28/2024											NFC Championship
2/11/2024											Super Bowl LVIII @ Las Vegas, NV

Pointspread Analysis vs NFC teams		Pointspread Analysis vs NFC teams
0-14 S/U vs NFC East as 7.5 point or more Dog since 1981		0-6 S/U @ home vs Atlanta as 3 point or less Dog since 1992
1-4 S/U & ATS @ home vs NFC East as 3.5-7 point Dog s/1988		1-5 S/U vs New Orleans as 3 point or less Dog since 2008
2-8 O/U on road vs NFC East as 3 point or less Dog since 1988		8-0 S/U vs Atlanta as 3 point or less favorite since 1997
1-5 O/U on road vs NFC East as 3 point or less favorite since 1990		7-0-1 ATS vs Atlanta as 3 point or less favorite since 1997
1-8-1 ATS vs NFC East as 3 point or less favorite since 1998		6-0 S/U & ATS vs Atlanta as 3.5 -7 point favorite since 1999
3-16-1 O/U vs NFC East as 3.5-10 point Dog since 1990		1-3 O/U vs Carolina as 7.5-10 point favorite since 2002
3-0 S/U & ATS vs Philadelphia as 3.5-7 point Dog since 2003		0-12 S/U vs NFC West as 10.5 point or more Dog since 1983
4-0 O/U vs Philadelphia as 3.5-7 point Dog since 2002		3-13 S/U on road vs NFC West as 3.5-7 point Dog since 1984
0-5 O/U vs Philadelphia as 3.5-7 point favorite since 1999		1-7 O/U @ home vs NFC West as 3 point or less favorite s/2006
2-15 S/U vs NFC North as 10.5 point or more Dog since 1986		1-7-1 ATS vs NFC West as 3 point or less favorite since 2006
0-6 S/U on road vs NFC North as 7.5-10 point Dog since 1993		4-0 S/U vs NFC West as 7.5-10 point favorite since 1984 {3-1 ATS}
7-1-1 ATS vs NFC North as 3.5-7 point Dog since 1998		0-6 S/U vs San Francisco as 10.5 point or more Dog since 1983
1-9-1 O/U vs NFC North as 3.5-7 point favorite since 2002		0-3 S/U & ATS @ San Francisco as 3.5-7 point favorite s/1979
14-4 S/U vs NFC North as 3.5-7 point favorite since 1998		**Grass/Turf**
6-1 S/U on road vs NFC North as 3.5-7 point favorite since 1998		2-21 S/U on Turf as 10.5 point or more Dog since 1992
6-1 S/U @ home vs NFC North as 7.5-10 point favorite since 1997		2-14 S/U on road on grass as 10.5 point or more Dog since 1983
1-5 S/U vs Chicago as 10.5 point or more Dog since 2006		1-17 S/U on road on grass as 7.5-10 point Dog since 1978
0-4 S/U vs Chicago as 7.5-10 point Dog since 1985		8-29 S/U on Turf as 7.5-10 point Dog since 1980
3-0 ATS @ home vs Chicago as 3.5-7 point Dog since 1991		0-9 S/U vs AFC on Turf as 7.5-10 point Dog since 1980
1-4 S/U & ATS vs Chicago as 3 point or less favorite since 1984		3-17-1 O/U on road on grass as 3.5-7 point Dog since 2005
8-3 S/U vs Chicago as 3.5 - 7 point favorite since 1981		11-1 O/U on road on grass as 3 point or less Dog since 2008
6-2 ATS vs Chicago as 3.5 - 7 point favorite since 1998		13-2 S/U on Turf as 3.5-7 point favorite since 1997
3-0 S/U & ATS @ home vs Detroit as 3 point or less Dog s/1985		4-0 S/U on Turf as 7.5-10 point favorite since 2000
5-1 O/U vs Detroit as 7.5-10 point Dog since 1983		1-7 ATS on road on grass as 7.5 point or more favorite s/2000
3-9 ATS vs Detroit as 3.5-7 point favorite since 1979		**Dog**
3-0 S/U vs Detroit as 7.5-10 point favorite since 2001		0-4 S/U & ATS @ home as 10.5 point or more Dog since 1986
0-5 S/U vs Green Bay as 10.5 point or more Dog since 1993		4-40 S/U as 10.5 point or more Dog since 1983
0-6 S/U @ Green Bay as 3.5 point Dog since 1991		5-24 S/U as 7.5-10 point Dog since 1993
1-5 S/U @ Minnesota as 3 point or less Dog since 1979		3-16 S/U @ home as 3.5-7 point Dog since 2009
4-12 S/U vs NFC South as 7.5 point or more Dog since 2006		7-1 O/U on road as 3.5-7 point Dog since 2017
4-14 S/U vs NFC South as 3.5-7 point Dog since 2012		3-12 S/U as 3.5-7 point dog since 2016
3-9 S/U on road vs NFC South as 3.5-7 point Dog since 2012		**Favorite**
2-11 S/U @ home vs NFC South as 3 point or less Dog since 2005		6-2 S/U on road as 7.5-10 point favorite since 2001
1-5 ATS vs NFC South as 7.5-10 point favorite since 2003		1-8 ATS on road as 7.5-10 point favorite since 2000
2-6 O/U vs NFC South as 7.5-10 point favorite since 2002		14-4 S/U as 10.5 point or more favorite since 2003
1-6 S/U vs New Orleans as 10.5 point or more Dog since 1988		
0-4 S/U vs Carolina as 7.5-10 point Dog since 2006	Hou, Ind, GB	7-1 S/U in 2nd of back to back road games last 8 times
2-13 S/U vs Atlanta as 3.5-7 point Dog since 1986	Ind	3-13 S/U prior to playing @ home vs Carolina since 2004
3-8 ATS @ Atlanta as 3.5-7 point Dog since 1988	SAINTS	7-15 S/U in final home game of season since 2001

2022

vs	N.Y. GIANTS		G	20	21	L	-5.5	L	44.0	U
@	Buffalo	M	A	7	41	L	10.0	L	47.0	O
vs	LAS VEGAS		G	24	22	W	2.0	W	45.5	O
@	Indianapolis		A	24	17	W	4.0	W	43.0	U
@	Washington		G	21	17	W	PK	W	43.0	U
	BYE									
vs	INDIANAPOLIS		G	19	10	W	-2.5	W	43.0	U
@	Houston		G	17	10	W	-1.0	W	39.5	U
@	Kansas City {OT}	Su	G	17	20	L	14.0	W	45.0	U
vs	DENVER		G	17	10	W	-2.5	W	39.5	U
@	Green Bay	T	G	27	17	W	3.0	W	40.5	O
vs	CINCINNATI		G	16	20	L	PK	L	42.5	U
@	Philadelphia		G	10	35	L	4.5	L	44.5	O
vs	JACKSONVILLE		G	22	36	L	-3.0	L	42.0	O
@	Los Angeles Chargers		G	14	17	L	3.0	T	48.5	U
vs	HOUSTON	Sa	G	14	19	L	-3.0	L	33.5	U
vs	DALLAS	T	G	13	27	L	13.5	L	40.5	U
@	Jacksonville	Sa	G	16	20	L	6.0	W	40.0	U

2021

vs	ARIZONA		G	13	38	L	-2.5	L	54.5	U
@	Seattle {OT}		A	33	30	W	6.0	W	53.5	O
vs	INDIANAPOLIS		G	25	16	W	-4.5	W	47.0	U
@	New York Jets {OT}		A	24	27	L	-5.5	L	44.5	O
@	Jacksonville		G	37	19	W	-4.0	W	48.5	O
vs	BUFFALO	M	G	34	31	W	6.0	W	53.0	O
vs	KANSAS CITY		G	27	3	W	4.0	W	59.0	U
@	Indianapolis {OT}		A	34	31	W	3.0	W	51.0	O
@	Los Angeles Rams	Su	A	28	16	W	7.0	W	53.0	U
vs	NEW ORLEANS		G	25	23	W	-3.0	L	42.5	O
vs	HOUSTON		G	13	22	L	-10.5	L	44.5	U
@	New England		A	13	36	L	7.0	L	43.5	O
	BYE									
vs	JACKSONVILLE		G	20	0	W	-9.0	W	44.5	U
@	Pittsburgh		G	13	19	L	1.0	L	44.0	U
vs	SAN FRANCISCO	T	G	20	17	W	3.5	W	45.0	U
vs	MIAMI		G	34	3	W	-3.0	W	41.0	U
@	Houston		G	28	25	W	-10.5	L	43.0	O
vs	CINCINNATI	Sa	G	16	19	L	-4.0	L	48.5	U

2020

@	Denver	M	G	16	14	W	-3.5	L	42.0	U	
vs	JACKSONVILLE		G	33	30	W	-7.0	L	44.5	O	
@	Minnesota		A	31	30	W	-3.0	L	49.5	O	
	BYE										
vs	BUFFALO	Tu	G	42	16	W	3.0	W	52.0	O	
vs	Houston {OT}		G	42	36	W	-4.0	W	52.0	O	
vs	PITTSBURGH		G	24	27	L	-1.0	L	51.0	T	
@	Cincinnati		A	20	31	L	-7.0	L	51.0	T	
vs	CHICAGO		G	24	17	W	-6.0	W	47.0	U	
vs	Indianapolis	T	G	17	34	L	1.0	L	49.0	O	
@	Baltimore {OT}		A	30	24	W	6.0	W	50.5	O	
@	Indianapolis		A	45	26	W	3.0	W	51.5	O	
vs	CLEVELAND		G	35	41	L	-4.0	L	54.5	O	
@	Jacksonville		G	31	10	W	-9.0	W	53.0	U	
vs	DETROIT		G	46	25	W	-10.0	W	54.5	O	
@	Green Bay	Su	G	14	40	L	3.0	L	52.0	O	
@	Houston		G	41	38	W	-7.5	W	55.5	O	
vs	Baltimore		G	13	20	L	3.5	L	53.5	U	

2019

@	Cleveland		G	43	13	W	5.5	W	44.0	O	
vs	Indianapolis		G	17	19	L	-3.0	L	43.5	U	
@	Jacksonville	T	G	7	20	L	-1.5	L	38.0	U	
@	Atlanta		A	24	10	W	3.0	W	46.0	U	
vs	BUFFALO		G	7	14	L	-3.0	L	39.5	U	
@	Denver		G	0	16	L	1.0	L	41.0	U	
vs	L.A. CHARGERS		G	23	20	W	-2.5	W	42.0	O	
vs	TAMPA BAY		G	27	23	W	-2.0	W	45.5	O	
@	Carolina		G	20	30	L	3.5	L	43.0	O	
vs	KANSAS CITY		G	35	32	W	5.5	W	48.5	O	
	BYE										
vs	JACKSONVILLE		G	42	20	W	-4.0	W	41.5	O	
@	Indianapolis		A	31	17	W	PK	W	41.5	O	
@	Oakland		G	42	21	W	-3.0	W	47.0	O	
vs	Houston		G	21	24	L	-3.0	L	50.0	U	
vs	NEW ORLEANS		G	28	38	L	3.5	L	49.0	O	
@	Houston		G	35	14	W	-10.0	W	42.5	O	
@	New England	Sa	A	20	13	W	4.5	W	45.0	U	
@	Baltimore	Sa	A	28	12	W	10.0	W	47.5	U	
@	Kansas City		G	24	35	L	7.0	L	51.0	O	

Pointspread Analysis vs NFC teams	
2-10 S/U vs NFC teams as 10.5 point or more Dog since 1984	
11-1 S/U vs NFC teams as 7.5-10 point favorite since 1980	
0-4 S/U @ home vs NFC South as a Dog since 2011	
12-0 S/U vs NFC South as a favorite since 1990	
3-0 S/U @ home vs Atlanta as 7.5-10 point favorite since 1993	
3-0 S/U & ATS vs New Orleans as 3.5-7 point favorite since 1990	
0-3 S/U vs NFC West as 10.5 point or more Dog since 1984	
1-5 S/U @ home vs NFC West as 3.5-7 point Dog since 1990	
5-2 O/U vs NFC West as 3.5-7 point Dog since 2005	
2-7 S/U vs NFC West as 3 point or less Dog since 1978	
4-0 O/U vs NFC West as 3 point or less Dog since 1999	
5-2 S/U vs NFC West as 3 point or less favorite since 1978	
4-0 S/U vs NFC West as 7.5-10 point favorite since 1978	
5-0 O/U vs NFC West as 7.5 or more favorite since 1993	
3-0 S/U vs Seattle as 3.5-7 point favorite since 1981	
Playoffs	
5-0 S/U on Saturday in Wild Card Playoffs since 1988	Steelers
2-5 S/U on road in Divisional Playoffs since 1987	
0-6 O/U in AFC Wild Card since 2000	Dolphins
7-1 ATS on road on Saturday in Playoffs since 1988	
0-4 O/U @ home in WILD Card since 1988	
4-1 O/U @ home in Divisional Playoffs since 1990	

Pointspread Analysis Grass/Turf
2-13 S/U on road on Turf as 10.5 point or more Dog since 1983
1-10 S/U on road on grass as 10.5 point or more Dog since 1984
7-2 O/U on road on grass as 10.5 point or more Dog since 1984
1-12 S/U on road on Turf as 7.5-10 point Dog since 1982
2-11 ATS on road on Turf as 7.5-10 point Dog since 1982
5-14 S/U on road on grass as 7.5-10 point Dog since 1978
2-14 S/U on road on grass as 3.5-7 point Dog since 2013
15-3 ATS on road on Turf as 3 point or less Dog since 1995
3-11 O/U on Turf as 3 point or less Dog since 1998
2-10 O/U on Turf as 3 point or less favorite since 2000
12-1 S/U on road on grass as 3.5-7 point favorite since 1989
8-3 O/U on road on grass as 3.5-7 point favorite since 1993
0-4 S/U on road on Turf as 3.5-7 point favorite since 2011
7-0 S/U on road on grass as 7.5 point or more favorite since 1999
4-0 S/U on road on Turf as 7.5-10 point favorite since 1992
THU-SAT-SNF-MNF
2-6 S/U on road on Thursday since 1997
vs Pittsburgh - HOME team 4-0 S/U on Thursday since 1980
8-3 ATS on Monday Night since 2008
12-3-1 O/U on MNF as Dog since 1982
4-1 S/U @ home in WILD Card since 1979
1-5 S/U @ home in Divisional Playoffs since 1990 {0-6 ATS}

Tennessee Titans   AFC South

LP Field   *2023 Schedule + Trends & Angles*   **Coach: Mike Vrabel**

DATE		OPPONENT	TURF	TN	OPP	S/U	LINE	ATS	TOT	O/U	Trends & Angles
9/10/2023	@	*New Orleans*	A								vs New Orleans - Titans leads series 9-6-1
9/17/2023	vs	L.A. CHARGERS	G								2-9-2 ATS vs Los Angeles Chargers since 1998
9/24/2023	@	Cleveland	G								vs Cleveland - Titans lead series 10-6
10/1/2023	vs	CINCINNATI	G								Game 1-6-1 O/U vs Bengals since 2007
10/8/2023	@	Indianapolis Colts	A								vs Indianapolis - Colts leads series 35-20
10/15/2023	vs	BALTIMORE {London}	G								0-9 ATS @ home vs AFC North as 3.5-7 point fav. s/2000
10/22/2023		BYE									
10/29/2023	vs	*ATLANTA*	G								12-0 S/U vs NFC South as a favorite since 1990
11/2/2023	@	Pittsburgh	G								vs Pittsburgh - Steelers leads series 48-32
11/12/2023	@	*Tampa Bay*	G								vs Tampa Bay - Titans lead series 11-2
11/19/2023	@	Jacksonville	G								vs Jacksonville - Titans leads series 34-23
11/26/2023	vs	*CAROLINA*	G								vs Carolina - Series tied 3-3
12/3/2023	vs	INDIANAPOLIS COLTS	G								3-8 S/U @ home vs Indianapolis since 2012
12/11/2023	@	Miami	G								Game 3-9 O/U @ Miami since 1991
12/17/2023	vs	HOUSTON TEXANS	G								vs Houston - Titans leads series 23-19
12/24/2023	vs	*SEATTLE*	G								vs Seattle - Seahawks leads series 10-8
12/31/2023	@	Houston Texans	G								2-8 ATS @ Houston since 2013
1/7/2024	vs	JACKSONVILLE	G								9-1 S/U @ home vs Jacksonville since 2014
1/14/2024											AFC Wild Card
1/21/2024											AFC Divisional Playoff
1/28/2024											AFC Championship
2/11/2024											Super Bowl LVIII @ Las Vegas, NV

Pointspread Analysis vs AFC teams		Pointspread Analysis vs AFC teams
0-5 S/U vs AFC East at 10.5 point or more Dog since 1983		1-6 ATS vs Pittsburgh as 3.5-7 point favorite since 1986
0-4 S/U & ATS vs AFC East as 7.5-10 point Dog since 1986		Game 6-1 O/U vs Cleveland since 2011
1-5 S/U & ATS vs AFC East as 3 point or less favorite since 2006		0-4 S/U vs AFC South as 10.5 point or more Dog since 2004
12-5 S/U vs AFC East as 3.5-7 point favorite since 1991		1-8 S/U @ home vs AFC South as 3.5-7 point Dog since 2005
6-1 O/U vs AFC East as 3.5-7 point favorite since 2003		2-11 ATS vs AFC South as 3.5-7 point Dog since 2013
6-1 S/U vs AFC East as 7.5-10 point favorite since 1978		1-17 S/U vs AFC South as 3.5-7 point Dog since 2009
1-5 O/U vs AFC East as 7.5-10 point favorite since 1990		13-2 S/U @ home vs AFC South as 3.5-7 point favorite since 2007
0-4 O/U @ Miami as 3.5-7 point Dog since 1992		10-0 S/U vs AFC South as 7.5-10 point favorite since 2002
0-3 S/U vs Miami as 10.5 point or more Dog since 1983		0-3 S/U @ Indianapolis as 10.5 point or more Dog since 2004
0-3 O/U vs Miami as 10.5 point or more Dog since 1983		0-3 O/U vs Indianapolis as 7.5-10 point Dog since 2006
vs Miami - Dolphins leads series 21-18		0-9 S/U vs Houston as 3.5-7 point Dog since 2010
1-11 S/U on road vs AFC North as 7.5 point or more Dog since 1978		0-6 ATS vs Houston as 3.5-7 point Dog since 2014
1-8 S/U on road vs AFC North as 7.5-10 point Dog since 1982		6-1 O/U vs Houston as 3.5-7 point Dog since 2013
6-2 O/U on road vs AFC North as 7.5-10 point Dog since 1983		1-9 S/U vs Indianapolis as 3.5-7 point Dog since 2005
2-10 S/U vs AFC North as 7.5-10 point Dog since 1982		1-7 ATS vs Indianapolis as 3.5-7 point Dog since 2009
2-6 S/U on road vs AFC North as 3.5-7 point Dog since 2001		3-0 S/U & ATS vs Houston as 3 point or less Dog since 2005
8-3 S/U on road vs AFC North as 3 point or less Dog since 1996		0-4 S/U @ home vs Indianapolis as 3 point or less Dog since 2013
8-3 ATS on road vs AFC North as 3 point or less Dog since 1996		4-0 O/U @ home vs Indianapolis as 3 point or less Dog s/2013
1-8 S/U @ home vs AFC North as 3.5-7 point favorite since 2000		0-3 S/U & ATS @ Jacksonville as 3 point or less Dog since 2002
0-9 ATS @ home vs AFC North as 3.5-7 point favorite since 2000		0-3 O/U @ Jacksonville as 3 point or less Dog since 2001
7-2 O/U @ home vs AFC North as 3.5-7 point favorite since 2000		3-0 S/U & ATS @ home vs Jacksonville as 3 point or less Dog since 2001
10-0 S/U vs AFC North as 7.5-10 point favorite since 1989		5-2 S/U @ home vs Jacksonville as 3 point or less favorite s/2001
11-2 S/U vs AFC North as 10.5 point or more favorite since 1990		6-1 S/U @ home vs Houston as 3.5-7 point favorite since 2005
1-4 S/U vs Baltimore as 7.5-10 point Dog since 1983		7-0 O/U @ home vs Indianapolis as 3.5-7 point favorite s/1984
4-1 ATS @ home vs Baltimore as 3.5-7 point Dog since 1983		5-0 S/U @ home vs Jacksonville as 3.5-7 point favorite since 2012
0-5 S/U & ATS @ home vs Baltimore as 3 point or less Dog since 1985		5-0 S/U vs Houston as 7.5-10 point favorite since 2002
1-4 O/U @ home vs Baltimore as 3 point or less Dog since 1985		3-0 S/U & ATS vs Indianapolis as 7.5-10 point favorite since 1990
0-4 S/U vs Cincinnati as 7.5-10 point Dog since 1982		0-3 O/U vs Indianapolis as 7.5-10 point favorite since 1990
3-0 O/U vs Cincinnati as 7.5-10 point Dog since 1983		5-11 S/U vs AFC West as a Dog since 1983
9-1 O/U vs Cincinnati as 3.5-7 point Dog since 1984		1-5 S/U ATS @ home vs AFC West as 3 point or less Dog s/2005
9-4 S/U vs Cincinnati as 3.5-7 point favorite since 1978		12-2 S/U @ home vs AFC West as 3.5-7 point favorite since 1979
6-2-1 O/U vs Cincinnati as 3.5-7 point favorite since 1989		**Dog**
5-0 S/U vs Cincinnati as 7.5-10 point favorite since 1993		3-27 S/U as 10.5 point or more Dog since 1983
4-0 S/U vs Cincinnati as 10.5 point or more favorite since 1991		7-23 S/U as 7.5-10 point or more Dog since 1985
4-0 O/U @ home vs Cincinnati as 3.5-7 point Dog since 1983		16-4-1 O/U @ home as 3 point or less Dog since 2005
4-0 S/U vs Cleveland as 10.5 point or more favorite since 1999		**Favorite**
0-4 O/U vs Cleveland as 10.5 point or more favorite since 1999		14-4 S/U @ home as 3.5-7 point favorite since 2011
7-2 O/U @ Pittsburgh as 3.5-7 point Dog since 1993		19-5 S/U on road as 3.5-7 point favorite since 1992
1-4 S/U @ Pittsburgh as 3.5-7 point Dog since 2005		24-0 S/U as 7.5-10 point favorite since 1999
3-0 O/U @ Pittsburgh as 3 point or less favorite since 1989		9-0 S/U on road as 7.5-10 point favorite since 1992
7-3 S/U vs Pittsburgh as 3 point or less favorite since 1980		11-2 S/U as 10.5 point or more favorite since 1993

    Copyright © 2023 by Steve's Football Bible, LLC

Last 4 seasons + Pointspread Analysis

2022

	Opponent	Day								
vs	JACKSONVILLE		G	28	22	W	-3.0	W	43.0	O
@	Detroit		A	27	36	L	PK	L	48.0	O
vs	PHILADELPHIA		G	8	24	L	5.5	L	47.5	U
@	Dallas		A	10	25	L	3.0	L	41.0	U
vs	TENNESSEE		G	17	21	L	PK	L	43.0	U
@	Chicago	T	G	12	7	W	-1.0	W	39.0	U
vs	GREEN BAY		G	23	21	W	4.0	W	41.0	O
@	Indianapolis		A	17	16	W	3.0	W	40.0	U
vs	MINNESOTA		G	17	20	L	3.0	T	43.0	U
@	Philadelphia	M	G	32	21	W	10.5	W	43.0	O
@	Houston		G	23	10	W	-3.0	W	41.0	U
vs	ATLANTA		G	19	13	W	-3.5	W	40.0	U
@	New York Giants		A	20	20	T	-2.5	L	40.0	T
	BYE									
vs	N.Y. GIANTS	Su	G	12	20	L	-4.0	L	40.0	U
@	San Francisco	Sa	G	20	37	L	6.0	L	37.0	O
vs	CLEVELAND		G	10	24	L	-1.0	L	41.0	U
vs	DALLAS		G	26	6	W	7.0	W	41.0	U

2021

	Opponent	Day								
vs	L.A. CHARGERS		G	16	20	L	-1.5	L	45.5	U
vs	N.Y. GIANTS	T	G	30	29	W	-4.0	L	41.0	O
@	Buffalo		A	21	43	L	7.0	L	45.5	O
@	Atlanta		A	34	30	W	-2.5	W	47.0	O
vs	NEW ORLEANS		G	22	33	L	2.5	L	43.5	O
vs	KANSAS CITY		G	13	31	L	6.5	L	54.0	U
@	Green Bay		G	10	24	L	9.0	L	48.0	U
@	Denver		G	10	17	L	3.5	L	44.5	U
	BYE									
vs	TAMPA BAY		G	29	19	W	9.5	W	51.0	U
@	Carolina		G	27	21	W	3.5	W	43.5	O
vs	SEATTLE	M	G	17	15	W	1.5	W	46.5	U
@	Las Vegas		G	17	15	W	1.0	W	47.5	U
vs	DALLAS		G	20	27	L	6.5	L	48.0	U
@	Philadelphia	Tu	G	17	27	L	10.0	T	39.5	O
@	Dallas	Su	A	14	56	L	10.0	L	46.0	O
vs	PHILADELPHIA		G	16	20	L	6.0	L	44.5	U
@	New York Giants		A	22	7	W	-6.0	W	35.5	U

2020

	Opponent	Day								
vs	PHILADELPHIA		G	27	17	W	5.5	W	41.5	O
@	Arizona		G	15	30	L	7.0	L	46.0	U
@	Cleveland		G	20	34	L	7.0	L	45.0	O
vs	Baltimore		G	17	31	L	14.5	L	45.0	U
vs	L.A. RAMS		G	10	30	L	7.0	L	44.5	U
@	New York Giants		A	19	20	L	2.0	W	42.0	U
vs	DALLAS		G	25	3	W	-1.0	W	44.5	U
	BYE									
vs	N.Y. GIANTS		G	20	23	L	-3.0	L	43.0	T
@	Detroit		A	27	30	L	2.5	L	45.5	O
vs	CINCINNATI		G	20	9	W	-1.0	W	48.0	U
@	Dallas	T	A	41	16	W	2.5	W	46.0	O
@	Pittsburgh	M	G	23	17	W	5.5	L	43.5	U
@	San Francisco		G	23	15	W	3.0	W	43.5	U
vs	SEATTLE		G	15	20	L	6.0	L	44.0	U
vs	CAROLINA		G	13	20	L	1.0	L	41.5	U
@	Philadelphia	Su	G	20	14	W	-6.5	W	43.5	U
vs	TAMPA BAY		G	23	31	L	10.5	W	45.0	O

2019

	Opponent	Day								
@	Philadelphia		G	27	32	L	10.0	W	44.0	O
vs	DALLAS		G	21	31	L	6.0	L	46.5	O
vs	CHICAGO	M	G	15	31	L	5.0	L	41.0	O
@	New York Giants		A	3	24	L	3.0	L	48.0	U
vs	NEW ENGLAND		G	7	33	L	16.5	L	41.5	U
@	Miami		G	17	16	W	-5.5	W	42.0	U
vs	SAN FRANCISCO		G	0	9	L	10.0	W	38.5	U
@	Minnesota	T	A	9	19	L	16.5	W	42.0	U
@	Buffalo		A	9	24	L	10.5	L	37.0	U
	BYE									
vs	N.Y. JETS		G	17	34	L	-1.5	L	38.0	O
vs	DETROIT		G	19	16	W	4.0	W	39.0	U
@	Carolina		G	29	21	W	10.5	W	39.5	O
@	Green Bay		G	15	20	L	12.5	W	42.0	O
vs	PHILADELPHIA		G	27	37	L	6.5	L	38.5	O
vs	N.Y. GIANTS {OT}		G	35	41	L	1.0	L	42.5	O
@	Dallas		A	16	47	L	12.5	L	47.5	O

Pointspread Analysis vs AFC teams

Analysis	
2-6 ATS vs AFC teams as 10.5 point or more Dog since 1979	
1-5 S/U vs AFC teams as 7.5-10 point Dog since 2004	BEARS
4-12 O/U vs AFC teams as 3.5-7 point Dog since 2010	Cowboys
9-3 O/U vs AFC teams as 3 point or less Dog since 2006	
14-4 S/U @ home vs AFC teams as 3 point or less favorite s/1990	Cowboys
0-5 S/U vs AFC East as 3.5-7 point Dog since 1999	Cowboys
0-3 S/U on road vs AFC East as 3 point or less Dog since 1987	
8-1 S/U vs AFC East as 3 point or less favorite since 1984	
0-5 O/U vs AFC East as 3 point or less favorite since 2000	
6-2 O/U vs AFC East as 3.5-7 point favorite since 1990	
0-5 ATS vs AFC East as 3.5-7 point favorite since 1993	
5-0 S/U & ATS vs AFC East as 7.5 point or more favorite s/1981	
0-5 S/U vs Miami as 3.5-7 point Dog since 1981	
3-0 S/U vs Miami as 3 point or less favorite since 1990	
1-4 S/U vs AFC West as 7.5 point or more Dog since 1995	
0-3 O/U vs AFC West as 7.5-10 point Dog since 1995	
7-2 O/U on road vs AFC West as 3.5-7 point Dog since 1986	
1-10 S/U on road vs AFC West as 3.5-7 point Dog since 1980	
6-1 S/U & ATS vs AFC West as 3 point or less favorite since 1998	
0-3 S/U & ATS vs AFC West as 3.5-7 point favorite since 1995	
4-1 O/U vs Denver as 3.5-7 point Dog since 1986	
0-4 S/U @ Denver as 3.5-7 point Dog since 1980	
3-1 ATS @ Denver as 3.5-7 point Dog since 1980	

Pointspread Analysis THU-SAT-SNF-MNF

- 5-1 S/U @ home on Thursday since 1937
- 3-12 S/U on road on Thursday since 1974
- 2-9 S/U @ Dallas on Thursday since 1968
- 2-7 S/U on Thursday as Dog since 1978
- 7-2 O/U on road on Thursday since 2012
- Game 6-0 O/U @ Dallas on Thursday since 2002

Playoffs

- 2-8 O/U in Playoffs on Saturday since 1991
- 13-4 S/U @ home in Playoffs since 1942 {3 L}
- 1-8-1 O/U on road in Playoffs since 1987
- 4-1 S/U @ home in Divisional Playoffs since 1972
- 0-4 S/U on road in Divisional Playoffs since 1991
- 0-4 O/U on road in Divisional Playoffs since 1991
- 5-1 S/U in NFC Championship since 1972
- 3-0 S/U vs Detroit in Playoffs since 1983
- 3-0 S/U & ATS vs Minnesota in Playoffs since 1983
- 0-3 S/U vs Seattle in Playoffs since 2006
- 0-3 S/U @ San Francisco in Playoffs since 1971
- vs Rams in Playoffs – Home team 4-0 S/U since 1945
- 3-0 S/U @ home in Playoffs on Saturday since 1983 {3-0 ATS}

Washington Commanders   NFC East

FedEx Field   *2023 Schedule + Trends & Angles*   **Coach: Ron Rivera**

DATE		OPPONENT	TURF	WAS	OPP	S/U	LINE	ATS	TOT	O/U	Trends & Angles
9/10/2023	vs	ARIZONA	G								vs Arizona - HOME team 7-1 S/U since 2007
9/17/2023	@	*Denver*	G								vs Denver - Broncos lead Series 8-7
9/24/2023	vs	*BUFFALO*	G								Game 5-1 O/U @ home vs Buffalo since 1972
10/1/2023	@	Philadelphia	G								Game 7-2 O/U @ Philadelphia since 2014
10/5/2023	vs	CHICAGO	G								vs Chicago - Commanders lead series 27-24-1
10/15/2023	@	Atlanta	A								2-6 S/U vs Atlanta since 2006
10/22/2023	@	New York Giants	A								4-10-1 S/U @ New York Giants since 2008
10/29/2023	vs	PHILADELPHIA	G								vs Philadelphia - Commanders leads series 89-83-6
11/5/2023	@	*New England*	A								vs New England - Commanders lead series 6-5 {4 L}
11/12/2023	@	Seattle	A								vs Seattle - Commanders leads series 13-9
11/19/2023	vs	NEW YORK GIANTS	G								vs New York Giants - Giants leads series 108-69-5
11/23/2023	@	Dallas	A								1-6 S/U @ Dallas since 2016
12/3/2023	vs	*MIAMI*	G								Game 0-4 O/U vs Miami since 2007
12/10/2023		BYE									
12/17/2023	@	Los Angeles Rams	G								Game 4-1 O/U @ Los Angeles Rams since 2006
12/24/2023	@	*New York Jets*	A								Game 3-0 O/U @ New York Jets since 1999
12/31/2023	vs	SAN FRANCISCO	G								vs San Francisco - 49ers lead series 21-12-1
1/7/2024	vs	DALLAS	G								3-7 S/U @ home vs Dallas since 2013
1/14/2024											NFC Wild Card
1/21/2024											NFC Divisional Playoff
1/28/2024											NFC Championship
2/11/2024											Super Bowl LVIII @ Las Vegas, NV

Pointspread Analysis		Pointspread Analysis
vs NFC teams		**vs NFC teams**
3-8 S/U on road vs NFC East as 10.5 point or more Dog since 1978		1-6 S/U & ATS vs NFC West as 3.5-7 point Dog since 2008
3-14 S/U on road vs NFC East as 7.5-10 point Dog since 1979		5-2 O/U on road vs NFC West as 3 point or less Dog since 1998
0-4 S/U @ home vs NFC East as 7.5-10 point Dog since 2003		0-5 O/U @ home vs NFC West as 3 point or less Dog since 2001
3-7 ATS vs NFC East as 3.5-7 point Dog since 2017		7-0 S/U vs NFC West as 3 point or less favorite since 1981
2-9 S/U vs NFC East as 3.5-7 point Dog since 2016		0-5 O/U vs NFC West as 3 point or less favorite since 1986
3-11-1 S/U on road vs NFC East as 3 point or less favorite s/1991		6-0-1 ATS vs NFC West as 3 point or less favorite since 1981
1-12 ATS vs NFC East as 10.5 point or more favorite since 1980		8-0 S/U @ home vs NFC West as 3.5-7 point favorite since 1986
5-1 ATS vs Dallas as 10.5 point or more Dog since 1995		7-2 S/U @ home vs NFC West as 7.5-10 point favorite since 1980
5-2 ATS vs Dallas as 7.5-10 point Dog since 1979		18-3 S/U vs NFC West as 3.5-7 point favorite since 1983
2-8 S/U @ Dallas as 3.5-7 point Dog since 1981		0-6 ATS vs NFC West as 7.5-10 point favorite since 1987
0-5 S/U & ATS @ Dallas as 3 point or less favorite since 1992		9-1 S/U vs NFC West as 10.5 point or more favorite since 1978
0-3 ATS vs Dallas as 3.5-7 point favorite since 2000		8-0 S/U @ home vs Arizona as 3.5-7 point favorite since 1980
3-12 S/U vs New York Giants as 3.5-7 point Dog since 1986		12-0 S/U @ home vs Arizona as 3.5-7 point favorite since 1979
2-9 O/U vs New York Giants as 3.5-7 point Dog since 2006		0-5 S/U vs San Francisco as 7.5-10 point Dog since 1991
7-1-1 O/U @ home vs NY Giants as 3 point or less favorite s/1985		0-5 O/U vs San Francisco as 7.5-10 point Dog since 1991
1-7-1 O/U vs NY Giants as 3.5-7 point favorite since 1997		0-8 S/U vs San Francisco as 3.5-7 point Dog since 1985
0-9 S/U vs Philadelphia as 7.5-10 point Dog since 2002		1-7 ATS vs San Francisco as 3.5-7 point Dog since 1985
1-7 O/U vs Philadelphia as 3 point or less Dog since 1995		4-0 S/U @ home vs San Francisco as 10.5 point or more favorite s/1978
1-4 O/U @ home vs Philadelphia as 3 point or less favorite s/1992		0-3 O/U vs Seattle as 7.5-10 point Dog since 1998
9-2 S/U @ home vs Philadelphia as 3.5-7 point favorite since 1978		**Dog**
3-1 O/U @ Philadelphia as 3.5-7 point favorite since 1987		5-16 S/U on road as 10.5 point or more Dog since 1978
3-0 S/U vs Philadelphia as 7.5-10 point favorite since 1984		5-19 S/U on road as 7.5-10 point Dog since 2002
0-4 S/U vs NFC North as 7.5 point or more Dog since 1993		1-7 S/U @ home as 7.5-10 point Dog since 2003
5-1 ATS vs NFC North as 3.5-7 point Dog since 2003		3-12 S/U on road as 3.5-7 point Dog since 2016 {4-11 ATS}
7-2 O/U vs NFC North as 3 point or less favorite since 2007		1-7 O/U @ home as 3.5-7 point dog since 2020
1-8 O/U vs NFC North as 3.5-7 point favorite since 1990		**Favorite**
0-4 ATS on road vs NFC North as 3.5-7 point favorite since 1983		32-8 S/U @ home as 7.5-10 point favorite since 1978
12-1 S/U vs NFC North as 7.5 point or more favorite since 1978		7-1 S/U on road as 7.5-10 point favorite since 1986
5-1 S/U @ home vs NFC North as 3 point or less favorite s/1981		1-7 ATS @ home as 10.5 point or more favorite since 1992
4-0 S/U & ATS vs Chicago as 3 point or less Dog since 1989		**Grass/Turf**
5-0 S/U & ATS vs Chicago as 3.5-7 point favorite since 1991		3-13 S/U on Turf as 10.5 point or more Dog since 1978
0-5 ATS vs Chicago as 3.5-7 point favorite since 1978		4-13 S/U on Turf as 7.5-10 point Dog since 2002
4-1 O/U vs NFC South as 7.5-10 point Dog since 2009		0-5 S/U on Turf vs AFC as 7.5-10 point Dog since 1988
2-8 S/U on road vs NFC South as 3.5-7 point Dog since 2000		2-12 S/U on road on grass as 7.5 or more Dog since 1993
8-3 ATS on road vs NFC South as 3.5-7 point Dog since 1982		7-22 S/U on road on grass as 3.5-7 point Dog since 2002
1-5 ATS vs NFC South as 3 point or less favorite since 2005		2-10 ATS on Turf as 3.5-7 point favorite since 1999
1-4 ATS vs NFC South as 7 point or more Dog since 1989		12-0 S/U on road on grass as 3.5-7 point favorite since 1988
0-3 S/U @ Atlanta as 3.5-7 point Dog since 1978		5-0 ATS on Turf as 7.5-10 point favorite since 1987
vs Atlanta - Commanders leads series 16-10-1		0-3 ATS on road on grass as 7.5-10 point favorite since 1980
1-7 O/U vs NFC West as 7.5-10 point Dog since 1991		12-2 S/U on Turf as 7.5 point or more favorite since 1978
4-1 O/U on road vs NFC West as 3.5-7 point Dog since 2001		

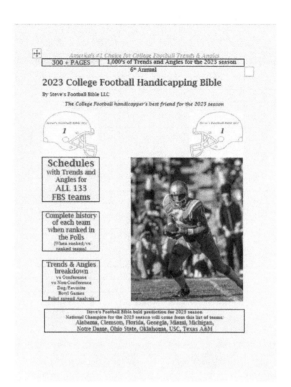

To order the College Football Bible go to: https://stevesfootballbible.com/

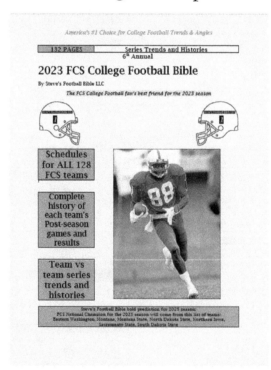

To order the FCS College Football Bible go to: https://stevesfootballbible.com/

2023 Thursday Night/Sunday Night/Monday Night Schedule

Prime Video			*2023 THURSDAY NIGHT FOOTBALL*									
	VISITOR		HOME	TURF	SC	ORE	S/U	LINE	ATS	TOTAL	O/U
9/7/2023	Detroit	@	KANSAS CITY	G							
9/14/2023	Minnesota	@	PHILADELPHIA	G							
9/21/2023	New York Giants	@	SAN FRANCISCO 49ers	G							
9/28/2023	Detroit	@	GREEN BAY	G							
10/5/2023	Chicago	@	WASHINGTON	G							
10/12/2023	Denver	@	KANSAS CITY	G							
10/19/2023	Jacksonville	@	NEW ORLEANS	A							
10/26/2023	Tampa Bay	@	BUFFALO	A							
11/2/2023	Tennessee	@	PITTSBURGH	G							
11/9/2023	Carolina	@	CHICAGO	G							
11/16/2023	Cincinnati	@	BALTIMORE	A							
11/23/2023	Green Bay	@	DETROIT	A							
11/23/2023	Washington	@	DALLAS	A							
11/23/2023	Seattle	@	SAN FRANCISCO 49ers	G							
11/30/2023	Seattle	@	DALLAS	A							
12/7/2023	New England	@	PITTSBURGH	G							
12/14/2023	Los Angeles Chargers	@	LAS VEGAS	G							
12/21/2023	New Orleans	@	LOS ANGELES RAMS	G							
12/28/2023	New York Jets	@	CLEVELAND	G							
NBC			*2023 SUNDAY NIGHT FOOTBALL*						8:20 PM EST			
9/10/2023	Dallas	@	NEW YORK GIANTS	A							
9/17/2023	Miami	@	NEW ENGLAND	A							
9/24/2023	Pittsburgh	@	LAS VEGAS	G							
10/1/2023	Kansas City	@	NEW YORK JETS	A							
10/8/2023	Dallas	@	SAN FRANCISCO 49ers	G							
10/15/2023	New York Giants	@	BUFFALO	A							
10/22/2023	Miami	@	PHILADELPHIA	G							
10/29/2023	Chicago	@	L.A. CHARGERS	G							
11/5/2023	Buffalo	@	CINCINNATI	A							
11/12/2023	New York Jets	@	LAS VEGAS	G							
11/19/2023	Minnesota	@	DENVER	G							
11/26/2023	Baltimore	@	L.A. CHARGERS	G							
12/3/2023	Kansas City	@	GREEN BAY	G							
12/10/2023	Philadelphia	@	DALLAS	A							
12/17/2023	Baltimore	@	JACKSONVILLE	G							
12/24/2023	New England	@	DENVER	G							
12/31/2023	Green Bay	@	MINNESOTA	A							
1/7/2024	TBD	@	TBD								

2023 Thursday Night/Sunday Night/Monday Night Schedule

ABC/ESPN			2023 MONDAY NIGHT FOOTBALL								8:15 PM EST	
9/11/2023	Buffalo	@	NEW YORK JETS	A								
9/18/2023	New Orleans	@	CAROLINA	G								
9/18/2023	Cleveland	@	PITTSBURGH	G								
9/25/2023	Philadelphia	@	TAMPA BAY	G								
9/25/2023	Los Angeles Rams	@	CINCINNATI	A								
10/2/2023	Seattle	@	NEW YORK GIANTS	A								
10/9/2023	Green Bay	@	LAS VEGAS	G								
10/16/2023	Dallas	@	L.A. CHARGERS	G								
10/23/2023	San Francisco	@	MINNESOTA	A								
10/30/2023	Las Vegas	@	DETROIT	A								
11/6/2023	Los Angeles Chargers	@	NEW YORK JETS	A								
11/13/2023	Denver	@	BUFFALO	A								
11/20/2023	Philadelphia	@	KANSAS CITY	G								
11/27/2023	Chicago	@	MINNESOTA	A								
12/4/2023	Cincinnati	@	JACKSONVILLE	G								
12/11/2023	Tennessee	@	MIAMI	G								
12/11/2023	Green Bay	@	NEW YORK GIANTS	A								
12/18/2023	Kansas City	@	NEW ENGLAND	A								
12/25/2023	Baltimore	@	SAN FRANCISCO	G								

Thursday Night Football History

	VISITOR		HOME	TURF	SC	ORE	S/U	LINE	ATS	TOTAL	O/U
12/29/2022	Dallas	@	TENNESSEE	G	27	13	W	-13.5	W	40.5	U
12/22/2022	Jacksonville	@	NEW YORK JETS	A	19	3	W	2.5	W	36.5	U
12/15/2022	San Francisco	@	SEATTLE	A	21	13	W	-3.0	W	42.5	U
12/8/2022	Las Vegas Raiders	@	LOS ANGELES RAMS	A	16	17	L	-6.0	L	42.5	U
12/1/2022	Buffalo	@	NEW ENGLAND	A	24	14	W	-4.0	W	44.0	U
11/24/2022	Buffalo	@	DETROIT	A	28	25	W	-9.5	L	54.0	U
11/24/2022	New York Giants	@	DALLAS	A	20	28	L	10.0	W	45.5	O
11/24/2022	New England	@	MINNESOTA	A	26	33	L	2.5	L	41.5	O
11/17/2022	Tennessee	@	GREEN BAY	G	27	17	W	3.0	W	40.5	O
11/10/2022	Atlanta	@	CAROLINA	G	15	25	L	-2.5	L	41.5	U
11/3/2022	Philadelphia	@	HOUSTON	G	29	17	W	-14.0	L	45.0	O
10/27/2022	Baltimore	@	TAMPA BAY	G	27	22	W	2.0	W	46.0	O
10/20/2022	New Orleans	@	ARIZONA	G	42	34	W	2.5	W	44.0	O
10/13/2022	Washington	@	CHICAGO	G	12	7	W	-1.0	W	39.0	U
10/6/2022	Indianapolis	@	DENVER	G	12	9	W	2.0	W	42.0	U
9/29/2022	Miami	@	CINCINNATI	A	15	27	L	4.0	L	48.5	U
9/22/2022	Pittsburgh	@	CLEVELAND	G	17	29	L	4.0	L	38.0	O
9/15/2022	Los Angeles Chargers	@	KANSAS CITY CHIEFS	G	24	27	L	4.0	W	51.5	U
9/8/2022	Buffalo	@	LOS ANGELES RAMS	A	31	10	W	-2.0	W	51.5	U
12/23/2021	San Francisco	@	TENNESSEE	G	17	20	L	-3.5	L	45.0	U
12/16/2021	Kansas City	@	L.A. CHARGERS	G	34	28	W	-3.0	W	53.5	O
12/9/2021	Pittsburgh	@	MINNESOTA	A	28	36	L	3.5	L	45.0	O
12/2/2021	Dallas	@	NEW ORLEANS	A	27	17	W	-6.5	W	45.5	U
11/25/2021	Chicago	@	DETROIT	A	16	14	W	-2.5	L	41.5	U
11/25/2021	Las Vegas Raiders	@	DALLAS	A	36	33	W	7.0	W	51.0	O
11/25/2021	Buffalo	@	NEW ORLEANS	A	31	6	W	-7.0	W	44.5	U
11/18/2021	New England	@	ATLANTA	A	25	0	W	-7.0	W	47.0	U
11/11/2021	Baltimore Ravens	@	MIAMI	G	10	22	L	-8.5	L	46.5	U
11/4/2021	New York Jets	@	INDIANAPOLIS COLTS	A	30	45	L	10.0	L	45.0	O
10/28/2021	Green Bay	@	ARIZONA	G	24	21	W	6.5	W	50.5	U
10/21/2021	Denver	@	CLEVELAND	G	14	17	L	2.0	L	40.5	U
10/14/2021	Tampa Bay	@	PHILADELPHIA	G	28	22	W	-7.0	L	52.0	U
10/7/2021	Los Angeles Rams	@	SEATTLE	A	26	17	W	-2.5	W	53.5	U
9/30/2021	Jacksonville	@	CINCINNATI	A	21	24	L	7.5	W	46.5	U
9/23/2021	Carolina	@	HOUSTON TEXANS	G	24	9	W	-8.5	W	43.5	U
9/16/2021	New York Giants	@	WASHINGTON	G	29	30	L	4.0	W	41.0	O
12/17/2020	Los Angeles Chargers	@	LAS VEGAS RAIDERS	G	30	27	W	3.0	W	52.0	O
12/10/2020	New England Patriots	@	LOS ANGELES RAMS	G	3	24	L	4.5	L	43.5	U
11/26/2020	Houston Texans	@	DETROIT LIONS	A	41	25	W	-3.0	W	52.5	W
11/26/2020	Washington Redskins	@	DALLAS COWBOYS	A	41	16	W	2.5	W	46.0	O
11/19/2020	Arizona Cardinals	@	SEATTLE SEAHAWKS	A	21	28	L	3.0	L	56.5	U
11/12/2020	Indianapolis Colts	@	TENNESSEE TITANS	G	34	17	W	-1.0	W	49.0	O
11/5/2020	Green Bay Packers	@	SAN FRANCISCO 49ERS	G	34	17	W	-5.5	W	48.5	O
10/29/2020	Atlanta Falcons	@	CAROLINA PANTHERS	G	25	17	W	1.0	W	52.0	U
10/22/2020	New York Giants	@	PHILADELPHIA EAGLES	G	21	22	L	4.5	W	44.5	U
10/8/2020	Tampa Bay Buccaneers	@	CHICAGO BEARS	G	19	20	L	-3.5	L	44.0	U
10/1/2020	Denver Broncos	@	NEW YORK JETS	G	37	28	W	1.0	W	41.0	O
9/24/2020	Miami Dolphins	@	JACKSONVILLE JAGUARS	G	31	13	W	2.5	W	49.5	U
9/17/2020	Cincinnati Bengals	@	CLEVELAND BROWNS	G	30	35	L	6.0	W	44.5	O
9/10/2020	Houston Texans	@	KANSAS CITY CHIEFS	G	20	34	L	9.5	L	53.5	O
12/12/2019	New York Jets	@	BALTIMORE RAVENS	A	21	42	L	17	L	43.5	O
12/5/2019	Dallas	@	CHICAGO	G	24	31	L	-3.0	L	43.0	O
11/28/2019	New Orleans	@	ATLANTA	A	26	18	W	-7.0	W	48.0	U
11/28/2019	Buffalo	@	DALLAS	A	26	15	W	6.5	W	46.5	U
11/28/2019	Chicago	@	DETROIT	A	24	20	W	-5.5	L	37.5	O
11/21/2019	Indianapolis Colts	@	HOUSTON TEXANS	G	17	20	L	3.5	W	46.5	U
11/14/2019	Pittsburgh	@	CLEVELAND	G	7	21	L	3.0	L	41.5	U

Thursday Night Football History

Date	Away		Home	Site	Away Score	Home Score	W/L	Line	ATS	Total	O/U
11/7/2019	Los Angeles Chargers	@	OAKLAND RAIDERS	G	24	26	L	-1.0	L	48.5	O
10/31/2019	San Francisco	@	ARIZONA CARDINALS	G	28	25	W	-10.0	L	43.5	O
10/24/2019	Washington	@	MINNESOTA	A	9	19	L	16.5	W	42.0	U
10/17/2019	Kansas City	@	DENVER	G	30	6	W	-3.0	W	49.5	U
10/10/2019	New York Giants	@	NEW ENGLAND PATRIOTS	A	14	35	L	16.5	L	43.0	O
10/3/2019	Los Angeles Rams	@	SEATTLE	A	29	30	L	1.5	W	49.0	O
9/26/2019	Philadelphia	@	GREEN BAY	G	34	27	W	3.5	W	46.5	O
9/19/2019	Tennessee	@	JACKSONVILLE	G	7	20	L	-1.5	L	38.0	U
9/12/2019	Tampa Bay	@	CAROLINA	G	20	14	W	6.5	W	48.0	U
9/5/2019	Green Bay	@	CHICAGO	G	10	3	W	3.0	W	46.5	U
12/13/2018	Los Angeles Chargers	@	KANSAS CITY	G	29	28	W	3.5	W	54.0	O
12/6/2018	Jacksonville	@	TENNESSEE TITANS	G	9	30	L	5.0	L	37.0	O
11/29/2018	New Orleans	@	DALLAS	A	10	13	L	-7.0	L	51.5	U
11/22/2018	Atlanta	@	NEW ORLEANS	A	17	31	L	12.0	L	61.0	U
11/22/2018	Washington Redskins	@	DALLAS	A	23	31	L	7.0	L	40.0	O
11/22/2018	Chicago	@	DETROIT	A	23	16	W	-3.0	W	42.5	U
11/15/2018	Green Bay	@	SEATTLE	A	24	27	L	3.0	T	49.0	O
11/8/2018	Carolina	@	PITTSBURGH	G	21	52	L	3.5	L	51.0	O
11/1/2018	Oakland Raiders	@	SAN FRANCISCO	G	3	34	L	-2.0	L	44.0	U
10/25/2018	Miami	@	HOUSTON TEXANS	G	23	42	L	7.5	L	45.0	O
10/18/2018	Denver	@	ARIZONA CARDINALS	G	45	10	W	-1.0	W	42.0	O
10/11/2018	Philadelphia	@	NEW YORK GIANTS	A	34	13	W	-2.0	W	45.5	O
10/4/2018	Indianapolis Colts	@	NEW ENGLAND PATRIOTS	A	24	38	L	10.5	L	49.5	O
9/27/2018	Minnesota	@	LOS ANGELES RAMS	G	31	38	L	7.0	T	48.0	O
9/20/2018	New York Jets	@	CLEVELAND	G	17	21	L	3.0	L	41.0	U
9/13/2018	Baltimore Ravens	@	CINCINNATI	A	23	34	L	PK	L	43.0	O
9/6/2018	Atlanta	@	PHILADELPHIA	G	12	18	L	PK	L	44.0	U
12/14/2017	Denver	@	INDIANAPOLIS COLTS	A	25	13	W	-2.5	W	40.5	U
12/7/2017	New Orleans	@	ATLANTA	A	17	20	L	2.5	L	51.5	U
11/30/2017	Washington Redskins	@	DALLAS	A	14	38	L	-1.5	L	46.5	O
11/23/2017	New York Giants	@	WASHINGTON REDSKINS	G	10	20	L	7.0	L	44.0	U
11/23/2017	Los Angeles Chargers	@	DALLAS	A	28	6	W	-1.0	W	46.5	U
11/23/2017	Minnesota	@	DETROIT	A	30	23	W	-2.5	W	45.0	O
11/16/2017	Tennessee Titans	@	PITTSBURGH	G	17	40	L	7.0	L	44.5	O
11/9/2017	Seattle	@	ARIZONA CARDINALS	G	22	16	W	-6.0	W	40.0	U
11/2/2017	Buffalo	@	NEW YORK JETS	A	21	34	L	-3.0	L	42.0	O
10/26/2017	Miami	@	BALTIMORE RAVENS	A	0	40	L	3.0	L	38.0	O
10/19/2017	Kansas City	@	OAKLAND RAIDERS	G	30	31	L	-3.0	L	46.5	O
10/12/2017	Philadelphia	@	CAROLINA	G	28	23	W	3.0	W	43.5	O
10/5/2017	New England Patriots	@	TAMPA BAY	G	19	14	W	-3.5	W	54.5	U
9/28/2017	Chicago	@	GREEN BAY	G	14	35	L	7.0	L	44.0	O
9/21/2017	Los Angeles Rams	@	SAN FRANCISCO	G	41	39	W	-3.0	L	40.5	O
9/14/2017	Houston Texans	@	CINCINNATI	A	13	9	W	5.5	W	38.5	U
9/7/2017	Kansas City	@	NEW ENGLAND PATRIOTS	A	42	27	W	8.0	W	47.5	O
12/22/2016	New York Giants	@	PHILADELPHIA	G	19	24	L	2.0	L	42.5	O
12/15/2016	Los Angeles Rams	@	SEATTLE	A	3	24	L	15.0	L	39.5	U
12/8/2016	Oakland Raiders	@	KANSAS CITY	G	13	21	L	3.5	L	46.0	U
12/1/2016	Dallas	@	MINNESOTA	A	17	15	W	-3.0	L	43.5	U
11/24/2016	Pittsburgh	@	INDIANAPOLIS COLTS	A	28	7	W	-8.0	W	50.0	U
11/24/2016	Washington Redskins	@	DALLAS	A	26	31	L	5.5	W	53.0	O
11/24/2016	Minnesota	@	DETROIT	A	13	16	L	2.0	L	42.0	U
11/17/2016	New Orleans	@	CAROLINA	G	20	23	L	3.5	W	52.5	U
11/10/2016	Cleveland	@	BALTIMORE RAVENS	A	7	28	L	7.5	L	44.0	U
11/3/2016	Atlanta	@	TAMPA BAY	G	43	28	W	-4.5	W	49.0	O
10/27/2016	Jacksonville	@	TENNESSEE TITANS	G	22	36	L	3.0	L	43.5	O
10/20/2016	Chicago	@	GREEN BAY	G	10	26	L	7.5	L	46.5	U
10/13/2016	Denver	@	SAN DIEGO CHARGERS	G	13	21	L	-3.0	L	44.0	U
10/6/2016	Arizona Cardinals	@	SAN FRANCISCO	G	31	21	W	-3.5	W	43.0	O

Thursday Night Football History

Date	Visitor	@	Home	G/A	V	H	W/L	Spread	W/L	Total	O/U
9/29/2016	Miami	@	**CINCINNATI**	A	7	22	L	7.5	L	46.5	U
9/22/2016	Houston Texans	@	**NEW ENGLAND PATRIOTS**	A	0	27	L	1.0	L	38.5	U
9/15/2016	**New York Jets**	@	BUFFALO	A	37	31	W	1.0	W	40.5	O
12/24/2015	San Diego	@	**OAKLAND RAIDERS**	G	20	23	L	4.0	W	45.0	U
12/17/2015	Tampa Bay	@	**ST. LOUIS RAMS**	A	23	31	L	1.0	L	41.5	O
12/10/2015	Minnesota	@	**ARIZONA CARDINALS**	G	20	23	L	10.0	W	46.0	U
12/3/2015	**Green Bay**	@	DETROIT	A	27	23	W	-2.5	W	46.0	O
11/26/2015	Philadelphia	@	**DETROIT**	A	14	45	L	3.0	L	47.0	O
11/26/2015	**Carolina**	@	DALLAS	A	33	14	W	-1.0	W	44.0	O
11/26/2015	**Chicago**	@	GREEN BAY	G	17	13	W	7.5	W	45.0	U
11/19/2015	Tennessee	@	**JACKSONVILLE**	G	13	19	L	3.0	L	41.5	U
11/12/2015	**Buffalo**	@	NEW YORK JETS	A	22	17	W	2.5	W	41.5	U
11/5/2015	Cleveland	@	**CINCINNATI**	A	10	31	L	13.0	L	46.0	U
10/29/2015	Miami	@	**NEW ENGLAND PATRIOTS**	A	7	36	L	8.0	L	51.0	U
10/22/2015	**Seattle**	@	SAN FRANCISCO	G	20	3	W	-6.5	W	42.0	U
10/15/2015	Atlanta	@	**NEW ORLEANS**	A	21	31	L	-3.0	L	52.0	T
10/8/2015	**Indianapolis**	@	HOUSTON TEXANS	G	27	20	W	4.5	W	40.5	O
10/1/2015	**Baltimore**	@	PITTSBURGH	G	23	20	W	-3.0	T	44.0	U
9/24/2015	Washington	@	**NEW YORK GIANTS**	A	21	32	L	3.0	L	45.0	O
9/17/2015	**Denver**	@	KANSAS CITY	G	31	24	W	3.0	W	42.0	O
9/10/2015	Pittsburgh	@	**NEW ENGLAND PATRIOTS**	A	21	28	L	7.0	T	51.0	U
12/18/2014	**Tennessee Titans**	@	JACKSONVILLE	G	21	13	W	-4.5	W	44.5	U
12/11/2014	Arizona Cardinals	@	**ST. LOUIS RAMS**	A	6	12	L	-6.0	L	40.5	U
12/4/2014	Dallas	@	**CHICAGO**	G	28	41	L	4.0	L	50.5	O
11/27/2014	Philadelphia	@	**DALLAS**	A	10	33	L	-3.0	L	56.0	U
11/27/2014	**Chicago**	@	DETROIT	A	34	17	W	-7.0	W	46.0	O
11/27/2014	Seattle	@	**SAN FRANCISCO**	G	3	19	L	-1.5	L	40.0	U
11/20/2014	**Kansas City**	@	OAKLAND RAIDERS	G	24	20	W	7.0	W	42.0	O
11/13/2014	**Buffalo**	@	MIAMI	G	22	9	W	-4.0	W	40.5	U
11/6/2014	Cleveland	@	**CINCINNATI**	A	3	24	L	-6.5	L	45.5	U
10/30/2014	New Orleans	@	**CAROLINA**	G	10	28	L	3.0	L	49.0	U
10/23/2014	**San Diego Chargers**	@	DENVER	G	35	21	W	-9.0	W	50.5	O
10/16/2014	**New York Jets**	@	NEW ENGLAND PATRIOTS	A	27	25	W	-9.5	L	44.0	O
10/9/2014	Indianapolis Colts	@	**HOUSTON TEXANS**	G	28	33	L	2.5	L	45.5	O
10/2/2014	**Minnesota**	@	GREEN BAY	G	42	10	W	-9.0	W	46.5	O
9/25/2014	New York Giants	@	**WASHINGTON REDSKINS**	G	14	45	L	-3.0	L	44.5	O
9/18/2014	**Tampa Bay**	@	ATLANTA	A	56	14	W	-6.5	W	47.0	O
9/11/2014	**Pittsburgh**	@	BALTIMORE RAVENS	A	26	6	W	-2.5	W	44.0	O
9/4/2014	**Green Bay**	@	SEATTLE	A	36	16	W	-4.5	W	46.5	O
12/12/2013	San Diego Chargers	@	**DENVER**	G	20	27	L	-10.0	L	56.5	U
12/5/2013	**Houston Texans**	@	JACKSONVILLE	G	27	20	W	3.0	W	42.5	O
11/28/2013	Pittsburgh	@	**BALTIMORE RAVENS**	A	22	20	W	-3.0	L	40.5	O
11/28/2013	**Oakland Raiders**	@	DALLAS	A	31	24	W	-9.5	L	51.0	O
11/28/2013	**Green Bay**	@	DETROIT	A	40	10	W	-6.5	W	48.0	O
11/21/2013	New Orleans	@	**ATLANTA**	A	13	17	L	7.5	W	53.0	U
11/14/2013	Indianapolis Colts	@	**TENNESSEE TITANS**	G	27	30	L	2.5	W	43.0	O
11/7/2013	**Washington Redskins**	@	MINNESOTA	A	34	27	W	1.0	W	48.5	O
10/31/2013	**Cincinnati (OT)**	@	MIAMI	G	22	20	W	3.0	W	43.0	U
10/24/2013	Carolina	@	**TAMPA BAY**	G	13	31	L	7.0	L	39.0	O
10/17/2013	Seattle	@	**ARIZONA CARDINALS**	G	22	34	L	5.0	L	40.5	O
10/10/2013	**New York Giants**	@	CHICAGO	G	27	21	W	-9.5	L	47.0	O
10/3/2013	**Buffalo**	@	CLEVELAND	G	37	24	W	-3.5	W	41.0	O
9/26/2013	San Francisco	@	**ST. LOUIS RAMS**	A	11	35	L	3.0	L	42.5	O
9/22/2013	Kansas City	@	**PHILADELPHIA**	A	14	26	L	-3.0	L	50.0	U
9/12/2013	**New York Jets**	@	NEW ENGLAND PATRIOTS	A	13	10	W	-10.5	L	43.0	U
9/5/2013	**Baltimore**	@	DENVER	G	49	27	W	-7.0	W	47.5	O
12/13/2012	Cincinnati	@	**PHILADELPHIA**	A	13	34	L	4.5	L	44.5	O
12/6/2012	Denver	@	**OAKLAND RAIDERS**	G	13	26	L	10.0	L	47.0	U

Thursday Night Football History

11/29/2012	New Orleans	@	ATLANTA	A	23	13	W	-3.5	W	54.0	U		
11/22/2012	Washington Redskins	@	DALLAS	A	31	38	L	-3.5	L	47.0	O		
11/22/2012	Houston {OT}	@	DETROIT	A	31	34	L	3.0	T	49.0	O		
11/22/2012	New England Patriots	@	NEW YORK JETS	A	19	49	L	7.0	L	48.5	O		
11/15/2012	Miami	@	BUFFALO	A	19	14	W	-2.5	W	46.5	U		
11/8/2012	Indianapolis Colts	@	JACKSONVILLE	G	10	27	L	3.0	L	43.5	U		
11/1/2012	Kansas City	@	SAN DIEGO CHARGERS	G	31	13	W	-7.0	W	41.0	O		
10/25/2012	Tampa Bay	@	MINNESOTA	A	17	36	L	-5.0	L	43.0	O		
10/18/2012	Seattle	@	SAN FRANCISCO	G	13	6	W	-7.5	L	37.5	U		
10/11/2012	Pittsburgh	@	TENNESSEE TITANS	G	26	23	W	5.5	W	42.5	O		
10/4/2012	Arizona	@	ST. LOUIS RAMS	A	17	3	W	1.5	W	38.0	U		
9/27/2012	Cleveland	@	BALTIMORE RAVENS	A	23	16	W	-11.0	L	43.5	U		
9/20/2012	New York Giants	@	CAROLINA	G	7	36	L	-3.0	L	48.5	U		
9/13/2012	Chicago	@	GREEN BAY	G	23	10	W	-5.0	W	50.5	U		
12/22/2011	Houston Texans	@	INDIANAPOLIS COLTS	A	19	16	W	6.5	W	40.5	U		
12/15/2011	Jacksonville	@	ATLANTA	A	41	14	W	-11.5	W	42.5	O		
12/8/2011	Cleveland	@	PITTSBURGH	G	14	3	W	-14.5	L	39.5	U		
12/1/2011	Philadelphia	@	SEATTLE	A	31	14	W	3.0	W	43.5	O		
11/24/2011	San Francisco	@	BALTIMORE RAVENS	A	16	6	W	-3.5	W	39.5	U		
11/24/2011	Miami	@	DALLAS	A	20	19	W	-7.5	L	45.0	U		
11/24/2011	Green Bay	@	DETROIT	A	15	27	L	5.5	L	55.0	U		
11/17/2011	New York Jets	@	DENVER	G	17	13	W	6.0	W	40.5	U		
11/10/2011	Oakland Raiders	@	SAN DIEGO CHARGERS	G	17	24	L	-7.5	L	47.5	U		
9/8/2011	New Orleans	@	GREEN BAY	G	42	34	W	-4.5	W	47.5	O		
12/23/2010	Carolina	@	PITTSBURGH	G	27	3	W	-14.5	W	37.0	U		
12/16/2010	San Francisco	@	SAN DIEGO CHARGERS	G	34	7	W	-10.5	W	44.5	U		
12/9/2010	Indianapolis Colts	@	TENNESSEE TITANS	G	28	30	L	3.0	W	44.5	O		
12/2/2010	Houston Texans	@	PHILADELPHIA	A	34	24	W	-8.5	W	51.0	O		
11/25/2010	New Orleans	@	DALLAS	A	27	30	L	+3.5	W	50.0	O		
11/25/2010	New England Patriots	@	DETROIT	A	24	45	L	7.0	L	50.5	O		
11/25/2010	Cincinnati	@	NEW YORK JETS	A	26	10	W	-10.0	W	43.0	U		
11/18/2010	Chicago	@	MIAMI	G	0	16	L	-2.0	L	40.0	U		
11/11/2010	Baltimore	@	ATLANTA	A	26	21	W	-1.0	W	43.5	O		
9/9/2010	Minnesota	@	NEW ORLEANS	A	14	9	W	-5.0	T	48.5	U		
12/17/2009	Indianapolis Colts	@	JACKSONVILLE	G	31	35	L	3.0	L	43.0	O		
12/10/2009	Pittsburgh	@	CLEVELAND	G	13	6	W	10.0	W	33.5	U		
12/3/2009	New York Jets	@	BUFFALO	A	13	19	L	3.0	L	37.0	U		
11/26/2009	Oakland Raiders	@	DALLAS	A	24	7	W	-13.5	W	40.0	U		
11/26/2009	New York Giants	@	DENVER	G	26	6	W	5.5	W	42.0	U		
11/26/2009	Green Bay	@	DETROIT	A	12	34	L	11.0	L	47.5	U		
11/19/2009	Miami	@	CAROLINA	G	17	24	L	-3.0	L	42.5	U		
11/12/2009	Chicago	@	SAN FRANCISCO	G	10	6	W	-3.0	W	43.0	U		
9/10/2009	Tennessee (OT)	@	PITTSBURGH	G	13	10	W	-6.0	L	35.5	U		
12/18/2008	Indianapolis Colts	@	JACKSONVILLE	G	24	31	L	6.5	L	44.0	O		
12/11/2008	New Orleans (OT)	@	CHICAGO	G	27	24	W	-3.0	T	45.0	O		
12/4/2008	Oakland Raiders	@	SAN DIEGO CHARGERS	G	34	7	W	-10.0	W	42.5	U		
11/27/2008	Seattle	@	DALLAS	A	34	9	W	-12.0	W	46.0	U		
11/27/2008	Tennessee	@	DETROIT	A	10	47	L	11.0	L	44.5	O		
11/27/2008	Arizona Cardinals	@	PHILADELPHIA	A	48	20	W	-3.0	W	48.0	O		
11/20/2008	Cincinnati	@	PITTSBURGH	G	27	10	W	-11.0	W	34.5	O		
11/13/2008	New York Jets (OT)	@	NEW ENGLAND PATRIOTS	A	31	34	L	-3.5	L	41.0	O		
11/6/2008	Denver	@	CLEVELAND	G	30	34	L	-3.0	L	46.5	O		
9/4/2008	Washington Redskins	@	NEW YORK GIANTS	A	16	7	W	-4.0	W	41.0	U		
12/20/2007	Pittsburgh	@	ST. LOUIS RAMS	A	24	41	L	8.0	L	43.0	O		
12/13/2007	Denver	@	HOUSTON TEXANS	G	31	13	W	1.5	W	47.0	O		
12/6/2007	Chicago	@	WASHINGTON REDSKINS	G	24	16	W	-3.0	W	38.0	O		
11/29/2007	Green Bay	@	DALLAS	A	37	27	W	-7.0	W	51.0	O		
11/22/2007	Indianapolis Colts	@	ATLANTA	A	13	31	L	12.0	L	41.5	O		

Thursday Night Football History

Date	Team		Opponent								
11/22/2007	New York Jets	@	DALLAS	A	34	3	W	-14.0	W	47.5	U
11/22/2007	Green Bay	@	DETROIT	A	26	37	L	3.5	L	47.0	O
9/6/2007	New Orleans	@	INDIANAPOLIS COLTS	A	41	10	W	-6.0	W	52.5	U
12/21/2006	Minnesota	@	GREEN BAY	G	9	7	W	-3.5	L	37.0	U
12/14/2006	San Francisco	@	SEATTLE	A	14	24	L	-10.0	L	39.0	U
12/7/2006	Cleveland	@	PITTSBURGH	G	27	7	W	-7.0	W	34.0	T
11/30/2006	Baltimore	@	CINCINNATI	A	13	7	W	-3.0	W	42.5	U
11/23/2006	Tampa Bay	@	DALLAS	A	38	10	W	-11.0	W	39.0	O
11/23/2006	Miami	@	DETROIT	A	10	27	L	3.0	L	40.0	U
11/23/2006	Denver	@	KANSAS CITY	G	19	10	W	-1.5	W	38.0	U
9/7/2006	Miami	@	PITTSBURGH	G	28	17	W	-1.0	W	35.5	O
11/24/2005	Denver (OT)	@	DALLAS	A	21	24	L	2.0	L	41.5	O
11/24/2005	Atlanta	@	DETROIT	A	7	27	L	3.0	L	42.0	U
9/8/2005	Oakland Raiders	@	NEW ENGLAND PATRIOTS	A	30	20	W	-7.5	W	49.5	O
11/25/2004	Chicago	@	DALLAS	A	21	7	W	-3.5	W	36.0	U
11/25/2004	Indianapolis Colts	@	DETROIT	A	9	41	L	9.0	L	53.5	U
9/9/2004	Indianapolis Colts	@	NEW ENGLAND PATRIOTS	A	27	24	W	-3.0	T	44.5	O
11/27/2003	Miami	@	DALLAS	A	21	40	L	-3.0	L	34.5	O
11/27/2003	Green Bay	@	DETROIT	A	22	14	W	7.0	W	44.5	U
9/4/2003	New York Jets	@	WASHINGTON REDSKINS	G	16	13	W	-3.0	T	40.0	U
11/28/2002	Washington Redskins	@	DALLAS	A	27	20	W	1.0	W	35.5	O
11/28/2002	New England Patriots	@	DETROIT	A	12	20	L	5.5	L	45.0	U
9/5/2002	San Francisco	@	NEW YORK GIANTS	A	13	16	L	3.5	W	39.5	U
11/29/2001	Philadelphia	@	KANSAS CITY	G	10	23	L	3.0	L	37.0	U
11/22/2001	Denver	@	DALLAS	A	24	26	L	6.5	W	39.5	O
11/22/2001	Green Bay	@	DETROIT	A	27	29	L	6.5	W	48.0	O
10/25/2001	Indianapolis Colts	@	KANSAS CITY	G	28	35	L	3.0	L	47.0	O
10/18/2001	Buffalo	@	JACKSONVILLE	G	10	13	L	-8.5	L	39.0	U
11/30/2000	Detroit	@	MINNESOTA	A	24	17	W	-9.0	L	48.0	U
11/23/2000	Minnesota	@	DALLAS	A	15	27	L	7.5	L	48.0	U
11/23/2000	New England Patriots	@	DETROIT	A	34	9	W	-6.5	W	38.5	O
10/19/2000	Detroit	@	TAMPA BAY	G	14	28	L	-8.0	L	37.5	O
12/9/1999	Oakland Raiders	@	TENNESSEE TITANS	G	21	14	W	-3.0	W	40.0	U
12/2/1999	Pittsburgh	@	JACKSONVILLE	G	20	6	W	-10.5	W	37.0	U
11/25/1999	Miami	@	DALLAS	A	20	0	W	-1.5	W	37.5	U
11/25/1999	Chicago	@	DETROIT	A	21	17	W	-6.0	W	44.5	U
10/21/1999	Kansas City	@	BALTIMORE RAVENS	A	8	35	L	1.0	L	35.5	O
12/3/1998	St. Louis Rams	@	PHILADELPHIA	A	17	14	W	-1.5	W	35.0	U
11/26/1998	Minnesota	@	DALLAS	A	36	46	L	3.0	L	46.5	O
11/26/1998	Pittsburgh (OT)	@	DETROIT	A	19	16	W	2.0	W	41.0	U
10/15/1998	Green Bay	@	DETROIT	A	27	20	W	7.0	W	45.0	O
12/4/1997	Tennessee	@	CINCINNATI	A	41	14	W	2.5	W	43.0	O
11/27/1997	Tennessee	@	DALLAS	A	14	27	L	-6.5	L	37.5	O
11/27/1997	Chicago	@	DETROIT	A	55	20	W	-8.0	W	44.0	O
10/16/1997	San Diego Chargers	@	KANSAS CITY	G	31	3	W	-6.0	W	40.5	O
12/5/1996	Philadelphia	@	INDIANAPOLIS COLTS	A	37	10	W	4.0	W	38.0	O
11/28/1996	Washington Redskins	@	DALLAS	A	21	10	W	-8.5	W	42.0	U
11/28/1996	Kansas City	@	DETROIT	A	24	28	L	2.0	L	42.0	O
10/17/1996	Seattle	@	KANSAS CITY	G	34	16	W	-9.0	W	37.5	O
11/30/1995	New York Giants	@	ARIZONA CARDINALS	G	6	10	L	-2.0	L	41.0	U
11/23/1995	Kansas City	@	DALLAS	A	24	12	W	-11.5	W	43.0	U
11/23/1995	Minnesota	@	DETROIT	A	44	38	W	-3.0	W	46.5	O
10/19/1995	Cincinnati	@	PITTSBURGH	A	9	27	L	-8.0	L	41.0	U
10/12/1995	Atlanta	@	ST. LOUIS RAMS	A	21	19	W	-3.0	L	43.5	U
12/1/1994	Chicago (OT)	@	MINNESOTA	A	33	27	W	-5.5	W	36.5	O
11/24/1994	Green Bay	@	DALLAS	A	42	31	W	-6.5	W	35.0	O
11/24/1994	Buffalo	@	DETROIT	A	35	21	W	1.5	W	39.0	O
10/20/1994	Green Bay (OT)	@	MINNESOTA	A	13	10	W	-4.5	L	37.0	U

Thursday Night Football History

Date	Visitor		Home		Score	Score		Line		Total	
10/13/1994	Cleveland Browns	@	HOUSTON OILERS	A	8	11	L	2.0	L	37.0	U
11/25/1993	Miami	@	DALLAS	A	14	16	L	-9.5	L	36.5	U
11/25/1993	Chicago	@	DETROIT	A	6	10	L	-7.5	L	36.5	U
10/14/1993	Los Angeles Rams	@	ATLANTA	A`	30	24	W	1.0	W	43.0	O
12/3/1992	Atlanta	@	NEW ORLEANS	A	22	14	W	-10.5	L	38.0	U
11/26/1992	New York Giants	@	DALLAS	A	30	3	W	-16.0	W	40.0	U
11/26/1992	Houston Oilers	@	DETROIT	A	21	24	L	1.0	L	40.0	O
10/15/1992	Detroit	@	MINNESOTA	A	31	14	W	-5.5	W	43.0	O
12/4/1991	Chicago	@	DETROIT	A	16	6	W	-3.0	W	41.0	U
11/28/1991	Pittsburgh	@	DALLAS	A	20	10	W	-6.5	W	39.5	U
10/21/1991	Chicago	@	GREEN BAY	G	0	10	L	3.5	L	35.5	U
11/22/1990	Washington Redskins	@	DALLAS	A	27	17	W	5.5	W	38.0	O
11/22/1990	Denver	@	DETROIT	A	40	27	W	-1.0	W	44.5	O
10/18/1990	New England Patriots	@	MIAMI	G	17	10	W	-10.0	L	42.0	U
11/23/1989	Philadelphia	@	DALLAS	A	0	27	L	6.5	L	39.5	U
11/23/1989	Cleveland	@	DETROIT	A	13	10	W	7.0	W	40.0	U
11/24/1988	Houston Oilers	@	DALLAS	A	17	25	L	6.0	L	47.0	U
11/24/1988	Minnesota	@	DETROIT	A	0	23	L	6.5	L	38.0	U
11/26/1987	Minnesota (OT)	@	DALLAS	A	38	44	L	1.5	L	44.0	O
11/26/1987	Kansas City	@	DETROIT	A	20	27	L	-6.0	L	43.0	O
11/27/1986	Seattle	@	DALLAS	A	14	31	L	-8.5	L	42.0	O
11/27/1986	Green Bay	@	DETROIT	A	40	44	L	-6.0	L	40.0	O
11/20/1986	Los Angeles Raiders (OT)	@	SAN DIEGO CHARGERS	G	31	37	L	6.5	W	43.0	O
9/18/1986	Cincinnati	@	CLEVELAND BROWNS	G	13	30	L	-4.5	U	46.5	U
9/11/1986	New England Patriots	@	NEW YORK JETS	A	6	20	L	-1.5	L	42.0	U
11/28/1985	St. Louis Cardinals	@	DALLAS	A	35	17	W	-14.0	W	41.0	O
11/28/1985	New York Jets	@	DETROIT	A	31	20	W	3.0	W	42.5	O
9/19/1985	Chicago	@	MINNESOTA	A	24	33	L	3.0	L	41.5	O
9/12/1985	Los Angeles Raiders	@	KANSAS CITY	G	20	36	L	-1.5	L	44.0	O
11/29/1984	Washington Redskins	@	MINNESOTA	A	17	31	L	12.0	L	46.0	O
11/22/1984	New England Patriots	@	DALLAS	A	20	17	W	-1.5	W	42.0	U
11/22/1984	Green Bay	@	DETROIT	A	31	28	W	4.0	W	44.5	O
9/6/1984	Pittsburgh	@	NEW YORK JETS	A	17	23	L	1.0	L	41.0	U
12/1/1983	Los Angeles Raiders	@	SAN DIEGO CHARGERS	G	10	42	L	2.0	L	54.5	U
11/24/1983	St. Louis Cardinals	@	DALLAS	A	35	17	W	-9.5	W	54.5	U
11/24/1983	Pittsburgh	@	DETROIT	A	45	3	W	3.0	W	41.0	O
9/15/1983	Cincinnati	@	CLEVELAND BROWNS	G	17	7	W	-3.5	W	41.5	U
9/8/1983	San Francisco	@	MINNESOTA	A	17	48	L	-3.5	L	44.0	O
12/30/1982	Los Angeles Rams	@	SAN FRANCISCO	G	20	21	L	-10.0	L		
12/2/1982	San Francisco	@	LOS ANGELES RAMS	G	24	30	L	3.0	L		
11/25/1982	Cleveland Browns	@	DALLAS	A	31	14	W	-7.0	W		
11/25/1982	New York Giants	@	DETROIT	A	6	13	L	-5.0	L		
9/16/1982	Minnesota	@	BUFFALO	A	23	22	W	-4.0	L		
12/7/1981	Cleveland Browns	@	HOUSTON OILERS	A	17	13	W	-2.5	W		
11/30/1981	Chicago	@	DALLAS	A	10	9	W	-13.5	L		
11/30/1981	Kansas City	@	DETROIT	A	27	10	W	-2.5	W		
9/17/1981	Philadelphia	@	BUFFALO	A	14	20	L	-4.0	L		
9/10/1981	Pittsburgh	@	MIAMI	G	30	10	W	-2.0	W		
12/4/1980	Pittsburgh	@	HOUSTON OILERS	A	6	0	W	-2.5	W		
11/27/1980	Seattle	@	DALLAS	A	51	7	W	-9.5	W		
11/27/1980	Chicago (OT)	@	DETROIT	A	17	23	L	-3.5	L		
11/20/1980	San Diego Chargers (OT)	@	MIAMI	G	24	27	L	3.5	W		
9/11/1980	Los Angeles Rams	@	TAMPA BAY	G	10	9	W	-3.0	L		
11/29/1979	New England Patriots	@	MIAMI	G	39	24	W	-3.0	W		
11/22/1979	Houston Oilers	@	DALLAS	A	24	30	L	-3.5	L		
11/22/1979	Chicago	@	DETROIT	A	20	0	W	4.0	W		
10/25/1979	San Diego Chargers	@	OAKLAND RAIDERS	G	45	22	W	1.0	W		
9/6/1979	Los Angeles Rams	@	DENVER	G	9	13	L	-3.0	L		

Thursday Night Football History

11/23/1978	Washington Redskins	@	DALLAS	A	37	10	W	-11.0	W			
11/23/1978	Denver	@	DETROIT	A	17	14	W	3.5	W			
10/26/1978	Minnesota	@	DALLAS	A	10	21	L	-7.5	L			
11/24/1977	Miami	@	ST. LOUIS CARDINALS	A	14	55	L					
11/24/1977	Chicago	@	DETROIT	A	14	31	L					
11/25/1976	St. Louis Cardinals	@	DALLAS	A	19	14	W					
11/25/1976	Buffalo	@	DETROIT	A	27	14	W					
11/27/1975	Buffalo	@	ST. LOUIS CARDINALS	A	14	32	L					
11/27/1975	Los Angeles Rams	@	DETROIT	A	0	20	L					
11/28/1974	Denver	@	DENVER	A	27	31	L					
11/27/1974	Washington Redskins	@	DALLAS	A	24	23	W					
11/22/1973	Miami	@	DALLAS	A	7	14	L					
11/22/1973	Washington Redskins	@	DETROIT	G	0	20	L					
11/23/1972	San Francisco	@	DALLAS	A	10	31	L					
11/23/1972	New York Jets	@	DETROIT	G	37	20	W					
11/25/1971	Los Angeles Rams	@	DALLAS	G	28	21	W					
11/25/1971	Kansas City	@	DETROIT	G	32	21	W					
11/26/1970	Green Bay	@	DALLAS	G	16	3	W					
11/26/1970	Oakland Raiders	@	DETROIT	G	28	14	W					
11/27/1969	San Francisco	@	DALLAS	G	24	24	T					
11/27/1969	Minnesota	@	DETROIT	G	0	27	L					
11/27/1969	San Diego Chargers	@	HOUSTON OILERS	A	17	21	L					
11/28/1968	Oakland Raiders	@	BUFFALO	G	10	13	L					
11/28/1968	Washington Redskins	@	DALLAS	G	29	20	W					
11/28/1968	Philadelphia	@	DETROIT	G	6	7	L					
11/28/1968	Houston Oilers	@	KANSAS CITY	G	24	10	W					
11/23/1967	St. Louis Cardinals	@	DALLAS	G	46	21	W					
11/23/1967	Los Angeles Rams	@	DETROIT	G	7	31	L					
11/23/1967	Oakland Raiders	@	KANSAS CITY	G	22	44	L					
11/23/1967	Denver	@	SAN DIEGO CHARGERS	G	24	20	W					
11/24/1966	Cleveland Browns	@	DALLAS	G	26	14	W					
11/24/1966	San Francisco	@	DETROIT	G	14	41	L					
11/24/1966	Buffalo	@	OAKLAND RAIDERS	G	10	31	L					
11/25/1965	Baltimore Colts	@	DETROIT	G	24	24	T					
11/25/1965	Buffalo	@	SAN DIEGO CHARGERS	G	20	20	T					
11/26/1964	Chicago	@	DETROIT	G	24	27	L					
11/26/1964	Buffalo	@	SAN DIEGO CHARGERS	G	24	27	L					
11/28/1963	Oakland Raiders	@	DENVER	G	10	26	L					
11/28/1963	Green Bay	@	DETROIT	G	13	13	T					
11/22/1962	Ny Titans	@	DENVER	G	45	46	L					
11/22/1962	Green Bay	@	DETROIT	G	26	14	W					
11/23/1961	Green Bay	@	DETROIT	G	9	17	L					
11/23/1961	Buffalo	@	NEW YORK TITANS	G	21	14	W					
11/24/1960	Green Bay	@	DETROIT	G	23	10	W					
11/24/1960	Dallas Texans	@	NEW YORK TITANS	G	41	35	W					
11/26/1959	Green Bay	@	DETROIT	G	17	24	L					
11/27/1958	Green Bay	@	DETROIT	G	24	14	W					
11/28/1957	Green Bay	@	DETROIT	G	18	6	W					
11/22/1956	Green Bay	@	DETROIT	G	20	24	L					
11/24/1955	Green Bay	@	DETROIT	G	24	10	W					
11/25/1954	Green Bay	@	DETROIT	G	28	24	W					
11/26/1953	Green Bay	@	DETROIT	G	34	15	W					
11/27/1952	Green Bay	@	DETROIT	G	48	24	W					
11/22/1951	Green Bay	@	DETROIT	G	52	35	W					
11/23/1950	Pittsburgh	@	CHICAGO CARDINALS	G	17	28	L					
11/23/1950	New York Yanks	@	DETROIT	G	49	14	W					
10/19/1950	Green Bay	@	NEW YORK YANKS	G	17	35	L					
11/24/1949	Cleveland Browns	@	CHICAGO HORNETS	G	14	6	W				AAFC

Thursday Night Football History

11/24/1949	Chicago	@	**DETROIT**	G	7	28	L					
9/22/1949	**Philadelphia**	@	NEW YORK BULLDOGS	G	7	0	W					
11/25/1948	Chicago Cardinals	@	**Detroit**	G	14	28	L					
11/25/1948	**Cleveland Browns**	@	Los Angeles Dons	G	31	14	W				AAFC	
9/23/1948	**New York Giants**	@	Boston Yanks	G	27	7	W					
11/27/1947	**Cleveland Browns**	@	Los Angeles Dons	G	27	17	W				AAFC	
11/27/1947	Chicago	@	**Detroit**	G	14	34	L					
11/28/1946	Boston Yanks	@	**Detroit**	G	10	34	L					
11/22/1945	Cleveland Rams	@	**Detroit**	G	21	28	L					
11/28/1940	**Pittsburgh**	@	Philadelphia	G	7	0	W					
11/23/1939	**Pittsburgh**	@	Philadelphia	G	17	14	W					
9/14/1939	Pittsburgh	@	**Brooklyn Dodgers**	G	7	12	L					
11/24/1938	**Chicago**	@	Detroit	G	14	7	W					
11/24/1938	New York Giants	@	Brooklyn Dodgers	G	7	7	**T**					
11/25/1937	Chicago	@	**Detroit**	G	0	13	L					
11/25/1937	New York Giants	@	**Brooklyn Dodgers**	G	13	13	**T**					
9/16/1937	**New York Giants**	@	Washington Redskins	G	13	3	W					
11/26/1936	**Chicago**	@	Detroit	G	13	7	W					
11/26/1936	**New York Giants**	@	Brooklyn Dodgers	G	14	0	W					
11/28/1935	**Green Bay**	@	Chicago Cardinals	G	9	7	W					
11/28/1935	**Chicago**	@	Detroit	G	14	2	W					
11/28/1935	**New York Giants**	@	Brooklyn Dodgers	G	21	0	W					
11/29/1934	**Green Bay**	@	Chicago Cardinals	G	6	0	W					
11/29/1934	Chicago	@	**Detroit**	G	16	19	L					
11/29/1934	**New York Giants**	@	Brooklyn Dodgers	G	27	0	W					
11/30/1933	Chicago	@	**Chicago Cardinals**	G	9	12	L					
11/30/1933	**New York Giants**	@	Brooklyn Dodgers	G	10	0	W					
11/24/1932	**Chicago Cardinals**	@	Chicago	G	34	0	W					
11/24/1932	**Green Bay**	@	Brooklyn Dodgers	G	7	0	W					
11/24/1932	New York Giants	@	Staten Island	G	13	13	**T**					
10/20/1932	**Detroit**	@	Staten Island	G	13	6	W					
11/26/1931	**Chicago Cardinals**	@	Chicago	G	18	7	W					
11/26/1931	**Green Bay**	@	Providence Steam Roller	G	38	7	W					
11/26/1931	New York Giants	@	**Staten Island**	G	6	9	L					
10/15/1931	**Frankford Yellow Jackets**	@	Detroit	G	19	0	W					
11/27/1930	**Chicago Cardinals**	@	Chicago	G	6	0	W					
11/27/1930	**Green Bay**	@	Frankford Yellow Jackets	G	25	7	W					
11/27/1930	New York Giants	@	**Staten Island**	G	6	7	L					
10/30/1930	**Newark**	@	New York Giants	G	34	7	W					
10/16/1930	**Chicago Cardinals**	@	New York Giants	G	25	12	W					
11/28/1929	Chicago Cardinals	@	Chicago	G	0	0	**T**					
11/28/1929	Green Bay	@	Frankford Yellow Jackets	G	0	0	**T**					
11/28/1929	**New York Giants**	@	Staten Island	G	21	7	W					
11/29/1928	**Chicago Cardinals**	@	Chicago	G	34	0	W					
11/29/1928	Green Bay	@	**Frankford Yellow Jackets**	G	0	2	L					
11/24/1927	Chicago Cardinals	@	**Chicago**	G	0	31	L					
11/24/1927	**Green Bay**	@	Frankford Yellow Jackets	G	17	9	W					
11/25/1926	Chicago Cardinals	@	Chicago	G	0	0	**T**					
11/25/1926	Green Bay	@	**Frankford Yellow Jackets**	G	14	20	L					
11/25/1926	**New York Giants**	@	Brooklyn Lions	G	17	0	W					
11/11/1926	Chicago Cardinals	@	**Chicago**	G	0	10	L					
11/11/1926	**Duluth Eskimos**	@	New York Giants	G	14	13	W					
11/26/1925	Chicago Cardinals	@	New York Giants	G	0	0	**T**					
11/26/1925	Green Bay	@	**Pottsville**	G	0	31	L					
11/27/1924	Chicago	@	**Chicago Cardinals**	G	0	21	L					
11/27/1924	**Green Bay**	@	Kansas City Blues	G	17	6	W					
11/29/1923	**Chicago Cardinals**	@	CHICAGO	G	31	0	W					
11/29/1923	**Green Bay**	@	HAMMOND PROS	G	19	0	W					

Thursday Night Football History

11/30/1922	Chicago	@	CHICAGO CARDINALS	G	6	0	W				
11/24/1921	Buffalo All-Americans	@	**CHICAGO**	G	6	7	L				
11/25/1920	Chicago	@	CHICAGO TIGERS	G	6	0	W				
11/25/1920	**Stambaugh Miners**	@	GREEN BAY	G	14	0	W				
11/11/1920	Chicago	@	CHAMPION LEGION	G	20	0	W				

Thanksgiving Day

Interesting Thursday Facts

Arizona is 2-9 at home on Thursday since 1950	Las Vegas is 4-1 at home on Thursday since 2014
Baltimore is 7-0 at home on Thursday since 2011	Philadelphia is 6-1 on Thanksgiving since 1939
Dallas is 9-2 at home vs Washington on Thursday since 1968	Pittsburgh is 8-1 at home on Thursday since 2006
Detroit is 0-8 at home vs AFC teams on Thursday since 2002	Seattle is 9-2 on Thursday since 2013
Miami is 1-7 on road on Thursday since 2011	Washington is 3-12 on road on Thursday since 1974
Minnesota is 4-0 at Dallas on Thursday since 1978	
New England is 7-1 @ home on Thursday since 2003	

College Football Blueblood Series available at: www.stevesfootballbible.com (Blueblood series)

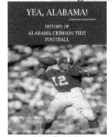 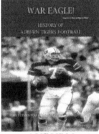  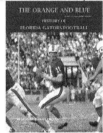 

ALABAMA AUBURN CLEMSON FLORIDA FLORIDA STATE

College Football Blueblood Series available at: www.stevesfootballbible.com (Blueblood series)

    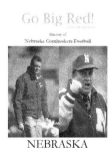

GEORGIA LSU MIAMI MICHIGAN NEBRASKA

College Football Patriot Series available at: www.stevesfootballbible.com (Patriot series)

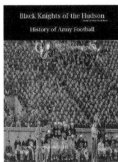  

ARMY AIR FORCE NAVY

Saturday Football History

DATE	VISITOR		HOME	SC	ORE	S/U W-L	LINE	ATS W-L	TOTAL	O/U	Saturday Trends
1/21/2023	Jacksonville	@	Kansas City	20	27	L	9.5	W	52.0	U	AFC Divisional Play-offs
1/21/2023	NY Giants	@	Philadelphia	7	38	L	8.0	L	47.5	U	NFC Divisional Play-offs
1/14/2023	Jacksonville	vs	L.A. CHARGERS	31	30	W	2.0	W	46.5	O	AFC WILD CARD
1/14/2023	San Francisco	vs	SEATTLE	41	23	W	-9.0	W	42.0	O	NFC WILD CARD
1/7/2023	Kansas City	@	Las Vegas Raiders	31	13	W	-8.0	W	51.5	U	
12/24/2022	Atlanta	@	Baltimore	9	17	L	6.5	L	35.5	U	
12/24/2022	Buffalo	@	Chicago	35	13	W	-8.0	W	40.5	O	
12/24/2022	Carolina	vs	DETROIT	37	23	W	1.5	W	43.5	O	
12/24/2022	Cincinnati	@	New England	22	18	W	-3.0	W	41.5	U	
12/24/2022	Cleveland	vs	NEW ORLEANS	10	17	L	-3.5	L	32.0	U	
12/24/2022	Dallas	vs	PHILADELPHIA	40	34	W	-3.5	W	48.0	O	
12/24/2022	Houston	@	Tennessee Titans	19	14	W	3.0	W	33.5	U	
12/24/2022	Las Vegas	@	Pittsburgh	10	13	L	2.5	L	37.5	U	
12/24/2022	Minnesota	vs	N.Y. GIANTS	27	24	W	-4.5	L	48.5	O	
12/24/2022	San Francisco	vs	WASHINGTON	37	20	W	-6.0	W	37.0	O	
12/24/2022	Kansas City	vs	SEATTLE	24	10	W	-10.5	W	51.0	U	
12/17/2022	Baltimore	@	Cleveland	3	13	L	3.0	L	39.0	U	
12/17/2022	Buffalo	vs	MIAMI	32	29	W	-7.0	L	45.0	O	
12/17/2022	Indianapolis	@	Minnesota {OT}	36	39	L	3.5	W	46.0	O	
1/22/2022	Cincinnati	@	Tennessee	19	16	W	4.0	W	48.5	U	AFC Divisional Play-offs
1/22/2022	GREEN BAY	vs	San Francisco	10	13	L	-6.0	L	47.0	U	NFC Divisional Play-offs
1/15/2022	BUFFALO	vs	New England	47	17	W	-4.5	W	43.0	O	AFC WILD CARD
1/15/2022	CINCINNATI	vs	Las Vegas Raiders	26	19	W	-6.0	W	48.5	U	AFC WILD CARD
1/8/2022	DENVER	vs	Kansas City	24	28	L	11.5	W	44.5	O	
1/8/2022	Dallas	@	PHILADELPHIA	51	26	W	-6.0	W	46.0	O	
12/25/2021	Cleveland	@	GREEN BAY	22	24	L	8.0	W	46.5	U	
12/25/2021	Indianapolis	@	ARIZONA	22	16	W	3.0	W	48.5	U	
12/18/2021	INDIANAPOLIS	vs	New England	27	17	W	-1.0	W	46.5	U	
1/16/2021	Buffalo	vs	Baltimore	17	3	W	-2.5	W	50.0	U	AFC Divisional Play-offs
1/16/2021	Green Bay	vs	Los Angeles Rams	32	18	W	-7.0	W	45.0	O	NFC Divisional Play-offs
1/9/2021	Tampa Bay	@	Washington	31	23	W	-10.5	L	45.0	O	NFC WILD CARD
1/9/2021	Los Angeles Rams	@	Seattle	30	20	W	3.0	W	42.0	O	NFC WILD CARD
1/9/2021	Buffalo	vs	Indianapolis	27	24	W	-6.5	L	50.5	O	AFC WILD CARD
12/26/2020	Las Vegas Raiders	vs	MIAMI	25	26	L	2.0	W	51.0	T	
12/26/2020	Detroit	vs	TAMPA BAY	7	47	L	12.0	L	55.0	U	
12/26/2020	Arizona	vs	SAN FRANCISCO	12	20	L	-5.5	L	49.5	U	
12/19/2020	Carolina	@	Green Bay	16	24	L	9.5	W	53.0	O	
12/19/2020	Denver	vs	BUFFALO	19	48	L	6.0	L	47.5	O	
12/19/2020	Buffalo	@	Denver	48	19	W	-6.0	W	47.5	O	
1/11/2020	Tennessee	@	Baltimore	28	12	W	10.0	W	47.5	U	AFC Divisional Play-offs
1/11/2020	Minnesota	@	San Francisco	10	27	L	7.0	L	44.5	U	NFC Divisional Play-offs
1/4/2020	Tennessee	@	New England	20	13	W	4.5	W	45.0	U	AFC WILD CARD
1/4/2020	Buffalo	@	Houston Texans	19	22	L	2.5	L	43.0	U	AFC WILD CARD
12/21/2019	Los Angeles Rams	@	San Francisco	31	34	L	7.0	W	45.5	O	
12/21/2019	Buffalo	@	New England	17	24	L	7.0	T	39.0	O	
12/21/2019	Houston Texans	@	Tampa Bay	23	20	W	-3.0	T	50.0	U	
1/12/2019	Dallas	@	Los Angeles Rams	22	30	L	7.0	L	48.0	O	NFC Divisional Play-offs
1/12/2019	Indianapolis	@	Kansas City	13	31	L	4.5	L	55.0	U	AFC Divisional Play-offs
1/5/2019	Seattle	@	Dallas	22	24	L	2.5	W	43.5	O	NFC WILD CARD
1/5/2019	Indianapolis	@	Houston Texans	21	7	W	2.0	W	48.5	U	AFC WILD CARD
12/22/2018	Baltimore	@	Los Angeles Chargers	22	10	W	4.0	W	42.5	U	
12/22/2018	Washington	@	Tennessee	16	25	L	12.0	W	38.0	O	
12/15/2018	Cleveland	@	Denver	17	16	W	1.0	W	47.5	U	
12/15/2018	Houston Texans	@	New York Jets	29	22	W	-7.0	T	44.5	O	
1/13/2018	Tennessee	@	New England	14	35	L	13.5	L	48.0	O	AFC Divisional Play-offs
1/13/2018	Atlanta	@	Philadelphia	10	15	L	-2.5	L	40.5	U	NFC Divisional Play-offs
1/6/2018	Atlanta	@	Los Angeles Rams	26	13	W	6.5	W	48.0	U	NFC WILD CARD
1/6/2018	Tennessee	@	Kansas City	22	21	W	8.5	W	44.0	U	AFC WILD CARD
12/23/2017	Minnesota	@	Green Bay	16	0	W	-8.5	W	40.5	U	
12/23/2017	Indianapolis	@	Baltimore	16	23	L	13.5	W	40.5	U	
12/16/2017	L.A. Chargers	@	Kansas City	13	30	L	1.0	L	47.0	U	
12/16/2017	Chicago	@	Detroit	10	20	L	4.5	L	43.5	U	
1/14/2017	Houston Texans	@	New England	16	34	L	16.0	L	44.0	O	AFC Divisional Play-offs

Saturday Football History

Date	Visitor		Home	V	H	W/L	Spread	W/L	Total	O/U	Notes
1/14/2017	Seattle	@	Atlanta	20	36	L	6.5	L	51.0	O	NFC Divisional Play-offs
1/7/2017	Detroit	@	Seattle	6	26	L	8.0	L	45.5	U	NFC WILD CARD
1/7/2017	Oakland Raiders	@	Houston Texans	14	27	L	4.0	L	37.5	O	AFC WILD CARD
12/24/2016	Cincinnati	@	Houston Texans	10	12	L	3.0	W	41.5	U	
12/24/2016	San Francisco	@	Los Angeles Rams	22	21	W	6.0	W	39.5	O	
12/24/2016	Arizona	@	Seattle	34	31	W	9.0	W	43.5	O	
12/24/2016	Indianapolis	@	Oakland Raiders	25	33	L	3.5	L	52.0	O	
12/24/2016	Atlanta	@	Carolina	33	16	W	-3.0	W	48.5	O	
12/24/2016	Washington	@	Chicago	41	21	W	-3.0	W	49.0	O	
12/24/2016	San Diego	@	Cleveland	17	20	L	-4.5	L	45.0	U	
12/24/2016	Minnesota	@	Green Bay	25	38	L	6.0	L	44.5	O	
12/24/2016	Tennessee	@	Jacksonville	17	38	L	-4.0	L	44.0	O	
12/24/2016	New York Jets	@	New England	3	41	L	17.0	L	45.0	U	
12/24/2016	Tampa Bay	@	New Orleans	24	31	L	3.0	L	53.0	O	
12/24/2016	Miami	@	Buffalo {OT}	34	31	W	4.5	W	44.5	O	
12/17/2016	Miami	@	New York Jets	34	13	W	-2.5	W	40.0	O	
1/16/2016	Green Bay	@	Arizona (OT)	20	26	L	7.0	W	49.0	U	NFC Divisional Play-offs
1/16/2016	Kansas City	@	New England	20	27	L	6.0	L	44.5	O	AFC Divisional Play-offs
1/9/2016	Pittsburgh	@	Cincinnati	18	16	W	-2.5	L	45.5	U	AFC WILD CARD
1/9/2016	Kansas City	@	Houston Texans	30	0	W	-3.0	W	39.5	U	AFC WILD CARD
12/26/2015	Washington	@	Philadelphia	38	24	W	3.5	W	48.5	O	
12/19/2015	New York Jets	@	Dallas	19	16	W	-3.0	T	51.0	U	
1/10/2015	Baltimore	@	New England	31	35	L	7.0	W	47.5	O	AFC Divisional Play-offs
1/10/2015	Carolina	@	Seattle	17	31	L	13.0	L	39.5	O	NFC Divisional Play-offs
1/3/2015	Arizona	@	Carolina	16	27	L	5.5	L	37.5	O	NFC WILD CARD
1/3/2015	Baltimore	@	Pittsburgh	30	17	W	3.0	W	47.0	T	AFC WILD CARD
12/20/2014	Philadelphia	@	Washington	24	27	L	-7.0	L	51.0	T	
12/20/2014	San Diego	@	San Francisco {OT}	38	35	W	1.5	W	40.5	O	
1/11/2014	Indianapolis	@	New England	22	43	L	7.0	L	51.5	O	AFC Divisional Play-offs
1/11/2014	New Orleans	@	Seattle	15	23	L	9.0	W	44.0	U	NFC Divisional Play-offs
1/4/2014	Kansas City	@	Indianapolis	44	45	L	-1.5	L	47.5	O	AFC WILD CARD
1/4/2014	New Orleans	@	Philadelphia	26	24	W	3.0	W	55.0	U	NFC WILD CARD
1/12/2013	Baltimore	@	Denver {OT}	38	35	W	9.0	W	44.0	O	AFC Divisional Play-offs
1/12/2013	Green Bay	@	San Francisco	31	45	L	3.0	L	45.0	O	NFC Divisional Play-offs
1/5/2013	Cincinnati	@	Houston Texans	13	19	L	4.0	L	42.5	U	AFC WILD CARD
1/5/2013	Minnesota	@	Green Bay	10	24	L	10.5	L	44.0	U	NFC WILD CARD
12/22/2012	Atlanta	@	Detroit	31	18	W	-3.5	W	50.0	U	
1/14/2012	Denver	@	New England	10	45	L	14.0	L	50.5	O	AFC Divisional Play-offs
1/14/2012	New Orleans	@	San Francisco	32	36	L	-3.0	L	46.0	O	NFC Divisional Play-offs
1/7/2012	Cincinnati	@	Houston Texans	10	31	L	4.0	L	38.0	O	AFC WILD CARD
1/7/2012	Detroit	@	New Orleans	28	45	L	10.0	L	59.0	O	NFC WILD CARD
12/24/2011	Arizona	@	Cincinnati	16	23	L	4.5	L	41.0	U	
12/24/2011	Cleveland	@	Baltimore	14	20	L	12.0	W	38.0	U	
12/24/2011	Denver	@	Buffalo	14	40	L	-3.0	L	42.5	O	
12/24/2011	Jacksonville	@	Tennessee	17	23	L	7.5	W	39.5	O	
12/24/2011	Miami	@	New England	24	27	L	8.5	W	48.5	O	
12/24/2011	Minnesota	@	Washington	33	26	W	6.5	W	43.5	O	
12/24/2011	New York Giants	@	New York Jets	29	14	W	3.0	W	45.5	U	
12/24/2011	Oakland Raiders	@	Kansas City (OT)	16	13	W	2.5	W	42.0	U	
12/24/2011	Philadelphia	@	Dallas	20	7	W	Pk	W	50.0	U	
12/24/2011	St. Louis Rams	@	Pittsburgh	0	27	L	10.0	L	34.0	U	
12/24/2011	San Diego	@	Detroit	10	38	L	2.0	L	52.5	U	
12/24/2011	San Francisco	@	Seattle	19	17	W	-2.5	L	37.5	U	
12/24/2011	Tampa Bay	@	Carolina	16	48	L	7.5	L	48.0	O	
12/17/2011	Dallas	@	Tampa Bay	31	15	W	-7.0	W	47.0	U	
1/15/2011	Green Bay	@	Atlanta	48	21	W	2.5	W	44.0	O	NFC Divisional Play-offs
1/15/2011	Baltimore	@	Pittsburgh	24	31	L	3.5	L	37.0	O	AFC Divisional Play-offs
1/8/2011	New Orleans	@	Seattle	36	41	L	-10.0	L	45.0	O	NFC WILD CARD
1/8/2011	New York Jets	@	Indianapolis	17	16	W	2.5	W	44.5	U	AFC WILD CARD
12/25/2010	Dallas	@	Arizona	26	27	L	-7.0	L	45.0	O	
1/16/2010	Arizona	@	New Orleans	14	45	L	7.0	L	57.0	O	NFC Divisional Play-offs
1/16/2010	Baltimore	@	Indianapolis	3	20	L	6.5	L	44.0	U	AFC Divisional Play-offs
1/9/2010	New York Jets	@	Cincinnati	24	14	W	2.5	W	34.0	O	AFC WILD CARD
1/9/2010	Philadelphia	@	Dallas	14	34	L	4.0	L	45.0	O	NFC WILD CARD

Saturday Football History

12/19/2009	Dallas	@	New Orleans	24	17	W	7.5	W	53.5	U	
1/10/2009	**Arizona**	@	**Carolina**	33	13	W	10.0	W	48.5	U	NFC Divisional Play-offs
1/10/2009	**Baltimore**	@	**Tennessee**	13	10	W	3.0	W	34.0	U	AFC Divisional Play-offs
1/3/2009	**Atlanta**	@	**Arizona**	24	30	L	-1.0	L	51.5	O	NFC WILD CARD
1/3/2009	**Indianapolis**	@	**San Diego (OT)**	17	23	L	-1.5	L	51.0	U	AFC WILD CARD
12/20/2008	Baltimore	@	Dallas	33	24	W	5.0	W	39.5	O	
1/12/2008	**Seattle**	@	**Green Bay**	20	42	L	7.5	L	43.0	O	NFC Divisional Play-offs
1/12/2008	**Jacksonville**	@	**New England**	20	31	L	13.5	W	50.0	O	AFC Divisional Play-offs
1/5/2008	**Washington**	@	**Seattle**	14	35	L	3.5	L	39.0	O	NFC WILD CARD
1/5/2008	**Jacksonville**	@	**Pittsburgh**	31	29	W	-2.5	L	39.5	O	AFC WILD CARD
12/29/2007	New England	@	New York Giants	38	35	W	-13.0	L	46.5	O	
12/22/2007	Dallas	@	Carolina	20	13	W	-10.5	L	42.5	U	
12/15/2007	Cincinnati	@	San Francisco	13	20	L	-8.0	L	42.5	U	
1/13/2007	**Indianapolis**	@	**Baltimore**	15	6	W	4.0	W	41.5	U	AFC Divisional Play-offs
1/13/2007	**Philadelphia**	@	**New Orleans**	24	27	L	5.5	W	49.0	O	NFC Divisional Play-offs
1/6/2007	**Dallas**	@	**Seattle**	20	21	L	2.0	W	48.0	U	NFC WILD CARD
1/6/2007	**Kansas City**	@	**Indianapolis**	8	23	L	7.0	L	50.5	U	AFC WILD CARD
12/30/2006	New York Giants	@	Washington	34	28	W	-2.0	W	42.5	O	
12/23/2006	Kansas City	@	Oakland Raiders	20	9	W	-7.0	W	36.5	U	
12/16/2006	Dallas	@	Atlanta	38	28	W	-3.5	W	44.5	O	
1/14/2006	**Washington**	@	**Seattle**	10	20	L	9.5	L	41.0	U	NFC Divisional Play-offs
1/14/2006	**New England**	@	**Denver**	13	27	L	3.0	L	44.0	U	AFC Divisional Play-offs
1/7/2006	**Jacksonville**	@	**New England**	3	28	L	7.5	L	37.0	U	AFC WILD CARD
1/7/2006	**Washington**	@	**Tampa Bay**	17	10	W	2.5	W	37.0	U	NFC WILD CARD
12/31/2005	New York Giants	@	Oakland Raiders	30	21	W	-8.0	W	42.0	O	
12/24/2005	Atlanta	@	Tampa Bay (OT)	24	27	L	3.0	**T**	36.5	O	
12/24/2005	Buffalo	@	Cincinnati	37	27	W	13.5	W	44.0	O	
12/24/2005	Dallas	@	Carolina	24	20	W	5.0	W	37.5	O	
12/24/2005	Detroit	@	New Orleans	13	12	W	3.0	W	38.0	U	
12/24/2005	Indianapolis	@	Seattle	13	28	L	9.5	L	44.0	U	
12/24/2005	Jacksonville	@	Houston Texans	38	20	W	-6.0	W	37.0	O	
12/24/2005	New York Giants	@	Washington	20	35	L	3.0	L	38.0	O	
12/24/2005	Philadelphia	@	Arizona	21	27	L	1.5	L	39.0	O	
12/24/2005	Pittsburgh	@	Cleveland	41	0	W	-7.0	W	32.5	O	
12/24/2005	San Diego	@	Kansas City	7	20	L	Pk	L	49.0	U	
12/24/2005	San Francisco	@	St. Louis Rams	24	20	W	9.5	W	42.0	O	
12/17/2005	**Denver**	@	Buffalo	28	17	W	-8.5	W	34.5	O	
1/15/2005	**New York Jets**	@	**Pittsburgh (OT)**	17	20	L	9.0	W	35.0	O	AFC Divisional Play-offs
1/15/2005	**St. Louis Rams**	@	**Atlanta**	17	47	L	7.0	L	48.5	O	NFC Divisional Play-offs
1/8/2005	**New York Jets**	@	**San Diego (OT)**	20	17	W	6.5	W	43.0	U	AFC WILD CARD
1/8/2005	**St. Louis Rams**	@	**Seattle**	27	20	W	4.0	W	50.5	U	NFC WILD CARD
12/25/2004	Denver	@	Tennessee	37	16	W	-4.0	W	50.5	O	
12/18/2004	Carolina	@	Atlanta (OT)	31	34	L	3.5	W	41.0	O	
12/18/2004	Pittsburgh	@	New York Giants	33	30	W	-10.0	L	35.0	O	
1/10/2004	**Tennessee**	@	**New England**	14	17	L	6.5	W	34.0	U	AFC Divisional Play-offs
1/10/2004	**Carolina**	@	**St. Louis Rams (OT)**	29	23	W	7.0	W	45.0	O	NFC Divisional Play-offs
1/3/2004	**Tennessee**	@	**Baltimore**	20	17	W	-1.0	W	39.5	U	AFC WILD CARD
1/3/2004	**Dallas**	@	**Carolina**	10	29	L	3.0	L	34.0	O	NFC WILD CARD
12/27/2003	Buffalo	@	New England	0	31	L	9.0	L	34.0	U	
12/27/2003	Philadelphia	@	Washington	31	7	W	-7.5	W	41.5	U	
12/27/2003	Seattle	@	San Francisco	24	17	W	1.5	W	45.0	U	
12/20/2003	Atlanta	@	Tampa Bay	30	28	W	7.5	W	38.0	O	
12/20/2003	Kansas City	@	Minnesota	20	45	L	-2.5	L	55.0	O	
12/20/2003	New England	@	New York Jets	21	16	W	-3.0	W	36.0	O	
1/11/2003	**Atlanta**	@	**Philadelphia**	6	20	L	7.5	L	38.5	U	NFC Divisional Play-offs
1/11/2003	**Pittsburgh**	@	**Tennessee (OT)**	31	34	L	4.0	W	44.0	O	AFC Divisional Play-offs
1/4/2003	**Atlanta**	@	**Green Bay**	27	7	W	6.5	W	40.0	U	NFC WILD CARD
1/4/2003	**Indianapolis**	@	**New York Jets**	0	41	L	6.0	L	41.0	**T**	AFC WILD CARD
12/28/2002	Kansas City	@	Oakland Raiders	0	24	L	8.0	L	47.0	U	
12/28/2002	Philadelphia	@	New York Giants (OT)	7	10	L	-1.0	L	37.5	U	
12/21/2002	Miami	@	Minnesota	17	20	L	-3.0	L	45.5	U	
12/21/2002	Philadelphia	@	Dallas	27	3	W	-6.5	W	36.5	U	
12/21/2002	San Francisco	@	Arizona	17	14	W	-4.0	L	41.0	U	
1/19/2002	**Oakland Raiders**	@	**New England (OT)**	13	16	L	3.0	**T**	38.0	U	AFC Divisional Play-offs

Saturday Football History

1/19/2002	Philadelphia	@	Chicago	33	19	W	3.0	W	31.5	O	NFC Divisional Play-offs
1/12/2002	New York Jets	@	Oakland Raiders	24	38	L	5.5	L	42.0	O	AFC WILD CARD
1/12/2002	Tampa Bay	@	Philadelphia	9	31	L	3.5	L	33.0	O	NFC WILD CARD
12/29/2001	Baltimore	@	Tampa Bay	10	22	L	1.5	L	34.0	U	
12/22/2001	Tennessee	@	Oakland Raiders	13	10	W	6.0	W	45.0	U	
1/6/2001	New Orleans	@	Minnesota	16	34	L	8.0	L	50.0	T	NFC Divisional Play-offs
1/6/2001	Miami	@	Oakland Raiders	0	27	L	8.5	L	42.0	U	AFC Divisional Play-offs
12/30/2000	Indianapolis	@	Miami (OT)	17	23	L	-1.5	L	41.5	U	AFC WILD CARD
12/30/2000	St. Louis Rams	@	New Orleans	28	31	L	-6.5	L	54.5	O	NFC WILD CARD
12/23/2000	Buffalo	@	Seattle	42	23	W	3.0	W	42.0	O	
12/23/2000	San Francisco	@	Denver	9	38	L	7.0	L	50.0	U	
12/16/2000	Oakland Raiders	@	Seattle	24	27	L	-6.5	L	46.5	O	
1/15/2000	Washington	@	Tampa Bay	13	14	L	5.0	W	37.5	U	NFC Divisional Play-offs
1/15/2000	Miami	@	Jacksonville	7	62	L	8.0	L	37.5	O	AFC Divisional Play-offs
1/8/2000	Buffalo	@	Tennessee	16	22	L	4.5	L	39.5	U	AFC WILD CARD
1/8/2000	Detroit	@	Washington	13	27	L	6.5	L	47.0	U	NFC WILD CARD
12/18/1999	Pittsburgh	@	Kansas City	19	35	L	8.5	L	36.5	O	
1/9/1999	Miami	@	Denver	3	38	L	13.5	L	47.5	U	AFC Divisional Play-offs
1/9/1999	San Francisco	@	Atlanta	18	20	L	3.5	W	53.0	U	NFC Divisional Play-offs
1/2/1999	Arizona	@	Dallas	20	7	W	7.0	W	42.0	U	NFC WILD CARD
1/2/1999	Buffalo	@	Miami	17	24	L	2.5	L	42.5	U	AFC WILD CARD
12/26/1998	Kansas City	@	Oakland Raiders	31	24	W	3.0	W	39.5	O	
12/26/1998	Minnesota	@	Tennessee	26	16	W	-7.0	W	48.5	U	
12/19/1998	Tampa Bay	@	Washington	16	20	L	-3.0	L	41.5	U	
1/3/1998	New England	@	Pittsburgh	6	7	L	7.5	W	41.0	U	AFC Divisional Play-offs
1/3/1998	Minnesota	@	San Francisco	22	38	L	14.0	L	41.5	O	NFC Divisional Play-offs
12/27/1997	Jacksonville	@	Denver	17	42	L	8.0	L	45.0	O	AFC WILD CARD
12/27/1997	Minnesota	@	New York Giants	23	22	W	4.5	W	37.0	O	NFC WILD CARD
12/20/1997	St. Louis Rams	@	Carolina	30	18	W	5.0	W	37.5	O	
12/13/1997	Pittsburgh	@	New England (OT)	24	21	W	1.5	W	42.0	O	
12/13/1997	Washington	@	New York Giants	10	30	L	3.0	L	36.5	O	
1/4/1997	Jacksonville	@	Denver	30	27	W	14.0	W	45.0	O	AFC Divisional Play-offs
1/4/1997	San Francisco	@	Green Bay	14	35	L	6.0	L	39.0	O	NFC Divisional Play-offs
12/28/1996	Jacksonville	@	Buffalo	30	27	W	8.5	W	39.0	O	AFC WILD CARD
12/28/1996	Minnesota	@	Dallas	15	40	L	10.0	L	39.0	O	NFC WILD CARD
12/21/1996	New England	@	New York Giants	23	22	W	-9.5	L	38.5	O	
12/21/1996	New Orleans	@	St. Louis Rams	13	14	L	5.0	W	41.0	U	
12/14/1996	Philadelphia	@	New York Jets	21	20	W	-7.5	L	38.5	O	
12/14/1996	San Diego	@	Chicago	14	27	L	3.0	L	37.5	O	
1/6/1996	Buffalo	@	Pittsburgh	21	40	L	6.5	L	42.5	O	AFC Divisional Play-offs
1/6/1996	Green Bay	@	San Francisco	27	17	W	10.0	W	52.0	U	NFC Divisional Play-offs
12/30/1995	Detroit	@	Philadelphia	37	58	L	-3.0	L	42.5	O	NFC WILD CARD
12/30/1995	Miami	@	Buffalo	22	37	L	3.5	L	43.0	O	AFC WILD CARD
12/23/1995	Detroit	@	Tampa Bay	37	10	W	-7.5	W	42.0	O	
12/23/1995	New England	@	Indianapolis	7	10	L	5.5	W	43.0	U	
12/23/1995	San Diego	@	New York Giants	27	17	W	-4.5	W	38.0	O	
12/16/1995	Green Bay	@	New Orleans	34	23	W	-5.0	W	46.0	O	
12/16/1995	New England	@	Pittsburgh	27	41	L	10.0	L	40.0	O	
12/9/1995	Arizona	@	San Diego	25	28	L	9.0	W	39.0	O	
12/9/1995	Cleveland Browns	@	Minnesota	11	27	L	9.5	L	44.0	U	
1/7/1995	Cleveland Browns	@	Pittsburgh	9	29	L	3.5	L	32.0	O	AFC Divisional Play-offs
1/7/1995	Chicago	@	San Francisco	15	44	L	17.5	L	44.0	O	NFC Divisional Play-offs
12/31/1994	Detroit	@	Green Bay	12	16	L	4.0	T	38.0	U	NFC WILD CARD
12/31/1994	Kansas City	@	Miami	17	27	L	3.0	L	43.5	O	AFC WILD CARD
12/24/1994	Arizona	@	Atlanta	6	10	L	-3.0	L	38.0	U	
12/24/1994	Buffalo	@	Indianapolis	9	10	L	3.0	W	41.0	U	
12/24/1994	Dallas	@	New York Giants	10	15	L	-3.0	L	34.0	U	
12/24/1994	Green Bay	@	Tampa Bay	34	19	W	-5.5	W	41.0	O	
12/24/1994	Kansas City	@	L.A. Raiders	19	9	W	-3.5	W	38.0	U	
12/24/1994	New England	@	Chicago	13	3	W	-2.0	W	36.5	U	
12/24/1994	New Orleans	@	Denver	30	28	W	4.5	W	45.0	O	
12/24/1994	New York Jets	@	Houston Oilers	10	24	L	-1.5	L	34.5	U	
12/24/1994	Philadelphia	@	Cincinnati	30	33	L	1.0	L	36.0	O	
12/24/1994	Pittsburgh	@	San Diego	34	37	L	3.5	W	35.0	O	

Saturday Football History

Date	Team	@/vs	Opponent	Score	Score	W/L	Spread	W/L/T	Total	O/U	Notes
12/24/1994	Seattle	@	Cleveland Browns	9	35	L	10.5	L	34.0	O	
12/24/1994	Washington	@	Los Angeles Rams	24	21	W	3.5	W	41.0	O	
12/17/1994	Denver	@	San Francisco	19	42	L	15.5	L	48.0	O	
12/17/1994	Minnesota	@	Detroit	19	41	L	1.5	L	41.5	O	
12/10/1994	Cleveland Browns	@	Dallas	19	14	W	10.5	W	39.0	U	
12/10/1994	Detroit	@	New York Jets	18	7	W	3.0	W	38.0	U	
1/15/1994	**New York Giants**	@	**San Francisco**	3	44	L	7.5	L	41.5	O	NFC Divisional Play-offs
1/15/1994	**Oakland Raiders**	@	**Buffalo**	23	29	L	6.5	W	34.0	O	AFC Divisional Play-offs
1/8/1994	**Green Bay**	@	**Detroit**	28	24	W	1.5	W	38.5	O	NFC WILD CARD
1/8/1994	**Pittsburgh**	@	**Kansas City (OT)**	24	27	L	8.0	W	35.5	O	AFC WILD CARD
12/25/1993	Houston Oilers	@	San Francisco	10	7	W	8.5	W	47.0	U	
12/18/1993	Denver	@	Chicago	13	3	W	-2.0	W	32.5	U	
12/18/1993	Dallas	@	New York Jets	28	7	W	-7.0	W	36.5	U	
12/11/1993	San Francisco	@	Atlanta	24	27	L	-8.5	L	47.0	O	
12/11/1993	NY JETS	@	Washington	3	0	W	-3.0	T	34.0	U	
1/9/1993	**Buffalo**	@	**Pittsburgh**	24	38	W	1.0	W	36.0	U	AFC Divisional Play-offs
1/9/1993	**San Francisco**	vs	**Washington**	20	13	W	-9.5	L	39.0	U	NFC Divisional Play-offs
1/2/1993	**San Diego**	vs	**KANSAS CITY**	17	0	W	-3.5	W	36.5	U	AFC WILD CARD
1/2/1993	**Washington**	@	**Minnesota**	24	7	W	3.5	W	37.0	U	NFC WILD CARD
12/26/1992	New Orleans	@	New York Jets	27	3	W	-7.5	W	34.0	U	
12/26/1992	L.A. Raiders	@	Washington	21	20	W	14.0	W	35.5	O	
12/19/1992	Kansas City	@	New York Giants	21	35	L	-7.0	L	35.5	O	
12/19/1992	Tampa Bay	@	San Francisco	14	21	L	20.5	W	41.0	U	
12/12/1992	Denver	@	Buffalo	17	27	L	14.0	W	37.5	O	
12/12/1992	New York Giants	@	Phoenix Cardinals	0	19	L	5.0	L	37.5	U	
1/4/1992	**Denver**	vs	**HOUSTON OILERS**	26	24	W	-3.5	L	37.0	O	AFC Divisional Play-offs
1/4/1992	**Washington**	vs	**ATLANTA**	24	7	W	-11.5	W	43.0	U	NFC Divisional Play-offs
12/28/1991	**Atlanta**	@	**New Orleans**	27	20	W	6.0	W	39.0	O	NFC WILD CARD
12/28/1991	**Kansas City**	vs	**L.A. Raiders**	10	6	W	-5.0	L	35.5	U	AFC WILD CARD
12/21/1991	Green Bay	@	Minnesota	27	7	W	6.0	W	43.0	U	
12/21/1991	Houston Oilers	@	New York Giants	20	24	L	-3.0	L	37.0	O	
12/14/1991	Kansas City	@	San Francisco	14	28	L	6.0	L	38.0	O	
1/12/1991	**Buffalo**	vs	**MIAMI**	44	34	W	-7.0	W	34.0	O	AFC Divisional Play-offs
1/12/1991	**San Francisco**	vs	**Washington**	28	10	W	-8.0	W	40.5	U	NFC Divisional Play-offs
1/5/1991	**Miami**	vs	**KANSAS CITY**	17	16	W	-2.5	L	40.5	U	AFC WILD CARD
1/5/1991	**Washington**	@	**Philadelphia**	20	6	W	4.0	W	39.5	U	NFC WILD CARD
12/29/1990	Kansas City	@	Chicago	21	10	W	-1.5	W	36.0	U	
12/29/1990	Philadelphia	@	Phoenix Cardinals	23	21	W	-7.5	L	43.0	O	
12/22/1990	Detroit	@	Green Bay	24	17	W	-3.0	W	36.5	U	
12/22/1990	L.A. Raiders	@	Minnesota	28	24	W	-1.0	T	41.0	O	
12/22/1990	Washington	@	Indianapolis	28	35	L	-6.5	L	40.5	U	
1/6/1990	**Cleveland Browns**	vs	**BUFFALO**	34	30	W	-3.5	W	35.5	O	AFC Divisional Play-offs
1/6/1990	**San Francisco**	vs	**MINNESOTA**	41	13	W	-8.0	W	43.5	O	NFC Divisional Play-offs
12/23/1989	Cleveland Browns	@	Houston Oilers	24	20	W	3.5	W	43.0	O	
12/23/1989	Buffalo	@	New York Jets	37	0	W	-8.0	W	34.5	O	
12/23/1989	Washington	@	Seattle	29	0	W	2.0	W	44.0	U	
12/16/1989	Dallas	@	New York Giants	0	15	L	11.5	L	35.0	U	
12/16/1989	Denver	@	Phoenix Cardinals	37	0	W	-7.0	W	38.5	U	
12/16/1989	L.A. Raiders	@	Seattle	17	23	L	Pk	L	38.0	O	
12/9/1989	New England	@	Miami	10	31	L	5.0	L	43.0	U	
11/25/1989	Los Angeles Rams	@	New Orleans	20	17	W	-1.0	W	43.0	U	
12/31/1988	**Chicago**	vs	**PHILADELPHIA**	20	12	W	-5.0	W	37.0	U	NFC Divisional Play-offs
12/31/1988	**Cincinnati**	vs	**SEATTLE**	21	13	W	-6.5	W	44.0	U	AFC Divisional Play-offs
12/24/1988	**Houston Oilers**	@	**Cleveland Browns**	24	23	W	3.0	W	38.0	O	AFC WILD CARD
12/17/1988	New England	@	Denver	10	21	L	-1.5	L	38.0	U	
12/17/1988	Washington	@	Cincinnati	17	20	L	7.5	W	44.0	U	
12/10/1988	Philadelphia	@	Phoenix Cardinals	23	17	W	2.0	W	47.5	U	
1/9/1988	**Cleveland Browns**	vs	**Indianapolis**	38	21	W	-7.0	W	37.0	O	AFC Divisional Play-offs
1/9/1988	**Minnesota**	@	**San Francisco**	36	24	W	11.0	W	48.0	O	NFC Divisional Play-offs
12/26/1987	Washington	@	Minnesota (OT)	27	24	W	3.0	W	45.5	O	
12/19/1987	Green Bay	@	New York Giants	10	20	L	7.0	L	40.0	U	
12/19/1987	Kansas City	@	Denver	17	20	L	11.0	W	43.5	U	
1/3/1987	**Cleveland Browns**	vs	**NEW YORK JETS**	23	20	W	-7.0	L	41.0	O	AFC Divisional Play-offs
1/3/1987	**Washington**	@	**Chicago**	27	13	W	7.0	W	34.0	O	NFC Divisional Play-offs

Saturday Football History

Date	Team		Opponent								
1/4/1986	Miami	vs	CLEVELAND	24	21	W	-10.5	L	45.0	T	AFC Divisional Play-offs
1/4/1986	Los Angeles Rams	vs	DALLAS	20	0	W	-2.0	W	40.5	U	NFC Divisional Play-offs
12/28/1985	New England	@	New York Jets	26	14	W	3.5	W	40.0	T	AFC WILD CARD
12/29/1984	Miami	vs	SEATTLE	31	10	W	-6.5	W	45.0	U	AFC Divisional Play-offs
12/29/1984	San Francisco	vs	NEW YORK GIANTS	21	10	W	-11.0	T	41.5	U	NFC Divisional Play-offs
12/22/1984	Seattle	vs	L.A. Raiders	13	7	W	1.5	W	40.0	U	AFC WILD CARD
12/31/1983	Seattle	@	Miami	27	20	W	8.0	W	43.0	O	AFC Divisional Play-offs
12/31/1983	San Francisco	vs	DETROIT	24	23	W	-7.0	L	43.0	O	NFC Divisional Play-offs
12/24/1983	Seattle	vs	DENVER	31	7	W	-4.0	W	44.0	U	AFC WILD CARD
1/15/1983	New York Jets	@	L.A. Raiders	17	14	W	3.5	W				AFC Divisional Play-offs
1/15/1983	Washington	vs	MINNESOTA	21	7	W	-6.5	W				NFC Divisional Play-offs
1/8/1983	Green Bay	vs	St. Louis Cardinals	41	16	W	-4.5	W				NFC WILD CARD
1/8/1983	Miami	vs	New England	28	13	W	-8.0	W				AFC WILD CARD
1/8/1983	L.A. Raiders	vs	CLEVELAND	27	10	W	-8.0	W				AFC WILD CARD
1/8/1983	Washington	vs	DETROIT	31	7	W	-5.5	W				NFC WILD CARD
1/2/1982	Dallas	vs	TAMPA BAY	38	0	W	-8.0	W				NFC Divisional Play-offs
1/2/1982	San Diego	@	Miami (OT)	41	38	W	3.0	W				AFC Divisional Play-offs
12/12/1981	Minnesota	@	Detroit	7	45	L	4.0	L				
1/3/1981	Philadelphia	vs	MINNESOTA	31	16	W						NFC Divisional Play-offs
1/3/1981	San Diego	vs	BUFFALO	20	14	W						AFC Divisional Play-offs
12/29/1979	Houston Oilers	@	San Diego	17	14	W						AFC Divisional Play-offs
12/29/1979	Tampa Bay	vs	PHILADELPHIA	24	17	W						NFC Divisional Play-offs
12/30/1978	Dallas	vs	ATLANTA	27	20	W						NFC Divisional Play-offs
12/30/1978	Pittsburgh	vs	DENVER	33	10	W						AFC Divisional Play-offs
12/24/1977	Oakland Raiders	@	Baltimore Colts (OT)	37	31	W						AFC Divisional Play-offs
12/24/1977	Pittsburgh	@	Denver	21	34	L						AFC Divisional Play-offs
12/17/1977	Buffalo	@	Miami	14	31	L						
12/17/1977	Minnesota	@	Detroit	30	21	W						
12/17/1977	Los Angeles Rams	@	Washington	14	17	L						
12/10/1977	Pittsburgh	@	Cincinnati	10	17	L						
12/10/1977	Washington	@	St. Louis Cardinals	26	20	W						
9/24/1977	Minnesota	@	Tampa Bay	9	3	W						
12/18/1976	New England	@	Oakland Raiders	21	24	L						AFC Divisional Play-offs
12/18/1976	Washington	@	Minnesota	20	35	L						NFC Divisional Play-offs
12/12/1976	St. Louis Cardinals	@	New York Giants	17	14	W						
12/11/1976	Los Angeles Rams	@	Detroit	20	17	W						
12/11/1976	Minnesota	@	Miami	29	7	W						
12/11/1976	Pittsburgh	@	Houston Oilers	21	0	W						
12/4/1976	Atlanta	@	Los Angeles Rams	0	59	L						
12/4/1976	Baltimore Colts	@	St. Louis Cardinals	17	24	L						
10/23/1976	Atlanta	@	San Francisco	0	15	L						
12/27/1975	Baltimore Colts	@	Pittsburgh	10	28	L						AFC Divisional Play-offs
12/27/1975	Los Angeles Rams	vs	St. Louis Cardinals	35	23	W						NFC Divisional Play-offs
12/20/1975	Denver	@	Miami	13	14	L						
12/20/1975	Minnesota	@	Buffalo	35	13	W						
12/13/1975	Cincinnati	@	Pittsburgh	14	35	L						
12/13/1975	Washington	@	Dallas	10	31	L						
11/1/1975	San Diego	@	New York Giants	24	35	L						
10/25/1975	St. Louis Cardinals	@	New York Giants	20	13	W						
12/21/1974	Minnesota	vs	St. Louis Cardinals	30	14	W						NFC Divisional Play-offs
12/21/1974	Oakland Raiders	vs	MIAMI	28	26	W						AFC Divisional Play-offs
12/14/1974	Cincinnati	@	Pittsburgh	3	27	L						
12/14/1974	Dallas	@	Oakland Raiders	23	27	L						
12/14/1974	Minnesota	@	Kansas City	35	15	W						
12/7/1974	Atlanta	@	Minnesota	10	23	L						
12/7/1974	Cleveland Browns	@	Dallas	17	41	L						
12/22/1973	Pittsburgh	@	Oakland Raiders	14	33	L						AFC Divisional Play-offs
12/22/1973	Washington	@	Minnesota	20	27	L						NFC Divisional Play-offs
12/15/1973	Detroit	@	Miami	7	34	L						
12/15/1973	Pittsburgh	@	San Francisco	37	14	W						
12/8/1973	Kansas City	@	Oakland Raiders	7	37	L						
12/8/1973	Minnesota	@	Green Bay	31	7	W						
12/23/1972	Dallas	@	San Francisco	30	28	W						NFC Divisional Play-offs
12/23/1972	Oakland Raiders	@	Pittsburgh	7	13	L						AFC Divisional Play-offs

Date	Team		Opponent								Notes
12/16/1972	Baltimore Colts	@	Miami	0	16	L					
12/16/1972	Minnesota	@	San Francisco	17	20	L					
12/9/1972	Cleveland Browns	@	Cincinnati	27	24	W					
12/9/1972	Washington	@	Dallas	24	34	L					
12/25/1971	**Dallas**	@	**Minnesota**	**20**	**12**	**W**					NFC Divisional Play-offs
12/25/1971	**Miami**	@	**Kansas City (2OT)**	**27**	**24**	**W**					AFC Divisional Play-offs
12/18/1971	St. Louis Cardinals	@	Dallas	12	31	L					
12/11/1971	Detroit	@	Minnesota	10	29	L					
12/11/1971	Miami	@	Baltimore Colts	3	14	L					
12/4/1971	New York Jets	@	Dallas	10	52	L					
10/23/1971	Buffalo	@	San Diego	3	20	L					
12/26/1970	**Cincinnati**	@	**Baltimore Colts**	**0**	**17**	**L**					AFC Divisional Play-offs
12/26/1970	**Detroit**	@	**Dallas**	**0**	**5**	**L**					NFC Divisional Play-offs
12/19/1970	New York Jets	@	Baltimore Colts	20	35	L					
12/12/1970	Dallas	@	Cleveland Browns	6	2	W					
12/12/1970	Kansas City	@	Oakland Raiders	6	20	L					
12/5/1970	Chicago	@	Minnesota	13	16	L					
10/10/1970	Miami	@	New York Jets	20	6	W					
10/3/1970	Oakland Raiders	@	Miami	13	20	L					
10/3/1970	Pittsburgh	@	Cleveland Browns	7	15	L					
9/19/1970	Chicago	@	New York Giants	24	16	W					
1/3/1970	**Dallas**	vs	**Los Angeles Rams**	**0**	**31**	**L**					NFL Play-off Bowl @ Miami, FL
12/27/1969	**Los Angeles Rams**	@	**Minnesota**	**20**	**23**	**L**					NFC Divisional Play-offs
12/20/1969	**Kansas City**	@	**New York Jets**	**13**	**6**	**W**					AFL Play-offs
12/13/1969	Baltimore Colts	@	Dallas	10	27	L					
12/13/1969	Kansas City	@	Oakland Raiders	6	10	L					
12/6/1969	Chicago	@	San Francisco	21	42	L					
12/6/1969	New York Jets	@	Houston Oilers	34	26	W					
10/18/1969	Pittsburgh	@	Cleveland Browns	31	42	L					
10/11/1969	Boston Patriots	@	Buffalo	16	23	L					
10/11/1969	San Diego	@	Miami	21	14	W					
10/4/1969	Cincinnati	@	San Diego	14	21	L					
10/4/1969	Oakland Raiders	@	Miami	20	20	T					
9/20/1969	Miami	@	Oakland Raiders	17	20	L					
12/21/1968	**Dallas**	@	**Cleveland**	**20**	**31**	**L**					NFL Play-offs
12/14/1968	Cleveland Browns	@	St. Louis Cardinals	16	27	L					
12/14/1968	Kansas City	@	Denver	30	7	W					
12/7/1968	Baltimore Colts	@	Green Bay	16	3	W					
10/12/1968	Buffalo	@	Miami	14	14	T					
10/5/1968	Kansas City	@	Buffalo	18	7	W					
10/5/1968	Pittsburgh	@	Cleveland Browns	24	31	L					
10/5/1968	San Diego	@	New York Jets	20	23	L					
9/28/1968	Kansas City	@	Miami	48	3	W					
9/21/1968	Oakland Raiders	@	Miami	47	21	W					
9/21/1968	Houston Oilers	@	San Diego	14	30	L					
9/14/1968	Atlanta	@	Minnesota	7	47	L					
9/14/1968	Houston Oilers	@	Miami	24	10	W					
12/23/1967	**Los Angeles Rams**	@	**Green Bay (Milwaukee)**	**7**	**28**	**L**					NFC Divisional Play-offs
12/23/1967	Houston Oilers	@	Miami	41	10	W					
12/16/1967	Dallas	@	San Francisco	16	24	L					
12/16/1967	San Diego	@	Houston Oilers	17	24	L					
12/9/1967	Buffalo	@	Boston Patriots	44	16	W					
10/7/1967	Oakland Raiders	@	New York Jets	14	27	L					
10/7/1967	Pittsburgh	@	Cleveland Browns	10	21	L					
9/9/1967	Kansas City	@	Houston Oilers	25	20	W					
9/9/1967	Boston Patriots	@	San Diego	14	28	L					
12/17/1966	Cleveland Browns	@	St. Louis Cardinals	38	10	W					
12/10/1966	Green Bay	@	Baltimore Colts	14	10	W					
12/3/1966	New York Jets	@	Oakland Raiders	28	28	T					
10/8/1966	Denver	@	Kansas City	10	37	L					
10/8/1966	Pittsburgh	@	Cleveland Browns	10	41	L					
10/8/1966	San Diego	@	New York Jets	16	17	L					
9/10/1966	Baltimore Colts	@	Green Bay (Milwaukee)	3	24	L					
9/10/1966	Oakland Raiders	@	Houston Oilers	0	31	L					

Saturday Football History

Date	Visitor		Home	V	H	Result					Notes
9/3/1966	Denver	@	Houston Oilers	7	45	L					
12/18/1965	Baltimore Colts	@	Los Angeles Rams	20	17	W					
12/18/1965	Houston Oilers	@	Boston Patriots	14	42	L					
12/11/1965	St. Louis Cardinals	@	Dallas	13	27	L					
12/4/1965	New York Jets	@	San Diego	7	38	L					
10/23/1965	San Diego	@	New York Jets	34	9	W					
10/16/1965	Oakland Raiders	@	New York Jets	24	24	T					
10/9/1965	New York Giants	@	Minnesota	14	40	L					
10/9/1965	Pittsburgh	@	Cleveland Browns	19	24	L					
9/25/1965	Chicago	@	Los Angeles Rams	28	30	L					
9/18/1965	Kansas City	@	New York Jets	14	10	W					
9/11/1965	Denver	@	San Diego	31	34	L					
9/11/1965	Boston Patriots	@	Buffalo	7	24	L					
12/26/1964	**San Diego**	@	**Buffalo**	**7**	**20**	**L**					AFL Championship
12/12/1964	Cleveland Browns	@	New York Giants	52	20	W					
12/5/1964	Green Bay	@	Chicago	17	3	W					
10/31/1964	Boston Patriots	@	New York Jets	14	35	L					
10/24/1964	New York Jets	@	Buffalo	24	34	L					
10/17/1964	Houston Oilers	@	New York Jets	21	24	L					
10/10/1964	Oakland Raiders	@	New York Jets	13	35	L					
10/10/1964	Pittsburgh	@	Cleveland Browns	23	7	W					
10/3/1964	Oakland Raiders	@	Buffalo	20	23	L					
10/3/1964	San Diego	@	New York Jets	17	17	T					
9/26/1964	San Diego	@	Buffalo	3	30	L					
9/19/1964	Detroit	@	Los Angeles Rams	17	17	T					
9/19/1964	Oakland Raiders	@	Houston Oilers	28	42	L					
9/12/1964	St. Louis Cardinals	@	Dallas	16	6	W					
9/12/1964	Denver	@	New York Jets	6	30	L					
9/12/1964	Houston Oilers	@	San Diego	21	27	L					
12/28/1963	**Boston Patriots**	@	**Buffalo**	**26**	**8**	**W**					AFL Play-offs
12/14/1963	Green Bay	@	San Francisco	21	17	W					
12/14/1963	Buffalo	@	New York Jets	19	10	W					
12/14/1963	Boston Patriots	@	Kansas City	3	35	L					
12/7/1963	Denver	@	Kansas City	21	52	L					
12/7/1963	Green Bay	@	Los Angeles Rams	31	14	W					
11/9/1963	Denver	@	Buffalo	17	27	L					
11/2/1963	San Diego	@	New York Jets	53	7	W					
10/26/1963	Denver	@	New York Jets	35	35	T					
10/26/1963	Boston Patriots	@	Buffalo	21	28	L					
10/5/1963	Boston Patriots	@	New York Jets	24	31	L					
10/5/1963	Oakland Raiders	@	Buffalo	0	12	L					
10/5/1963	Pittsburgh	@	Cleveland Browns	23	35	L					
9/28/1963	Oakland Raiders	@	New York Jets	7	10	L					
9/28/1963	Houston Oilers	@	Buffalo	31	20	W					
9/21/1963	Washington	@	Los Angeles Rams	37	14	W					
9/14/1963	St. Louis Cardinals	@	Dallas	34	7	W					
9/14/1963	Denver	@	Houston Oilers	14	20	L					
9/14/1963	Detroit	@	Los Angeles Rams	23	2	W					
9/14/1963	Boston Patriots	@	San Diego	13	17	L					
9/7/1963	Kansas City	@	Denver	59	7	W					
9/7/1963	Oakland Raiders	@	Houston Oilers	24	13	W					
12/15/1962	Cleveland Browns	@	San Francisco	13	10	W					
12/15/1962	Houston Oilers	@	New York Titans	44	10	W					
12/8/1962	Buffalo	@	New York Titans	20	3	W					
12/8/1962	Washington	@	Baltimore Colts	21	34	L					
11/3/1962	Boston Patriots	@	Buffalo	28	28	T					
10/20/1962	Oakland Raiders	@	Buffalo	6	14	L					
10/13/1962	San Diego	@	Buffalo	10	35	L					
10/6/1962	Boston Patriots	@	New York Titans	43	14	W					
10/6/1962	Philadelphia	@	Pittsburgh	7	13	L					
9/29/1962	Houston Oilers	@	San Diego	42	17	W					
9/22/1962	New York Titans	@	Buffalo	17	6	W					
9/15/1962	Denver	@	Buffalo	23	20	W					
9/8/1962	Boston Patriots	@	Dallas Texans	28	48	L					

Saturday Football History

Date	Team		Opponent	Score	Score	W/L					Notes
1/6/1962	**Detroit**	vs	**Philadelphia**	**38**	**10**	**W**					**NFL Play-off Bowl @ Miami, FL**
12/16/1961	Baltimore Colts	@	San Francisco	27	24	W					
12/9/1961	Baltimore Colts	@	Los Angeles Rams	17	34	L					
12/9/1961	Boston Patriots	@	Oakland Raiders	35	21	W					
11/11/1961	Oakland Raiders	@	New York Titans	12	23	L					
10/7/1961	San Diego	@	Boston Patriots	38	27	W					
9/30/1961	San Diego	@	Buffalo	19	11	W					
9/23/1961	Boston Patriots	@	Buffalo	23	21	W					
9/23/1961	Chicago	@	Los Angeles Rams	21	17	W					
9/16/1961	Denver	@	Boston Patriots	17	45	L					
9/9/1961	New York Titans	@	Boston Patriots	21	20	W					
9/9/1961	Oakland Raiders	@	Houston Oilers	0	55	L					
1/7/1961	**Detroit**	vs	**Cleveland Browns**	**17**	**16**	**W**					**NFL Play-off Bowl @ Miami, FL**
12/17/1960	Green Bay	@	Los Angeles Rams	35	21	W					
12/17/1960	Denver	@	Oakland Raiders	10	48	L					
12/10/1960	Denver	@	Los Angeles Chargers	33	41	L					
12/10/1960	Green Bay	@	San Francisco	13	0	W					
10/8/1960	Boston Patriots	@	Los Angeles Chargers	35	0	W					
9/24/1960	Pittsburgh	@	Dallas	35	28	W					
9/17/1960	Boston Patriots	@	New York Titans	28	24	W					
9/10/1960	Dallas Texan	@	Los Angeles Chargers	20	21	L					
12/12/1959	Baltimore Colts	@	Los Angeles Rams	45	26	W					
12/5/1959	Baltimore Colts	@	San Francisco	34	14	W					
10/3/1959	Chicago	@	Baltimore Colts	26	21	W					
9/26/1959	Cleveland Browns	@	Pittsburgh	7	17	L					
9/26/1959	New York Giants	@	Los Angeles Rams	23	21	W					
12/13/1958	Chicago Cardinals	@	Pittsburgh	21	38	L					
12/6/1958	Baltimore Colts	@	Los Angeles Rams	28	30	L					
10/4/1958	Chicago	@	Baltimore Colts	38	51	L					
10/4/1958	Washington	@	Chicago Cardinals	10	37	L					
12/14/1957	Chicago Cardinals	@	Philadelphia	31	27	W					
12/7/1957	New York Giants	@	Pittsburgh	10	21	L					
10/5/1957	Cleveland Browns	@	Pittsburgh	23	12	W					
10/5/1957	Chicago	@	Baltimore Colts	10	21	L					
10/5/1957	New York Giants	@	Philadelphia	24	20	W					
12/15/1956	New York Giants	@	Philadelphia	21	7	W					
12/8/1956	Green Bay	@	San Francisco	20	38	L					
10/6/1956	Cleveland Browns	@	Pittsburgh	14	10	W					
10/6/1956	Detroit	@	Baltimore Colts	31	14	W					
10/6/1956	Washington	@	Philadelphia	9	13	L					
11/5/1955	Baltimore Colts	@	Detroit	14	24	L					
11/5/1955	Pittsburgh	@	Chicago Cardinals	13	27	L					
10/29/1955	Green Bay	@	Baltimore Colts	10	14	L					
10/15/1955	Philadelphia	@	Pittsburgh	7	13	L					
10/8/1955	Baltimore Colts	@	Green Bay (Milwaukee)	24	20	W					
10/1/1955	Detroit	@	Baltimore Colts	13	28	L					
10/1/1955	Washington	@	Philadelphia	31	30	W					
9/24/1955	New York Giants	@	Philadelphia	17	27	L					
12/11/1954	Baltimore Colts	@	San Francisco	7	10	L					
12/4/1954	Baltimore Colts	@	Los Angeles Rams	22	21	W					
11/20/1954	San Francisco	@	Pittsburgh	31	3	W					
11/13/1954	Baltimore Colts	@	Green Bay (Milwaukee)	13	24	L					
11/6/1954	Detroit	@	Baltimore Colts	27	3	W					
10/30/1954	Green Bay	@	Philadelphia	37	14	W					
10/23/1954	Philadelphia	@	Pittsburgh	7	17	L					
10/16/1954	Baltimore Colts	@	Detroit	0	35	L					
10/9/1954	Pittsburgh	@	Philadelphia	22	24	L					
10/2/1954	New York Giants	@	Baltimore Colts	14	20	L					
10/2/1954	Washington	@	Pittsburgh	7	37	L					
12/12/1953	Green Bay	@	Los Angeles Rams	17	33	L					
12/5/1953	Baltimore Colts	@	Los Angeles Rams	2	45	L					
11/21/1953	Chicago Cardinals	@	Philadelphia	0	38	L					
11/7/1953	Baltimore Colts	@	Detroit	7	17	L					
10/31/1953	Green Bay	@	Baltimore Colts	35	24	W					

Saturday Football History

Date	Team	@	Opponent			Result					Notes
10/24/1953	Green Bay	@	Pittsburgh	14	31	L					
10/17/1953	Pittsburgh	@	Philadelphia	7	23	L					
10/10/1953	Philadelphia	@	Cleveland Browns	13	37	L					
10/3/1953	Detroit	@	Baltimore Colts	27	17	W					
10/3/1953	New York Giants	@	Pittsburgh	14	24	L					
12/13/1952	Dallas Texans	@	Detroit	6	41	L					
10/18/1952	Green Bay	@	Dallas Texans	24	14	W					
10/4/1952	Cleveland Browns	@	Pittsburgh	21	20	W					
10/4/1952	New York Giants	@	Philadelphia	31	7	W					
10/4/1952	San Francisco	@	Dallas Texans	37	14	W					
10/6/1951	San Francisco	@	Philadelphia	14	21	L					
10/1/1951	New York Giants	@	Pittsburgh	13	13	T					
10/7/1950	Cleveland Browns	@	Pittsburgh	30	17	W					
10/7/1950	Los Angeles Rams	@	Philadelphia	20	56	L					
9/16/1950	Cleveland Browns	@	Philadelphia	35	10	W					
10/8/1949	Chicago Cardinals	@	Philadelphia	3	28	L					
10/8/1949	Detroit	@	Pittsburgh	7	14	L					
10/9/1948	Boston Yanks	@	Detroit	17	14	W					
11/30/1946	Chicago Rockets	@	San Francisco	0	14	L					AAFC
11/2/1946	Buffalo Bills	@	San Francisco	14	27	L					AAFC
10/19/1946	San Francisco	@	Buffalo Bills	14	17	L					AAFC
10/12/1946	San Francisco	@	Los Angeles Dons	23	14	W					AAFC
10/9/1943	New York Giants	@	Steagles	14	28	L					
10/2/1943	**Brooklyn Dodgers**	@	**Steagles**	**10**	**17**	**L**					**Shibe Park**
9/27/1941	Detroit	@	Chicago Cardinals	14	14	T					
9/27/1941	Brooklyn Dodgers	@	Philadelphia	24	13	W					
9/13/1941	New York Giants	@	Philadelphia	24	0	W					
10/5/1940	Chicago Cardinals	@	Detroit	14	43	L					
9/28/1940	New York Giants	@	Philadelphia	20	14	W					
9/17/1938	Chicago Cardinals	@	Cleveland Rams	7	6	W					
10/31/1931	Detroit	@	Frankford Yellow Jackets	14	0	W					
11/22/1930	Chicago	@	Frankford Yellow Jackets	13	6	W					
11/15/1930	Detroit	@	Frankford Yellow Jackets	6	7	L					
10/25/1930	Chicago Cardinals	@	Frankford Yellow Jackets	34	7	W					
12/7/1929	New York Giants	@	Frankford Yellow Jackets	12	0	W					
11/16/1929	Chicago	@	Frankford Yellow Jackets	14	20	L					
11/2/1929	Chicago Cardinals	@	Frankford Yellow Jackets	0	8	L					
12/15/1928	Chicago	@	Frankford Yellow Jackets	0	19	L					
12/8/1928	New York Giants	@	Frankford Yellow Jackets	0	7	L					
11/24/1928	Chicago Cardinals	@	Frankford Yellow Jackets	0	19	L					
12/3/1927	Chicago	@	Frankford Yellow Jackets	0	0	T					
11/19/1927	Chicago Cardinals	@	Frankford Yellow Jackets	8	12	L					
10/22/1927	New York Giants	@	Frankford Yellow Jackets	13	0	W					
12/4/1926	Chicago	@	Frankford Yellow Jackets	6	7	L					
11/6/1926	Chicago Cardinals	@	Frankford Yellow Jackets	7	33	L					
10/16/1926	New York Giants	@	Frankford Yellow Jackets	0	6	L					
12/12/1925	Hammond Pros	@	Chicago Cardinals	0	13	L					
12/12/1925	Chicago	@	Detroit Panthers	0	21	L					
12/5/1925	Chicago	@	Frankford Yellow Jackets	14	7	W					
11/28/1925	Green Bay	@	Frankford Yellow Jackets	7	13	L					
10/17/1925	New York Giants	@	Frankford Yellow Jackets	3	5	L					

Interesting Saturday Facts

Baltimore is 6-0 at home vs Pittsburgh since 1965

Chicago is 1-6 on road on Saturday since 1965

Cincinnati is 2-8 on road on Saturday since 1969

Dallas is 1-5 at home on Saturday since 1994 (Reg. season)

Indianapolis is 3-15 on road on Saturday since 1969

Indianapolis is 10-2 at home on Saturday since 1970

Miami is 9-0 at home on Saturday since 1984

New England is 15-2 at home on Saturday since 2002

New York Jets are 2-11 at home on Saturday since 1969

Philadelphia is 0-5 at home on Saturday since 1956 (Reg season)

Pittsburgh is 16-4 at home on Saturday since 1958

San Francisco is 19-5 at home on Saturday since 1976

Seattle is 7-1 at home in Playoffs on Saturday since 2006

Seattle is 1-8 on road on Saturday since 1984

Tampa Bay is 1-7 on road on Saturday since 1982 {1-7 ATS}

Washington is 0-5 vs AFC teams on Saturday since 1988

Sunday Night Football History

	VISITOR		HOME	SC	ORE	S/U W-L	LINE	ATS W-L	TOTAL	O/U
1/08/2023	Detroit	@	GREEN BAY	20	16	W	4.0	W	48.0	U
1/1/2023	Pittsburgh	@	BALTIMORE	16	13	W	1.5	W	35.5	U
12/25/2022	Tampa Bay	@	ARIZONA	19	16	W	-7.5	W	36.5	U
12/18/2022	New York Giants	@	WASHINGTON	20	12	W	4.0	W	40.0	U
12/11/2022	Miami	@	LOS ANGELES CHARGERS	17	23	L	3.0	L	55.0	U
12/4/2022	Indianapolis	@	DALLAS	19	54	L	11.0	L	44.0	O
11/27/2022	Green Bay	@	PHILADELPHIA	33	40	L	6.0	L	46.0	O
11/20/2022	Kansas City	@	LOS ANGELES CHARGERS	30	27	W	-4.5	L	52.5	O
11/13/2022	Los Angeles Chargers	@	SAN FRANCISCO	16	22	L	8.5	W	45.5	U
11/6/2022	Tennessee	@	KANSAS CITY	17	20	L	14.0	W	45.0	U
10/30/2022	Green Bay	@	BUFFALO	17	27	L	10.5	W	47.0	U
10/23/2022	Pittsburgh	@	MIAMI	13	16	L	7.5	W	44.0	U
10/16/2022	Dallas	@	PHILADELPHIA	17	26	L	6.5	L	42.5	O
10/9/2022	Cincinnati	@	BALTIMORE	17	19	L	3.0	W	47.5	U
10/2/2022	Kansas City	@	TAMPA BAY	41	31	W	2.0	W	47.5	O
9/25/2022	San Francisco	@	DENVER	10	11	L	-1.5	L	44.5	U
9/18/2022	Chicago	@	GREEN BAY	10	27	L	10.0	L	42.0	U
9/11/2022	Tampa Bay	@	DALLAS	19	3	W	-2.5	W	49.5	U
1/9/2022	Los Angeles Chargers	@	LAS VEGAS RAIDERS	32	35	L	-3.0	L	50.0	O
1/2/2022	Minnesota	@	GREEN BAY	10	37	L	12.5	L	42.5	O
12/26/2021	Washington	@	DALLAS	14	56	L	10.0	L	46.0	O
12/19/2021	New Orleans	@	TAMPA BAY	9	0	W	11.5	W	46.5	U
12/12/2021	Chicago	@	GREEN BAY	30	45	L	12.0	L	43.0	O
12/5/2021	Denver	@	KANSAS CITY	9	22	L	8.5	L	47.0	U
11/28/2021	Cleveland	@	BALTIMORE RAVENS	10	16	L	3.0	L	47.5	U
11/21/2021	Pittsburgh	@	LOS ANGELES CHARGERS	37	41	L	6.0	W	47.5	O
11/14/2021	Kansas City	@	LAS VEGAS RAIDERS	41	14	W	-2.5	W	53.5	O
11/7/2021	Tennessee	@	LOS ANGELES RAMS	28	16	W	7.0	W	53.0	U
10/31/2021	Dallas	@	MINNESOTA	20	16	W	4.0	W	49.0	U
10/24/2021	Indianapolis Colts	@	SAN FRANCISCO	30	18	W	3.5	W	41.5	O
10/17/2021	Seattle	@	PITTSBURGH	20	23	L	5.5	W	43.0	T
10/10/2021	Buffalo	@	KANSAS CITY	38	20	W	2.5	W	57.5	O
10/3/2021	Tampa Bay	@	NEW ENGLAND	19	17	W	-6.5	L	49.0	U
9/26/2021	Green Bay	@	SAN FRANCISCO	30	28	W	3.0	W	50.5	O
9/19/2021	Kansas City	@	BALTIMORE RAVENS	35	36	L	-3.5	L	53.5	O
9/12/2021	Chicago	@	LOS ANGELES RAMS	14	34	L	9.5	L	46.5	O
1/3/2021	Washington Redskins	@	PHILADELPHIA EAGLES	20	14	W	-6.5	L	43.5	U
12/27/2020	Tennessee Titans	@	GREEN BAY PACKERS	14	40	L	3.0	L	52.0	O
12/20/2020	Cleveland	@	NEW YORK GIANTS	20	6	W	-6.0	W	44.5	U
12/13/2020	Pittsburgh Steelers	@	BUFFALO BILLS	15	26	L	1.5	L	49.0	U
12/6/2020	Denver Broncos	@	KANSAS CITY CHIEFS	16	22	L	13.0	W	51.0	U
11/29/2020	Chicago Bears	@	GREEN BAY PACKERS	25	41	L	7.5	L	44.5	O
11/22/2020	Kansas City Chiefs	@	LAS VEGAS RAIDERS	35	31	W	-7.5	L	56.5	O
11/15/2020	Baltimore Ravens	@	NEW ENGLAND PATRIOTS	17	23	L	-7.0	L	44.0	U
11/8/2020	New Orleans Saints	@	TAMPA BAY BUCCANEERS	38	3	W	3.0	W	51.0	U
11/1/2020	Dallas Cowboys	@	PHILADELPHIA EAGLES	9	23	L	10.0	L	43.5	U
10/25/2020	Seattle Seahawks	@	ARIZONA CARDINALS {OT}	34	37	L	-3.5	L	55.5	O
10/18/2020	Los Angeles Rams	@	SAN FRANCISCO 49ERS	16	24	L	-2.0	L	51.0	U
10/11/2020	Minnesota Vikings	@	SEATTLE SEAHAWKS	26	27	L	6.5	W	53.5	U
10/4/2020	Philadelphia Eagles	@	SAN FRANCISCO 49ERS	25	20	W	7.5	W	45.5	U
9/27/2020	Green Bay Packers	@	NEW ORLEANS SAINTS	37	30	W	3.0	W	51.5	O
9/20/2020	New England Patriots	@	SEATTLE SEAHAWKS	30	35	L	4.5	L	45.0	O
9/13/2020	Dallas Cowboys	@	LOS ANGELES RAMS	17	20	L	PK	L	51.5	U
12/22/2019	Kansas City	@	CHICAGO	26	3	W	-6.5	W	45.5	U
12/15/2019	Buffalo	@	PITTSBURGH	17	10	W	1.0	W	37.0	U
12/8/2019	Seattle	@	LOS ANGELES RAMS	12	28	L	1.0	L	48.0	U
12/1/2019	New England Patriots	@	HOUSTON	22	28	L	-3.0	L	46.5	O
11/24/2019	Green Bay	@	SAN FRANCISCO	8	37	L	3.0	L	47.5	U
11/17/2019	Chicago	@	LOS ANGELES RAMS	7	17	L	5.5	L	39.5	U
11/10/2019	Minnesota	@	DALLAS	28	24	W	3.0	W	48.0	O
11/3/2019	New England Patriots	@	BALTIMORE RAVENS	20	37	L	-3.0	L	44.5	O

Sunday Night Football History

10/27/2019	**Green Bay**	@	KANSAS CITY	31	24	W	-5.0	W	48.0	O
10/20/2019	Philadelphia	@	**DALLAS**	10	37	L	3.0	L	50.0	U
10/13/2019	**Pittsburgh**	@	LOS ANGELES CHARGERS	24	17	W	6.0	W	42.5	U
10/6/2019	**Indianapolis Colts**	@	KANSAS CITY	19	13	W	10.5	W	55.5	U
9/29/2019	Dallas	@	**NEW ORLEANS**	10	12	L	-2.5	L	47.0	U
9/22/2019	**Los Angeles Rams**	@	CLEVELAND	20	13	W	-4.0	W	47.5	U
9/15/2019	Philadelphia	@	**ATLANTA**	20	24	L	-1.0	L	53.0	U
9/8/2019	Pittsburgh	@	**NEW ENGLAND PATRIOTS**	3	33	L	5.5	L	49.0	U
12/30/2018	**Indianapolis Colts**	@	TENNESSEE TITANS	33	17	W	-4.5	W	43.0	O
12/23/2018	Kansas City	@	**SEATTLE**	31	38	L	-1.0	L	54.5	O
12/16/2018	**Philadelphia**	@	LOS ANGELES RAMS	30	23	W	13.5	W	53.0	T
12/9/2018	Los Angeles Rams	@	**CHICAGO**	6	15	L	-3.0	L	51.0	U
12/2/2018	**Los Angeles Chargers**	@	PITTSBURGH	33	30	W	3.0	W	53.5	O
11/25/2018	Green Bay	@	**MINNESOTA**	17	24	L	3.5	L	48.5	U
11/18/2018	Minnesota	@	**CHICAGO**	20	25	L	2.5	L	44.0	O
11/11/2018	**Dallas**	@	PHILADELPHIA	27	20	W	7.5	W	45.0	O
11/4/2018	Green Bay	@	**NEW ENGLAND PATRIOTS**	17	31	L	5.0	L	56.0	U
10/28/2018	**New Orleans**	@	MINNESOTA	30	20	W	-2.5	W	54.0	U
10/21/2018	Cincinnati	@	**KANSAS CITY**	10	45	L	6.5	L	56.0	U
10/14/2018	Kansas City	@	**NEW ENGLAND PATROITS**	40	43	L	4.0	W	59.0	O
10/7/2018	Dallas	@	**HOUSTON TEXANS {OT}**	16	19	L	3.5	W	45.5	U
9/30/2018	**Baltimore Ravens**	@	PITTSBURGH	26	14	W	3.0	W	51.0	U
9/23/2018	New England Patriots	@	**DETROIT**	10	26	L	-7.0	L	55.5	U
9/16/2018	New York Giants	@	**DALLAS**	13	20	L	3.0	L	42.0	U
9/9/2018	Chicago	@	**GREEN BAY**	23	24	L	7.0	W	45.0	O
12/17/2017	**Dallas**	@	OAKLAND RAIDERS	20	17	W	-3.0	T	46.0	U
12/10/2017	Baltimore Ravens	@	**PITTSBURGH**	38	39	L	6.0	W	43.0	O
12/3/2017	Philadelphia	@	**SEATTLE**	10	24	L	-3.5	L	46.5	U
11/26/2017	Green Bay	@	**PITTSBURGH**	28	31	L	14.0	W	43.0	O
11/19/2017	**Philadelphia**	@	DALLAS	37	9	W	-6.0	W	47.5	U
11/12/2017	**New England Patriots**	@	DENVER	41	16	W	-7.0	W	45.0	O
11/5/2017	**Oakland Raiders**	@	MIAMI	27	24	W	-3.0	T	44.5	O
10/29/2017	**Pittsburgh**	@	DETROIT	20	15	W	-3.0	W	44.5	U
10/22/2017	Atlanta	@	**NEW ENGLAND PATRIOTS**	7	23	L	2.5	L	55.5	U
10/15/2017	**New York Giants**	@	DENVER	23	10	W	13.5	W	37.5	U
10/8/2017	**Kansas City**	@	HOUSTON TEXANS	42	34	W	-2.0	W	44.5	O
10/1/2017	Indianapolis Colts	@	**SEATTLE**	18	46	L	12.5	L	41.5	O
9/24/2017	Oakland Raiders	@	**WASHINGTON REDSKINS**	27	10	W	3.5	W	53.5	U
9/17/2017	Green Bay	@	**ATLANTA**	23	34	L	3.0	L	54.5	O
9/10/2017	New York Giants	@	**DALLAS**	3	19	L	6.0	L	46.0	U
1/1/2017	**Green Bay**	@	DETROIT	31	24	W	-3.5	W	50.0	O
12/25/2016	Denver	@	**KANSAS CITY**	10	33	L	3.5	L	38.5	O
12/18/2016	Tampa Bay	@	**DALLAS**	20	26	L	7.0	W	47.5	U
12/11/2016	Dallas	@	**NEW YORK GIANTS**	7	10	L	-3.5	L	44.0	U
12/4/2016	Carolina	@	**SEATTLE**	7	40	L	8.5	L	44.0	O
11/27/2016	**Kansas City**	@	DENVER {OT}	30	27	W	3.5	W	40.0	O
11/20/2016	Green Bay	@	**WASHINGTON REDSKINS**	24	42	L	2.5	L	48.5	O
11/13/2016	**Seattle**	@	NEW ENGLAND PATRIOTS	31	24	W	7.5	W	49.5	O
11/6/2016	Denver	@	**OAKLAND RAIDERS**	20	30	L	1.0	L	44.5	O
10/30/2016	Philadelphia	@	**DALLAS {OT}**	23	29	L	5.0	L	44.0	O
10/23/2016	Seattle	@	ARIZONA CARDINALS {OT}	6	6	T	2.5	W	43.0	U
10/16/2016	Indianapolis Colts	@	**HOUSTON TEXANS**	23	26	L	3.0	T	47.5	O
10/9/2016	New York Giants	@	**GREEN BAY**	16	23	L	7.0	T	49.0	U
10/2/2016	Kansas City	@	**PITTSBURGH**	14	43	L	3.5	L	48.5	O
9/25/2016	Chicago	@	**DALLAS**	17	31	L	6.5	L	45.0	O
9/18/2016	Green Bay	@	**MINNESOTA**	14	17	L	-2.0	L	42.5	U
9/11/2016	**New England Patriots**	@	ARIZONA CARDINALS	23	21	W	9.0	W	44.5	U
1/3/2016	**Minnesota**	@	GREEN BAY	20	13	W	3.0	W	44.0	U
12/27/2015	New York Giants	@	**MINNESOTA**	17	49	L	7.0	L	45.0	O
12/20/2015	**Arizona Cardinals**	@	PHILADELPHIA	40	17	W	-3.5	W	51.0	O
12/13/2015	**New England Patriots**	@	HOUSTON TEXANS	27	6	W	-5.0	W	46.5	U
12/6/2015	Indianapolis Colts	@	**PITTSBURGH**	10	45	L	9.5	L	50.5	O
11/29/2015	New England Patriots	@	**DENVER {OT}**	24	30	L	-2.5	L	43.0	O
11/22/2015	Cincinnati	@	**ARIZONA CARDINALS**	31	34	L	4.0	W	47.5	O

Sunday Night Football History

11/15/2015	**Arizona Cardinals**	@	SEATTLE	39	32	W	3.0	W	43.5	O
11/8/2015	**Philadelphia**	@	DALLAS {OT}	33	27	W	-3.0	W	44.0	O
11/1/2015	Green Bay	@	**DENVER**	10	29	L	-2.5	L	46.0	U
10/25/2015	Philadelphia	@	**CAROLINA**	16	27	L	3.0	L	45.5	U
10/18/2015	**New England Patriots**	@	INDIANAPOLIS COLTS	34	27	W	-8.5	L	53.5	O
10/11/2015	San Francisco	@	**NEW YORK GIANTS**	27	30	L	7.5	W	44.0	O
10/4/2015	Dallas	@	**NEW ORLEANS {OT}**	20	26	L	3.0	L	48.0	U
9/27/2015	**Denver**	@	DETROIT	24	12	W	-3.0	W	45.0	U
9/20/2015	Seattle	@	**GREEN BAY**	17	27	L	3.5	L	49.0	U
9/13/2015	New York Giants	@	**DALLAS**	26	27	L	7.0	W	52.0	O
12/28/2014	Cincinnati	@	**PITTSBURGH**	17	27	L	3.0	L	48.5	U
12/21/2014	**Seattle**	@	ARIZONA CARDINALS	35	6	W	-9.0	W	36.5	O
12/14/2014	**Dallas**	@	PHILADELPHIA	38	27	W	3.0	W	54.0	O
12/7/2014	**New England Patriots**	@	SAN DIEGO CHARGERS	23	14	W	-4.0	W	53.0	U
11/30/2014	**Denver**	@	KANSAS CITY	29	16	W	1.0	W	49.0	U
11/23/2014	**Dallas**	@	NEW YORK GIANTS	31	28	W	-4.0	L	49.0	O
11/16/2014	**New England Patriots**	@	INDIANAPOLIS COLTS	42	20	W	3.0	W	57.5	O
11/9/2014	Chicago	@	**GREEN BAY**	14	55	L	9.5	L	53.5	O
11/2/2014	Baltimore Ravens	@	**PITTSBURGH**	23	43	L	2.0	L	47.5	O
10/26/2014	Green Bay	@	**NEW ORLEANS**	23	44	L	2.5	L	54.5	O
10/19/2014	San Francisco	@	**DENVER**	17	42	L	6.5	L	47.5	O
10/12/2014	New York Giants	@	**PHILADELPHIA**	0	27	L	1.5	L	50.0	U
10/5/2014	Cincinnati	@	**NEW ENGLAND PATRIOTS**	17	43	L	-2.5	L	46.0	O
9/28/2014	New Orleans	@	**DALLAS**	17	38	L	-3.0	L	53.5	O
9/21/2014	**Pittsburgh**	@	CAROLINA	37	19	W	3.0	W	42.5	O
9/14/2014	**Chicago**	@	SAN FRANCISCO	28	20	W	7.0	W	47.0	O
9/7/2014	Indianapolis Colts	@	**DENVER**	24	31	L	9.0	W	53.0	O
12/29/2013	**Philadelphia**	@	DALLAS	24	22	W	-7.0	L	52.0	U
12/22/2013	Chicago	@	**PHILADELPHIA**	11	54	L	3.5	L	54.0	O
12/15/2013	Cincinnati	@	**PITTSBURGH**	20	30	L	-2.5	L	43.5	O
12/8/2013	Carolina	@	**NEW ORLEANS**	13	31	L	3.0	L	46.5	U
12/1/2013	**New York Giants**	@	WASHINGTON REDSKINS	24	17	W	Pk	W	45.0	U
11/24/2013	Denver	@	**NEW ENGLAND PATRIOTS (OT)**	31	34	L	-2.0	L	54.5	O
11/17/2013	Kansas City	@	**DENVER**	17	27	L	7.0	L	49.0	U
11/10/2013	Dallas	@	**NEW ORLEANS**	17	49	L	6.5	L	54.5	O
11/3/2013	**Indianapolis Colts**	@	HOUSTON TEXANS	27	24	W	Pk	W	42.5	O
10/27/2013	**Green Bay**	@	MINNESOTA	44	31	W	-7.0	W	47.5	O
10/20/2013	Denver	@	**INDIANAPOLIS COLTS**	33	39	L	-6.0	L	55.0	O
10/13/2013	Washington Redskins	@	**DALLAS**	16	31	L	5.5	L	52.5	U
10/6/2013	Houston Texans	@	**SAN FRANCISCO**	3	34	L	4.0	L	43.0	U
9/29/2013	**New England Patriots**	@	ATLANTA	30	23	W	3.5	W	49.0	O
9/22/2013	**Chicago**	@	PITTSBURGH	40	23	W	-2.0	W	41.0	O
9/15/2013	San Francisco	@	**SEATTLE**	3	29	L	3.0	L	44.0	U
9/8/2013	New York Giants	@	**DALLAS**	31	36	L	3.0	L	49.5	O
12/30/2012	Dallas	@	**WASHINGTON REDSKINS**	18	28	L	3.0	L	48.5	U
12/23/2012	San Francisco	@	**SEATTLE**	13	42	L	2.5	L	41.0	O
12/16/2012	**San Francisco**	@	NEW ENGLAND PATRIOTS	41	34	W	4.0	W	47.5	O
12/9/2012	Detroit	@	**GREEN BAY**	20	27	L	6.5	L	50.0	U
12/2/2012	Philadelphia	@	**DALLAS**	33	38	L	10.5	W	44.5	O
11/25/2012	Green Bay	@	**NEW YORK GIANTS**	10	38	L	1.5	L	50.0	U
11/18/2012	**Baltimore Ravens**	@	PITTSBURGH	13	10	W	-3.0	T	41.0	U
11/11/2012	**Houston Texans**	@	CHICAGO	13	6	W	1.0	W	37.0	U
11/4/2012	Dallas	@	**ATLANTA**	13	19	L	3.5	L	47.5	U
10/28/2012	New Orleans	@	**DENVER**	14	34	L	6.0	L	55.0	U
10/21/2012	**Pittsburgh**	@	CINCINNATI	24	17	W	-1.0	W	47.0	U
10/14/2012	**Green Bay**	@	HOUSTON TEXANS	42	24	W	4.0	W	46.5	O
10/7/2012	San Diego Chargers	@	**NEW ORLEANS**	24	31	L	3.5	L	53.5	O
9/30/2012	New York Giants	@	**PHILADELPHIA**	17	19	L	1.5	L	46.0	U
9/23/2012	New England Patriots	@	**BALTIMORE RAVENS**	30	31	L	3.0	W	48.0	O
9/16/2012	Detroit	@	**SAN FRANCISCO**	19	27	L	7.0	L	46.0	T
9/9/2012	Pittsburgh	@	**DENVER**	19	31	L	3.0	L	45.5	O
1/1/2012	Dallas	@	**NEW YORK GIANTS**	14	31	L	3.0	L	47.5	U
12/18/2011	Baltimore Ravens	@	**SAN DIEGO CHARGERS**	14	34	L	-2.5	L	44.5	O
12/11/2011	**New York Giants**	@	DALLAS	37	34	W	4.0	W	50.0	O

Sunday Night Football History

12/4/2011	Detroit	@	NEW ORLEANS	17	31	L	9.0	L	54.0	U
11/27/2011	**Pittsburgh**	@	KANSAS CITY	13	9	W	-10.5	L	41.0	U
11/20/2011	**Philadelphia**	@	NEW YORK GIANTS	17	10	W	5.5	W	45.5	U
11/13/2011	**New England Patriots**	@	NEW YORK JETS	37	16	W	2.0	W	47.5	O
11/6/2011	**Baltimore Ravens**	@	PITTSBURGH	23	20	W	3.5	W	42.0	O
10/30/2011	Dallas	@	**PHILADELPHIA**	7	34	L	3.0	L	48.5	U
10/23/2011	Indianapolis Colts	@	**NEW ORLEANS**	7	62	L	13.5	L	48.5	O
10/16/2011	Minnesota	@	**CHICAGO**	10	39	L	2.5	L	41.5	O
10/9/2011	**Green Bay**	@	ATLANTA	25	14	W	-6.0	W	53.5	U
10/2/2011	New York Jets	@	**BALTIMORE RAVENS**	17	34	L	4.5	L	43.0	O
9/25/2011	**Pittsburgh**	@	INDIANAPOLIS COLTS	23	20	W	-10.5	L	39.5	O
9/18/2011	Philadelphia	@	**ATLANTA**	31	35	L	-2.5	L	49.5	O
9/11/2011	Dallas	@	**NEW YORK JETS**	24	27	L	6.0	W	40.5	O
1/2/2011	St. Louis Rams	@	**SEATTLE**	6	16	L	-3.0	L	41.5	U
12/26/2010	New York Giants	@	**GREEN BAY**	17	45	L	3.0	L	43.5	O
12/19/2010	Green Bay	@	**NEW ENGLAND PATRIOTS**	27	31	L	14.0	W	43.5	O
12/12/2010	**Philadelphia**	@	DALLAS	30	27	W	-3.5	L	50.5	O
12/5/2010	**Pittsburgh**	@	BALTIMORE RAVENS	13	10	W	3.0	W	39.5	U
11/28/2010	**San Diego Chargers**	@	INDIANAPOLIS COLTS	36	14	W	2.5	W	51.0	U
11/21/2010	New York Giants	@	**PHILADELPHIA**	17	27	L	3.5	L	48.0	U
11/14/2010	**New England Patriots**	@	PITTSBURGH	39	26	W	5.0	W	45.0	O
11/7/2010	Dallas	@	**GREEN BAY**	7	45	L	7.5	L	45.5	O
10/31/2010	Pittsburgh	@	**NEW ORLEANS**	10	20	L	1.5	L	44.5	U
10/24/2010	Minnesota	@	**GREEN BAY**	24	28	L	3.0	L	44.0	O
10/17/2010	**Indianapolis Colts**	@	WASHINGTON REDSKINS	27	24	W	-3.0	T	44.5	O
10/10/2010	**Philadelphia**	@	SAN FRANCISCO	27	24	W	3.0	W	38.5	O
10/3/2010	Chicago	@	**NEW YORK GIANTS**	3	17	L	3.5	L	44.0	U
9/26/2010	**New York Jets**	@	MIAMI	31	23	W	2.0	W	35.5	O
9/19/2010	New York Giants	@	**INDIANAPOLIS COLTS**	14	38	L	4.5	L	48.0	O
9/12/2010	Dallas	@	**WASHINGTON REDSKINS**	7	13	L	-3.5	L	40.0	U
12/27/2009	**Dallas**	@	WASHINGTON REDSKINS	17	0	W	-7.0	W	42.0	U
12/20/2009	Minnesota	@	**CAROLINA**	7	26	L	-9.0	L	42.5	U
12/13/2009	**Philadelphia**	@	NEW YORK GIANTS	45	38	W	-1.0	W	44.0	O
12/6/2009	Minnesota	@	**ARIZONA CARDINALS**	17	30	L	-3.5	L	48.5	U
11/29/2009	Pittsburgh	@	**BALTIMORE RAVENS (OT)**	17	20	L	7.5	W	34.0	O
11/22/2009	**Philadelphia**	@	CHICAGO	24	20	W	-3.0	W	45.0	U
11/15/2009	New England Patriots	@	**INDIANAPOLIS COLTS**	34	35	L	3.0	W	49.0	O
11/8/2009	**Dallas**	@	PHILADELPHIA	20	16	W	3.0	W	50.0	U
10/25/2009	**Arizona Cardinals**	@	NEW YORK GIANTS	24	17	W	7.0	W	46.5	U
10/25/2009	**New England Patriots**	@	TAMPA BAY	35	7	W	-15.0	W	45.0	U
10/18/2009	Chicago	@	**ATLANTA**	14	21	L	3.5	L	45.5	U
10/11/2009	**Indianapolis Colts**	@	TENNESSEE TITANS	31	9	W	-4.0	W	45.0	U
10/4/2009	San Diego Chargers	@	**PITTSBURGH**	28	38	L	6.5	L	43.0	O
9/27/2009	**Indianapolis Colts**	@	ARIZONA CARDINALS	31	10	W	3.0	W	48.5	U
9/20/2009	**New York Giants**	@	DALLAS	33	31	W	2.5	W	44.5	O
9/13/2009	Chicago	@	**GREEN BAY**	15	21	L	4.5	L	46.5	U
12/28/2008	Denver	@	**SAN DIEGO CHARGERS**	21	52	L	7.5	L	50.0	O
12/21/2008	Carolina	@	**NEW YORK GIANTS (OT)**	28	34	L	3.5	L	37.5	O
12/14/2008	New York Giants	@	**DALLAS**	8	20	L	3.0	L	45.0	U
12/7/2008	Washington Redskins	@	**BALTIMORE RAVENS**	10	24	L	6.0	L	35.0	U
11/30/2008	Chicago	@	**MINNESOTA**	14	34	L	3.5	L	42.0	O
11/23/2008	**Indianapolis Colts**	@	SAN DIEGO CHARGERS	23	20	W	3.0	W	49.0	U
11/16/2008	**Dallas**	@	WASHINGTON REDSKINS	14	10	W	-1.5	W	43.0	U
11/9/2008	**New York Giants**	@	PHILADELPHIA	36	31	W	3.0	W	43.0	O
11/2/2008	New England Patriots	@	**INDIANAPOLIS COLTS**	15	18	L	6.0	W	44.0	U
10/26/2008	**New Orleans**	@	SAN DIEGO CHARGERS	37	32	W	3.0	W	45.5	O
10/26/2008	San Diego Chargers	@	**NEW ORLEANS**	32	37	L	-3.0	L	45.5	O
10/19/2008	Seattle	@	**TAMPA BAY**	10	20	L	10.5	W	38.0	U
10/12/2008	New England Patriots	@	**SAN DIEGO CHARGERS**	10	30	L	6.0	L	45.0	U
10/5/2008	**Pittsburgh**	@	JACKSONVILLE	26	21	W	5.0	W	36.5	O
9/28/2008	Philadelphia	@	**CHICAGO**	20	24	L	-3.0	L	39.0	O
9/21/2008	**Dallas**	@	GREEN BAY	27	16	W	-3.0	W	51.0	U
9/14/2008	**Pittsburgh**	@	CLEVELAND	10	6	W	-6.5	L	44.0	U
9/7/2008	**Chicago**	@	INDIANAPOLIS COLTS	29	13	W	9.5	W	44.0	U

Copyright © 2023 by Steve's Football Bible, LLC

Sunday Night Football History

12/30/2007	**Tennessee Titans**	@	INDIANAPOLIS COLTS	16	10	W	-4.5	W	39.5	U		
12/23/2007	**Washington Redskins**	@	MINNESOTA	32	21	W	6.5	W	40.5	O		
12/16/2007	**Washington Redskins**	@	NEW YORK GIANTS	22	10	W	5.0	W	36.0	U		
12/9/2007	**Indianapolis Colts**	@	BALTIMORE RAVENS	44	20	W	-9.0	W	41.5	O		
12/2/2007	Cincinnati	@	**PITTSBURGH**	10	24	L	7.0	L	40.0	U		
11/29/2007	Green Bay	@	**DALLAS**	27	37	L	7.0	L	51.0	O		
11/25/2007	Philadelphia	@	**NEW ENGLAND PATRIOTS**	28	31	L	24.0	W	51.0	O		
11/18/2007	**New England Patriots**	@	BUFFALO	56	10	W	-15.5	W	46.5	O		
11/11/2007	Indianapolis Colts	@	**SAN DIEGO CHARGERS**	21	23	L	-3.5	L	48.0	U		
11/4/2007	**Dallas**	@	PHILADELPHIA	38	17	W	-3.0	W	46.5	O		
10/21/2007	Pittsburgh	@	**DENVER**	28	31	L	-3.5	L	38.0	O		
10/14/2007	**New Orleans**	@	SEATTLE	28	17	W	6.5	W	42.5	O		
10/7/2007	**Chicago**	@	GREEN BAY	27	20	W	3.0	W	40.5	O		
9/30/2007	Philadelphia	@	**NEW YORK GIANTS**	3	16	L	-2.5	L	47.5	U		
9/23/2007	**Dallas**	@	CHICAGO	34	10	W	3.0	W	41.0	O		
9/16/2007	San Diego Chargers	@	**NEW ENGLAND PATRIOTS**	14	38	L	3.5	L	46.0	O		
9/9/2007	New York Giants	@	**DALLAS**	35	45	L	6.0	L	44.0	O		
12/31/2006	**Green Bay**	@	CHICAGO	26	7	W	3.0	W	36.5	U		
12/17/2006	Kansas City	@	**SAN DIEGO CHARGERS**	9	20	L	8.5	L	46.5	U		
12/10/2006	**New Orleans**	@	DALLAS	42	17	W	7.5	W	47.5	O		
12/3/2006	**Seattle**	@	DENVER	23	20	W	4.0	W	40.0	O		
11/26/2006	Philadelphia	@	**INDIANAPOLIS COLTS**	21	45	L	9.0	L	44.5	O		
11/19/2006	**San Diego Chargers**	@	DENVER	35	27	W	2.5	W	43.0	O		
11/12/2006	**Chicago**	@	NEW YORK GIANTS	38	20	W	1.0	W	37.5	O		
11/5/2006	**Indianapolis Colts**	@	NEW ENGLAND PATRIOTS	27	20	W	3.0	W	48.5	U		
10/29/2006	**Dallas**	@	CAROLINA	35	14	W	4.5	W	41.0	O		
10/15/2006	Oakland Raiders	@	**DENVER**	3	13	L	14.0	W	36.0	U		
10/8/2006	Pittsburgh	@	**SAN DIEGO CHARGERS**	13	23	L	3.5	L	37.0	U		
10/1/2006	Seattle	@	**CHICAGO**	6	37	L	3.5	L	35.5	O		
9/24/2006	**Denver**	@	NEW ENGLAND PATRIOTS	17	7	W	6.5	W	38.5	U		
9/17/2006	Washington Redskins	@	**DALLAS**	10	27	L	6.5	L	37.0	T		
9/10/2006	**Indianapolis Colts**	@	NEW YORK GIANTS	26	21	W	-3.0	W	48.0	U		
1/1/2006	**St. Louis Rams**	@	DALLAS	20	10	W	12.5	W	44.0	U		
12/25/2005	**Chicago**	@	GREEN BAY	24	17	W	-6.5	W	33.5	O		
12/25/2005	Minnesota	@	**BALTIMORE RAVENS**	23	30	L	3.0	L	35.0	O		
12/18/2005	Atlanta	@	**CHICAGO**	3	16	L	3.5	L	31.5	U		
12/17/2005	**Denver**	@	BUFFALO	28	17	W	-8.5	W	34.5	O		
12/11/2005	Detroit	@	**GREEN BAY (OT)**	13	16	L	6.5	W	35.5	U		
12/4/2005	Oakland Raiders	@	**SAN DIEGO CHARGERS**	10	34	L	11.0	L	50.5	U		
11/27/2005	**New Orleans**	@	NEW YORK JETS	21	19	W	2.0	W	37.0	O		
11/20/2005	**Kansas City**	@	HOUSTON TEXANS	45	17	W	-7.0	W	43.5	O		
11/13/2005	Cleveland	@	**PITTSBURGH**	21	34	L	7.5	L	34.5	O		
11/6/2005	Philadelphia	@	**WASHINGTON REDSKINS**	10	17	L	3.0	L	40.0	U		
10/30/2005	Buffalo	@	**NEW ENGLAND PATRIOTS**	16	21	L	9.0	W	44.0	U		
10/16/2005	Houston Texans	@	**SEATTLE**	10	45	L	9.5	L	45.5	O		
10/9/2005	Cincinnati	@	**JACKSONVILLE**	20	23	L	3.0	T	37.0	O		
10/2/2005	San Francisco	@	**ARIZONA CARDINALS**	14	31	L	2.5	L	44.0	O		
9/25/2005	New York Giants	@	**SAN DIEGO CHARGERS**	23	45	L	6.5	L	43.0	O		
9/18/2005	**Kansas City**	@	OAKLAND RAIDERS	23	17	W	-1.0	W	53.5	U		
9/11/2005	**Indianapolis Colts**	@	BALTIMORE RAVENS	24	7	W	-3.0	W	45.5	U		
1/2/2005	Dallas	@	**NEW YORK GIANTS**	24	28	L	2.5	L	37.5	O		
12/26/2004	Cleveland	@	**MIAMI**	7	10	L	8.0	W	40.5	U		
12/19/2004	Baltimore Ravens	@	**INDIANAPOLIS COLTS**	10	20	L	7.5	L	49.5	U		
12/12/2004	**Philadelphia**	@	WASHINGTON REDSKINS	17	14	W	-9.0	L	37.5	U		
12/5/2004	**Pittsburgh**	@	JACKSONVILLE	17	16	W	-3.0	L	35.0	U		
11/28/2004	**Oakland Raiders**	@	DENVER	25	24	W	11.5	W	43.0	O		
11/21/2004	**Green Bay**	@	HOUSTON TEXANS	16	13	W	-3.0	T	50.5	U		
11/14/2004	Buffalo	@	**NEW ENGLAND PATRIOTS**	6	29	L	7.0	L	37.5	U		
11/7/2004	Cleveland	@	**BALTIMORE RAVENS**	13	27	L	6.0	L	35.0	O		
10/31/2004	San Francisco	@	**CHICAGO**	13	23	L	2.0	L	35.5	O		
10/17/2004	**Minnesota**	@	NEW ORLEANS	38	31	W	-3.5	W	51.5	O		
10/10/2004	**Baltimore Ravens**	@	WASHINGTON REDSKINS	17	10	W	-1.0	W	34.0	U		
10/3/2004	**St. Louis Rams**	@	SAN FRANCISCO	24	14	W	-3.5	W	44.5	U		
9/26/2004	**Pittsburgh**	@	MIAMI	13	3	W	2.0	W	31.5	U		

Sunday Night Football History

9/26/2004	Tampa Bay	@	**OAKLAND RAIDERS**	20	30	L	3.5	L	35.0	O
9/19/2004	Miami	@	**CINCINNATI**	13	16	L	5.0	W	39.0	U
9/12/2004	Kansas City	@	**DENVER**	24	34	L	3.0	L	48.0	O
12/28/2003	Pittsburgh	@	**BALTIMORE RAVENS**	10	13	L	7.5	W	38.0	U
12/21/2003	**Denver**	@	INDIANAPOLIS COLTS	31	17	W	6.5	W	48.0	T
12/14/2003	New York Giants	@	**NEW ORLEANS**	7	45	L	7.0	L	39.0	O
12/7/2003	Carolina	@	**ATLANTA (OT)**	14	20	L	-1.0	L	41.0	U
11/30/2003	Tampa Bay	@	**JACKSONVILLE**	10	17	L	-3.5	L	37.0	U
11/23/2003	Washington Redskins	@	**MIAMI**	23	24	L	6.5	W	35.0	O
11/16/2003	Dallas	@	**NEW ENGLAND PATRIOTS**	0	12	L	4.0	L	35.0	U
11/9/2003	Baltimore Ravens	@	**ST. LOUIS RAMS**	22	33	L	7.0	L	43.0	O
11/2/2003	**Green Bay**	@	MINNESOTA	30	27	W	5.0	W	49.0	O
10/26/2003	Buffalo	@	**KANSAS CITY**	5	38	L	6.0	L	43.5	U
10/12/2003	San Francisco	@	**SEATTLE**	19	20	L	3.5	W	45.5	U
10/5/2003	**Cleveland**	@	PITTSBURGH	33	13	W	7.0	W	42.0	O
9/28/2003	**Indianapolis Colts**	@	NEW ORLEANS	55	21	W	-2.0	W	42.0	O
9/21/2003	Buffalo	@	**MIAMI**	7	17	L	3.0	L	40.5	U
9/14/2003	Chicago	@	**MINNESOTA**	13	24	L	9.0	L	45.0	U
9/7/2003	Oakland Raiders	@	**TENNESSEE TITANS**	20	25	L	3.0	L	46.5	U
12/29/2002	**Tampa Bay**	@	CHICAGO	15	0	W	-7.0	W	32.0	U
12/22/2002	**New York Jets**	@	NEW ENGLAND PATRIOTS	30	17	W	3.5	W	41.5	O
12/15/2002	Arizona Cardinals	@	**ST. LOUIS RAMS**	28	30	L	10.5	W	43.5	O
12/8/2002	Minnesota	@	**GREEN BAY**	22	26	L	9.5	W	44.0	O
12/1/2002	Tampa Bay	@	**NEW ORLEANS**	20	23	L	-1.0	L	40.0	O
11/24/2002	**Indianapolis Colts**	@	DENVER (OT)	23	20	W	6.5	W	43.0	T
11/17/2002	New England Patriots	@	**OAKLAND RAIDERS**	20	27	L	4.0	L	48.0	U
11/10/2002	Miami	@	**NEW YORK JETS**	10	13	L	2.5	L	40.0	U
11/3/2002	Jacksonville	@	**NEW YORK GIANTS**	17	24	L	3.0	L	35.5	O
10/27/2002	Indianapolis Colts	@	**WASHINGTON REDSKINS**	21	26	L	Pk	L	46.5	O
10/20/2002	Dallas	@	**ARIZONA CARDINALS (OT)**	6	9	L	3.5	W	36.5	U
10/13/2002	**Miami**	@	DENVER	24	22	W	3.5	W	41.0	O
10/6/2002	**Baltimore Ravens**	@	CLEVELAND	26	21	W	7.0	W	36.0	O
9/29/2002	Minnesota	@	**SEATTLE**	23	48	L	3.0	L	44.0	O
9/22/2002	Cincinnati	@	**ATLANTA**	3	30	L	7.0	L	41.5	U
9/15/2002	**Oakland Raiders**	@	PITTSBURGH	30	17	W	3.5	W	40.0	O
9/8/2002	Dallas	@	**HOUSTON TEXANS**	10	19	L	-8.0	L	33.5	U
1/6/2002	Philadelphia	@	TAMPA BAY	17	13	W	3.5	W	33.0	U
12/30/2001	**Washington Redskins**	@	NEW ORLEANS	40	10	W	5.0	W	39.5	O
12/23/2001	**New York Jets**	@	INDIANAPOLIS COLTS	29	28	W	1.0	W	47.0	O
12/16/2001	Pittsburgh	@	BALTIMORE RAVENS	26	21	W	3.0	W	33.0	O
12/9/2001	Seattle	@	**DENVER**	7	20	L	6.5	L	41.0	U
12/2/2001	Buffalo	@	**SAN FRANCISCO**	0	35	L	8.0	L	42.5	U
11/25/2001	**Chicago**	@	MINNESOTA	13	6	W	3.0	W	45.0	U
11/18/2001	**St. Louis Rams**	@	NEW ENGLAND PATRIOTS	24	17	W	-8.0	L	47.0	U
11/11/2001	Oakland Raiders	@	**SEATTLE**	27	34	L	-6.0	L	43.0	O
11/4/2001	**New York Jets**	@	NEW ORLEANS	16	9	W	6.0	W	41.5	U
10/14/2001	**Oakland Raiders**	@	INDIANAPOLIS COLTS	23	18	W	3.5	W	52.5	U
10/7/2001	Carolina	@	**SAN FRANCISCO**	14	24	L	7.0	L	44.5	U
9/30/2001	Dallas	@	**PHILADELPHIA**	18	40	L	14.0	L	35.0	O
9/23/2001	**Denver**	@	ARIZONA CARDINALS	38	17	W	-8.0	W	45.5	O
9/9/2001	**Miami**	@	TENNESSEE TITANS	31	23	W	6.0	W	34.0	O
12/17/2000	**New York Giants**	@	DALLAS	17	13	W	-6.5	L	36.0	U
12/10/2000	New York Jets	@	**OAKLAND RAIDERS**	7	31	L	3.5	L	46.5	U
12/3/2000	**Green Bay**	@	CHICAGO	28	6	W	-2.0	W	39.0	U
11/26/2000	**New York Giants**	@	ARIZONA CARDINALS	31	7	W	-7.0	W	38.0	T
11/19/2000	Jacksonville	@	PITTSBURGH	34	24	W	3.5	W	37.0	O
11/12/2000	New York Jets	@	**INDIANAPOLIS COLTS**	15	23	L	6.0	L	52.5	U
11/5/2000	**Carolina**	@	ST. LOUIS RAMS	27	24	W	13.5	W	59.5	U
10/29/2000	**Oakland Raiders**	@	SAN DIEGO CHARGERS	15	13	W	-7.0	L	42.0	U
10/15/2000	**Minnesota**	@	CHICAGO	28	16	W	-6.0	W	45.0	U
10/8/2000	**Baltimore Ravens**	@	JACKSONVILLE	15	10	W	2.5	W	37.5	U
10/1/2000	Atlanta	@	**PHILADELPHIA**	10	38	L	3.0	L	41.0	O
9/24/2000	**Washington Redskins**	@	NEW YORK GIANTS	16	6	W	1.5	W	41.5	U
9/17/2000	Baltimore Ravens	@	**MIAMI**	6	19	L	-2.5	L	33.0	U

Sunday Night Football History

9/10/2000	Dallas	@	**ARIZONA CARDINALS**	31	32	L	3.0	W	38.0	O
9/3/2000	Tennessee Titans	@	**BUFFALO**	13	16	L	Pk	L	40.0	U
12/26/1999	**Washington Redskins**	@	SAN FRANCISCO (OT)	26	20	W	-7.0	L	48.0	U
12/19/1999	**Buffalo**	@	ARIZONA CARDINALS	31	21	W	-3.0	W	37.0	O
12/12/1999	Minnesota	@	**KANSAS CITY**	28	31	L	1.5	L	41.5	O
12/5/1999	Dallas	@	**NEW ENGLAND PATRIOTS**	6	13	L	2.5	L	37.5	U
11/28/1999	Atlanta	@	**CAROLINA**	28	34	L	4.5	L	40.5	O
11/21/1999	New Orleans	@	**JACKSONVILLE**	23	41	L	12.5	L	35.0	O
11/14/1999	Denver	@	**SEATTLE**	17	20	L	6.0	W	41.0	U
11/7/1999	Tennessee Titans	@	**MIAMI**	0	17	L	3.0	L	36.5	U
10/31/1999	Tampa Bay	@	**DETROIT**	3	20	L	-2.0	L	35.0	U
10/17/1999	**Washington Redskins**	@	ARIZONA CARDINALS	24	10	W	-3.5	W	47.0	U
10/10/1999	Tampa Bay	@	**GREEN BAY**	23	26	L	6.0	W	40.5	O
10/3/1999	Oakland Raiders	@	**SEATTLE**	21	22	L	3.5	W	40.5	O
9/26/1999	New York Giants	@	**NEW ENGLAND PATRIOTS**	14	16	L	6.0	W	43.5	U
9/19/1999	New York Jets	@	**BUFFALO**	3	17	L	4.0	L	41.5	U
9/12/1999	**Pittsburgh**	@	CLEVELAND	43	0	W	-6.0	W	37.0	O
12/27/1998	Washington Redskins	@	**DALLAS**	7	23	L	-1.5	L	41.5	U
12/20/1998	Jacksonville	@	**MINNESOTA**	10	50	L	13.5	L	48.0	O
12/13/1998	**New York Jets**	@	MIAMI	21	16	W	3.0	W	40.5	U
12/6/1998	Chicago	@	**MINNESOTA**	22	48	L	16.0	L	46.0	O
11/29/1998	**Denver**	@	SAN DIEGO CHARGERS	31	16	W	-13.5	W	44.5	O
11/22/1998	New Orleans	@	**SAN FRANCISCO**	20	31	L	12.5	W	44.0	O
11/15/1998	Chicago	@	**DETROIT**	3	26	L	6.5	L	39.0	U
11/8/1998	**Tennessee Titans**	@	TAMPA BAY	31	22	W	3.0	W	37.0	O
11/1/1998	**Oakland Raiders**	@	SEATTLE	31	18	W	7.0	W	40.0	O
10/25/1998	**Buffalo**	@	CAROLINA	30	14	W	2.0	W	39.0	O
10/11/1998	**Atlanta**	@	NEW YORK GIANTS	34	20	W	2.5	W	37.5	O
10/4/1998	Seattle	@	**KANSAS CITY**	6	17	L	3.5	L	36.5	U
9/27/1998	Cincinnati	@	**BALTIMORE RAVENS**	24	31	L	4.5	L	40.5	O
9/20/1998	Philadelphia	@	**ARIZONA CARDINALS**	3	17	L	4.5	L	39.0	U
9/13/1998	Indianapolis Colts	@	**NEW ENGLAND PATRIOTS**	6	29	L	10.5	L	40.0	U
9/6/1998	Oakland Raiders	@	**KANSAS CITY**	8	28	L	7.5	L	41.0	U
12/21/1997	San Francisco	@	**SEATTLE**	9	38	L	3.0	L	41.5	O
12/14/1997	**Chicago**	@	ST. LOUIS RAMS	13	10	W	4.0	W	42.0	U
12/7/1997	Detroit	@	**MIAMI**	30	33	L	3.0	T	44.5	O
11/30/1997	**Denver**	@	SAN DIEGO CHARGERS	38	28	W	-9.5	W	43.5	O
11/23/1997	New York Giants	@	WASHINGTON REDSKINS	7	7	T	5.5	W	36.0	U
11/16/1997	**Oakland Raiders**	@	SAN DIEGO CHARGERS	38	13	W	-1.0	W	44.5	O
11/9/1997	Baltimore Ravens	@	**PITTSBURGH**	0	37	L	7.0	L	44.0	U
11/2/1997	Detroit	@	**GREEN BAY**	10	20	L	10.0	T	44.5	U
10/26/1997	Atlanta	@	**CAROLINA**	12	21	L	8.5	L	37.5	U
10/12/1997	Indianapolis Colts	@	**PITTSBURGH**	22	24	L	11.0	W	41.5	O
10/5/1997	**New Orleans**	@	CHICAGO	20	17	W	3.5	W	36.5	O
9/28/1997	Philadelphia	@	**MINNESOTA**	19	28	L	2.5	L	43.5	O
9/21/1997	Miami	@	**TAMPA BAY**	21	31	L	3.5	L	36.5	O
9/14/1997	New York Jets	@	**NEW ENGLAND PATRIOTS (OT)**	24	27	L	10.0	W	45.0	O
8/31/1997	**Washington Redskins**	@	CAROLINA	24	10	W	4.0	W	38.0	U
12/22/1996	Denver	@	**SAN DIEGO CHARGERS**	10	16	L	-1.5	L	40.5	U
12/15/1996	Seattle	@	**JACKSONVILLE**	13	20	L	5.0	L	43.0	U
12/8/1996	**Minnesota**	@	DETROIT	24	22	W	2.5	W	44.0	O
12/1/1996	**New England Patriots**	@	SAN DIEGO CHARGERS	45	7	W	1.0	W	46.0	O
11/24/1996	**Green Bay**	@	ST. LOUIS RAMS	24	9	W	-9.5	W	43.5	U
11/17/1996	**Minnesota**	@	OAKLAND RAIDERS (OT)	16	13	W	6.5	W	40.0	U
11/10/1996	New York Giants	@	**CAROLINA**	17	27	L	5.5	L	35.5	O
11/3/1996	**San Francisco**	@	NEW ORLEANS	24	17	W	-8.5	L	41.0	T
10/27/1996	Buffalo	@	**NEW ENGLAND PATRIOTS**	25	28	L	4.0	W	40.0	O
10/13/1996	Baltimore Ravens	@	**INDIANAPOLIS COLTS**	21	26	L	8.0	W	40.0	O
10/6/1996	**Houston Oilers**	@	CINCINNATI (OT)	30	27	W	1.0	W	42.0	O
9/29/1996	New York Jets	@	**WASHINGTON REDSKINS**	16	31	L	8.0	L	38.0	O
9/22/1996	**Philadelphia**	@	ATLANTA	33	18	W	2.5	W	43.5	O
9/15/1996	Tampa Bay	@	**DENVER**	23	27	L	13.5	W	40.5	O
9/8/1996	**Miami**	@	ARIZONA CARDINALS	38	10	W	-6.0	W	39.0	O
9/1/1996	**Buffalo**	@	NEW YORK GIANTS (OT)	23	20	W	-5.0	L	38.0	O

Sunday Night Football History

12/17/1995	Oakland Raiders	@	**SEATTLE**	10	44	L	-3.0	L		42.5	O
12/10/1995	Green Bay	@	**TAMPA BAY (OT)**	10	13	L	-7.0	L		43.0	U
12/3/1995	Buffalo	@	**SAN FRANCISCO**	17	27	L	13.5	W		46.5	U
11/26/1995	Carolina	@	**NEW ORLEANS**	26	34	L	5.0	L		40.0	O
11/19/1995	Houston Oilers	@	**KANSAS CITY**	13	20	L	9.5	W		38.5	U
11/12/1995	Denver	@	**PHILADELPHIA**	13	31	L	-1.0	L		39.0	O
11/5/1995	**Miami**	@	SAN DIEGO CHARGERS	24	14	W	2.0	W		43.0	U
10/29/1995	**New York Giants**	@	WASHINGTON REDSKINS	24	15	W	3.0	W		42.0	U
10/8/1995	**Denver**	@	NEW ENGLAND PATRIOTS	37	3	W	4.0	W		43.0	U
10/1/1995	**Oakland Raiders**	@	NEW YORK JETS	47	10	W	-7.5	W		38.5	O
9/24/1995	**Green Bay**	@	JACKSONVILLE	24	14	W	-11.0	L		37.0	O
9/17/1995	**Dallas**	@	MINNESOTA (OT)	23	17	W	-8.5	L		42.5	U
9/10/1995	**Philadelphia**	@	ARIZONA CARDINALS	31	19	W	3.5	W		35.0	O
9/3/1995	Buffalo	@	**DENVER**	7	22	L	5.5	L		44.0	U
12/25/1994	Detroit	@	**MIAMI**	20	27	L	3.5	L		45.5	O
12/18/1994	**Oakland Raiders**	@	SEATTLE	17	16	W	-6.5	L		36.0	U
12/11/1994	**New Orleans**	@	ATLANTA	29	20	W	4.0	W		46.5	O
12/4/1994	**Buffalo**	@	MIAMI	42	31	W	3.5	W		42.0	O
11/27/1994	**New England Patriots**	@	INDIANAPOLIS COLTS	12	10	W	Pk	W		40.0	U
11/20/1994	Los Angeles Rams	@	**SAN FRANCISCO**	27	31	L	14.0	W		43.0	O
11/13/1994	Tampa Bay	@	**DETROIT**	9	14	L	10.0	W		38.0	U
11/6/1994	Oakland Raiders	@	**KANSAS CITY**	3	13	L	3.5	L		42.0	U
10/30/1994	Pittsburgh	@	**ARIZONA CARDINALS (OT)**	17	20	L	2.5	L		34.0	O
10/9/1994	Washington Redskins	@	**PHILADELPHIA**	17	21	L	12.5	W		41.5	U
10/2/1994	**Miami**	@	CINCINNATI	23	7	W	-7.5	W		44.5	U
9/25/1994	**Chicago**	@	NEW YORK JETS	19	7	W	8.0	W		39.0	U
9/18/1994	**Kansas City**	@	ATLANTA	30	10	W	-2.5	W		47.0	U
9/11/1994	**New York Giants**	@	ARIZONA CARDINALS	20	17	W	3.5	W		36.5	O
9/4/1994	**San Diego Chargers**	@	DENVER	37	34	W	7.0	W		46.0	O
1/2/1994	New York Jets	@	**HOUSTON OILERS**	0	24	L	5.5	L		38.5	U
12/26/1993	Kansas City	@	**MINNESOTA**	10	30	L	-3.0	L		37.0	O
12/19/1993	**Philadelphia**	@	INDIANAPOLIS COLTS	20	10	W	-2.0	W		33.0	U
12/12/1993	**Green Bay**	@	SAN DIEGO CHARGERS	20	13	W	3.0	W		36.0	U
12/5/1993	Cincinnati	@	**SAN FRANCISCO**	8	21	L	24.0	W		44.0	U
11/28/1993	Pittsburgh	@	**HOUSTON OILERS**	3	23	L	3.0	L		40.0	U
11/21/1993	Minnesota	@	**TAMPA BAY**	10	23	L	-8.0	L		38.0	U
11/14/1993	**Chicago**	@	SAN DIEGO CHARGERS	16	13	W	8.5	W		34.5	U
11/7/1993	Indianapolis Colts	@	**WASHINGTON REDSKINS**	24	30	L	6.5	W		37.5	O
10/31/1993	**Detroit**	@	MINNESOTA	30	27	W	4.0	W		35.0	O
10/24/1993	Indianapolis Colts	@	**MIAMI**	27	41	L	6.5	L		35.0	O
10/10/1993	Denver	@	**GREEN BAY**	27	30	L	3.0	T		40.0	O
10/3/1993	New York Giants	@	**BUFFALO**	14	17	L	5.5	L		40.0	U
9/26/1993	New England Patriots	@	**NEW YORK JETS**	7	45	L	9.5	L		36.5	O
9/19/1993	**Dallas**	@	PHOENIX CARDINALS	17	10	W	-6.5	W		38.0	U
9/12/1993	**Los Angeles Raiders**	@	SEATTLE	17	13	W	-3.0	W		33.0	U
9/5/1993	Houston Oilers	@	**NEW ORLEANS**	21	33	L	2.5	L		39.0	O
12/27/1992	Buffalo	@	**HOUSTON OILERS**	3	27	L	-3.5	L		42.0	U
12/20/1992	New York Jets	@	**MIAMI**	17	19	L	11.0	W		37.5	U
12/13/1992	**Green Bay**	@	HOUSTON OILERS	16	14	W	7.5	W		40.0	U
12/6/1992	**Los Angeles Rams**	@	TAMPA BAY	31	27	W	1.0	W		39.0	O
11/29/1992	Los Angeles Raiders	@	**SAN DIEGO CHARGERS**	3	27	L	3.5	L		34.5	U
11/22/1992	**Kansas City**	@	SEATTLE	24	14	W	-11.5	L		31.5	O
11/15/1992	New York Giants	@	**DENVER**	13	27	L	3.5	L		37.0	O
11/8/1992	**Cincinnati**	@	CHICAGO (OT)	31	28	W	9.0	W		38.5	O
11/1/1992	**New York Giants**	@	WASHINGTON REDSKINS	24	7	W	10.5	W		38.0	U
10/25/1992	**Pittsburgh**	@	KANSAS CITY	27	3	W	8.0	W		35.5	U
10/11/1992	Los Angeles Rams	@	**NEW ORLEANS**	10	13	L	9.0	W		34.0	U
10/4/1992	New England Patriots	@	**NEW YORK JETS**	21	30	L	9.0	T		34.5	O
9/27/1992	**San Francisco**	@	NEW ORLEANS	16	10	W	-3.0	W		36.5	U
9/20/1992	Indianapolis Colts	@	**BUFFALO**	0	38	L	19.5	L		42.0	U
9/13/1992	**Philadelphia**	@	PHOENIX CARDINALS	31	14	W	-7.0	W		34.0	O
9/6/1992	Los Angeles Raiders	@	**DENVER**	13	17	L	3.0	L		37.0	U
12/29/1991	Los Angeles Rams	@	**SEATTLE**	9	23	L	6.5	L		39.5	U
12/22/1991	**Buffalo**	@	INDIANAPOLIS COLTS	35	7	W	-13.5	W		42.0	T

Sunday Night Football History

Date	Away		Home	Away Score	Home Score	W/L	Spread	ATS	Total	O/U
12/15/1991	**Minnesota**	@	TAMPA BAY	26	24	W	-4.0	L	39.0	O
12/8/1991	**Los Angeles Raiders**	@	SAN DIEGO CHARGERS	9	7	W	-5.0	L	36.0	U
12/1/1991	**Atlanta**	@	NEW ORLEANS (OT)	23	20	W	6.5	W	35.5	O
11/24/1991	Cleveland Browns	@	**HOUSTON OILERS**	24	28	L	13.5	W	45.0	O
11/17/1991	New England Patriots	@	**MIAMI**	20	30	L	6.5	L	35.0	O
11/10/1991	Pittsburgh	@	**DENVER**	13	20	L	-6.5	L	34.5	U
11/3/1991	**Washington Redskins**	@	NEW YORK GIANTS	17	13	W	-2.5	W	38.5	U
10/20/1991	**Los Angeles Raiders**	@	SEATTLE (OT)	23	20	W	2.5	W	34.5	O
10/13/1991	**Pittsburgh**	@	INDIANAPOLIS COLTS	21	3	W	-7.0	W	36.0	U
10/6/1991	**Denver**	@	MINNESOTA	13	6	W	5.0	W	40.5	U
9/29/1991	**Dallas**	@	PHOENIX CARDINALS	17	9	W	1.0	W	37.0	U
9/22/1991	Los Angeles Rams	@	**NEW ORLEANS**	7	24	L	3.0	L	37.5	U
9/15/1991	**Houston Oilers**	@	CINCINNATI	30	7	W	2.0	W	51.0	U
9/8/1991	Detroit	@	**WASHINGTON REDSKINS**	0	45	L	8.0	L	44.0	O
12/30/1990	Pittsburgh	@	**HOUSTON OILERS**	14	34	L	-2.0	L	37.5	O
12/23/1990	Denver	@	**SEATTLE**	12	17	L	5.0	T	41.5	U
12/16/1990	Chicago	@	**DETROIT**	21	38	L	-3.0	L	44.0	O
12/9/1990	Philadelphia	@	**MIAMI**	20	23	L	1.0	L	42.5	O
12/2/1990	Green Bay	@	**MINNESOTA**	7	23	L	5.5	L	42.0	U
11/25/1990	**Seattle**	@	SAN DIEGO CHARGERS (OT)	13	10	W	3.5	W	37.0	U
11/18/1990	Pittsburgh	@	**CINCINNATI**	3	27	L	2.5	L	41.5	U
11/11/1990	**San Francisco**	@	DALLAS	24	6	W	-9.5	W	40.0	U
11/4/1990	Denver	@	**MINNESOTA**	22	27	L	-1.0	L	44.0	O
10/28/1990	Cincinnati	@	**ATLANTA**	17	38	L	Pk	L	53.0	O
10/14/1990	Los Angeles Rams	@	**CHICAGO**	9	38	L	1.5	L	41.0	O
10/7/1990	Los Angeles Raiders	@	**BUFFALO**	24	38	L	3.0	L	37.0	O
9/30/1990	**Washington Redskins**	@	PHOENIX CARDINALS	38	10	W	-6.5	W	36.5	O
9/23/1990	Detroit	@	**TAMPA BAY**	20	23	L	3.0	T	47.5	U
9/16/1990	Houston Oilers	@	**PITTSBURGH**	9	20	L	2.5	L	41.0	U
9/9/1990	Philadelphia	@	**NEW YORK GIANTS**	20	27	L	4.0	L	37.5	O
12/17/1989	Los Angeles Raiders	@	**SEATTLE**	17	23	L	Pk	L	38.0	O
12/3/1989	Chicago	@	**MINNESOTA**	16	27	L	6.0	L	37.5	O
11/26/1989	**Los Angeles Rams**	@	NEW ORLEANS	20	17	W	-1.0	W	43.0	U
11/19/1989	New York Jets	@	**INDIANAPOLIS COLTS**	10	27	L	6.0	L	41.0	U
11/12/1989	Los Angeles Raiders	@	**SAN DIEGO CHARGERS**	12	14	L	-2.5	L	38.0	U
11/5/1989	**Dallas**	@	WASHINGTON REDSKINS	13	3	W	14.0	W	45.5	U
12/18/1988	**Los Angeles Rams**	@	SAN FRANCISCO	38	16	W	6.0	W	42.0	O
12/11/1988	Denver	@	**SEATTLE**	14	42	L	3.5	L	44.5	O
12/4/1988	**Pittsburgh**	@	HOUSTON OILERS	37	34	W	11.0	W	46.5	O
11/28/1988	**New York Giants**	@	NEW ORLEANS	13	12	W	6.0	W	38.0	U
11/20/1988	**New England Patriots**	@	MIAMI	6	3	W	3.0	W	41.0	U
11/13/1988	**Minnesota**	@	DALLAS	43	3	W	-3.5	W	43.0	O
11/6/1988	**Los Angeles Raiders**	@	SAN DIEGO CHARGERS	13	3	W	-3.0	W	38.0	U
10/30/1988	Washington Redskins	@	**HOUSTON OILERS**	17	41	L	-1.0	L	46.5	O
12/27/1987	Los Angeles Rams	@	**SAN FRANCISCO**	0	48	L	10.0	L	41.5	O
12/20/1987	Washington Redskins	@	**MIAMI**	21	23	L	3.0	W	49.0	U
12/13/1987	Denver	@	**SEATTLE**	21	28	L	3.5	L	48.0	O
12/6/1987	**Chicago**	@	MINNESOTA	30	24	W	1.5	W	45.5	O
11/29/1987	Cleveland Browns	@	**SAN FRANCISCO**	24	38	L	3.0	L	45.0	O
11/22/1987	**Miami**	@	DALLAS	20	14	W	1.5	W	48.0	U
11/15/1987	Los Angeles Raiders	@	**SAN DIEGO CHARGERS**	14	16	L	3.5	W	45.5	U
11/8/1987	New England Patriots	@	**NEW YORK GIANTS**	10	17	L	4.5	L	40.0	U
12/7/1986	Dallas	@	**LOS ANGELES RAMS**	10	29	L	4.5	L	39.0	T
12/8/1985	Pittsburgh	@	**SAN DIEGO CHARGERS**	44	54	L	6.0	L	49.5	O
10/6/1985	**Dallas**	@	NEW YORK GIANTS	30	29	W	1.5	W	38.0	O
10/21/1984	New Orleans	@	**DALLAS**	27	30	L	6.5	W	42.0	O
9/16/1984	**Denver**	@	CLEVELAND BROWNS	24	14	W	4.5	W	39.5	U
10/23/1983	**Los Angeles Raiders**	@	DALLAS	40	38	W	4.0	W	46.5	O
12/19/1982	**Atlanta**	@	SAN FRANCISCO	17	7	W	4.0	W		
10/18/1981	Los Angeles Rams	@	**DALLAS**	17	29	L	5.0	L		
10/26/1980	San Diego Chargers	@	**DALLAS**	31	42	L	2.0	L		
10/14/1979	Los Angeles Rams	@	**DALLAS**	6	30	L	5.0	L		
12/3/1978	**Denver**	@	OAKLAND RAIDERS	21	6	W	3.5	W		
11/12/1978	Pittsburgh	@	**LOS ANGELES RAMS**	7	10	L	3.0	T		

Sunday Night Football History

9/24/1978	New England Patriots	@	OAKLAND RAIDERS	21	14	W	6.5	W	

Interesting Sunday Night Football Facts

Atlanta is 0-4 on road on Sunday Night since 1999	Cincinnati is 0-11 on road on Sunday Night since 1993
Baltimore is 0-4 vs Indianapolis on Sunday Night since 1996	Cleveland is 0-4 at home on Sunday Night since 1999
Buffalo is 0-4 vs New England on Sunday Night since 1996	Dallas is 2-7 vs AFC teams on Sunday Night since 1983
Carolina is 0-5 on road on Sunday Night since 2001	Dallas is 4-0 at home vs N.Y. Giants on Sunday Night since 2013
Chicago is 1-12 on road vs NFC teams on Sunday Night since 2008	Detroit is 1-7 on road on Sunday Night since 1994
Chicago is 4-0 on road vs AFC teams on Sunday Night s/1993	Green Bay is 12-2 at home on Sunday Night since 2009

Interesting Sunday Night Football Facts

Green Bay is 3-11 on road on Sunday Night since 2014	N.Y. Jets are 3-0 vs Miami on Sunday Night since 1998
L.A. Chargers are 1-6 vs NFC teams on Sunday Night since 1980	Pittsburgh is 4-0 vs Indianapolis on Sunday Night since 1991
Miami is 7-1 vs NFC teams on Sunday Night since 1987	San Francisco is 2-9 on road on Sunday Night since 1997
New England is 9-3 at home on Sunday Night since 2007	Seattle is 8-1 vs AFC teams on Sunday Night since 1999
New Orleans is 8-0 at home on Sunday Night since 2010	Washington is 0-4 vs AFC teams on Sunday Night since 1987
N.Y. Giants are 0-5 vs Philadelphia on Sunday Night since 2009	

NFL Football Series available at: www.stevesfootballbible.com

  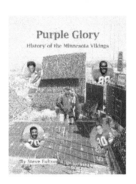 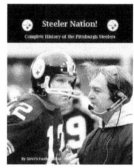

DALLAS	GREEN BAY	MINNESOTA	PITTSBURGH

Monday Night Football History

DATE	VISITOR		HOME	SC	ORE	S/U W-L	LINE	ATS W-L	TOTAL	O/U
9/12/2022	Denver	@	SEATTLE	16	17	L	-6.0	L	43.5	U
9/19/2022	Tennessee	@	BUFFALO	7	41	L	10.0	L	47.0	O
9/19/2022	Minnesota	@	PHILADELPHIA	7	24	L	3.0	L	49.5	U
9/26/2022	Dallas	@	NEW YORK GIANTS	23	16	W	1.0	W	38.5	O
10/3/2022	Los Angeles Rams	@	SAN FRANCISCO	9	24	L	2.0	L	42.0	U
10/10/2022	Las Vegas Raiders	@	KANSAS CITY	29	30	L	7.0	W	51.5	O
10/17/2022	Denver	@	LOS ANGELES CHARGERS	16	19	L	4.0	W	45.5	U
10/24/2022	Chicago	@	NEW ENGLAND	33	14	W	8.5	W	40.0	O
10/31/2022	Cincinnati	@	CLEVELAND	13	32	L	-3.0	L	45.0	T
11/7/2022	Baltimore	@	NEW ORLEANS	27	13	W	-1.5	W	46.5	U
11/14/2022	Washington	@	PHILADELPHIA	32	21	W	10.5	W	43.0	O
11/21/2022	San Francisco	@	ARIZONA	10	38	L	9.5	L	43.0	O
11/28/2022	Pittsburgh	@	INDIANAPOLIS	24	17	W	2.0	W	39.5	O
12/5/2022	New Orleans	@	TAMPA BAY	16	17	L	3.0	L	41.0	U
12/12/2022	New England	@	ARIZONA	13	27	L	2.0	L	44.0	U
12/19/2022	Los Angeles Rams	@	GREEN BAY	12	24	L	7.5	L	39.5	U
12/26/2022	Los Angeles Chargers	@	INDIANAPOLIS	20	3	W	-3.5	W	44.5	U
1/17/2022	Arizona	@	LOS ANGELES RAMS	11	34	L	3.0	L	49.0	U
1/3/2022	Cleveland	@	PITTSBURGH	14	26	L	-2.0	L	43.0	U
12/27/2021	Miami	@	NEW ORLEANS	20	3	W	-3.5	W	37.0	U
12/20/2021	Minnesota	@	CHICAGO	17	9	W	-7.0	W	47.5	U
12/20/2021	Las Vegas Raiders	@	CLEVELAND	16	14	W	-2.5	L	41.5	U
12/13/2021	Los Angeles Rams	@	ARIZONA	30	23	W	3.0	W	51.0	O
12/6/2021	New England	@	BUFFALO	14	10	W	3.0	W	40.0	U
11/29/2021	Seattle	@	WASHINGTON	15	17	L	-1.5	L	46.5	U
11/22/2021	New York Giants	@	TAMPA BAY	10	30	L	10.5	L	50.0	U
11/15/2021	Los Angeles Rams	@	SAN FRANCISCO	10	31	L	-3.5	L	50.0	U
11/8/2021	Chicago	@	PITTSBURGH	27	29	L	7.0	W	39.5	O
11/1/2021	New York Giants	@	KANSAS CITY	17	20	L	11.0	W	53.0	U
10/25/2021	New Orleans	@	SEATTLE	13	10	W	-6.0	L	42.0	U
10/18/2021	Buffalo	@	TENNESSEE	31	34	L	-6.0	L	53.0	O
10/11/2021	Indianapolis Colts	@	BALTIMORE RAVENS	25	31	L	7.5	W	47.5	O
10/4/2021	Las Vegas Raiders	@	LOS ANGELES CHARGERS	14	28	L	3.0	L	51.5	U
9/27/2021	Philadelphia	@	DALLAS	21	41	L	3.5	L	51.5	O
9/20/2021	Detroit	@	GREEN BAY	17	35	L	11.5	L	49.5	O
9/13/2021	Baltimore Ravens	@	LAS VEGAS RAIDERS	27	33	L	-3.0	L	50.0	O
12/28/2020	Buffalo	@	NEW ENGLAND	38	9	W	-7.0	W	47.0	T
12/21/2020	Pittsburgh Steelers	@	CINCINNATI BENGALS	17	27	L	-14.0	L	44.5	U
12/14/2020	Baltimore Ravens	@	CLEVELAND BROWNS	47	42	W	-3.0	W	45.5	O
12/7/2020	Buffalo Bills	@	SAN FRANCISCO 49ERS	34	24	W	2.0	W	48.0	O
12/7/2020	Washington Redskins	@	PITTSBURGH	23	17	W	5.5	W	43.5	U
11/30/2020	Seattle Seahawks	@	PHILADELPHIA EAGLES	23	17	W	-6.5	L	50.5	U
11/23/2020	Los Angeles Rams	@	TAMPA BAY BUCCANEERS	27	24	W	4.0	W	47.5	O
11/16/2020	Minnesota Vikings	@	CHICAGO BEARS	19	13	W	-3.0	W	44.0	U
11/9/2020	New England Patriots	@	NEW YORK JETS	30	27	W	-9.0	L	42.0	O
11/2/2020	Tampa Bay Buccaneers	@	NEW YORK GIANTS	25	23	W	-1.0	L	47.0	O
10/26/2020	Chicago Bears	@	LOS ANGELES RAMS	10	24	L	6.5	L	44.0	U
10/19/2020	Arizona Cardinals	@	DALLAS COWBOYS	38	10	W	1.0	W	56.0	U
10/19/2020	Kansas City Chiefs	@	BUFFALO	26	17	W	-5.5	W	55.0	U
10/12/2020	Los Angeles Chargers	@	NEW ORLEANS SAINTS {OT}	27	30	L	7.0	W	49.0	O
10/5/2020	Atlanta Falcons	@	GREEN BAY PACKERS	16	30	L	5.0	L	56.5	U
10/5/2020	New England Patriots	@	KANSAS CITY	10	26	L	11.5	L	48.5	U
9/28/2020	Kansas City Chiefs	@	BALTIMORE RAVENS	34	20	W	3.0	W	54.5	U

Monday Night Football History

Date	Away Team	@	Home Team	Away	Home	W/L	Spread	W/L	Total	O/U
9/21/2020	New Orleans Saints	@	**LAS VEGAS RAIDERS**	24	34	L	-4.0	L	47.5	O
9/14/2020	**Pittsburgh Steelers**	@	NEW YORK GIANTS	26	16	W	-6.0	W	43.5	U
9/14/2020	**Tennessee Titans**	@	DENVER BRONCOS	16	14	W	-3.5	L	42.0	U
12/23/2019	**Green Bay**	@	MINNESOTA	23	10	W	4.0	W	47.5	U
12/16/2019	Indianapolis Colts	@	**NEW ORLEANS**	7	34	L	8.5	L	49.0	U
12/9/2019	New York Giants	@	**PHILADELPHIA**	17	23	L	9.0	W	45.0	U
12/2/2019	Minnesota	@	**SEATTLE**	30	37	L	3.0	L	48.5	O
11/25/2019	**Baltimore Ravens**	@	LOS ANGELES RAMS	45	6	W	-3.0	W	46.5	O
11/18/2019	**Kansas City**	@	LOS ANGELES CHARGERS	24	17	W	-5.5	W	52.5	U
11/11/2019	**Seattle**	@	SAN FRANCISCO {OT}	27	24	W	6.5	W	47.0	O
11/4/2019	**Dallas**	@	NEW YORK GIANTS	37	18	W	-6.5	W	48.5	O
10/28/2019	Miami	@	**PITTSBURGH**	14	27	L	14.0	W	43.5	U
10/21/2019	**New England Patriots**	@	NEW YORK JETS	33	0	W	-10.0	W	43.0	U
10/14/2019	Detroit	@	**GREEN BAY**	22	23	L	3.5	W	46.0	U
10/7/2019	Cleveland	@	**SAN FRANCISCO**	3	31	L	5.0	L	47.5	U
9/30/2019	Cincinnati	@	**PITTSBURGH**	3	27	L	3.5	L	45.0	U
9/23/2019	**Chicago**	@	WASHINGTON	31	15	W	-5.0	W	41.0	O
9/16/2019	**Cleveland**	@	NEW YORK JETS	23	3	W	-6.5	W	45.0	U
9/9/2019	Denver	@	**OAKLAND RAIDERS**	16	24	L	-3.0	L	42.5	U
9/9/2019	Houston Texans	@	**NEW ORLEANS**	28	30	L	6.5	W	52.0	O
12/24/2018	Denver	@	**OAKLAND RAIDERS**	14	27	L	-3.5	L	42.5	U
12/17/2018	**New Orleans**	@	CAROLINA	12	9	W	-6.0	L	50.5	U
12/10/2018	Minnesota	@	**SEATTLE**	7	21	L	3.0	L	45.5	U
12/3/2018	Washington Redskins	@	**PHILADELPHIA**	13	28	L	5.5	L	45.0	U
11/26/2018	Tennessee Titans	@	**HOUSTON TEXANS**	17	34	L	3.5	L	42.5	O
11/19/2018	Kansas City	@	**LOS ANGELES RAMS**	51	54	L	3.0	T	63.5	O
11/12/2018	**New York Giants**	@	SAN FRANCISCO	27	23	W	3.0	W	45.0	O
11/5/2018	**Tennessee Titans**	@	DALLAS	28	14	W	4.5	W	40.0	O
10/29/2018	**New England Patriots**	@	BUFFALO	25	6	W	-14.0	W	43.5	U
10/22/2018	New York Giants	@	**ATLANTA**	20	23	L	4.0	W	52.5	U
10/15/2018	San Francisco	@	**GREEN BAY**	30	33	L	9.0	W	46.5	O
10/8/2018	Washington Redskins	@	**NEW ORLEANS**	19	43	L	5.5	L	51.5	O
10/1/2018	**Kansas City**	@	DENVER	27	23	W	-3.5	L	53.0	U
9/24/2018	**Pittsburgh**	@	TAMPA BAY	30	27	W	1.0	W	55.0	O
9/17/2018	Seattle	@	**CHICAGO**	17	24	L	5.0	L	42.0	U
9/10/2018	**Los Angeles Rams**	@	OAKLAND RAIDERS	33	13	W	-6.0	W	47.5	U
9/10/2018	**New York Jets**	@	DETROIT	48	17	W	7.0	W	44.0	O
12/25/2017	Oakland Raiders	@	**PHILADELPHIA**	10	19	L	10.0	W	46.0	U
12/25/2017	**Pittsburgh**	@	HOUSTON TEXANS	34	6	W	-9.0	W	45.5	U
12/18/2017	**Atlanta**	@	TAMPA BAY	24	21	W	-7.0	L	49.5	U
12/11/2017	New England Patriots	@	**MIAMI**	20	27	L	-10.5	L	48.0	U
12/4/2017	**Pittsburgh**	@	CINCINNATI	23	20	W	-4.5	L	42.5	O
11/27/2017	Houston Texans	@	**BALTIMORE RAVENS**	16	23	L	7.5	W	39.0	T
11/20/2017	**Atlanta**	@	SEATTLE	34	31	W	PK	W	46.0	O
11/13/2017	Miami	@	**CAROLINA**	21	45	L	8.0	L	38.5	O
11/6/2017	**Detroit**	@	GREEN BAY	30	17	W	-2.0	W	42.5	O
10/30/2017	Denver	@	**KANSAS CITY**	19	29	L	7.0	L	42.0	O
10/23/2017	Washington Redskins	@	**PHILADELPHIA**	24	34	L	5.0	L	48.5	O
10/16/2017	Indianapolis Colts	@	**HOUSTON TEXANS**	22	36	L	7.0	L	46.0	O
10/9/2017	**Minnesota**	@	CHICAGO	20	17	W	-3.5	L	41.5	U
10/2/2017	Washington Redskins	@	**KANSAS CITY**	20	29	L	6.5	L	47.5	O
9/25/2017	**Dallas**	@	ARIZONA CARDINALS	28	17	W	-3.0	W	46.0	O
9/18/2017	**Detroit**	@	NEW YORK GIANTS	24	10	W	3.0	W	42.5	U
9/11/2017	Los Angeles Chargers	@	**DENVER**	21	24	L	3.0	T	41.5	O

Monday Night Football History

Date	Away		Home	Away Score	Home Score	W/L	Spread	ATS	Total	O/U
9/11/2017	New Orleans	@	**MINNESOTA**	19	29	L	3.0	L	47.5	O
12/26/2016	Detroit	@	**DALLAS**	21	42	L	6.5	L	47.0	O
12/19/2016	**Carolina**	@	WASHINGTON	26	15	W	7.0	W	50.5	U
12/12/2016	Baltimore Ravens	@	**NEW ENGLAND**	23	30	L	6.0	L	45.5	O
12/5/2016	**Indianapolis Colts**	@	NEW YORK JETS	41	10	W	1.0	W	48.5	O
11/28/2016	**Green Bay**	@	PHILADELPHIA	27	13	W	4.0	W	47.0	U
11/21/2016	Houston Texans	vs	**OAKLAND RAIDERS (@ MEXICO CITY)**	20	27	L	6.5	L	45.5	O
11/14/2016	Cincinnati	@	**NEW YORK GIANTS**	20	21	L	-1.0	L	49.5	U
11/7/2016	Buffalo	@	**SEATTLE**	25	31	L	5.5	L	43.5	O
10/31/2016	Minnesota	@	**CHICAGO**	10	20	L	-5.5	L	39.5	U
10/24/2016	Houston Texans	@	**DENVER**	9	27	L	8.5	L	40.0	U
10/17/2016	New York Jets	@	**ARIZONA CARDINALS**	3	28	L	7.5	L	46.0	U
10/10/2016	**Tampa Bay**	@	CAROLINA	17	14	W	5.5	W	47.0	U
10/3/2016	New York Giants	@	**MINNESOTA**	10	24	L	4.0	L	42.5	U
9/26/2016	**Atlanta**	@	NEW ORLEANS	45	32	W	2.5	W	54.5	O
9/19/2016	**Philadelphia**	@	CHICAGO	29	14	W	3.0	W	43.0	T
9/12/2016	Los Angeles Rams	@	**SAN FRANCISCO**	0	28	L	-2.5	L	43.5	U
9/12/2016	**Pittsburgh**	@	WASHINGTON	38	16	W	-2.5	W	49.5	O
12/28/2015	Cincinnati	@	**DENVER**	17	20	L	3.5	W	39.0	U
12/21/2015	**Detroit**	@	NEW ORLEANS	35	27	W	2.5	W	52.5	O
12/14/2015	**New York Giants**	@	MIAMI	31	24	W	-2.0	W	48.0	O
12/7/2015	**Dallas**	@	WASHINGTON	19	16	W	2.0	W	43.0	U
11/30/2015	**Baltimore Ravens**	@	CLEVELAND	33	27	W	6.0	W	41.0	O
11/23/2015	Buffalo	@	**NEW ENGLAND**	13	20	L	7.0	T	47.5	U
11/16/2015	**Houston Texans**	@	CINCINNATI	10	6	W	10.0	W	46.5	U
11/9/2015	**Chicago**	@	SAN DIEGO CHARGERS	22	19	W	3.5	W	49.5	U
11/2/2015	Indianapolis Colts	@	**CAROLINA {OT}**	26	29	L	5.0	W	45.5	O
10/26/2015	Baltimore Ravens	@	**ARIZONA CARDINALS**	18	26	L	9.5	W	49.5	U
10/19/2015	New York Giants	@	**PHILADLEPHIA**	7	27	L	3.5	L	50.5	U
10/12/2015	**Pittsburgh**	@	SAN DIEGO CHARGERS	24	20	W	4.0	W	45.5	U
10/5/2015	Detroit	@	**SEATTLE**	10	13	L	10.0	W	43.0	U
9/28/2015	Kansas City	@	**GREEN BAY**	28	38	L	5.5	L	45.5	O
9/21/2015	**New York Jets**	@	INDIANAPOLIS COLTS	20	7	W	6.0	W	45.5	U
9/14/2015	Philadelphia	@	**ATLANTA**	24	26	L	-3.5	L	55.0	U
9/14/2015	Minnesota	@	**SAN FRANCISCO**	3	20	L	-3.0	L	42.5	U
12/22/2014	Denver	@	**CINCINNATI**	28	37	L	-3.5	L	47.0	O
12/15/2014	**New Orleans**	@	CHICAGO	31	15	W	-3.5	W	53.0	U
12/8/2014	Atlanta	@	**GREEN BAY**	37	43	L	13.5	W	54.5	O
12/1/2014	**Miami**	@	NEW YORK JETS	16	13	W	-7.0	L	41.5	U
11/24/2014	**Baltimore Ravens**	@	NEW ORLEANS	34	27	W	2.5	W	51.0	O
11/24/2014	New York Jets	vs	**BUFFALO (@ DETROIT, MI)**	3	38	L	2.5	L	42.0	U
11/17/2014	**Pittsburgh**	@	TENNESSEE TITANS	27	24	W	-7.0	L	46.5	O
11/10/2014	Carolina	@	**PHILADELPHIA**	21	45	L	7.0	L	48.5	O
11/3/2014	**Indianapolis Colts**	@	NEW YORK GIANTS	40	24	W	-3.0	W	51.0	O
10/27/2014	**Washington Redskins**	@	DALLAS {OT}	20	17	W	9.5	W	49.0	U
10/20/2014	Houston Texans	@	**PITTSBURGH**	23	30	L	3.0	L	44.0	O
10/13/2014	**San Francisco**	@	ST. LOUIS RAMS	31	17	W	-3.5	W	44.0	O
10/6/2014	**Seattle**	@	WASHINGTON	27	17	W	-7.0	W	45.5	U
9/29/2014	New England Patriots	@	**KANSAS CITY**	14	41	L	-3.0	L	45.0	O
9/22/2014	**Chicago**	@	NEW YORK JETS	27	19	W	2.0	W	45.0	O
9/15/2014	**Philadelphia**	@	INDIANAPOLIS COLTS	30	27	W	3.0	W	53.5	O
9/8/2014	New York Giants	@	**DETROIT**	14	35	L	6.5	L	46.0	O
9/8/2014	San Diego	@	**ARIZONA CARDINALS**	17	18	L	3.0	W	45.5	U
12/22/2013	Atlanta	@	**SAN FRANCISCO**	24	34	L	13.5	W	46.0	O

Monday Night Football History

12/16/2013	**Baltimore Ravens**	@	DETROIT	18	16	W	4.5	W	49.0	U
12/9/2013	Dallas	@	**CHICAGO**	28	45	L	1.5	L	49.0	O
12/1/2013	New Orleans	@	**SEATTLE**	7	34	L	4.5	L	47.5	U
11/25/2013	**San Francisco**	@	WASHINGTON	27	6	W	-6.0	W	46.0	U
11/18/2013	New England Patriots	@	**CAROLINA**	20	24	L	3.0	L	47.5	U
11/11/2013	Miami	@	**TAMPA BAY**	19	22	L	-2.0	L	39.0	O
11/4/2013	Chicago	@	GREEN BAY	27	20	W	9.5	W	51.0	U
10/28/2013	**Seattle**	@	ST. LOUIS RAMS	14	9	W	-13.0	L	43.5	U
10/21/2013	Minnesota	@	**NEW YORK GIANTS**	7	23	L	3.5	L	47.5	U
10/14/2013	Indianapolis Colts	@	**SAN DIEGO CHARGERS**	9	19	L	-1.0	L	50.5	U
10/7/2013	**New York Jets**	@	ATLANTA	30	28	W	10.0	W	45.0	O
9/30/2013	Miami	@	**NEW ORLEANS**	17	38	L	7.0	L	48.5	O
9/23/2013	Oakland Raiders	@	**DENVER**	21	37	L	16.0	T	48.5	O
9/16/2013	Pittsburgh	@	**CINCINNATI**	10	20	L	6.0	L	40.5	U
9/9/2013	**Houston Texans**	@	SAN DIEGO CHARGERS	31	28	W	-5.0	L	44.0	O
9/9/2013	**Philadelphia**	@	WASHINGTON	33	27	W	4.0	W	52.0	O
12/17/2012	New York Jets	@	**TENNESSEE TITANS**	10	14	L	Pk	L	40.0	U
12/10/2012	Houston Texans	@	**NEW ENGLAND**	14	42	L	5.5	L	50.5	O
12/3/2012	New York Giants	@	**WASHINGTON**	16	17	L	-3.0	L	50.5	U
11/26/2012	**Carolina**	@	PHILADELPHIA	30	22	W	-3.0	W	41.5	O
11/19/2012	Chicago	@	**SAN FRANCISCO**	7	32	L	3.5	L	34.0	O
11/12/2012	Kansas City	@	**PITTSBURGH {OT}**	13	16	L	12.5	W	39.5	U
11/5/2012	Philadelphia	@	**NEW ORLEANS**	13	28	L	3.0	L	52.5	U
10/29/2012	**San Francisco**	@	ARIZONA CARDINALS	24	3	W	-7.0	W	38.5	U
10/22/2012	Detroit	@	**CHICAGO**	7	13	L	6.5	W	45.0	U
10/15/2012	**Denver**	@	SAN DIEGO CHARGERS	35	24	W	Pk	W	48.0	O
10/8/2012	**Houston Texans**	@	NEW YORK JETS	23	17	W	-9.5	L	40.0	T
10/1/2012	**Chicago**	@	DALLAS	34	18	W	3.0	W	41.0	O
9/24/2012	Green Bay	@	**SEATTLE**	12	14	L	-3.0	L	45.5	U
9/17/2012	Denver	@	**ATLANTA**	21	27	L	3.0	L	50.0	U
9/10/2012	Cincinnati	@	**BALTIMORE RAVENS**	13	44	L	7.0	L	43.0	O
9/10/2012	**San Diego**	@	OAKLAND RAIDERS	22	14	W	1.0	W	47.0	U
12/26/2011	Atlanta	@	**NEW ORLEANS**	16	45	L	7.0	L	52.5	O
12/19/2011	Pittsburgh	@	**SAN FRANCISCO**	3	20	L	2.5	L	37.0	U
12/12/2011	St. Louis Rams	@	**SEATTLE**	13	30	L	9.5	L	38.0	O
12/5/2011	**San Diego**	@	JACKSONVILLE	38	14	W	-3.0	W	39.0	O
11/28/2011	New York Giants	@	**NEW ORLEANS**	24	49	L	7.5	L	51.0	O
11/21/2011	Kansas City	@	**NEW ENGLAND**	3	34	L	16.5	L	46.5	U
11/14/2011	Minnesota	@	**GREEN BAY**	7	45	L	13.5	L	49.5	O
11/7/2011	**Chicago**	@	PHILADELPHIA	30	24	W	8.0	W	47.5	O
10/31/2011	San Diego	@	**KANSAS CITY (OT)**	20	23	L	-3.5	L	44.5	U
10/24/2011	Baltimore Ravens	@	**JACKSONVILLE**	7	12	L	-9.5	L	39.0	U
10/17/2011	Miami	@	**NEW YORK JETS**	6	24	L	7.5	L	41.5	U
10/10/2011	Chicago	@	**DETROIT**	13	24	L	6.0	L	47.5	U
10/3/2011	Indianapolis Colts	@	**TAMPA BAY**	17	24	L	10.0	W	40.5	O
9/26/2011	Washington Redskins	@	**DALLAS**	16	18	L	3.5	W	45.0	U
9/19/2011	St. Louis Rams	@	**NEW YORK GIANTS**	16	28	L	6.5	L	43.5	O
9/12/2011	**New England Patriots**	@	MIAMI	38	24	W	-7.0	W	46.0	O
9/12/2011	**Oakland Raiders**	@	DENVER	23	20	W	3.0	W	42.0	O
12/27/2010	**New Orleans**	@	ATLANTA	17	14	W	2.5	W	49.0	U
12/20/2010	**Chicago**	@	MINNESOTA	40	14	W	-6.5	W	35.0	O
12/13/2010	**Baltimore Ravens**	@	HOUSTON TEXANS (OT)	34	28	W	-3.0	W	45.5	O
12/13/2010	**New York Giants**	vs	MINNESOTA (@ DETROI)	21	3	W	-4.5	W	43.5	U
12/6/2010	New York Jets	@	**NEW ENGLAND**	3	45	L	3.5	L	45.0	O

Monday Night Football History

Date	Away		Home								
11/29/2010	San Francisco	@	ARIZONA CARDINALS	27	6	W	-1.5	W	41.0	U
11/22/2010	Denver	@	SAN DIEGO CHARGERS	14	35	L	9.5	L	50.5	U
11/15/2010	Philadelphia	@	WASHINGTON	59	28	W	-3.5	W	43.0	O
11/8/2010	Pittsburgh	@	CINCINNATI	27	21	W	-4.5	W	41.5	O
11/1/2010	Houston Texans	@	INDIANAPOLIS COLTS	17	30	L	5.5	L	51.0	U
10/25/2010	New York Giants	@	DALLAS	41	35	W	3.5	W	44.5	O
10/18/2010	Tennessee Titans	@	JACKSONVILLE	30	3	W	-3.0	W	45.0	U
10/11/2010	Minnesota	@	NEW YORK JETS	20	29	L	4.5	L	38.5	O
10/4/2010	New England Patriots	@	MIAMI	41	14	W	-1.0	W	47.5	O
9/27/2010	Green Bay	@	CHICAGO	17	20	L	-3.0	L	46.0	U
9/20/2010	New Orleans	@	SAN FRANCISCO	25	22	W	-5.5	L	44.0	O
9/13/2010	Baltimore Ravens	@	NEW YORK JETS	10	9	W	2.0	W	36.0	U
9/13/2010	San Diego	@	KANSAS CITY	14	21	L	-4.5	L	45.0	U
12/28/2009	Minnesota	@	CHICAGO (OT)	30	36	L	-7.5	L	41.5	O
12/21/2009	New York Giants	@	WASHINGTON	45	12	W	-3.0	W	43.5	O
12/14/2009	Arizona	@	SAN FRANCISCO	9	24	L	-3.5	L	44.5	U
12/7/2009	Baltimore Ravens	@	GREEN BAY	14	27	L	3.5	L	42.5	U
11/30/2009	New England Patriots	@	NEW ORLEANS	17	38	L	2.0	L	56.5	U
11/23/2009	Tennessee Titans	@	HOUSTON TEXANS	20	17	W	4.0	W	48.0	U
11/16/2009	Baltimore Ravens	@	CLEVELAND	16	0	W	-10.5	W	40.0	U
11/9/2009	Pittsburgh	@	DENVER	28	10	W	-3.0	W	39.5	U
11/2/2009	Atlanta	@	NEW ORLEANS	27	35	L	11.0	W	54.5	O
10/26/2009	Philadelphia	@	WASHINGTON	27	17	W	-7.5	W	37.5	O
10/19/2009	Denver	@	SAN DIEGO CHARGERS	34	23	W	3.5	W	44.0	O
10/12/2009	New York Jets	@	MIAMI	27	31	L	-2.5	L	36.0	O
10/5/2009	Green Bay	@	MINNESOTA	23	30	L	3.5	L	45.5	O
9/28/2009	Carolina	@	DALLAS	7	21	L	8.5	L	47.5	U
9/21/2009	Indianapolis Colts	@	MIAMI	27	23	W	-3.0	W	42.0	O
9/14/2009	Buffalo	@	NEW ENGLAND	24	25	L	10.5	W	47.5	O
9/14/2009	San Diego	@	OAKLAND RAIDERS	24	20	W	-9.5	L	43.0	O
12/22/2008	Green Bay	@	CHICAGO (OT)	17	20	L	4.0	W	40.5	U
12/15/2008	Cleveland	@	PHILADELPHIA	10	30	L	14.5	L	39.0	O
12/8/2008	Tampa Bay	@	CAROLINA	23	38	L	3.0	L	39.0	O
12/1/2008	Jacksonville	@	HOUSTON TEXANS	17	30	L	3.0	L	48.5	U
11/24/2008	Green Bay	@	NEW ORLEANS	29	51	L	2.0	L	51.5	O
11/17/2008	Cleveland	@	BUFFALO	29	27	W	5.5	W	41.0	O
11/10/2008	San Francisco	@	ARIZONA CARDINALS	24	29	L	9.5	W	47.0	O
11/3/2008	Pittsburgh	@	WASHINGTON	23	6	W	2.5	W	37.0	U
10/27/2008	Indianapolis Colts	@	TENNESSEE TITANS	21	31	L	4.0	L	40.5	O
10/20/2008	Denver	@	NEW ENGLAND	7	41	L	3.0	L	48.0	T
10/13/2008	New York Giants	@	CLEVELAND	14	35	L	-8.5	L	43.5	O
10/6/2008	Minnesota	@	NEW ORLEANS	30	27	W	3.0	W	46.5	O
9/29/2008	Baltimore Ravens	@	*PITTSBURGH (OT)*	20	23	L	5.0	W	33.5	O
9/22/2008	New York Jets	@	SAN DIEGO CHARGERS	29	48	L	8.5	L	44.5	O
9/15/2008	Philadelphia	@	DALLAS	37	41	L	7.0	W	46.5	O
9/8/2008	Denver	@	OAKLAND RAIDERS	41	14	W	-3.0	W	41.0	O
9/8/2008	Minnesota	@	GREEN BAY	19	24	L	2.5	L	38.0	O
12/24/2007	Denver	@	SAN DIEGO CHARGERS	3	23	L	9.0	L	47.0	U
12/17/2007	Chicago	@	MINNESOTA	13	20	L	10.5	W	43.0	U
12/10/2007	New Orleans	@	ATLANTA	34	14	W	-3.5	W	42.5	O
12/3/2007	New England Patriots	@	BALTIMORE RAVENS	27	24	W	-19.5	L	48.0	O
11/26/2007	Miami	@	PITTSBURGH	0	3	L	16.0	W	39.0	U
11/19/2007	Tennessee Titans	@	DENVER	20	34	L	2.0	L	38.0	O
11/12/2007	San Francisco	@	SEATTLE	0	24	L	9.5	L	38.5	U

Monday Night Football History

11/5/2007	Baltimore Ravens	@	*PITTSBURGH*	7	38	L	9.0	L	36.0	O
10/29/2007	**Green Bay**	@	DENVER (OT)	19	13	W	3.0	W	42.5	U
10/22/2007	**Indianapolis Colts**	@	JACKSONVILLE	29	7	W	-3.0	W	44.5	U
10/15/2007	**New York Giants**	@	ATLANTA	31	10	W	-4.0	W	43.5	U
10/8/2007	**Dallas**	@	BUFFALO	25	24	W	-10.0	L	45.0	O
10/1/2007	**New England Patriots**	@	CINCINNATI	34	13	W	-7.5	W	53.5	U
9/24/2007	**Tennessee Titans**	@	NEW ORLEANS	31	14	W	4.5	W	45.0	T
9/17/2007	**Washington Redskins**	@	PHILADELPHIA	20	12	W	6.5	W	39.0	U
9/10/2007	Arizona	@	**SAN FRANCISCO**	17	20	L	3.0	T	45.0	U
9/10/2007	Baltimore Ravens	@	**CINCINNATI**	20	27	L	2.5	L	40.0	O
12/25/2006	**New York Jets**	@	MIAMI	13	10	W	2.5	W	36.5	U
12/25/2006	**Philadelphia**	@	DALLAS	23	7	W	7.0	W	47.5	U
12/18/2006	Cincinnati	@	**INDIANAPOLIS COLTS**	16	34	L	3.5	L	54.5	U
12/11/2006	**Chicago**	@	ST. LOUIS RAMS	42	27	W	-6.5	W	40.5	O
12/4/2006	Carolina	@	**PHILADELPHIA**	24	27	L	-3.0	L	37.5	O
11/27/2006	Green Bay	@	**SEATTLE**	24	34	L	9.5	L	43.5	O
11/20/2006	New York Giants	@	**JACKSONVILLE**	10	26	L	3.5	L	38.5	U
11/13/2006	Tampa Bay	@	**CAROLINA**	10	24	L	9.5	L	37.0	U
11/6/2006	Oakland Raiders	@	**SEATTLE**	0	16	L	7.0	L	36.0	U
10/30/2006	**New England Patriots**	@	MINNESOTA	31	7	W	-1.5	W	39.0	U
10/23/2006	**New York Giants**	@	DALLAS	36	22	W	3.5	W	44.5	O
10/16/2006	**Chicago**	@	ARIZONA CARDINALS	24	23	W	-11.0	L	40.0	O
10/9/2006	Baltimore Ravens	@	**DENVER**	3	13	L	4.5	L	33.0	U
10/2/2006	Green Bay	@	**PHILADELPHIA**	9	31	L	11.5	L	48.5	U
9/25/2006	Atlanta	@	**NEW ORLEANS**	3	23	L	-3.5	L	43.5	U
9/18/2006	Pittsburgh	@	**JACKSONVILLE**	0	9	L	-2.5	L	37.5	U
9/11/2006	**Minnesota**	@	WASHINGTON	19	16	W	4.5	W	36.0	U
9/11/2006	**San Diego**	@	OAKLAND RAIDERS	27	0	W	-3.0	W	43.0	U
12/26/2005	**New England Patriots**	@	NEW YORK JETS	31	21	W	-6.5	W	37.0	O
12/19/2005	Green Bay	@	**BALTIMORE RAVENS**	3	48	L	3.5	L	33.5	O
12/12/2005	New Orleans	@	**ATLANTA**	17	36	L	10.5	L	44.0	O
12/5/2005	**Seattle**	@	PHILADELPHIA	42	0	W	-3.5	W	42.0	T
11/28/2005	Pittsburgh	@	**INDIANAPOLIS COLTS**	7	26	L	8.5	L	47.0	U
11/21/2005	**Minnesota**	@	GREEN BAY	20	17	W	5.0	W	44.5	U
11/14/2005	**Dallas**	@	PHILADELPHIA	21	20	W	3.0	W	39.5	O
11/7/2005	**Indianapolis Colts**	@	NEW ENGLAND	40	21	W	-4.0	W	48.0	O
10/31/2005	Baltimore Ravens	@	*PITTSBURGH*	19	20	L	11.0	W	33.5	O
10/24/2005	New York Jets	@	**ATLANTA**	14	27	L	8.0	L	40.5	O
10/17/2005	St. Louis Rams	@	**INDIANAPOLIS COLTS**	28	45	L	13.5	L	51.0	O
10/10/2005	**Pittsburgh**	@	SAN DIEGO CHARGERS	24	22	W	3.0	W	46.0	T
10/3/2005	Green Bay	@	**CAROLINA**	29	32	L	7.5	W	43.0	O
9/26/2005	Kansas City	@	**DENVER**	10	30	L	3.0	L	47.5	U
9/19/2005	New Orleans	@	**NEW YORK GIANTS**	10	27	L	3.5	L	43.5	U
9/19/2005	**Washington Redskins**	@	DALLAS	14	13	W	5.5	W	36.0	U
9/12/2005	Philadelphia	@	**ATLANTA**	10	14	L	-1.0	L	42.0	U
12/27/2004	Philadelphia	@	**ST. LOUIS RAMS**	7	20	L	3.0	L	45.5	U
12/20/2004	New England Patriots	@	**MIAMI**	28	29	L	-9.5	L	42.0	O
12/13/2004	**Kansas City**	@	TENNESSEE TITANS	49	38	W	1.5	W	52.5	O
12/6/2004	**Dallas**	@	SEATTLE	43	39	W	7.0	W	42.0	O
11/29/2004	St. Louis Rams	@	**GREEN BAY**	17	45	L	6.5	L	51.5	O
11/22/2004	**New England Patriots**	@	KANSAS CITY	27	19	W	-3.0	W	53.0	U
11/15/2004	**Philadelphia**	@	DALLAS	49	21	W	-6.5	W	42.0	O
11/8/2004	Minnesota	@	**INDIANAPOLIS COLTS**	28	31	L	7.0	W	57.5	O
11/1/2004	Miami	@	**NEW YORK JETS**	14	41	L	7.0	L	35.0	O

Monday Night Football History

10/25/2004	Denver	@	**CINCINNATI**	10	23	L	-6.5	L	43.5	U
10/18/2004	Tampa Bay	@	**ST. LOUIS RAMS**	21	28	L	6.5	L	42.5	O
10/11/2004	**Tennessee Titans**	@	GREEN BAY	48	27	W	3.0	W	44.0	O
10/4/2004	**Kansas City**	@	BALTIMORE RAVENS	27	24	W	5.5	W	41.5	O
9/27/2004	**Dallas**	@	WASHINGTON	21	18	W	1.5	W	36.0	O
9/20/2004	Minnesota	@	**PHILADELPHIA**	16	27	L	3.0	L	50.5	U
9/13/2004	**Green Bay**	@	CAROLINA	24	14	W	3.0	W	43.5	U
12/22/2003	**Green Bay**	@	OAKLAND RAIDERS	41	7	W	-5.0	W	44.0	O
12/15/2003	Philadelphia	@	MIAMI	34	27	W	2.5	W	37.0	O
12/8/2003	**St. Louis Rams**	@	CLEVELAND	26	20	W	-4.5	W	43.0	O
12/1/2003	Tennessee Titans	@	**NEW YORK JETS**	17	24	L	-2.0	L	42.5	U
11/24/2003	New York Giants	@	**TAMPA BAY**	13	19	L	5.5	L	37.5	U
11/17/2003	Pittsburgh	@	**SAN FRANCISCO**	14	30	L	4.0	L	41.5	O
11/10/2003	Philadelphia	@	**GREEN BAY**	17	14	W	4.5	W	43.5	U
11/3/2003	**New England Patriots**	@	DENVER	30	26	W	2.5	W	35.5	O
10/27/2003	**Miami**	@	SAN DIEGO CHARGERS	26	10	W	-6.5	W	38.0	U
10/20/2003	**Kansas City**	@	OAKLAND RAIDERS	17	10	W	-4.0	W	47.0	U
10/13/2003	Atlanta	@	*ST. LOUIS RAMS*	0	36	L	11.0	L	45.5	U
10/6/2003	**Indianapolis Colts**	@	TAMPA BAY (OT)	38	35	W	4.5	W	37.5	O
9/29/2003	**Green Bay**	@	CHICAGO	38	23	W	-4.0	W	41.5	O
9/22/2003	Oakland Raiders	@	**DENVER**	10	31	L	5.0	L	45.0	U
9/15/2003	**Dallas**	@	NEW YORK GIANTS (OT)	35	32	W	7.5	W	37.0	O
9/8/2003	**Tampa Bay**	@	PHILADELPHIA	17	0	W	3.0	W	36.0	U
12/30/2002	San Francisco	@	**ST. LOUIS RAMS**	20	31	L	Pk	L	39.5	O
12/23/2002	**Pittsburgh**	@	TAMPA BAY	17	7	W	4.5	W	39.0	U
12/16/2002	New England Patriots	@	**TENNESSEE TITANS**	7	24	L	2.5	L	43.5	U
12/9/2002	Chicago	@	**MIAMI**	9	27	L	10.0	L	37.5	U
12/2/2002	New York Jets	@	**OAKLAND RAIDERS**	20	26	L	6.5	W	48.0	U
11/25/2002	**Philadelphia**	@	SAN FRANCISCO	38	17	W	7.0	W	37.5	O
11/18/2002	Chicago	@	**ST. LOUIS RAMS**	16	21	L	10.5	W	44.0	U
11/11/2002	**Oakland Raiders**	@	DENVER	34	10	W	5.5	W	46.0	U
11/4/2002	Miami	@	**GREEN BAY**	10	24	L	4.5	L	41.5	U
10/28/2002	New York Giants	@	**PHILADELPHIA**	3	17	L	7.0	L	38.5	U
10/21/2002	Indianapolis Colts	@	**PITTSBURGH**	10	28	L	4.0	L	46.0	U
10/14/2002	**San Francisco**	@	SEATTLE	28	21	W	-3.0	W	43.0	O
10/7/2002	**Green Bay**	@	CHICAGO	34	21	W	1.0	W	44.0	O
9/30/2002	Denver	@	**BALTIMORE RAVENS**	23	34	L	-7.5	L	35.5	O
9/23/2002	St. Louis Rams	@	**TAMPA BAY**	14	26	L	-3.0	L	43.0	U
9/16/2002	**Philadelphia**	@	WASHINGTON	37	7	W	-3.0	W	44.5	U
9/9/2002	Pittsburgh	@	**NEW ENGLAND**	14	30	L	-2.5	L	37.5	O
1/7/2002	Minnesota	@	**BALTIMORE RAVENS**	3	19	L	12.5	L	37.0	U
12/17/2001	**St. Louis Rams**	@	NEW ORLEANS	34	21	W	-6.0	W	51.0	O
12/10/2001	Indianapolis Colts	@	**MIAMI**	6	41	L	4.5	L	45.0	O
12/3/2001	**Green Bay**	@	JACKSONVILLE	28	21	W	-3.5	W	43.0	O
11/26/2001	Tampa Bay	@	ST. LOUIS RAMS	24	17	W	10.0	W	47.0	U
11/19/2001	New York Giants	@	**MINNESOTA**	16	28	L	2.0	L	45.0	U
11/12/2001	**Baltimore Ravens**	@	TENNESSEE TITANS	16	10	W	-2.0	W	35.5	U
11/5/2001	Denver	@	**OAKLAND RAIDERS**	28	38	L	5.5	L	45.0	O
10/29/2001	Tennessee Titans	@	**PITTSBURGH**	7	34	L	3.0	L	36.5	O
10/22/2001	Philadelphia	@	NEW YORK GIANTS	10	9	W	3.0	W	35.5	U
10/15/2001	Washington Redskins	@	**DALLAS**	7	9	L	3.0	L	36.5	U
10/8/2001	**St. Louis Rams**	@	DETROIT	35	0	W	-13.5	W	48.5	U
10/1/2001	**San Francisco**	@	NEW YORK JETS	19	17	W	3.0	W	44.5	U
9/24/2001	Washington Redskins	@	**GREEN BAY**	0	37	L	9.0	L	40.5	U

Monday Night Football History

9/10/2001	New York Giants	@	**DENVER**	20	31	L	6.5	L		44.0	O
12/25/2000	Dallas	@	**TENNESSEE TITANS**	0	31	L	14.0	L		37.5	U
12/18/2000	St. Louis Rams	@	**TAMPA BAY**	35	38	L	-2.0	L		48.5	O
12/11/2000	Buffalo	@	**INDIANAPOLIS COLTS**	20	44	L	6.5	L		45.5	O
12/4/2000	Kansas City	@	**NEW ENGLAND**	24	30	L	-1.0	L		40.0	O
11/27/2000	Green Bay	@	**CAROLINA**	14	31	L	-2.0	L		44.0	O
11/20/2000	**Washington Redskins**	@	ST. LOUIS RAMS	33	20	W	6.0	W		56.0	U
11/13/2000	Oakland Raiders	@	**DENVER**	24	27	L	3.5	W		48.0	O
11/6/2000	Minnesota	@	**GREEN BAY (OT)**	20	26	L	-3.5	L		47.5	U
10/30/2000	**Tennessee Titans**	@	WASHINGTON	27	21	W	3.5	W		38.5	O
10/23/2000	Miami	@	**NEW YORK JETS (OT)**	37	40	L	3.0	T		35.5	O
10/16/2000	Jacksonville	@	**TENNESSEE TITANS**	13	27	L	6.5	L		39.0	O
10/9/2000	Tampa Bay	@	**MINNESOTA**	23	30	L	1.0	L		38.5	O
10/2/2000	Seattle	@	**KANSAS CITY**	17	24	L	4.0	L		38.0	O
9/25/2000	Jacksonville	@	**INDIANAPOLIS COLTS**	14	43	L	3.5	L		46.0	O
9/18/2000	**Dallas**	@	WASHINGTON	27	21	W	10.0	W		43.5	O
9/11/2000	New England Patriots	@	**NEW YORK JETS**	19	20	L	6.0	W		39.0	T
9/4/2000	Denver	@	**ST. LOUIS RAMS**	36	41	L	6.5	W		49.5	O
1/3/2000	San Francisco	@	**ATLANTA**	29	34	L	6.5	W		46.5	O
12/27/1999	**New York Jets**	@	MIAMI	38	31	W	3.5	W		37.0	O
12/20/1999	Green Bay	@	**MINNESOTA**	20	24	L	5.0	W		49.0	U
12/13/1999	Denver	@	**JACKSONVILLE**	24	27	L	9.0	W		37.0	O
12/6/1999	Minnesota	@	**TAMPA BAY**	17	24	L	-2.5	L		38.5	O
11/29/1999	**Green Bay**	@	SAN FRANCISCO	20	3	W	-6.0	W		40.5	U
11/22/1999	Oakland Raiders	@	DENVER (OT)	21	27	L	1.5	L		35.5	O
11/15/1999	**New York Jets**	@	NEW ENGLAND	24	17	W	6.0	W		37.0	O
11/8/1999	Dallas	@	**MINNESOTA**	17	27	L	7.0	L		47.5	U
11/1/1999	**Seattle**	@	GREEN BAY	27	7	W	5.5	W		42.5	U
10/25/1999	Atlanta	@	**PITTSBURGH**	9	13	L	5.5	W		37.0	U
10/18/1999	Dallas	@	**NEW YORK GIANTS**	10	13	L	-3.0	L		37.0	U
10/11/1999	**Jacksonville**	@	NEW YORK JETS	16	6	W	-3.0	W		40.0	U
10/4/1999	**Buffalo**	@	MIAMI	23	18	W	5.5	W		40.0	O
9/27/1999	**San Francisco**	@	ARIZONA CARDINALS	24	10	W	-2.5	W		46.0	U
9/20/1999	Atlanta	@	**DALLAS**	7	24	L	6.5	L		42.5	U
9/13/1999	**Miami**	@	DENVER	38	21	W	6.0	W		43.0	O
12/28/1998	Pittsburgh	@	**JACKSONVILLE**	3	21	L	3.0	L		40.0	U
12/21/1998	Denver	@	**MIAMI**	21	31	L	-4.0	L		44.0	O
12/14/1998	Detroit	@	**SAN FRANCISCO**	13	35	L	10.0	L		48.5	U
12/7/1998	Green Bay	@	**TAMPA BAY**	22	24	L	-3.5	L		42.0	O
11/30/1998	New York Giants	@	**SAN FRANCISCO**	7	31	L	13.5	L		44.0	U
11/23/1998	Miami	@	**NEW ENGLAND**	23	26	L	3.0	T		36.5	O
11/16/1998	**Denver**	@	KANSAS CITY	30	7	W	-4.0	W		40.5	U
11/9/1998	Green Bay	@	**PITTSBURGH**	20	27	L	-3.5	L		41.5	O
11/2/1998	**Dallas**	@	PHILADELPHIA	34	0	W	-7.0	W		37.0	U
10/26/1998	**Pittsburgh**	@	KANSAS CITY	20	13	W	6.0	W		36.5	U
10/19/1998	**New York Jets**	@	NEW ENGLAND	24	14	W	6.5	W		43.5	U
10/12/1998	Miami	@	**JACKSONVILLE**	21	28	L	6.5	L		40.0	O
10/5/1998	**Minnesota**	@	GREEN BAY	37	24	W	7.0	W		47.0	O
9/28/1998	Tampa Bay	@	**DETROIT**	6	27	L	-1.5	L		38.0	U
9/21/1998	**Dallas**	@	NEW YORK GIANTS	31	7	W	4.0	W		36.5	O
9/14/1998	**San Francisco**	@	WASHINGTON	45	10	W	-6.0	W		44.0	O
9/7/1998	New England Patriots	@	**DENVER**	21	27	L	7.5	W		44.5	O
12/22/1997	**New England Patriots**	@	MIAMI	14	12	W	2.5	W		44.5	U
12/15/1997	Denver	@	**SAN FRANCISCO**	17	34	L	3.5	L		45.0	O

Monday Night Football History

Date	Visitor	@	Home	V	H		Line		Total	
12/8/1997	**Carolina**	@	DALLAS	23	13	W	6.5	W	37.0	U
12/1/1997	**Green Bay**	@	MINNESOTA	27	11	W	-3.0	W	45.5	U
11/24/1997	Oakland Raiders	@	DENVER	3	31	L	10.0	L	47.5	U
11/17/1997	Buffalo	@	MIAMI	13	30	L	5.5	L	38.0	O
11/10/1997	**San Francisco**	@	PHILADELPHIA	24	12	W	-3.5	W	38.5	U
11/3/1997	Pittsburgh	@	KANSAS CITY	10	13	L	3.0	T	41.5	U
10/27/1997	**Chicago**	@	MIAMI (OT)	36	33	W	8.5	W	39.5	O
10/27/1997	**Green Bay**	@	NEW ENGLAND	28	10	W	2.0	W	45.0	U
10/20/1997	**Buffalo**	@	INDIANAPOLIS COLTS	9	6	W	1.0	W	38.0	U
10/13/1997	Dallas	@	WASHINGTON	16	21	L	-2.5	L	40.0	U
10/6/1997	New England Patriots	@	DENVER	13	34	L	5.5	L	45.5	O
9/29/1997	**San Francisco**	@	CAROLINA	34	21	W	-3.5	W	38.0	O
9/22/1997	Pittsburgh	@	JACKSONVILLE	21	30	L	3.5	L	40.5	O
9/15/1997	Philadelphia	@	DALLAS	20	21	L	9.0	W	41.5	U
9/8/1997	**Kansas City**	@	OAKLAND RAIDERS	28	27	W	5.0	W	40.5	O
9/1/1997	Chicago	@	GREEN BAY	24	38	L	16.0	W	42.5	O
12/23/1996	Detroit	@	SAN FRANCISCO	14	24	L	10.0	T	42.0	U
12/16/1996	Buffalo	@	MIAMI	14	16	L	-2.0	L	41.0	U
12/9/1996	Kansas City	@	OAKLAND RAIDERS	7	26	L	2.5	L	39.0	U
12/2/1996	**San Francisco**	@	ATLANTA	34	10	W	-10.0	W	45.0	U
11/25/1996	**Pittsburgh**	@	MIAMI	24	17	W	2.5	W	42.0	U
11/18/1996	Green Bay	@	DALLAS	6	21	L	4.0	L	43.0	U
11/11/1996	Detroit	@	SAN DIEGO CHARGERS	21	27	L	4.0	L	43.5	O
11/4/1996	**Denver**	@	OAKLAND RAIDERS	22	21	W	2.0	W	44.5	U
10/28/1996	**Chicago**	@	MINNESOTA	15	13	W	6.5	W	39.5	U
10/21/1996	**Oakland Raiders**	@	SAN DIEGO CHARGERS	23	14	W	3.5	W	42.0	U
10/14/1996	San Francisco	@	GREEN BAY (OT)	20	23	L	5.5	T	45.0	U
10/7/1996	**Pittsburgh**	@	KANSAS CITY	17	7	W	4.5	W	38.0	U
9/30/1996	**Dallas**	@	PHILADELPHIA	23	19	W	3.0	W	38.0	O
9/23/1996	Miami	@	INDIANAPOLIS COLTS	6	10	L	2.5	L	42.5	U
9/16/1996	Buffalo	@	PITTSBURGH	6	24	L	3.0	L	40.0	U
9/9/1996	Philadelphia	@	GREEN BAY	13	39	L	8.5	L	42.0	O
9/2/1996	Dallas	@	CHICAGO	6	22	L	-3.0	L	44.0	U
12/25/1995	**Dallas**	@	ARIZONA CARDINALS	37	13	W	-10.0	W	42.0	O
12/18/1995	Minnesota	@	SAN FRANCISCO	30	37	L	13.5	W	48.0	O
12/11/1995	Kansas City	@	MIAMI	6	13	L	3.0	L	43.5	U
12/4/1995	Chicago	@	DETROIT	7	27	L	3.0	L	49.0	U
11/27/1995	Oakland Raiders	@	SAN DIEGO CHARGERS	6	12	L	-1.0	L	39.0	U
11/20/1995	**San Francisco**	@	MIAMI	44	20	W	2.0	W	44.0	O
11/13/1995	Cleveland Browns	@	*PITTSBURGH*	3	20	L	6.0	L	39.0	U
11/6/1995	Philadelphia	@	DALLAS	12	34	L	14.0	L	43.5	O
10/30/1995	**Chicago**	@	MINNESOTA	14	6	W	3.5	W	45.0	U
10/23/1995	Buffalo	@	NEW ENGLAND	14	27	L	1.0	L	41.0	T
10/16/1995	Oakland Raiders	@	DENVER	0	27	L	-3.0	L	46.0	U
10/9/1995	San Diego	@	KANSAS CITY (OT)	23	29	L	3.5	L	38.0	O
10/2/1995	**Buffalo**	@	CLEVELAND BROWNS	22	19	W	7.0	W	37.0	O
9/25/1995	San Francisco	@	DETROIT	24	27	L	-11.5	L	48.0	O
9/18/1995	Pittsburgh	@	MIAMI	10	23	L	7.5	L	40.5	U
9/11/1995	**Green Bay**	@	CHICAGO	27	24	W	3.0	W	38.5	O
9/4/1995	**Dallas**	@	NEW YORK GIANTS	35	0	W	-7.0	W	38.0	U
12/26/1994	San Francisco	@	MINNESOTA	14	21	L	-7.0	L	47.5	U
12/19/1994	**Dallas**	@	NEW ORLEANS	24	16	W	-9.5	L	45.5	U
12/12/1994	Kansas City	@	MIAMI	28	45	L	4.5	L	39.5	O
12/5/1994	**Oakland Raiders**	@	SAN DIEGO CHARGERS	24	17	W	4.0	W	37.0	O

Monday Night Football History

11/28/1994	**San Francisco**	@	NEW ORLEANS	35	14	W	-8.5	W		47.0	O
11/21/1994	**New York Giants**	@	HOUSTON OILERS	13	10	W	3.0	W		35.5	U
11/14/1994	Buffalo	@	**PITTSBURGH**	10	23	L	2.5	L		36.5	U
11/7/1994	New York Giants	@	**DALLAS**	10	38	L	13.5	L		38.0	O
10/31/1994	**Green Bay**	@	CHICAGO	33	6	W	-1.0	W		34.0	O
10/24/1994	Houston Oilers	@	**PHILADELPHIA**	6	21	L	11.0	L		37.0	U
10/17/1994	**Kansas City**	@	DENVER	31	28	W	2.5	W		42.0	O
10/10/1994	**Minnesota**	@	NEW YORK GIANTS	27	10	W	2.5	W		40.0	U
10/3/1994	Houston Oilers	@	**PITTSBURGH**	14	30	L	8.0	L		39.5	O
9/26/1994	Denver	@	**BUFFALO**	20	27	L	7.0	T		48.0	U
9/19/1994	**Detroit**	@	DALLAS (OT)	20	17	W	13.5	W		44.5	U
9/12/1994	Chicago	@	**PHILADELPHIA**	22	30	L	4.0	L		37.0	O
9/5/1994	Oakland Raiders	@	**SAN FRANCISCO**	14	44	L	7.0	L		47.0	O
1/3/1994	**Philadelphia**	@	SAN FRANCISCO (OT)	37	34	W	11.0	W		41.0	O
12/27/1993	Miami	@	**SAN DIEGO CHARGERS**	20	45	L	1.0	L		38.0	O
12/20/1993	**New York Giants**	@	NEW ORLEANS	24	14	W	1.5	W		35.5	O
12/13/1993	**Pittsburgh**	@	MIAMI	21	20	W	3.5	W		36.5	O
12/6/1993	Philadelphia	@	**DALLAS**	17	23	L	16.0	W		37.0	O
11/29/1993	**San Diego**	@	INDIANAPOLIS COLTS	31	0	W	-2.0	W		37.0	U
11/22/1993	New Orleans	@	**SAN FRANCISCO**	7	42	L	8.5	L		41.5	O
11/15/1993	Buffalo	@	**PITTSBURGH**	0	23	L	3.0	L		39.0	U
11/8/1993	Green Bay	@	**KANSAS CITY**	16	23	L	3.0	L		36.5	O
11/1/1993	Washington Redskins	@	**BUFFALO**	10	24	L	9.0	L		40.0	U
10/25/1993	**Minnesota**	@	CHICAGO	19	12	W	3.5	W		33.5	U
10/18/1993	**Oakland Raiders**	@	DENVER	23	20	W	6.5	W		38.0	O
10/11/1993	Houston Oilers	@	**BUFFALO**	7	35	L	3.5	L		41.5	O
10/4/1993	Washington Redskins	@	**MIAMI**	10	17	L	4.5	L		40.0	U
9/27/1993	**Pittsburgh**	@	ATLANTA	45	17	W	3.0	W		43.0	O
9/20/1993	Denver	@	**KANSAS CITY**	7	15	L	6.5	L		41.5	U
9/13/1993	San Francisco	@	**CLEVELAND BROWNS**	13	23	L	-6.5	L		39.0	U
9/6/1993	Dallas	@	**WASHINGTON**	16	35	L	2.5	L		40.0	O
12/28/1992	Detroit	@	**SAN FRANCISCO**	6	24	L	13.5	L		37.0	U
12/21/1992	**Dallas**	@	ATLANTA	41	17	W	-7.0	W		42.0	O
12/14/1992	Los Angeles Raiders	@	**MIAMI**	7	20	L	6.0	L		38.0	U
12/7/1992	Chicago	@	**HOUSTON OILERS**	7	24	L	11.5	L		41.5	U
11/30/1992	Denver	@	**SEATTLE (OT)**	13	16	L	-4.0	L		32.5	U
11/23/1992	Washington Redskins	@	**NEW ORLEANS**	3	20	L	5.0	L		37.0	U
11/16/1992	**Buffalo**	@	MIAMI	26	20	W	-1.0	W		47.0	U
11/9/1992	**San Francisco**	@	ATLANTA	41	3	W	-8.5	W		44.5	U
11/2/1992	**Minnesota**	@	CHICAGO	38	10	W	3.5	W		40.0	O
10/26/1992	**Buffalo**	@	NEW YORK JETS	24	20	W	-8.5	L		42.5	O
10/19/1992	Cincinnati	@	**PITTSBURGH**	0	20	L	9.5	L		37.5	U
10/12/1992	Denver	@	**WASHINGTON**	3	34	L	8.5	L		38.0	U
10/5/1992	Dallas	@	**PHILADELPHIA**	7	31	L	6.0	L		39.0	U
9/28/1992	Los Angeles Raiders	@	**KANSAS CITY**	7	27	L	7.0	L		36.5	U
9/21/1992	**New York Giants**	@	CHICAGO	27	14	W	5.5	W		37.0	O
9/14/1992	**Miami**	@	CLEVELAND BROWNS	27	23	W	-3.0	W		37.5	O
9/7/1992	Washington Redskins	@	**DALLAS**	10	23	L	-2.5	L		43.0	U
12/30/1991	Chicago	@	**SAN FRANCISCO**	14	52	L	3.5	L		37.5	O
12/23/1991	Los Angeles Raiders	@	**NEW ORLEANS**	0	27	L	3.0	L		37.0	U
12/16/1991	Cincinnati	@	**MIAMI**	13	37	L	8.0	L		47.0	O
12/9/1991	**Philadelphia**	@	HOUSTON OILERS	13	6	W	6.5	W		41.5	U
12/2/1991	**San Francisco**	@	LOS ANGELES RAMS	33	10	W	-3.0	W		37.0	O
11/25/1991	**Buffalo**	@	MIAMI	41	27	W	-4.0	W		46.5	O

Date	Away	@	Home							
11/18/1991	**Chicago**	@	MINNESOTA	34	17	W	3.5	W	36.5	O
11/11/1991	New York Giants	@	PHILADELPHIA	7	30	L	-3.5	L	31.5	O
11/4/1991	Los Angeles Raiders	@	KANSAS CITY	21	24	L	6.5	W	35.5	O
10/28/1991	Cincinnati	@	BUFFALO	16	35	L	13.5	L	49.5	O
10/21/1991	**New York Giants**	@	PITTSBURGH	23	20	W	-3.5	L	35.0	O
10/14/1991	Buffalo	@	KANSAS CITY	6	33	L	-2.5	L	40.5	U
10/7/1991	Philadelphia	@	WASHINGTON	0	23	L	6.5	L	39.0	U
9/30/1991	New York Jets	@	CHICAGO (OT)	13	19	L	8.0	W	36.0	U
9/29/1991	Kansas City	@	HOUSTON OILERS	7	17	L	5.0	L	43.0	U
9/16/1991	**Washington Redskins**	@	DALLAS	33	31	W	-2.5	L	40.5	O
9/9/1991	San Francisco	@	NEW YORK GIANTS	14	16	L	1.0	L	36.5	U
12/31/1990	Los Angeles Rams	@	NEW ORLEANS	17	20	L	6.0	W	40.0	U
12/17/1990	**San Francisco**	@	LOS ANGELES RAMS	26	10	W	-6.0	W	46.0	U
12/10/1990	**Los Angeles Raiders**	@	DETROIT	38	31	W	-3.0	W	43.0	O
12/3/1990	New York Giants	@	SAN FRANCISCO	3	7	L	3.5	L	41.5	U
11/26/1990	Buffalo	@	HOUSTON OILERS	24	27	L	3.0	T	46.0	O
11/19/1990	**Los Angeles Raiders**	@	MIAMI	13	10	W	3.5	W	36.5	U
11/12/1990	Washington Redskins	@	PHILADELPHIA	14	28	L	3.0	L	44.0	U
11/5/1990	**New York Giants**	@	INDIANAPOLIS COLTS	24	7	W	-10.0	W	37.0	U
10/29/1990	Los Angeles Rams	@	PITTSBURGH	10	41	L	Pk	L	44.0	O
10/22/1990	**Cincinnati**	@	CLEVELAND BROWNS	34	13	W	2.5	W	43.5	O
10/15/1990	Minnesota	@	PHILADELPHIA	24	32	L	4.5	L	41.0	O
10/8/1990	**Cleveland Browns**	@	DENVER	30	29	W	9.0	W	39.0	O
10/1/1990	Cincinnati	@	SEATTLE	16	31	L	-2.5	L	43.0	U
9/24/1990	**Buffalo**	@	NEW YORK JETS	30	7	W	-1.5	W	43.0	O
9/17/1990	Kansas City	@	DENVER	23	24	L	6.0	W	38.5	O
9/10/1990	**San Francisco**	@	NEW ORLEANS	13	12	W	-4.5	L	43.5	U
12/25/1989	Cincinnati	@	MINNESOTA	21	29	L	5.0	L	43.5	O
12/18/1989	Philadelphia	@	NEW ORLEANS	20	30	L	1.5	L	39.0	O
12/11/1989	**San Francisco**	@	LOS ANGELES RAMS	30	27	W	-2.5	W	44.5	O
12/4/1989	Buffalo	@	SEATTLE	16	17	L	-5.5	L	38.0	U
11/27/1989	New York Giants	@	SAN FRANCISCO	24	34	L	5.5	L	41.0	O
11/27/1989	**San Francisco**	@	NEW YORK GIANTS	34	24	W	-5.5	W	41.0	O
11/20/1989	**Denver**	@	WASHINGTON	14	10	W	2.0	W	42.0	U
11/13/1989	Cincinnati	@	HOUSTON OILERS	24	26	L	5.5	W	44.5	O
11/6/1989	New Orleans	@	SAN FRANCISCO	13	21	L	5.5	L	43.5	U
10/30/1989	Minnesota	@	NEW YORK GIANTS	14	24	L	2.0	L	39.5	U
10/23/1989	Chicago	@	CLEVELAND BROWNS	7	27	L	2.0	L	41.5	U
10/16/1989	Los Angeles Rams	@	BUFFALO	20	23	L	-4.0	L	41.5	O
10/9/1989	**Los Angeles Raiders**	@	NEW YORK JETS	14	7	W	3.0	W	44.5	U
10/2/1989	Philadelphia	@	CHICAGO	13	27	L	3.5	L	45.5	U
9/25/1989	Cleveland Browns	@	CINCINNATI	14	21	L	4.0	L	46.0	U
9/18/1989	**Denver**	@	BUFFALO	28	14	W	6.5	W	42.0	T
9/11/1989	**New York Giants**	@	WASHINGTON	27	24	W	4.0	W	42.0	O
12/19/1988	Chicago	@	MINNESOTA	27	28	L	7.0	L	38.0	O
12/12/1988	Cleveland Browns	@	MIAMI	31	38	L	-5.0	L	44.0	O
12/5/1988	Chicago	@	LOS ANGELES RAMS	3	23	L	3.0	L	37.0	U
11/28/1988	Los Angeles Raiders	@	SEATTLE	27	35	L	3.5	L	38.5	O
11/21/1988	Washington Redskins	@	SAN FRANCISCO	21	37	L	3.5	L	40.0	O
11/14/1988	**Buffalo**	@	MIAMI	31	6	W	Pk	W	41.5	U
11/7/1988	Cleveland Browns	@	HOUSTON OILERS	17	24	L	Pk	L	43.0	U
10/31/1988	Denver	@	INDIANAPOLIS COLTS	23	55	L	1.5	L	40.5	O
10/24/1988	San Francisco	@	CHICAGO	9	10	L	2.5	W	39.0	U
10/17/1988	**Buffalo**	@	NEW YORK JETS	37	14	W	2.0	W	39.5	O

Monday Night Football History

Date	Team	@	Opponent	Score1	Score2	W/L	Spread	ATS	Total	O/U
10/10/1988	New York Giants	@	PHILADELPHIA	13	24	L	2.0	L	43.5	U
10/3/1988	Dallas	@	NEW ORLEANS	17	20	L	6.0	L	43.0	U
9/26/1988	**Los Angeles Raiders**	@	DENVER (OT)	30	27	W	6.0	W	42.5	O
9/19/1988	Indianapolis Colts	@	CLEVELAND BROWNS	17	23	L	2.0	L	35.5	O
9/12/1988	**Dallas**	@	PHOENIX CARDINALS	17	14	W	2.5	W	45.0	U
9/5/1988	Washington Redskins	@	NEW YORK GIANTS	20	27	L	2.0	L	42.5	O
12/28/1987	**New England Patriots**	@	MIAMI	24	10	W	6.0	W	48.5	U
12/21/1987	**Dallas**	@	LOS ANGELES RAMS	29	21	W	8.0	W	44.0	O
12/14/1987	Chicago	@	SAN FRANCISCO	0	41	L	5.5	L	44.5	U
12/7/1987	New York Jets	@	MIAMI	28	37	L	5.0	L	48.0	O
11/30/1987	**Los Angeles Raiders**	@	SEATTLE	37	14	W	9.5	W	43.5	O
11/23/1987	**Los Angeles Rams**	@	WASHINGTON	30	26	W	9.5	W	41.5	O
11/16/1987	Chicago	@	DENVER	29	31	L	2.0	**T**	42.5	O
11/9/1987	Seattle	@	NEW YORK JETS	14	30	L	-3.5	L	46.0	U
11/2/1987	New York Giants	@	DALLAS	24	33	L	-7.5	L	41.5	O
10/26/1987	Denver	@	MINNESOTA	27	34	L	2.5	L	35.5	O
10/26/1987	Los Angeles Rams	@	CLEVELAND BROWNS	17	30	L	6.5	L	42.0	O
10/19/1987	**Washington Redskins**	@	DALLAS	13	7	W	7.5	W	N/T	
10/12/1987	Los Angeles Raiders	@	DENVER	14	30	L	-10.5	L	N/T	
9/22/1987	New England Patriots	@	NEW YORK JETS	24	43	L	-2.0	L	46.0	O
9/15/1987	New York Giants	@	CHICAGO	19	34	L	-1.0	L	34.5	O
12/22/1986	**New England Patriots**	@	MIAMI	34	27	W	3.5	W	48.0	O
12/15/1986	**Chicago**	@	DETROIT	16	13	W	-9.5	L	38.5	U
12/8/1986	Los Angeles Raiders	@	SEATTLE	0	37	L	-2.0	L	41.0	U
12/1/1986	**New York Giants**	@	SAN FRANCISCO	21	17	W	4.0	W	39.5	U
11/24/1986	New York Jets	@	MIAMI	3	45	L	-1.5	L	52.5	U
11/17/1986	San Francisco	@	WASHINGTON	6	14	L	2.0	L	44.0	U
11/10/1986	Miami	@	CLEVELAND BROWNS	16	26	L	3.0	L	43.5	U
11/3/1986	**Los Angeles Rams**	@	CHICAGO	20	17	W	8.5	W	35.5	O
10/27/1986	Washington Redskins	@	NEW YORK GIANTS	20	27	L	3.5	L	37.0	O
10/20/1986	Denver	@	NEW YORK JETS	10	22	L	-3.5	L	45.5	U
10/13/1986	Pittsburgh	@	CINCINNATI	22	24	L	8.5	W	44.0	O
10/6/1986	San Diego	@	SEATTLE	7	33	L	7.0	L	49.0	U
9/29/1986	**Dallas**	@	ST. LOUIS CARDINALS	31	7	W	-7.0	W	44.0	U
9/22/1986	**Chicago**	@	GREEN BAY	25	12	W	-11.5	W	39.0	U
9/15/1986	**Denver**	@	PITTSBURGH	21	10	W	-6.0	W	40.5	U
9/8/1986	New York Giants	@	DALLAS	28	31	L	-1.0	L	42.0	O
12/23/1985	**Los Angeles Raiders**	@	LOS ANGELES RAMS	16	6	W	-3.5	W	41.0	U
12/16/1985	New England Patriots	@	MIAMI	27	30	L	7.0	W	47.0	O
12/9/1985	**Los Angeles Rams**	@	SAN FRANCISCO	27	20	W	10.0	W	41.0	O
12/2/1985	Chicago	@	MIAMI	24	38	L	-3.5	L	45.0	O
11/25/1985	Seattle	@	SAN FRANCISCO	6	19	L	-7.5	L	42.0	U
11/18/1985	New York Giants	@	WASHINGTON	21	23	L	2.0	**T**	37.5	O
11/11/1985	San Francisco	@	DENVER	16	17	L	-3.5	L	39.0	U
11/4/1985	Dallas	@	ST. LOUIS CARDINALS	10	21	L	-4.0	L	43.5	U
10/28/1985	San Diego	@	LOS ANGELES RAIDERS	21	34	L	6.5	L	48.0	O
10/21/1985	Green Bay	@	CHICAGO	7	23	L	9.5	L	46.0	U
10/14/1985	Miami	@	NEW YORK JETS	7	23	L	-3.5	L	48.0	U
10/7/1985	St. Louis Cardinals	@	WASHINGTON	10	27	L	-1.5	L	48.5	U
9/30/1985	**Cincinnati**	@	PITTSBURGH	37	24	W	6.5	W	46.5	O
9/23/1985	**Los Angeles Rams**	@	SEATTLE	35	24	W	7.5	W	44.0	O
9/16/1985	Pittsburgh	@	CLEVELAND BROWNS	7	17	L	-2.5	L	41.5	U
9/9/1985	Washington Redskins	@	DALLAS	14	44	L	-1.0	L	43.5	O
12/17/1984	Dallas	@	MIAMI	21	28	L	4.0	L	47.0	O

Monday Night Football History

Date	Away	@	Home	AS	HS	W/L	Spread	W/L	Total	O/U
12/10/1984	**Los Angeles Raiders**	@	DETROIT	24	3	W	-7.5	W	46.0	U
12/3/1984	Chicago	@	SAN DIEGO CHARGERS	7	20	L	-2.5	L	45.0	U
11/26/1984	New York Jets	@	MIAMI	17	28	L	13.0	W	47.0	U
11/19/1984	Pittsburgh	@	NEW ORLEANS	24	27	L	-1.5	L	39.5	O
11/12/1984	Los Angeles Raiders	@	SEATTLE	14	17	L	3.5	W	42.0	U
11/5/1984	Atlanta	@	WASHINGTON	14	27	L	Pk	L	46.5	U
10/29/1984	**Seattle**	@	SAN DIEGO CHARGERS	24	0	W	Pk	W	51.0	U
10/22/1984	**Los Angeles Rams**	@	ATLANTA	24	10	W	1.0	W	44.5	U
10/15/1984	Green Bay	@	DENVER	14	17	L	6.5	W	37.0	U
10/8/1984	**San Francisco**	@	NEW YORK GIANTS	31	10	W	-5.0	W	44.0	U
10/1/1984	Cincinnati	@	PITTSBURGH	17	38	L	4.5	L	41.0	O
9/24/1984	San Diego	@	LOS ANGELES RAIDERS	30	33	L	6.0	W	51.0	O
9/17/1984	**Miami**	@	BUFFALO	21	17	W	-9.0	L	42.0	U
9/10/1984	Washington Redskins	@	SAN FRANCISCO	31	37	L	2.0	L	51.0	O
9/3/1984	**Dallas**	@	LOS ANGELES RAMS	20	13	W	2.0	W	48.0	U
12/19/1983	Dallas	@	SAN FRANCISCO	17	42	L	1.0	L	48.5	O
12/12/1983	**Green Bay**	@	TAMPA BAY	12	9	W	-5.5	L	48.0	U
12/5/1983	Minnesota	@	DETROIT	2	13	L	5.0	L	45.0	U
11/28/1983	Cincinnati	@	MIAMI	14	38	L	5.0	L	44.0	O
11/21/1983	**New York Jets**	@	NEW ORLEANS	31	28	W	3.0	W	43.0	O
11/14/1983	**Los Angeles Rams**	@	ATLANTA	36	13	W	2.0	W	43.0	O
11/7/1983	New York Giants	@	DETROIT	9	15	L	5.5	L	44.5	U
10/31/1983	**Washington Redskins**	@	SAN DIEGO CHARGERS	27	24	W	-6.5	L	52.0	U
10/24/1983	New York Giants	@	ST. LOUIS CARDINALS (OT)	20	20	T	1.5	W	43.0	U
10/17/1983	Washington Redskins	@	GREEN BAY	47	48	L	-5.5	L	52.5	O
10/10/1983	**Pittsburgh**	@	CINCINNATI	24	14	W	-1.0	W	43.0	U
10/3/1983	**New York Jets**	@	BUFFALO	34	10	W	Pk	W	44.0	T
9/26/1983	Green Bay	@	NEW YORK GIANTS	3	27	L	1.5	L	42.0	U
9/19/1983	Miami	@	LOS ANGELES RAIDERS	14	27	L	3.0	L	38.5	O
9/12/1983	**San Diego**	@	KANSAS CITY	17	14	W	-5.0	L	46.5	U
9/5/1983	**Dallas**	@	WASHINGTON	31	30	W	-3.0	L	40.0	O
1/3/1983	Dallas	@	MINNESOTA	27	31	L	-5.0	L		
12/27/1982	Buffalo	@	MIAMI	10	27	L	3.0	L		
12/20/1982	Cincinnati	@	SAN DIEGO CHARGERS	34	50	L	3.0	L		
12/13/1982	**Dallas**	@	HOUSTON OILERS	37	7	W	-9.0	W		
12/6/1982	**New York Jets**	@	DETROIT	28	13	W	-1.0	W		
11/29/1982	Miami	@	TAMPA BAY	17	23	L	-2.0	L		
11/22/1982	San Diego	@	LOS ANGELES RAIDERS	24	28	L	1.0	L		
9/20/1982	**Green Bay**	@	NEW YORK GIANTS	27	19	W	3.0	W		
9/13/1982	**Pittsburgh**	@	DALLAS	36	28	W	6.0	W		
12/20/1981	Oakland Raiders	@	SAN DIEGO CHARGERS	10	23	L	7.5	L		
12/14/1981	Atlanta	@	*LOS ANGELES RAMS*	16	21	L	-3.5	L		
12/7/1981	Pittsburgh	@	OAKLAND RAIDERS	27	30	L	-4.0	L		
11/30/1981	Philadelphia	@	MIAMI	10	13	L	-2.5	L		
11/23/1981	Minnesota	@	ATLANTA	30	31	L	5.0	W		
11/16/1981	San Diego	@	SEATTLE	23	44	L	-6.0	L		
11/9/1981	Buffalo	@	DALLAS	14	27	L	3.5	L		
11/2/1981	Minnesota	@	DENVER	17	19	L	-5.5	L		
10/26/1981	Houston Oilers	@	PITTSBURGH	13	26	L	5.5	L		
10/19/1981	Chicago	@	DETROIT	17	48	L	6.0	L		
10/12/1981	Miami	@	BUFFALO	21	31	L	4.0	L		
10/5/1981	Atlanta	@	PHILADELPHIA	13	16	L	2.0	L		
9/28/1981	**Los Angeles Rams**	@	CHICAGO	24	7	W	-1.0	W		
9/21/1981	**Dallas**	@	NEW ENGLAND	35	21	W	-2.0	W		

Monday Night Football History

Date	Away Team		Home Team	Away Score	Home Score	W/L	Spread	W/L		
9/14/1981	**Oakland Raiders**	@	MINNESOTA	36	10	W	2.5	W		
9/7/1981	**San Diego**	@	CLEVELAND BROWNS	44	14	W	2.0	W		
12/22/1980	Pittsburgh	@	**SAN DIEGO CHARGERS**	17	26	L	5.0	L		
12/15/1980	Dallas	@	**LOS ANGELES RAMS**	14	38	L	-2.5	L		
12/8/1980	New England Patriots	@	**MIAMI**	13	16	L	-3.0	L		
12/1/1980	Denver	@	**OAKLAND RAIDERS**	3	9	L	4.5	L		
11/24/1980	**Los Angeles Rams**	@	NEW ORLEANS	27	7	W	-11.0	W		
11/17/1980	**Oakland Raiders**	@	SEATTLE	19	17	W	-2.5	L		
11/10/1980	New England Patriots	@	**HOUSTON OILERS**	34	38	L	3.5	L		
11/3/1980	Chicago	@	**CLEVELAND**	21	27	L	5.5	L		
10/27/1980	Miami	@	**NEW YORK JETS**	14	17	L	1.0	L		
10/20/1980	**Oakland Raiders**	@	PITTSBURGH	45	34	W	10.0	W		
10/13/1980	Washington Redskins	@	**DENVER**	17	20	L	5.0	W		
10/6/1980	Tampa Bay	@	**CHICAGO**	0	23	L	Pk	L		
9/29/1980	Denver	@	**NEW ENGLAND**	14	23	L	5.0	L		
9/22/1980	New York Giants	@	**PHILADELPHIA**	3	35	L	10.0	L		
9/15/1980	**Houston Oilers**	@	CLEVELAND BROWNS	16	7	W	-3.5	W		
9/8/1980	**Dallas**	@	WASHINGTON	17	3	W	3.0	W		
12/17/1979	Denver	@	**SAN DIEGO CHARGERS**	7	17	L	6.5	L		
12/10/1979	Pittsburgh	@	**HOUSTON OILERS**	17	20	L	-3.5	L		
12/3/1979	**Oakland Raiders**	@	NEW ORLEANS	42	35	W	3.5	W		
11/26/1979	New York Jets	@	**SEATTLE**	7	30	L	6.5	L		
11/19/1979	Atlanta	@	*LOS ANGELES RAMS*	14	20	L	7.0	W		
11/12/1979	**Philadelphia**	@	DALLAS	31	21	W	9.5	W		
11/5/1979	**Houston Oilers**	@	MIAMI	9	6	W	4.5	W		
10/29/1979	**Seattle**	@	ATLANTA	31	28	W	1.5	W		
10/22/1979	Denver	@	**PITTSBURGH**	7	42	L	9.0	L		
10/15/1979	Minnesota	@	**NEW YORK JETS**	7	14	L	5.5	L		
10/8/1979	Miami	@	**OAKLAND RAIDERS**	3	13	L	-1.0	L		
10/1/1979	New England Patriots	@	**GREEN BAY**	14	27	L	-8.0	L		
9/24/1979	Dallas	@	**CLEVELAND BROWNS**	7	26	L	-3.0	L		
9/17/1979	New York Giants	@	**WASHINGTON**	0	27	L	6.0	L		
9/10/1979	**Atlanta**	@	PHILADELPHIA	14	10	W	5.0	W		
9/3/1979	**Pittsburgh**	@	NEW ENGLAND (OT)	16	13	W	-2.0	W		
12/18/1978	New England Patriots	@	**MIAMI**	3	23	L	3.5	L		
12/11/1978	**Cincinnati**	@	LOS ANGELES RAMS	20	19	W	6.0	W		
12/4/1978	Chicago	@	**SAN DIEGO CHARGERS**	7	40	L	6.0	L		
11/27/1978	**Pittsburgh**	@	SAN FRANCISCO	24	7	W	-8.0	W		
11/20/1978	Miami	@	**HOUSTON OILERS**	30	35	L	2.0	L		
11/13/1978	**Oakland Raiders**	@	CINCINNATI	34	21	W	-6.0	W		
11/6/1978	Washington Redskins	@	**BALTIMORE COLTS**	17	21	L	-3.5	L		
10/30/1978	Los Angeles Rams	@	**ATLANTA**	7	15	L	-6.5	L		
10/23/1978	**Houston Oilers**	@	PITTSBURGH	24	17	W	7.5	W		
10/16/1978	Chicago	@	**DENVER**	7	16	L	6.5	L		
10/9/1978	Cincinnati	@	**MIAMI**	0	21	L	10.5	L		
10/2/1978	Dallas	@	**WASHINGTON**	5	9	L	-5.0	L		
9/25/1978	**Minnesota**	@	CHICAGO	24	20	W	3.0	W		
9/18/1978	**Baltimore Colts**	@	NEW ENGLAND	34	27	W	1.0	W		
9/11/1978	Denver	@	**MINNESOTA (OT)**	9	12	L	1.0	L		
9/4/1978	Baltimore Colts	@	**DALLAS**	0	38	L	11.5	L		
12/26/1977	**Minnesota**	@	**LOS ANGELES RAMS**	**14**	**7**	**W**				
12/12/1977	**Dallas**	@	SAN FRANCISCO	42	35	W				
12/5/1977	Baltimore Colts	@	**MIAMI**	6	17	L				
11/28/1977	Buffalo	@	**OAKLAND RAIDERS**	13	34	L				

Monday Night Football History

Date	Visitor	@	Home	V	H	Result				
11/21/1977	Green Bay	@	**WASHINGTON**	9	10	L				
11/14/1977	**St. Louis Cardinals**	@	DALLAS	24	17	W				
11/7/1977	Washington Redskins	@	**BALTIMORE COLTS**	3	10	L				
10/31/1977	New York Giants	@	**ST. LOUIS CARDINALS**	0	28	L				
10/24/1977	Minnesota	@	**LOS ANGELES RAMS**	3	35	L				
10/17/1977	Cincinnati	@	**PITTSBURGH**	14	20	L				
10/10/1977	Los Angeles Rams	@	**CHICAGO**	23	24	L				
10/3/1977	**Oakland Raiders**	@	KANSAS CITY	37	28	W				
9/26/1977	New England Patriots	@	**CLEVELAND BROWNS (OT)**	27	30	L				
9/19/1977	San Francisco	@	**PITTSBURGH**	0	27	L				
12/6/1976	Cincinnati	@	**OAKLAND RAIDERS**	20	35	L				
12/6/1976	New Orleans	@	**NEW ENGLAND**	6	27	L				
11/29/1976	Minnesota	@	**SAN FRANCISCO**	16	20	L				
11/22/1976	**Baltimore Colts**	@	MIAMI	17	16	W				
11/15/1976	Buffalo	@	**DALLAS**	10	17	L				
11/8/1976	Los Angeles Rams	@	**CINCINNATI**	12	20	L				
11/1/1976	Houston Oilers	@	**BALTIMORE COLTS**	14	38	L				
10/25/1976	St. Louis Cardinals	@	**WASHINGTON**	10	20	L				
10/18/1976	New York Jets	@	**NEW ENGLAND**	7	41	L				
10/11/1976	**San Francisco**	@	LOS ANGELES RAMS	16	0	W				
10/4/1976	Pittsburgh	@	**MINNESOTA**	6	17	L				
9/27/1976	**Washington Redskins**	@	PHILADELPHIA	20	17	W				
9/20/1976	**Oakland Raiders**	@	KANSAS CITY	24	21	W				
9/13/1976	**Miami**	@	BUFFALO	30	21	W				
12/15/1975	New York Jets	@	**SAN DIEGO CHARGERS**	16	24	L				
12/8/1975	Denver	@	**OAKLAND RAIDERS**	10	17	L				
12/1/1975	New England Patriots	@	**MIAMI**	7	20	L				
11/24/1975	**Pittsburgh**	@	HOUSTON OILERS	32	9	W				
11/17/1975	Buffalo	@	**CINCINNATI**	24	33	L				
11/10/1975	**Kansas City**	@	DALLAS	34	31	W				
11/3/1975	**Los Angeles Rams**	@	PHILADELPHIA	42	3	W				
10/27/1975	**Minnesota**	@	CHICAGO	13	9	W				
10/20/1975	**New York Giants**	@	BUFFALO	17	14	W				
10/13/1975	St. Louis Cardinals	@	**WASHINGTON**	17	27	L				
10/6/1975	**Dallas**	@	DETROIT	36	10	W				
9/29/1975	Green Bay	@	**DENVER**	13	23	L				
9/22/1975	**Oakland Raiders**	@	MIAMI	31	21	W				
12/9/1974	**Washington Redskins**	@	LOS ANGELES RAMS	23	17	W				
12/2/1974	Cincinnati	@	**MIAMI**	3	24	L				
11/25/1974	**Pittsburgh**	@	NEW ORLEANS	28	7	W				
11/18/1974	**Kansas City**	@	DENVER	42	34	W				
11/11/1974	**Minnesota**	@	ST. LOUIS CARDINALS	28	24	W				
11/4/1974	**Los Angeles Rams**	@	SAN FRANCISCO	15	13	W				
10/28/1974	Atlanta	@	**PITTSBURGH**	17	24	L				
10/21/1974	Green Bay	@	**CHICAGO**	9	10	L				
10/14/1974	San Francisco	@	**DETROIT**	13	17	L				
10/7/1974	New York Jets	@	**MIAMI**	17	21	L				
9/30/1974	Denver	@	**WASHINGTON**	3	30	L				
9/23/1974	Dallas	@	**PHILADELPHIA**	10	13	L				
9/16/1974	Oakland Raiders	@	**BUFFALO**	20	21	L				
12/10/1973	New York Giants	@	**LOS ANGELES RAMS**	6	40	L				
12/3/1973	Pittsburgh	@	**MIAMI**	26	30	L				
11/26/1973	Green Bay	@	**SAN FRANCISCO**	6	20	L				
11/19/1973	Minnesota	@	**ATLANTA**	14	20	L				

Monday Night Football History

Date	Visitor	@	Home	V	H	Result					
11/12/1973	Chicago	@	**KANSAS CITY**	7	19	L					
11/5/1973	Washington Redskins	@	**PITTSBURGH**	16	21	L					
10/29/1973	Kansas City	@	**BUFFALO**	14	23	L					
10/22/1973	Oakland Raiders	@	DENVER	23	23	**T**					
10/15/1973	**Miami**	@	CLEVELAND BROWNS	17	9	W					
10/8/1973	Dallas	@	**WASHINGTON**	7	14	L					
10/1/1973	Atlanta	@	**DETROIT**	6	31	L					
9/24/1973	New Orleans	@	**DALLAS**	3	40	L					
9/17/1973	New York Jets	@	**GREEN BAY**	7	23	L					
12/11/1972	New York Jets	@	**OAKLAND RAIDERS**	16	24	L					
12/4/1972	**Los Angeles Rams**	@	SAN FRANCISCO	26	16	W					
11/27/1972	St. Louis Cardinals	@	**MIAMI**	10	31	L					
11/20/1972	Atlanta	@	**WASHINGTON**	13	24	L					
11/13/1972	Cleveland Browns	@	**SAN DIEGO CHARGERS**	21	27	L					
11/6/1972	**Baltimore Colts**	@	NEW ENGLAND	24	17	W					
10/30/1972	Detroit	@	**DALLAS**	24	28	L					
10/23/1972	Minnesota	@	**CHICAGO**	10	13	L					
10/16/1972	**Green Bay**	@	DETROIT	24	23	W					
10/9/1972	**Oakland Raiders**	@	HOUSTON OILERS	34	0	W					
10/2/1972	**New York Giants**	@	PHILADELPHIA	27	12	W					
9/25/1972	**Kansas City**	@	NEW ORLEANS	20	17	W					
9/18/1972	**Washington Redskins**	@	MINNESOTA	24	21	W					
12/13/1971	**Washington Redskins**	@	LOS ANGELES RAMS	38	24	W					
12/6/1971	**Kansas City**	@	SAN FRANCISCO	26	17	W					
11/29/1971	Chicago	@	**MIAMI**	3	34	L					
11/22/1971	Green Bay	@	**ATLANTA**	21	28	L					
11/15/1971	St. Louis Cardinals	@	**SAN DIEGO CHARGERS**	17	20	L					
11/8/1971	Los Angeles Rams	@	**BALTIMORE COLTS**	17	24	L					
11/1/1971	Detroit	@	GREEN BAY	14	14	**T**					
10/25/1971	Baltimore Colts	@	**MINNESOTA**	3	10	L					
10/18/1971	Pittsburgh	@	**KANSAS CITY**	16	38	L					
10/11/1971	New York Giants	@	**DALLAS**	13	20	L					
10/4/1971	**Oakland Raiders**	@	CLEVELAND BROWNS	34	20	W					
9/27/1971	New York Jets	@	**ST. LOUIS CARDINALS**	10	17	L					
9/20/1971	**Minnesota**	@	DETROIT	16	13	W					
12/14/1970	**Detroit**	@	LOS ANGELES RAMS	28	23	W					
12/7/1970	**Cleveland Browns**	@	HOUSTON OILERS	21	10	W					
11/30/1970	**Miami**	@	ATLANTA	20	7	W					
11/23/1970	New York Giants	@	**PHILADELPHIA**	20	23	L					
11/16/1970	**St. Louis Cardinals**	@	DALLAS	38	0	W					
11/9/1970	**Baltimore Colts**	@	GREEN BAY (MILWAUKEE)	13	10	W					
11/2/1970	Cincinnati	@	**PITTSBURGH**	10	21	L					
10/26/1970	Los Angeles Rams	@	**MINNESOTA**	3	13	L					
10/19/1970	Washington Redskins	@	**OAKLAND RAIDERS**	20	34	L					
10/12/1970	**Green Bay**	@	SAN DIEGO CHARGERS	22	20	W					
10/5/1970	Chicago	@	**DETROIT**	14	28	L					
9/28/1970	**Kansas City**	@	BALTIMORE COLTS	44	24	W					
9/21/1970	New York Jets	@	**CLEVELAND BROWNS**	21	31	L					
10/27/1969	New York Giants	@	**DALLAS**	3	25	L					
10/20/1969	Houston Oilers	@	**NEW YORK JETS**	17	26	L					
10/13/1969	Philadelphia	@	**BALTIMORE COLTS**	20	24	L					
10/28/1968	**Green Bay**	@	DALLAS	28	17	W					
9/16/1968	**Los Angeles Rams**	@	ST. LOUIS CARDINALS	24	13	W					
10/30/1967	**Green Bay**	@	ST. LOUIS CARDINALS	31	23	W					

Monday Night Football History

Date	Away		Home	Score1	Score2	Result					Notes
10/31/1966	Chicago	@	ST. LOUIS CARDINALS	17	24	L					
10/4/1965	Dallas	@	ST. LOUIS CARDINALS	13	20	L					
11/23/1964	**Baltimore Colts**	@	LOS ANGELES RAMS	24	7	W					
10/12/1964	St. Louis Cardinals	@	BALTIMORE COLTS	27	47	L					
9/28/1964	**Green Bay**	@	DETROIT	14	10	W					
12/26/1960	Green Bay	@	PHILADELPHIA	**13**	**17**	**L**					Playoffs
12/26/1955	**Cleveland Browns**	@	LOS ANGELES RAMS	**38**	**14**	**W**					Playoffs
9/26/1955	Chicago Cardinals	@	PITTSBURGH	7	14	L					
10/8/1951	New York Yanks	@	DETROIT	10	37	L					
10/2/1950	Baltimore Colts	@	CHICAGO CARDINALS	13	55	L					
10/3/1949	**Philadelphia**	@	DETROIT	22	14	W					
10/3/1949	**Washington Redskins**	@	PITTSBURGH	27	14	W					
9/26/1949	**Cleveland Browns**	@	BALTIMORE COLTS	28	20	W					AAFC
9/5/1949	Cleveland Browns	@	BUFFALO BILLS	28	28	**T**					AAFC
10/4/1948	**Chicago**	@	CHICAGO CARDINALS	28	17	W					
9/29/1947	New York Giants	@	BOSTON YANKS	7	7	**T**					
9/29/1947	**Los Angeles Rams**	@	PITTSBURGH	48	7	W					
9/30/1946	Detroit	@	CHICAGO CARDINALS	14	34	L					
11/6/1939	Pittsburgh	@	BROOKLYN DODGERS	13	17	L					
10/2/1939	**Chicago**	@	PITTSBURGH	32	0	W					
10/3/1938	**Pittsburgh**	@	NEW YORK GIANTS	13	10	W					
10/4/1937	**Chicago**	@	PITTSBURGH	7	0	W					
9/28/1936	Chicago Cardinals	@	DETROIT	0	39	L					
10/24/1921	**Chicago Cardinals**	@	CHICAGO STAYM-FORESTERS	27	0	W					
10/24/1921	Gary Elks	@	CHICAGO CARDINALS	0	21	L					
10/10/1921	Rock Island	@	CHICAGO	10	14	L					

Interesting Monday Night Football Facts

Arizona is 4-1 at home vs AFC on Monday Night since 1971
Arizona is 2-8 on road on Monday Night since 1971
Atlanta is 0-5 vs L.A. Rams on Monday Night since 1979
Baltimore is 7-0 at home vs NFC on Monday Night since 1979
Baltimore is 0-4 at Pittsburgh on Monday Night since 1995
Cincinnati is 3-20 on road on Monday Night since 1970
Dallas is 9-1 on road on Monday Night since 2003
Denver is 3-16 on road on Monday Night since 1998
Detroit is 0-6 vs AFC on Monday Night since 1982
Kansas City is 8-0 at home on Monday Night since 2010
Miami is 6-22 on road on Monday Night since 1978
Miami is 2-8 vs NFC on Monday Night since 1995
Minnesota is 3-9 on road on Monday Night since 1999
Minnesota is 0-5 vs NY Giants on Monday Night since 1989
New England is 7-2 at home on Monday Night since 2008
New England is 2-6 vs NFC on Monday Night since 1979
N.Y. Giants are 0-6 at Philadelphia on Monday Night since 1980

N.Y. Jets are 0-7 at home on Monday Night since 2012
Las Vegas is 1-6 vs NFC on Monday Night since 1991
Philadelphia is 7-0 vs N.Y. Giants on Monday Night since 1980
Philadelphia is 5-0 vs AFC on Monday Night since 1991
Pittsburgh is 20-0 at home on Monday Night since 1992
Pittsburgh is 13-1 on Monday Night since 2014
Pittsburgh is 4-0 vs Tennessee on Monday Night since 1981
San Francisco is 6-1 at home vs AFC on Monday since 1985
Seattle is 11-2 at home on Monday Night since 2006
Seattle is 12-2 at home vs AFC on Monday Night since 1979
Tennessee is 6-0 vs NFC on Monday Night since 2000
Washington is 2-17 at home on Monday Night since 1998
Washington is 2-8 on Monday Night since 2015
Washington is 0-6 vs AFC on Monday Night since 1989
Washington is 1-8 on road vs AFC on Monday Night since 1970

Playoffs History

Date				SC	ORE	S/U W-L	LINE	ATS W-L	TOTAL	O/U	PLAY-OFF GAME
2/12/2023	**Kansas City**	vs	Philadelphia	**38**	**35**	**W**	**1.0**	**W**	**51.5**	**O**	Super Bowl LVII @ Glendale, AZ
1/29/2023	**Philadelphia**	vs	San Francisco	31	7	W	-2.5	W	44.5	U	NFC CHAMPIONSHIP
1/29/2023	**Kansas City**	vs	Cincinnati	**23**	**20**	W	-2.5	W	48.0	U	AFC CHAMPIONSHIP
1/22/2023	**San Francisco**	vs	Dallas	19	12	W	-3.5	W	47.0	U	NFC Divisional Play-offs
1/22/2023	**Cincinnati**	@	Buffalo	27	10	W	6.0	W	48.0	U	AFC Divisional Play-offs
1/21/2023	**Philadelphia**	vs	New York Giants	38	7	W	-8.0	W	47.5	U	NFC Divisional Play-offs
1/21/2023	**Kansas City**	vs	Jacksonville	27	20	W	-9.5	L	52.0	U	AFC Divisional Play-offs
1/16/2023	**Dallas**	@	Tampa Bay	31	14	W	-2.5	W	44.5	O	NFC WILD CARD
1/15/2023	**Cincinnati**	vs	Baltimore Ravens	24	17	W	-7.5	L	40.0	O	AFC WILD CARD
1/15/2023	**New York Giants**	@	Minnesota	31	24	W	2.5	W	48.0	O	NFC WILD CARD
1/15/2023	**Buffalo**	vs	Miami	34	31	W	-14.0	L	44.5	O	AFC WILD CARD
1/14/2023	**Jacksonville**	vs	Los Angeles Chargers	31	30	W	2.0	W	46.5	O	AFC WILD CARD
1/14/2023	**San Francisco**	vs	Seattle	41	23	W	-9.0	W	42.0	O	NFC WILD CARD
2/13/2022	**Los Angeles Rams**	vs	Cincinnati	**23**	**20**	**W**	**-4.5**	**L**	**49.0**	**U**	Super Bowl LVI @ Los Angeles, CA
1/30/2022	**Los Angeles Rams**	vs	San Francisco	20	17	W	-3.5	L	46.0	U	NFC CHAMPIONSHIP
1/30/2022	**Cincinnati**	@	Kansas City {OT}	27	24	W	7.0	W	54.5	U	AFC CHAMPIONSHIP
1/23/2022	**Los Angeles Rams**	@	Tampa Bay	30	27	W	3.0	W	48.0	O	NFC Divisional Play-offs
1/23/2022	**Kansas City**	vs	Buffalo	42	36	W	-2.5	W	54.0	O	AFC Divisional Play-offs
1/22/2022	**Cincinnati**	@	Tennessee	19	16	W	4.0	W	48.5	U	AFC Divisional Play-offs
1/22/2022	**San Francisco**	@	Green Bay	13	10	W	6.0	W	47.0	U	NFC Divisional Play-offs
1/17/2022	**Los Angeles Rams**	vs	Arizona	34	11	W	-3.0	W	49.0	U	NFC WILD CARD
1/16/2022	**Kansas City**	vs	Pittsburgh	42	21	W	-12.0	W	46.5	O	AFC WILD CARD
1/16/2022	**Tampa Bay**	vs	Philadelphia	31	15	W	-7.0	W	47.5	U	NFC WILD CARD
1/16/2022	**San Francisco**	@	Dallas	23	17	W	3.0	W	51.5	U	NFC WILD CARD
1/15/2022	**Buffalo**	vs	New England	47	17	W	-4.5	W	43.0	O	AFC WILD CARD
1/15/2022	**Cincinnati**	vs	Las Vegas Raiders	26	19	W	-6.0	W	48.5	U	AFC WILD CARD
2/7/2021	**Tampa Bay**	vs	Kansas City	**31**	**9**	**W**	**3.0**	**W**	**55.5**	**U**	Super Bowl LV @ Tampa, FL
1/24/2021	**Kansas City**	vs	Buffalo	38	24	W	-3.0	W	55.0	O	AFC CHAMPIONSHIP
1/24/2021	**Tampa Bay**	@	Green Bay	31	26	W	3.0	W	53.0	O	NFC CHAMPIONSHIP
1/17/2021	**Tampa Bay**	@	New Orleans	30	20	W	2.5	W	53.0	U	NFC Divisional Play-offs
1/17/2021	**Kansas City**	vs	Cleveland	22	17	W	-7.5	L	56.0	U	AFC Divisional Play-offs
1/16/2021	**Buffalo**	vs	Baltimore Ravens	17	3	W	-2.5	W	50.0	U	AFC Divisional Play-offs
1/16/2021	**Green Bay**	vs	Los Angeles Rams	32	18	W	-7.0	W	45.0	O	NFC Divisional Play-offs
1/10/2021	**Cleveland**	@	Pittsburgh	48	37	W	5.0	W	47.0	O	AFC WILD CARD
1/10/2021	**New Orleans**	vs	Chicago	21	9	W	-11.0	W	47.5	U	NFC WILD CARD
1/10/2021	**Baltimore Ravens**	@	Tennessee	20	13	W	-3.5	W	53.5	U	AFC WILD CARD
1/9/2021	**Tampa Bay**	@	Washington	31	23	W	-10.5	L	45.0	O	NFC WILD CARD
1/9/2021	**Los Angeles Rams**	@	Seattle	30	20	W	3.0	W	42.0	O	NFC WILD CARD
1/9/2021	**Buffalo**	vs	Indianapolis	27	24	W	-6.5	L	50.5	O	AFC WILD CARD
2/2/2020	**Kansas City**	vs	San Francisco	**31**	**20**	**W**	**-1.5**	**W**	**52.5**	**U**	Super Bowl LIV @ Miami Gardens,
1/19/2020	Tennessee	@	**Kansas City**	24	35	L	7.0	L	51.0	O	AFC CHAMPIONSHIP
1/19/2020	Green Bay	@	**San Francisco**	20	37	L	8.0	L	46.5	O	NFC CHAMPIONSHIP
1/12/2020	Seattle	@	**Green Bay**	23	28	L	4.5	L	45.5	O	NFC Divisional Play-offs
1/12/2020	Houston Texans	@	**Kansas City**	31	51	L	10.0	L	50.5	O	AFC Divisional Play-offs
1/11/2020	**Tennessee**	@	Baltimore Ravens	28	12	W	10.0	W	47.5	U	AFC Divisional Play-offs
1/11/2020	Minnesota	@	**San Francisco**	10	27	L	7.0	L	44.5	U	NFC Divisional Play-offs
1/5/2020	**Seattle**	@	Philadelphia	17	9	W	-1.0	W	44.5	U	NFC WILD CARD
1/5/2020	**Minnesota**	@	New Orleans {OT}	26	20	W	7.0	W	50.0	U	NFC WILD CARD
1/4/2020	**Tennessee**	@	New England	20	13	W	4.5	W	45.0	U	AFC WILD CARD
1/4/2020	Buffalo	@	**Houston {OT}**	19	22	L	2.5	L	43.0	U	AFC WILD CARD
2/3/2019	**New England**	vs	Los Angeles Rams	**13**	**3**	**W**	**-2.0**	**W**	**55.5**	**U**	Super Bowl LIII @ Atlanta, GA
1/20/2019	**New England**	@	Kansas City	37	31	W	3.0	W	56.0	O	AFC CHAMPIONSHIP
1/20/2019	**Los Angeles Rams**	@	New Orleans	26	23	W	3.0	W	55.0	U	NFC CHAMPIONSHIP

Playoffs History

1/13/2019	Philadelphia	@	New Orleans	14	20	L	8.5	W	51.5	U	NFC Divisional Play-offs
1/13/2019	Los Angeles Chargers	@	New England	28	41	L	4.0	L	47.5	O	AFC Divisional Play-offs
1/12/2019	Dallas	@	Los Angeles Rams	22	30	L	7.0	L	48.0	O	NFC Divisional Play-offs
1/12/2019	Indianapolis	@	Kansas City	13	31	L	4.5	L	55.0	U	AFC Divisional Play-offs
1/6/2019	**Philadelphia**	@	Chicago	16	15	W	6.5	W	42.0	U	NFC WILD CARD
1/6/2019	**Los Angeles Chargers**	@	Baltimore Ravens	23	17	W	3.0	W	42.5	U	AFC WILD CARD
1/5/2019	Seattle	@	**Dallas**	22	24	L	2.5	W	43.5	O	NFC WILD CARD
1/5/2019	**Indianapolis**	@	Houston Texans	21	7	W	2.0	W	48.5	U	AFC WILD CARD
2/4/2018	**Philadelphia**	vs	New England	41	33	W	4.5	W	49.0	O	Super Bowl LII @ Minneapolis
1/21/2018	Minnesota	@	**Philadelphia**	7	38	L	3.0	L	39.0	O	NFC CHAMPIONSHIP
1/21/2018	Jacksonville	@	**New England**	20	24	L	7.5	W	45.5	U	AFC CHAMPIONSHIP
1/14/2018	New Orleans	@	**Minnesota**	24	29	L	5.5	W	46.5	O	NFC Divisional Play-offs
1/14/2018	**Jacksonville**	@	Pittsburgh	45	42	W	7.0	W	40.5	O	AFC Divisional Play-offs
1/13/2018	Tennessee	@	**New England**	14	35	L	13.5	L	48.0	O	AFC Divisional Play-offs
1/13/2018	Atlanta	@	**Philadelphia**	10	15	L	-2.5	L	40.5	U	NFC Divisional Play-offs
1/7/2018	Carolina	@	**New Orleans**	26	31	L	6.5	W	47.5	O	NFC WILD CARD
1/7/2018	Buffalo	@	**Jacksonville**	3	10	L	8.5	W	40.0	U	AFC WILD CARD
1/6/2018	**Atlanta**	@	Los Angeles Rams	26	13	W	6.5	W	48.0	U	NFC WILD CARD
1/6/2018	**Tennessee**	@	Kansas City	22	21	W	8.5	W	44.0	U	AFC WILD CARD
2/5/2017	**New England**	vs	Atlanta {OT}	34	28	W	-3.0	W	56.0	O	Super Bowl LI @ Houston, TX
1/22/2017	Pittsburgh	@	**New England**	17	36	L	5.5	L	49.5	O	AFC CHAMPIONSHIP
1/22/2017	Green Bay	@	**Atlanta**	21	44	L	6.5	L	59.5	O	NFC CHAMPIONSHIP
1/15/2017	**Green Bay**	@	Dallas	34	31	W	5.5	W	52.5	O	NFC Divisional Play-offs
1/15/2017	**Pittsburgh**	@	Kansas City	18	16	W	2.5	W	45.5	U	AFC Divisional Play-offs
1/14/2017	Houston Texans	@	**New England**	16	34	L	16.0	L	44.0	O	AFC Divisional Play-offs
1/14/2017	Seattle	@	**Atlanta**	20	36	L	6.5	L	51.0	O	NFC Divisional Play-offs
1/8/2017	New York Giants	@	**Green Bay**	13	38	L	5.0	L	46.5	O	NFC WILD CARD
1/8/2017	Miami	@	**Pittsburgh**	12	30	L	11.0	L	47.5	U	AFC WILD CARD
1/7/2017	Detroit	@	**Seattle**	6	26	L	8.0	L	45.5	U	NFC WILD CARD
1/7/2017	Oakland Raiders	@	**Houston Texans**	14	27	L	4.0	L	37.5	O	AFC WILD CARD
2/7/2016	**Denver**	vs	Carolina	24	10	W	4.5	W	43.0	U	Super Bowl 50 @ Santa Clara, CA
1/24/2016	Arizona	@	**Carolina**	15	49	L	-3.0	L	47.5	O	NFC CHAMPIONSHIP
1/24/2016	New England	@	**Denver**	18	20	L	-2.5	L	45.0	U	AFC CHAMPIONSHIP
1/17/2016	Pittsburgh	@	**Denver**	16	23	L	7.0	T	41.5	U	AFC Divisional Play-offs
1/17/2016	Seattle	@	**Carolina**	24	31	L	2.5	L	41.5	U	NFC Divisional Play-offs
1/16/2016	Green Bay	@	**Arizona (OT)**	20	26	L	7.0	W	49.0	U	NFC Divisional Play-offs
1/16/2016	Kansas City	@	**New England**	20	27	L	6.0	L	44.5	O	AFC Divisional Play-offs
1/10/2016	**Green Bay**	@	Washington	35	18	W	2.0	W	47.5	O	NFC WILD CARD
1/10/2016	**Seattle**	@	Minnesota	10	9	W	-4.5	L	40.0	U	NFC WILD CARD
1/9/2016	**Pittsburgh**	@	Cincinnati	18	16	W	-2.5	L	45.5	U	AFC WILD CARD
1/9/2016	**Kansas City**	@	Houston Texans	30	0	W	-3.0	W	39.5	U	AFC WILD CARD
2/1/2015	**New England**	vs	Seattle	28	24	W	1.0	W	47.0	O	Super Bowl XLIX @ Glendale, AZ
1/18/2015	Green Bay	@	**Seattle {OT}**	22	28	L	8.5	W	45.0	O	NFC CHAMPIONSHIP
1/18/2015	Indianapolis	@	**New England**	7	45	L	7.0	L	51.5	O	AFC CHAMPIONSHIP
1/11/2015	Dallas	@	**Green Bay**	21	26	L	5.5	W	52.5	U	NFC Divisional Play-offs
1/11/2015	**Indianapolis**	@	Denver	24	13	W	9.0	W	53.5	U	AFC Divisional Play-offs
1/10/2015	Baltimore Ravens	@	**New England**	31	35	L	7.0	W	47.5	O	AFC Divisional Play-offs
1/10/2015	Carolina	@	**Seattle**	17	31	L	13.0	L	39.5	O	NFC Divisional Play-offs
1/4/2015	Cincinnati	@	**Indianapolis**	10	26	L	3.5	L	47.0	U	AFC WILD CARD
1/4/2015	Detroit	@	**Dallas**	20	24	L	6.0	W	47.5	U	NFC WILD CARD
1/3/2015	Arizona	@	**Carolina**	16	27	L	5.5	L	37.5	O	NFC WILD CARD
1/3/2015	**Baltimore Ravens**	@	Pittsburgh	30	17	W	3.0	W	47.0	T	AFC WILD CARD
2/2/2014	**Seattle**	vs	Denver	43	8	W	2.0	W	47.5	O	Super Bowl XLVIII @ East Rutherford, NJ
1/19/2014	New England	@	**Denver**	16	26	L	5.0	L	56.5	U	AFC CHAMPIONSHIP

Playoffs History

Date	Team	@/vs	Opponent	Score1	Score2	W/L	Line	ATS	Total	O/U	Round
1/19/2014	San Francisco	@	**Seattle**	17	23	L	4.0	L	40.5	U	NFC CHAMPIONSHIP
1/12/2014	San Diego	@	**Denver**	17	24	L	8.0	W	54.5	U	AFC Divisional Play-offs
1/12/2014	**San Francisco**	@	Carolina	23	10	W	-1.0	W	41.5	U	NFC Divisional Play-offs
1/11/2014	Indianapolis	@	**New England**	22	43	L	7.0	L	51.5	O	AFC Divisional Play-off
1/11/2014	New Orleans	@	**Seattle**	15	23	L	9.0	W	44.0	U	NFC Divisional Play-offs
1/5/2014	**San Diego**	@	Cincinnati	27	10	W	6.5	W	47.5	U	AFC WILD CARD
1/5/2014	**San Francisco**	@	Green Bay	23	20	W	-3.0	T	46.5	U	NFC WILD CARD
1/4/2014	Kansas City	@	**Indianapolis**	44	45	L	-1.5	L	47.5	O	AFC WILD CARD
1/4/2014	**New Orleans**	@	Philadelphia	26	24	W	3.0	W	55.0	U	NFC WILD CARD
2/3/2013	**Baltimore Ravens**	vs	San Francisco	**34**	**31**	**W**	**4.5**	**W**	**47.5**	**O**	Super Bowl XLVII @ New Orleans
1/20/2013	**Baltimore Ravens**	@	New England	28	13	W	8.0	W	50.0	U	AFC CHAMPIONSHIP
1/20/2013	**San Francisco**	@	Atlanta	28	24	W	-3.5	W	47.0	O	NFC CHAMPIONSHIP
1/13/2013	Houston Texans	@	**New England**	28	41	L	9.5	L	50.5	O	AFC Divisional Play-offs
1/13/2013	Seattle	@	**Atlanta**	28	30	L	3.0	L	46.5	O	NFC Divisional Play-offs
1/12/2013	**Baltimore Ravens**	@	Denver (OT)	38	35	W	9.0	W	44.0	O	AFC Divisional Play-offs
1/12/2013	Green Bay	@	**San Francisco**	31	45	L	3.0	L	45.0	O	NFC Divisional Play-offs
1/6/2013	Indianapolis	@	**Baltimore Ravens**	9	24	L	7.5	L	47.5	U	AFC WILD CARD
1/6/2013	**Seattle**	@	Washington	24	14	W	-3.0	W	44.5	U	NFC WILD CARD
1/5/2013	Cincinnati	@	**Houston Texans**	13	19	L	4.0	L	42.5	U	AFC WILD CARD
1/5/2013	Minnesota	@	**Green Bay**	10	24	L	10.5	L	44.0	U	NFC WILD CARD
2/5/2012	**New York Giants**	vs	New England	**21**	**17**	**W**	**3.0**	**W**	**53.0**	**U**	Super Bowl XLVI @ Indianapolis
1/22/2012	Baltimore Ravens	@	**New England**	20	23	L	7.0	W	49.0	U	AFC CHAMPIONSHIP
1/22/2012	**New York Giants**	@	San Francisco (OT)	20	17	W	2.0	W	41.0	U	NFC CHAMPIONSHIP
1/15/2012	Houston Texans	@	**Baltimore Ravens**	13	20	L	7.5	W	37.5	U	AFC Divisional Play-offs
1/15/2012	**New York Giants**	@	Green Bay	37	20	W	8.5	W	54.0	O	NFC Divisional Play-offs
1/14/2012	Denver	@	**New England**	10	45	L	14.0	L	50.5	O	AFC Divisional Play-offs
1/14/2012	New Orleans	@	**San Francisco**	32	36	L	-3.0	L	46.0	O	NFC Divisional Play-offs
1/8/2012	Atlanta	@	**New York Giants**	2	24	L	3.0	L	47.0	U	NFC WILD CARD
1/8/2012	Pittsburgh	@	**Denver (OT)**	23	29	L	-7.5	L	34.0	O	AFC WILD CARD
1/7/2012	**Houston Texans**	vs	Cincinnati	31	10	W	-4.0	W	38.0	O	AFC WILD CARD
1/7/2012	**New Orleans**	vs	Detroit	45	28	W	-10.0	W	59.0	O	NFC WILD CARD
2/6/2011	**Green Bay**	vs	Pittsburgh	**31**	**25**	**W**	**-2.5**	**W**	**45.0**	**O**	Super Bowl XLV @ Dallas, TX
1/23/2011	**Green Bay**	@	Chicago	21	14	W	-3.5	W	43.0	U	NFC CHAMPIONSHIP
1/23/2011	**Pittsburgh**	vs	New York Jets	24	19	W	-3.5	W	38.0	O	AFC CHAMPIONSHIP
1/16/2011	**Chicago**	vs	Seattle	35	24	W	-10.0	W	41.5	O	NFC Divisional Play-offs
1/16/2011	**New York Jets**	@	New England	28	21	W	9.0	W	44.5	O	AFC Divisional Play-offs
1/15/2011	**Green Bay**	@	Atlanta	48	21	W	2.5	W	44.0	O	NFC Divisional Play-offs
1/15/2011	**Pittsburgh**	vs	Baltimore	31	24	W	-3.5	W	37.0	O	AFC Divisional Play-offs
1/9/2011	**Baltimore Ravens**	@	Kansas City	30	7	W	-3.0	W	40.5	U	AFC WILD CARD
1/9/2011	**Green Bay**	@	Philadelphia	21	16	W	2.5	W	46.5	U	NFC WILD CARD
1/8/2011	**New York Jets**	@	Indianapolis	17	16	W	2.5	W	44.5	U	AFC WILD CARD
1/8/2011	**Seattle**	vs	New Orleans	41	36	W	10.0	W	45.0	O	NFC WILD CARD
2/7/2010	**New Orleans**	vs	Indianapolis	**31**	**17**	**W**	**4.5**	**W**	**56.5**	**U**	Super Bowl XLIV @ Miami, FL
1/24/2010	**Indianapolis**	vs	New York Jets	30	17	W	-8.0	W	40.0	O	AFC CHAMPIONSHIP
1/24/2010	**New Orleans**	vs	Minnesota (OT)	31	28	W	-3.5	L	54.0	O	NFC CHAMPIONSHIP
1/17/2010	**Minnesota**	vs	Dallas	34	3	W	-3.0	W	45.5	U	NFC Divisional Play-offs
1/17/2010	**New York Jets**	@	San Diego	17	14	W	8.5	W	42.0	U	AFC Divisional Play-offs
1/16/2010	**Indianapolis**	vs	Baltimore	20	3	W	-6.5	W	44.0	U	AFC Divisional Play-offs
1/16/2010	**New Orleans**	vs	Arizona	45	14	W	-7.0	W	57.0	O	NFC Divisional Play-offs
1/10/2010	**Arizona**	vs	Green Bay (OT)	51	45	W	-1.0	W	47.5	O	NFC WILD CARD
1/10/2010	**Baltimore Ravens**	@	New England	33	14	W	3.5	W	43.5	O	AFC WILD CARD
1/9/2010	**Dallas**	vs	Philadelphia	34	14	W	-4.0	W	45.0	O	NFC WILD CARD
1/9/2010	**New York Jets**	@	Cincinnati	24	14	W	2.5	W	34.0	O	AFC WILD CARD
2/1/2009	**Pittsburgh**	vs	Arizona	**27**	**23**	**W**	**-7.0**	**L**	**46.5**	**O**	Super Bowl XLIII @ Tampa, FL

Playoffs History

1/18/2009	**Arizona**	vs	Philadelphia	32	25	W	3.5	W	47.0	O	NFC CHAMPIONSHIP
1/18/2009	**Pittsburgh**	vs	Baltimore	23	14	W	-6.0	W	34.5	O	AFC CHAMPIONSHIP
1/11/2009	**Philadelphia**	@	New York Giants	23	11	W	4.0	W	39.0	U	NFC Divisional Play-offs
1/11/2009	**Pittsburgh**	vs	San Diego	35	24	W	-6.0	W	37.5	O	AFC Divisional Play-offs
1/10/2009	**Arizona**	@	Carolina	33	13	W	10.0	W	48.5	U	NFC Divisional Play-offs
1/10/2009	**Baltimore Ravens**	@	Tennessee	13	10	W	3.0	W	34.0	U	AFC Divisional Play-offs
1/4/2009	**Baltimore Ravens**	@	Miami	27	9	W	-3.5	W	37.5	U	AFC WILD CARD
1/4/2009	**Philadelphia**	@	Minnesota	26	14	W	-3.0	W	41.0	U	NFC WILD CARD
1/3/2009	**Arizona**	vs	Atlanta	30	24	W	1.0	W	51.5	O	NFC WILD CARD
1/3/2009	**San Diego**	vs	Indianapolis (OT)	23	17	W	1.5	W	51.0	U	AFC WILD CARD
2/3/2008	**New York Giants**	vs	New England	**17**	**14**	W	12.5	W	54.5	U	Super Bowl XLII @ Phoenix, AZ
1/20/2008	**New England**	vs	San Diego	21	12	W	-13.5	L	47.0	U	AFC CHAMPIONSHIP
1/20/2008	**New York Giants**	@	Green Bay (Ot)	23	20	W	7.5	W	41.0	O	NFC CHAMPIONSHIP
1/13/2008	**New York Giants**	@	Dallas	21	17	W	7.5	W	46.5	U	NFC Divisional Play-offs
1/13/2008	**San Diego**	@	Indianapolis	28	24	W	9.0	W	45.5	O	AFC Divisional Play-offs
1/12/2008	**Green Bay**	vs	Seattle	42	20	W	-7.5	W	43.0	O	NFC Divisional Play-offs
1/12/2008	**New England**	vs	Jacksonville	31	20	W	-13.5	L	50.0	O	AFC Divisional Play-offs
1/6/2008	**New York Giants**	@	Tampa Bay	24	14	W	3.0	W	39.5	U	NFC WILD CARD
1/6/2008	**San Diego**	vs	Tennessee	17	6	W	-10.0	W	39.0	U	AFC WILD CARD
1/5/2008	**Jacksonville**	@	Pittsburgh	31	29	W	-2.5	L	39.5	O	AFC WILD CARD
1/5/2008	**Seattle**	vs	Washington	35	14	W	-3.5	W	39.0	O	NFC WILD CARD
2/4/2007	**Indianapolis**	vs	Chicago	**29**	**17**	W	-7.0	W	48.0	U	Super Bowl XLI @ Miami, FL
1/21/2007	**Chicago**	vs	New Orleans	39	14	W	-2.5	W	43.0	O	NFC CHAMPIONSHIP
1/21/2007	**Indianapolis**	vs	New England	38	34	W	-3.0	W	47.5	O	AFC CHAMPIONSHIP
1/14/2007	**Chicago**	vs	Seattle (Ot)	27	24	W	-9.0	L	37.5	O	NFC Divisional Play-offs
1/14/2007	**New England**	@	San Diego	24	21	W	4.5	W	46.5	U	AFC Divisional Play-offs
1/13/2007	**Indianapolis**	@	Baltimore Ravens	15	6	W	4.0	W	41.5	U	AFC Divisional Play-offs
1/13/2007	**New Orleans**	vs	Philadelphia	27	24	W	-5.5	L	49.0	O	NFC Divisional Play-offs
1/7/2007	**New England**	vs	New York Jets	37	16	W	-9.0	W	38.5	O	AFC WILD CARD
1/7/2007	**Philadelphia**	vs	New York Giants	23	20	W	-7.0	L	46.0	U	NFC WILD CARD
1/6/2007	**Indianapolis**	vs	Kansas City	23	8	W	-7.0	W	50.5	U	AFC WILD CARD
1/6/2007	**Seattle**	vs	Dallas	21	20	W	-2.0	L	48.0	U	NFC WILD CARD
2/5/2006	**Pittsburgh**	vs	Seattle	**21**	**10**	W	-4.0	W	47.0	U	Super Bowl XL @ Detroit, MI
1/22/2006	**Pittsburgh**	@	Denver	34	17	W	3.0	W	41.0	O	AFC CHAMPIONSHIP
1/22/2006	**Seattle**	vs	Carolina	34	14	W	-3.5	W	43.5	O	NFC CHAMPIONSHIP
1/15/2006	**Carolina**	@	Chicago	29	21	W	2.5	W	30.5	O	NFC Divisional Play-offs
1/15/2006	**Pittsburgh**	@	Indianapolis	21	18	W	9.5	W	47.5	U	AFC Divisional Play-offs
1/14/2006	**Denver**	vs	New England	27	13	W	-3.0	W	44.0	U	AFC Divisional Play-offs
1/14/2006	**Seattle**	vs	Washington	20	10	W	-9.5	W	41.0	U	NFC Divisional Play-offs
1/8/2006	**Carolina**	@	New York Giants	23	0	W	2.5	W	43.5	U	NFC WILD CARD
1/8/2006	**Pittsburgh**	@	Cincinnati	31	17	W	-3.0	W	46.5	O	AFC WILD CARD
1/7/2006	**New England**	vs	Jacksonville	28	3	W	-7.5	W	37.0	U	AFC WILD CARD
1/7/2006	**Washington**	@	Tampa Bay	17	10	W	2.5	W	37.0	U	NFC WILD CARD
2/6/2005	**New England**	vs	Philadelphia	**24**	**21**	W	-7.0	L	47.5	U	Super Bowl XXXIX @ Jacksonville
1/23/2005	**New England**	@	Pittsburgh	41	27	W	-3.0	W	35.0	O	AFC CHAMPIONSHIP
1/23/2005	**Philadelphia**	vs	Atlanta	27	10	W	-5.5	W	37.5	U	NFC CHAMPIONSHIP
1/16/2005	**New England**	vs	Indianapolis	20	3	W	-1.0	W	52.5	U	AFC Divisional Play-offs
1/16/2005	**Philadelphia**	vs	Minnesota	27	14	W	-8.0	W	47.5	U	NFC Divisional Play-offs
1/15/2005	**Atlanta**	vs	St. Louis Rams	47	17	W	-7.0	W	48.5	O	NFC Divisional Play-offs
1/15/2005	**Pittsburgh**	vs	New York Jets (Ot)	20	17	W	-9.0	L	35.0	O	AFC Divisional Play-offs
1/9/2005	**Indianapolis**	vs	Denver	49	24	W	-10.0	W	56.0	O	AFC WILD CARD
1/9/2005	**Minnesota**	@	Green Bay	31	17	W	6.5	W	49.5	U	NFC WILD CARD
1/8/2005	**New York Jets**	@	San Diego (Ot)	20	17	W	6.5	W	43.0	U	AFC WILD CARD
1/8/2005	**St. Louis Rams**	@	Seattle	27	20	W	4.0	W	50.5	U	NFC WILD CARD

Playoffs History

Date	Team		Opponent									Round
2/1/2004	New England	vs	Carolina	32	29	W	-7.0	L	37.5	O		Super Bowl XXXVIII @ Houston
1/18/2004	Carolina	@	Philadelphia	14	3	W	4.0	W	36.5	U		NFC CHAMPIONSHIP
1/18/2004	New England	vs	Indianapolis	24	14	W	-3.0	W	43.0	U		AFC CHAMPIONSHIP
1/11/2004	Indianapolis	@	Kansas City	38	31	W	3.0	W	51.5	O		AFC Divisional Play-offs
1/11/2004	Philadelphia	vs	Green Bay (Ot)	20	17	W	-5.0	L	42.5	U		NFC Divisional Play-offs
1/10/2004	Carolina	@	St. Louis Rams (Ot)	29	23	W	7.0	W	45.0	O		NFC Divisional Play-offs
1/10/2004	New England	vs	Tennessee	17	14	W	-6.5	L	34.0	U		AFC Divisional Play-offs
1/4/2004	Green Bay	vs	Seattle (Ot)	33	27	W	-7.5	L	44.0	O		NFC WILD CARD
1/4/2004	Indianapolis	vs	Denver	41	10	W	-3.0	W	49.0	O		AFC WILD CARD
1/3/2004	Carolina	vs	Dallas	29	10	W	-3.0	W	34.0	O		NFC WILD CARD
1/3/2004	Tennessee	@	Baltimore Ravens	20	17	W	-1.0	W	39.5	U		AFC WILD CARD
1/26/2003	Tampa Bay	vs	Oakland	48	21	W	4.0	W	44.0	O		Super Bowl XXXVII @ San Diego
1/19/2003	Oakland Raiders	vs	Tennessee	41	24	W	-8.0	W	47.0	O		AFC CHAMPIONSHIP
1/19/2003	Tampa Bay	@	Philadelphia	27	10	W	4.0	W	34.0	O		NFC CHAMPIONSHIP
1/12/2003	Oakland Raiders	vs	New York Jets	30	10	W	-5.5	W	47.5	U		AFC Divisional Play-offs
1/12/2003	Tampa Bay	vs	San Francisco	31	6	W	-6.0	W	39.0	U		NFC Divisional Play-offs
1/11/2003	Philadelphia	vs	Atlanta	20	6	W	-7.5	W	38.5	U		NFC Divisional Play-offs
1/11/2003	Tennessee	vs	Pittsburgh (Ot)	34	31	W	-4.0	L	44.0	O		AFC Divisional Play-offs
1/5/2003	Pittsburgh	vs	Cleveland	36	33	W	-8.0	L	41.0	O		AFC WILD CARD
1/5/2003	San Francisco	vs	New York Giants	39	38	W	-3.0	L	40.0	O		NFC WILD CARD
1/4/2003	Atlanta	@	Green Bay	27	7	W	6.5	W	40.0	U		NFC WILD CARD
1/4/2003	New York Jets	vs	Indianapolis	41	0	W	-6.0	W	41.0	T		AFC WILD CARD
2/3/2002	New England	vs	St. Louis	20	17	W	14.0	W	53.0	U		Super Bowl XXXVI @ New Orleans, LA
1/27/2002	New England	@	Pittsburgh	24	17	W	10.0	W	37.0	O		AFC CHAMPIONSHIP
1/27/2002	St. Louis Rams	vs	Philadelphia	29	24	W	-10.5	L	49.0	O		NFC CHAMPIONSHIP
1/20/2002	Pittsburgh	vs	Baltimore	27	10	W	-6.0	W	32.0	O		AFC Divisional Play-offs
1/20/2002	St. Louis Rams	vs	Green Bay	45	17	W	-11.5	W	55.0	O		NFC Divisional Play-offs
1/19/2002	New England	vs	Oakland Raiders (Ot)	16	13	W	-3.0	T	38.0	U		AFC Divisional Play-offs
1/19/2002	Philadelphia	@	Chicago	33	19	W	3.0	W	31.5	O		NFC Divisional Play-offs
1/13/2002	Baltimore Ravens	@	Miami	20	3	W	2.5	W	32.5	U		AFC WILD CARD
1/13/2002	Green Bay	vs	San Francisco	25	15	W	-3.5	W	42.0	U		NFC WILD CARD
1/12/2002	Oakland Raiders	vs	New York Jets	38	24	W	-5.5	W	42.0	O		AFC WILD CARD
1/12/2002	Philadelphia	vs	Tampa Bay	31	9	W	-3.5	W	33.0	O		NFC WILD CARD
1/28/2001	Baltimore Ravens	vs	New York Giants	34	7	W	-3.0	W	33.0	O		Super Bowl XXXV @ Tampa, FL
1/14/2001	Baltimore Ravens	@	Oakland Raiders	16	3	W	6.0	W	36.5	U		AFC CHAMPIONSHIP
1/14/2001	New York Giants	vs	Minnesota	41	0	W	2.5	W	42.0	U		NFC CHAMPIONSHIP
1/7/2001	Baltimore Ravens	@	Tennessee	24	10	W	6.0	W	33.5	O		AFC Divisional Play-offs
1/7/2001	New York Giants	vs	Philadelphia	20	10	W	-4.5	W	33.5	U		NFC Divisional Play-offs
1/6/2001	Minnesota	vs	New Orleans	34	16	W	-8.0	W	50.0	T		NFC Divisional Play-offs
1/6/2001	Oakland Raiders	vs	Miami	27	0	W	-8.5	W	42.0	U		AFC Divisional Play-offs
12/31/2000	Baltimore Ravens	vs	Denver	21	3	W	-3.0	W	40.0	U		AFC WILD CARD
12/31/2000	Philadelphia	vs	Tampa Bay	21	3	W	3.0	W	33.5	U		NFC WILD CARD
12/30/2000	Miami	vs	Indianapolis (OT)	23	17	W	1.5	W	41.5	U		AFC WILD CARD
12/30/2000	New Orleans	vs	St. Louis Rams	31	28	W	6.5	W	54.5	O		NFC WILD CARD
1/30/2000	St. Louis Rams	vs	Tennessee	23	16	W	-7.0	T	48.0	U		Super Bowl XXXIV @ Atlanta, GA
1/23/2000	St. Louis Rams	vs	Tampa Bay	11	6	W	-14.0	L	44.0	U		NFC CHAMPIONSHIP
1/23/2000	Tennessee	@	Jacksonville	33	14	W	7.0	W	40.0	O		AFC CHAMPIONSHIP
1/16/2000	St. Louis Rams	vs	Minnesota	49	37	W	-7.0	W	53.0	O		NFC Divisional Play-offs
1/16/2000	Tennessee	@	Indianapolis	19	16	W	5.5	W	46.5	U		AFC Divisional Play-offs
1/15/2000	Jacksonville	vs	Miami	62	7	W	-8.0	W	37.5	O		AFC Divisional Play-offs
1/15/2000	Tampa Bay	vs	Washington	14	13	W	-5.0	L	37.5	U		NFC Divisional Play-offs
1/9/2000	Miami	@	Seattle	20	17	W	3.5	W	39.5	U		AFC WILD CARD
1/9/2000	Minnesota	vs	Dallas	27	10	W	-7.0	W	46.0	U		NFC WILD CARD
1/8/2000	Tennessee	vs	Buffalo	22	16	W	-4.5	W	39.5	U		AFC WILD CARD

Playoffs History

1/8/2000	Washington	vs	Detroit	27	13	W	-6.5	W	47.0	U	NFC WILD CARD
1/31/1999	Denver	vs	Atlanta	34	19	W	-7.5	W	53.0	T	Super Bowl XXXIII @ Miami, FL
1/17/1999	Atlanta	@	Minnesota (OT)	30	27	W	11.0	W	55.5	O	NFC CHAMPIONSHIP
1/17/1999	Denver	vs	New York Jets	23	10	W	-9.0	W	51.0	U	AFC CHAMPIONSHIP
1/10/1999	Minnesota	vs	Arizona	41	21	W	-16.0	W	52.5	O	NFC Divisional Play-offs
1/10/1999	New York Jets	vs	Jacksonville	34	24	W	-8.5	W	43.0	O	AFC Divisional Play-offs
1/9/1999	Atlanta	vs	San Francisco	20	18	W	-3.5	L	53.0	U	NFC Divisional Play-offs
1/9/1999	Denver	vs	Miami	38	3	W	-13.5	W	47.5	U	AFC Divisional Play-offs
1/3/1999	Jacksonville	vs	New England	25	10	W	-8.5	W	41.0	U	AFC WILD CARD
1/3/1999	San Francisco	vs	Green Bay	30	27	W	-3.0	T	50.0	O	NFC WILD CARD
1/2/1999	Arizona	@	Dallas	20	7	W	7.0	W	42.0	U	NFC WILD CARD
1/2/1999	Miami	vs	Buffalo	24	17	W	-2.5	W	42.5	U	AFC WILD CARD
1/25/1998	Denver	vs	Green Bay	31	24	W	11.5	W	49.0	O	Super Bowl XXXII @ San Diego
1/11/1998	Denver	@	Pittsburgh	24	21	W	-2.5	W	41.5	O	AFC CHAMPIONSHIP
1/11/1998	Green Bay	@	San Francisco	23	10	W	-2.5	W	44.0	U	NFC CHAMPIONSHIP
1/4/1998	Denver	@	Kansas City	14	10	W	1.5	W	41.0	U	AFC Divisional Play-offs
1/4/1998	Green Bay	vs	Tampa Bay	21	7	W	-14.0	T	37.5	U	NFC Divisional Play-offs
1/3/1998	Pittsburgh	vs	New England	7	6	W	-7.5	L	41.0	U	AFC Divisional Play-offs
1/3/1998	San Francisco	vs	Minnesota	38	22	W	-14.0	W	41.5	O	NFC Divisional Play-offs
12/28/1997	New England	vs	Miami	17	3	W	-5.0	W	40.0	U	AFC WILD CARD
12/28/1997	Tampa Bay	vs	Detroit	20	10	W	-2.5	W	38.5	U	NFC WILD CARD
12/27/1997	Denver	vs	Jacksonville	42	17	W	-8.0	W	45.0	O	AFC WILD CARD
12/27/1997	Minnesota	@	New York Giants	23	22	W	4.5	W	37.0	O	NFC WILD CARD
1/26/1997	Green Bay	vs	New England	35	21	W	-14.0	T	49.5	O	Super Bowl XXXI @ New Orleans
1/12/1997	Green Bay	vs	Carolina	30	13	W	-12.5	W	38.0	O	NFC CHAMPIONSHIP
1/12/1997	New England	vs	Jacksonville	20	6	W	-7.0	W	44.0	U	AFC CHAMPIONSHIP
1/5/1997	Carolina	vs	Dallas	26	17	W	3.0	W	37.5	O	NFC Divisional Play-offs
1/5/1997	New England	vs	Pittsburgh	28	3	W	-3.0	W	40.0	U	AFC Divisional Play-offs
1/4/1997	Green Bay	vs	San Francisco	35	14	W	-6.0	W	39.0	O	NFC Divisional Play-offs
1/4/1997	Jacksonville	@	Denver	30	27	W	14.0	W	45.0	O	AFC Divisional Play-offs
12/29/1996	Pittsburgh	vs	Indianapolis	42	14	W	-8.0	W	37.0	O	AFC WILD CARD
12/29/1996	San Francisco	vs	Philadelphia	14	0	W	-10.5	W	39.5	U	NFC WILD CARD
12/28/1996	Dallas	vs	Minnesota	40	15	W	-10.0	W	39.0	O	NFC WILD CARD
12/28/1996	Jacksonville	@	Buffalo	30	27	W	8.5	W	39.0	O	AFC WILD CARD
1/28/1996	Dallas	vs	Pittsburgh	27	17	W	-13.5	L	52.0	U	Super Bowl XXX @ Phoenix, AZ
1/14/1996	Dallas	vs	Green Bay	38	27	W	-8.5	W	50.0	O	NFC CHAMPIONSHIP
1/14/1996	Pittsburgh	vs	Indianapolis	20	16	W	-11.5	L	41.0	U	AFC CHAMPIONSHIP
1/7/1996	Dallas	vs	Philadelphia	30	11	W	-13.5	W	45.5	U	NFC Divisional Play-offs
1/7/1996	Indianapolis	@	Kansas City	10	7	W	10.5	W	41.0	U	AFC Divisional Play-offs
1/6/1996	Green Bay	@	San Francisco	27	17	W	10.0	W	52.0	U	NFC Divisional Play-offs
1/6/1996	Pittsburgh	vs	Buffalo	40	21	W	-6.5	W	42.5	O	AFC Divisional Play-offs
12/31/1995	Green Bay	vs	Atlanta	37	20	W	-9.5	W	44.5	O	NFC WILD CARD
12/31/1995	Indianapolis	@	San Diego	35	20	W	6.0	W	40.5	O	AFC WILD CARD
12/30/1995	Buffalo	vs	Miami	37	22	W	-3.5	W	43.0	O	AFC WILD CARD
12/30/1995	Philadelphia	vs	Detroit	58	37	W	3.0	W	42.5	O	NFC WILD CARD
1/29/1995	San Francisco	vs	San Diego	49	26	W	-18.0	W	54.0	O	Super Bowl XXIX @ Miami, FL
1/15/1995	San Diego	@	Pittsburgh	17	13	W	9.0	W	36.0	U	AFC CHAMPIONSHIP
1/15/1995	San Francisco	vs	Dallas	38	28	W	-7.5	W	46.5	O	NFC CHAMPIONSHIP
1/8/1995	Dallas	vs	Green Bay	35	9	W	-11.0	W	43.0	O	NFC Divisional Play-offs
1/8/1995	San Diego	vs	Miami	22	21	W	-2.0	L	45.5	U	AFC Divisional Play-offs
1/7/1995	Pittsburgh	vs	Cleveland	29	9	W	-3.5	W	32.0	O	AFC Divisional Play-offs
1/7/1995	San Francisco	vs	Chicago	44	15	W	-17.5	W	44.0	O	NFC Divisional Play-offs
1/1/1995	Cleveland Browns	vs	New England	20	13	W	-3.0	W	34.0	U	AFC WILD CARD
1/1/1995	Chicago	@	Minnesota	35	18	W	6.5	W	37.5	O	NFC WILD CARD

Playoffs History

Date	Team		Opponent	Score								Notes
12/31/1994	Green Bay	vs	Detroit	16	12	W	-4.0	T		38.0	U	NFC WILD CARD
12/31/1994	Miami	vs	Kansas City	27	17	W	-3.0	W		43.5	O	AFC WILD CARD
1/30/1994	Dallas	vs	Buffalo	30	13	W	-10.5	W		50.5	U	Super Bowl XXVII @ Atlanta, GA
1/23/1994	Buffalo	vs	Kansas City	30	13	W	-3.0	W		38.0	O	AFC CHAMPIONSHIP
1/23/1994	Dallas	vs	San Francisco	38	21	W	-3.5	W		48.0	O	NFC CHAMPIONSHIP
1/16/1994	Dallas	vs	Green Bay	27	17	W	-14.0	L		42.5	O	NFC Divisional Play-offs
1/16/1994	Kansas City	@	Houston Oilers	28	20	W	7.0	W		41.5	O	AFC Divisional Play-offs
1/15/1994	Buffalo	vs	L.A. Raiders	29	23	W	-6.5	L		34.0	O	AFC Divisional Play-offs
1/15/1994	San Francisco	vs	New York Giants	44	3	W	-7.5	W		41.5	O	NFC Divisional Play-offs
1/9/1994	New York Giants	vs	Minnesota	17	10	W	-6.5	W		31.5	U	NFC WILD CARD
1/9/1994	L.A. Raiders	vs	Denver	42	24	W	-1.5	W		41.0	O	AFC WILD CARD
1/8/1994	Green Bay	@	Detroit	28	24	W	1.5	W		38.5	O	NFC WILD CARD
1/8/1994	Kansas City	vs	Pittsburgh (OT)	27	24	W	-8.0	L		35.5	O	AFC WILD CARD
1/31/1993	Dallas	vs	Buffalo	52	17	W	-6.5	W		45.0	O	Super Bowl XXVII @ Pasadena
1/17/1993	Buffalo	@	Miami	29	10	W	-2.5	W		41.5	U	AFC CHAMPIONSHIP
1/17/1993	Dallas	@	San Francisco	30	20	W	4.0	W		37.0	O	NFC CHAMPIONSHIP
1/10/1993	Dallas	vs	Philadelphia	34	10	W	-6.5	W		37.5	O	NFC Divisional Play-offs
1/10/1993	Miami	vs	San Diego	31	0	W	-1.0	W		37.0	O	AFC Divisional Play-offs
1/9/1993	Buffalo	@	Pittsburgh	24	3	W	1.0	W		36.0	U	AFC Divisional Play-offs
1/9/1993	San Francisco	vs	Washington	20	13	W	-9.5	L		39.0	U	NFC Divisional Play-offs
1/3/1993	Buffalo	vs	Houston (OT)	41	38	W	-3.0	T		35.0	O	AFC WILD CARD
1/3/1993	Philadelphia	@	New Orleans	36	20	W	3.5	W		34.5	O	NFC WILD CARD
1/2/1993	San Diego	vs	Kansas City	17	0	W	-3.5	W		36.5	U	AFC WILD CARD
1/2/1993	Washington	@	Minnesota	24	7	W	3.5	W		37.0	U	NFC WILD CARD
1/26/1992	Washington	vs	Buffalo	37	24	W	-7.0	W		48.0	O	Super Bowl XXVI @ Minneapolis
1/12/1992	Buffalo	vs	Denver	10	7	W	-11.5	L		45.0	U	AFC CHAMPIONSHIP
1/12/1992	Washington	vs	Detroit	41	10	W	-13.5	W		43.0	O	NFC CHAMPIONSHIP
1/5/1992	Buffalo	vs	Kansas City	37	14	W	-10.5	W		41.5	O	AFC Divisional Play-offs
1/5/1992	Detroit	vs	Dallas	38	6	W	Pk	W		43.0	O	NFC Divisional Play-offs
1/4/1992	Denver	vs	Houston Oilers	26	24	W	-3.5	L		37.0	O	AFC Divisional Play-offs
1/4/1992	Washington	vs	Atlanta	24	7	W	-11.5	W		43.0	U	NFC Divisional Play-offs
12/29/1991	Dallas	@	Chicago	17	13	W	2.5	W		36.0	U	NFC WILD CARD
12/29/1991	Houston Oilers	vs	New York Jets	17	10	W	-9.5	L		43.5	U	AFC WILD CARD
12/28/1991	Atlanta	@	New Orleans	27	20	W	6.0	W		39.0	O	NFC WILD CARD
12/28/1991	Kansas City	vs	L.A. Raiders	10	6	W	-5.0	L		35.5	U	AFC WILD CARD
1/27/1991	New York Giants	vs	Buffalo	20	19	W	7.0	W		40.5	U	Super Bowl XL @ Tampa, FL
1/20/1991	Buffalo	vs	L.A. Raiders	51	3	W	-7.0	W		36.0	O	AFC CHAMPIONSHIP
1/20/1991	New York Giants	@	San Francisco	15	13	W	8.0	W		37.0	U	NFC CHAMPIONSHIP
1/13/1991	New York Giants	vs	Chicago	31	3	W	-6.5	W		35.5	U	NFC Divisional Play-offs
1/13/1991	L.A. Raiders	vs	Cincinnati	20	10	W	-7.0	W		41.0	U	AFC Divisional Play-offs
1/12/1991	Buffalo	vs	Miami	44	34	W	-7.0	W		34.0	O	AFC Divisional Play-offs
1/12/1991	San Francisco	vs	Washington	28	10	W	-8.0	W		40.5	U	NFC Divisional Play-offs
1/6/1991	Chicago	vs	New Orleans	16	6	W	-6.5	W		32.0	U	NFC WILD CARD
1/6/1991	Cincinnati	vs	Houston Oilers	41	14	W	-3.5	W		42.0	O	AFC WILD CARD
1/5/1991	Miami	vs	Kansas City	17	16	W	-2.5	L		40.5	U	AFC WILD CARD
1/5/1991	Washington	@	Philadelphia	20	6	W	4.0	W		39.5	U	NFC WILD CARD
1/28/1990	San Francisco	vs	Denver	55	10	W	-12.0	W		48.0	O	Super Bowl @ New Orleans, LA
1/14/1990	Denver	vs	Cleveland	37	21	W	-3.5	W		40.0	O	AFC CHAMPIONSHIP
1/14/1990	San Francisco	vs	Los Angeles Rams	30	3	W	-7.0	W		46.0	U	NFC CHAMPIONSHIP
1/7/1990	Denver	vs	Pittsburgh	24	23	W	-10.0	L		38.0	O	AFC Divisional Play-offs
1/7/1990	Los Angeles Rams	@	New York Giants (OT)	19	13	W	3.0	W		39.0	U	NFC Divisional Play-offs
1/6/1990	Cleveland Browns	vs	Buffalo	34	30	W	-3.5	W		35.5	O	AFC Divisional Play-offs
1/6/1990	San Francisco	vs	Minnesota	41	13	W	-8.0	W		43.5	O	NFC Divisional Play-offs
12/31/1989	Pittsburgh	@	Houston Oilers (OT)	26	23	W	6.5	W		43.0	O	AFC WILD CARD

Playoffs History

Date	Team		Opponent									Round
12/31/1989	Los Angeles Rams	@	Philadelphia	21	7	W	3.0	W	39.0	U		NFC WILD CARD
1/22/1989	San Francisco	vs	Cincinnati	20	16	W	-7.0	L	48.0	U		Super Bowl XXIII @ Miami, FL
1/8/1989	Cincinnati	vs	Buffalo	21	10	W	-4.0	W	41.0	U		AFC CHAMPIONSHIP
1/8/1989	San Francisco	@	Chicago	28	3	W	Pk	W	35.0	U		NFC CHAMPIONSHIP
1/1/1989	Buffalo	vs	Houston Oilers	17	10	W	-3.5	W	37.0	U		AFC Divisional Play-offs
1/1/1989	San Francisco	vs	Minnesota	34	9	W	-3.5	W	44.0	U		NFC Divisional Play-offs
12/31/1988	Chicago	vs	Philadelphia	20	12	W	-5.0	W	37.0	U		NFC Divisional Play-offs
12/31/1988	Cincinnati	vs	Seattle	21	13	W	-6.5	W	44.0	U		AFC Divisional Play-offs
12/26/1988	Minnesota	vs	Los Angeles Rams	28	17	W	-4.5	W	43.0	O		NFC WILD CARD
12/24/1988	Houston Oilers	@	Cleveland Browns	24	23	W	3.0	W	38.0	O		AFC WILD CARD
1/31/1988	Washington	vs	Denver	42	10	W	3.0	W	47.0	O		Super Bowl XXII @ San Diego, CA
1/17/1988	Denver	vs	Cleveland	38	33	W	-3.0	W	44.0	O		AFC CHAMPIONSHIP
1/17/1988	Washington	vs	Minnesota	17	10	W	-3.0	W	44.0	U		NFC CHAMPIONSHIP
1/10/1988	Denver	vs	Houston Oilers	34	10	W	-10.0	W	43.0	O		AFC Divisional Play-offs
1/10/1988	Washington	@	Chicago	21	17	W	4.5	W	38.0	T		NFC Divisional Play-offs
1/9/1988	Cleveland Browns	vs	Indianapolis	38	21	W	-7.0	W	37.0	O		AFC Divisional Play-offs
1/9/1988	Minnesota	@	San Francisco	36	24	W	11.0	W	48.0	O		NFC Divisional Play-offs
1/3/1988	Minnesota	@	New Orleans	44	10	W	6.5	W	46.0	O		NFC WILD CARD
1/3/1988	Houston Oilers	vs	Seattle (OT)	23	20	W	-2.0	W	46.0	U		AFC WILD CARD
1/25/1987	New York Giants	vs	Denver	39	20	W	-9.5	W	10.0	O		Super Bowl XXI @ Pasadena, CA
1/11/1987	Denver	@	Cleveland Browns (OT)	23	20	W	3.0	W	39.0	O		AFC CHAMPIONSHIP
1/11/1987	New York Giants	vs	Washington	17	0	W	-7.0	W	39.0	U		NFC CHAMPIONSHIP
1/4/1987	Denver	vs	New England	22	17	W	-4.0	T	43.0	U		AFC Divisional Play-offs
1/4/1987	New York Giants	vs	San Francisco	49	3	W	-3.5	W	39.0	O		NFC Divisional Play-offs
1/3/1987	Cleveland Browns	vs	New York Jets	23	20	W	-7.0	L	41.0	O		AFC Divisional Play-offs
1/3/1987	Washington	@	Chicago	27	13	W	7.0	W	34.0	O		NFC Divisional Play-offs
12/28/1986	New York Jets	vs	Kansas City	35	15	W	-3.0	W	40.0	O		AFC WILD CARD
12/28/1986	Washington	vs	Los Angeles Rams	19	7	W	-4.5	W	39.0	U		NFC WILD CARD
1/26/1986	Chicago	vs	New England	46	10	W	-10.0	W	37.5	O		Super Bowl XX @ New Orleans, LA
1/12/1986	Chicago	vs	Los Angeles Rams	24	0	W	-10.5	W	34.0	U		NFC CHAMPIONSHIP
1/12/1986	New England	@	Miami	31	14	W	6.0	W	46.0	U		AFC CHAMPIONSHIP
1/5/1986	Chicago	vs	New York Giants	21	0	W	-9.0	W	35.0	U		NFC Divisional Play-offs
1/5/1986	New England	@	L.A. Raiders	27	20	W	5.5	W	38.0	O		AFC Divisional Play-offs
1/4/1986	Miami	vs	Cleveland	24	21	W	-10.5	L	45.0	T		AFC Divisional Play-offs
1/4/1986	Los Angeles Rams	vs	Dallas	20	0	W	-2.0	W	40.5	U		NFC Divisional Play-offs
12/29/1985	New York Giants	vs	San Francisco	17	3	W	3.0	W	38.0	U		NFC WILD CARD
12/28/1985	New England	@	New York Jets	26	14	W	3.5	W	40.0	T		AFC WILD CARD
1/20/1985	San Francisco	vs	Miami	38	16	W	-3.0	W	53.5	O		Super Bowl XIX @ Stanford, CA
1/6/1985	Miami	vs	Pittsburgh	45	28	W	-9.5	W	43.5	O		AFC CHAMPIONSHIP
1/6/1985	San Francisco	vs	Chicago	23	0	W	-9.0	W	39.0	U		NFC CHAMPIONSHIP
12/30/1984	Chicago	@	Washington	23	19	W	7.0	W	38.0	O		NFC Divisional Play-offs
12/30/1984	Pittsburgh	@	Denver	24	17	W	5.5	W	36.0	O		AFC Divisional Play-offs
12/29/1984	Miami	vs	Seattle	31	10	W	-6.5	W	45.0	U		AFC Divisional Play-offs
12/29/1984	San Francisco	vs	New York Giants	21	10	W	-11.0	T	41.5	U		NFC Divisional Play-offs
12/23/1984	New York Giants	@	Los Angeles Rams	16	13	W	5.5	W	38.0	U		NFC WILD CARD
12/22/1984	Seattle	vs	L.A. Raiders	13	7	W	1.5	W	40.0	U		AFC WILD CARD
1/22/1984	L.A. Raiders	vs	Washington	38	9	W	3.0	W	48.0	U		Super Bowl XVIII @ Tampa, FL
1/8/1984	L.A. Raiders	vs	Seattle	30	14	W	-7.5	W	47.0	U		AFC CHAMPIONSHIP
1/8/1984	Washington	vs	San Francisco	24	21	W	-10.5	L	50.5	U		NFC CHAMPIONSHIP
1/1/1984	L.A. Raiders	vs	Pittsburgh	38	10	W	-7.0	W	43.0	O		AFC Divisional Play-offs
1/1/1984	Washington	vs	Los Angeles Rams	51	7	W	-9.5	W	47.0	O		NFC Divisional Play-offs
12/31/1983	Seattle	@	Miami	27	20	W	8.0	W	43.0	O		AFC Divisional Play-offs
12/31/1983	San Francisco	vs	Detroit	24	23	W	-7.0	L	43.0	O		NFC Divisional Play-offs
12/26/1983	Los Angeles Rams	@	Dallas	24	17	W	8.0	W	46.0	U		NFC WILD CARD

Playoffs History

Date	Team		Opponent									Round
12/24/1983	Seattle	vs	Denver	31	7	W	-4.0	W	44.0	U		AFC WILD CARD
1/30/1983	Washington	vs	Miami	27	17	W	3.0	W	36.5	O		Super Bowl XVII @ Pasadena, CA
1/23/1983	Miami	vs	New York Jets	14	0	W	-1.5	W	38.5	U		AFC CHAMPIONSHIP
1/23/1983	Washington	vs	Dallas	31	17	W	2.5	W	38.5	O		NFC CHAMPIONSHIP
1/16/1983	Dallas	vs	Green Bay	37	26	W	-7.0	W	48.0	O		NFC Divisional Play-offs
1/16/1983	Miami	vs	San Diego	34	13	W	2.0	W	53.0	U		AFC Divisional Play-offs
1/15/1983	New York Jets	@	L.A. Raiders	17	14	W	3.5	W	48.0	U		AFC Divisional Play-offs
1/15/1983	Washington	vs	Minnesota	21	7	W	-6.5	W	43.5	U		NFC Divisional Play-offs
1/9/1983	Dallas	vs	Tampa Bay	30	17	W	-8.0	W	38.5	O		NFC WILD CARD
1/9/1983	Minnesota	vs	Atlanta	30	24	W	-2.0	W	46.5	O		NFC WILD CARD
1/9/1983	New York Jets	@	Cincinnati	44	17	W	4.0	W	44.5	O		AFC WILD CARD
1/9/1983	San Diego	@	Pittsburgh	31	28	W	1.5	W	53.0	O		AFC WILD CARD
1/8/1983	Green Bay	vs	St. Louis Cardinals	41	16	W	-4.5	W	37.5	O		NFC WILD CARD
1/8/1983	Miami	vs	New England	28	13	W	-8.0	W	36.0	O		AFC WILD CARD
1/8/1983	L.A. Raiders	vs	Cleveland	27	10	W	-8.0	W	44.5	U		AFC WILD CARD
1/8/1983	Washington	vs	Detroit	31	7	W	-5.5	W	37.0	O		NFC WILD CARD
1/24/1982	San Francisco	vs	Cincinnati	26	21	W	1.0	W	48.0	U		Super Bowl XVI @ Pontiac, MI
1/10/1982	Cincinnati	vs	San Diego	27	7	W	-4.5	W	45.0	U		AFC CHAMPIONSHIP
1/10/1982	San Francisco	vs	Dallas	28	27	W	3.0	W	42.0	O		NFC CHAMPIONSHIP
1/3/1982	Cincinnati	vs	Buffalo	28	21	W	-5.5	W	41.0	O		AFC Divisional Play-offs
1/3/1982	San Francisco	vs	New York Giants	38	24	W	-5.5	W	38.0	O		NFC Divisional Play-offs
1/2/1982	Dallas	vs	Tampa Bay	38	0	W	-8.0	W	37.0	O		NFC Divisional Play-offs
1/2/1982	San Diego	@	Miami (OT)	41	38	W	3.0	W	43.0	O		AFC Divisional Play-offs
12/27/1981	Buffalo	@	New York Jets	31	27	W	3.0	W	33.0	O		AFC WILD CARD
12/27/1981	New York Giants	@	Philadelphia	27	21	W	7.0	W	31.5	O		NFC WILD CARD
1/25/1981	Oakland Raiders	vs	Philadelphia	27	10	W	3.0	W	37.5	U		Super Bowl XV @ New Orleans, LA
1/11/1981	Oakland Raiders	@	San Diego	34	27	W	4.0	W	45.0	O		AFC CHAMPIONSHIP
1/11/1981	Philadelphia	vs	Dallas	20	7	W	1.0	W	43.0	U		NFC CHAMPIONSHIP
1/4/1981	Dallas	@	Atlanta	30	27	W	2.5	W	45.0	O		NFC Divisional Play-offs
1/4/1981	Oakland Raiders	@	Cleveland Browns	14	12	W	3.5	W	38.0	U		AFC Divisional Play-offs
1/3/1981	Philadelphia	vs	Minnesota	31	16	W	-7.0	W	38.0	O		NFC Divisional Play-offs
1/3/1981	San Diego	vs	Buffalo	20	14	W	6.0	W	41.0	U		AFC Divisional Play-offs
12/28/1980	Dallas	@	Los Angeles Rams	34	13	W	-3.0	W	46.0	O		NFC WILD CARD
12/28/1980	Oakland Raiders	vs	Houston Oilers	27	7	W	1.0	W	38.0	U		AFC WILD CARD
1/21/1980	Pittsburgh	vs	Los Angeles Rams	31	19	W	-10.5	W	36.0	O		Super Bowl XIV @ Pasadena, CA
1/7/1980	Pittsburgh	vs	Houston Oilers	27	13	W	-9.5	W				AFC CHAMPIONSHIP
1/7/1980	Los Angeles Rams	@	Tampa Bay	9	0	W	-3.5	W				NFC CHAMPIONSHIP
12/30/1979	Pittsburgh	vs	Miami	34	14	W	-9.5	W				AFC Divisional Play-offs
12/30/1979	Los Angeles Rams	@	Dallas	21	19	W	8.5	W				NFC Divisional Play-offs
12/29/1979	Tampa Bay	vs	Philadelphia	24	17	W	4.5	W				NFC Divisional Play-offs
12/29/1979	Houston Oilers	@	San Diego	17	14	W	8.0	W				AFC Divisional Play-offs
12/23/1979	Philadelphia	vs	Chicago	27	17	W	-6.5	W				NFC WILD CARD
12/23/1979	Houston Oilers	vs	Denver	13	7	W	-7.0	L				AFC WILD CARD
1/21/1979	Pittsburgh	vs	Dallas	35	31	W	-3.5	W	37.0	O		Super Bowl XIII @ Miami, FL
1/7/1979	Dallas	@	Los Angeles Rams	28	0	W	-3.5	W				NFC CHAMPIONSHIP
1/7/1979	Pittsburgh	vs	Houston Oilers	34	5	W	-7.0	W				AFC CHAMPIONSHIP
12/31/1978	Los Angeles Rams	vs	Minnesota	34	10	W	-7.5	W				NFC Divisional Play-offs
12/31/1978	Houston Oilers	@	New England	31	14	W	6.0	W				AFC Divisional Play-offs
12/30/1978	Dallas	vs	Atlanta	27	20	W	-15.0	L				NFC Divisional Play-offs
12/30/1978	Pittsburgh	vs	Denver	33	10	W	-7.0	W				AFC Divisional Play-offs
12/24/1978	Atlanta	vs	Philadelphia	14	13	W	-2.5	L				NFC WILD CARD
12/24/1978	Houston Oilers	@	Miami	17	9	W	6.5	W				AFC WILD CARD
1/15/1978	Dallas	vs	Denver	27	10	W	-6.0	W	39.0	U		Super Bowl XII @ New Orleans
1/1/1978	Dallas	vs	Minnesota	23	6	W	-11.0	W				NFC CHAMPIONSHIP

Playoffs History

Date	Team		Opponent	PF	PA	W/L	Spread	ATS	Total	O/U	Round
1/1/1978	**Denver**	vs	Oakland Raiders	20	17	W	-4.0	L			AFC CHAMPIONSHIP
12/26/1977	**Dallas**	vs	Chicago	37	7	W	-10.0	W			NFC Divisional Play-offs
12/26/1977	**Minnesota**	@	Los Angeles Rams	14	7	W	8.0	W			NFC Divisional Play-offs
12/24/1977	**Denver**	vs	Pittsburgh	34	21	W	-2.0	W			AFC Divisional Play-offs
12/24/1977	**Oakland Raiders**	@	Baltimore Colts (OT)	37	31	W	-3.0	W			AFC Divisional Play-offs
1/9/1977	**Oakland Raiders**	vs	Minnesota	32	14	W	-4.5	W	38.0	O	Super Bowl XI @ Pasadena, CA
12/26/1976	**Minnesota**	vs	Los Angeles Rams	24	13	W	-5.0	W			NFC CHAMPIONSHIP
12/26/1976	**Oakland Raiders**	vs	Pittsburgh	24	7	W	4.0	W			AFC CHAMPIONSHIP
12/19/1976	**Pittsburgh**	@	Baltimore Colts	40	14	W	-3.5	W			AFC Divisional Play-offs
12/19/1976	**Los Angeles Rams**	@	Dallas	14	12	W	3.5	W			NFC Divisional Play-offs
12/18/1976	**Minnesota**	vs	Washington	35	20	W	-6.0	W			NFC Divisional Play-offs
12/18/1976	**Oakland Raiders**	vs	New England	24	21	W	-8.0	L			AFC Divisional Play-offs
1/18/1976	**Pittsburgh**	vs	Dallas	21	17	W	-7.0	L	36.0	O	Super Bowl X @ Miami, FL
1/4/1976	**Dallas**	@	Los Angeles Rams	37	7	W	6.5	W			NFC CHAMPIONSHIP
1/4/1976	**Pittsburgh**	vs	Oakland Raiders	16	10	W	-6.5	L			AFC CHAMPIONSHIP
12/28/1975	**Dallas**	@	Minnesota	17	14	W	8.0	W			NFC Divisional Play-offs
12/28/1975	**Oakland Raiders**	vs	Cincinnati	31	28	W	-6.5	L			AFC Divisional Play-offs
12/27/1975	**Pittsburgh**	vs	Baltimore Colts	28	10	W	-10.5	W			AFC Divisional Play-offs
12/27/1975	**Los Angeles Rams**	vs	St. Louis Cardinals	35	23	W	-6.5	W			NFC Divisional Play-offs
1/12/1975	**Pittsburgh**	vs	Minnesota	16	6	W	-3.0	W	33.0	U	Super Bowl IX @ New Orleans, LA
12/29/1974	**Minnesota**	vs	Los Angeles Rams	14	10	W	-5.5	L			NFC CHAMPIONSHIP
12/29/1974	**Pittsburgh**	@	Oakland Raiders	24	13	W	5.5	W			AFC CHAMPIONSHIP
12/22/1974	**Pittsburgh**	vs	Buffalo	32	14	W	-6.5	W			AFC Divisional Play-offs
12/22/1974	**Los Angeles Rams**	vs	Washington	19	10	W	-2.5	W			NFC Divisional Play-offs
12/21/1974	**Minnesota**	vs	St. Louis Cardinals	30	14	W	-7.0	W			NFC Divisional Play-offs
12/21/1974	**Oakland Raiders**	vs	Miami	28	26	W	-3.0	L			AFC Divisional Play-offs
1/13/1974	**Miami**	vs	Minnesota	24	7	W	-6.5	W	33.0	U	Super Bowl VIII @ Houston, TX
12/30/1973	**Miami**	vs	Oakland Raiders	27	10	W	-7.0	W			AFC CHAMPIONSHIP
12/30/1973	**Minnesota**	@	Dallas	27	10	W	1.0	W			NFC CHAMPIONSHIP
12/23/1973	**Dallas**	vs	Los Angeles Rams	27	16	W	-2.5	W			NFC Divisional Play-offs
12/23/1973	**Miami**	vs	Cincinnati	34	16	W	-10.0	W			AFC Divisional Play-offs
12/22/1973	**Minnesota**	vs	Washington	27	20	W	-8.0	L			NFC Divisional Play-offs
12/22/1973	**Oakland Raiders**	vs	Pittsburgh	33	14	W	-3.5	W			AFC Divisional Play-offs
1/14/1973	**Miami**	vs	Washington	14	7	W	1.5	W	33.0	U	Super Bowl VII @ Los Angeles, CA
12/31/1972	**Miami**	@	Pittsburgh	21	17	W	-3.0	W			AFC CHAMPIONSHIP
12/31/1972	**Washington**	vs	Dallas	26	3	W	-3.0	W			NFC CHAMPIONSHIP
12/24/1972	**Miami**	vs	Cleveland	20	14	W	-12.5	L			AFC Divisional Play-offs
12/24/1972	**Washington**	vs	Green Bay	16	3	W	-5.0	W			NFC Divisional Play-offs
12/23/1972	**Dallas**	@	San Francisco	30	28	W	PK	W			NFC Divisional Play-offs
12/23/1972	**Pittsburgh**	vs	Oakland Raiders	13	7	W	-2.0	W			AFC Divisional Play-offs
1/16/1972	**Dallas**	vs	Miami	24	3	W	-6.0	W	34.0	U	Super Bowl VI @ New Orleans, LA
1/2/1972	**Dallas**	vs	San Francisco	14	3	W	-5.0	W			NFC CHAMPIONSHIP
1/2/1972	**Miami**	vs	Baltimore Colts	21	0	W	-1.0	W			AFC CHAMPIONSHIP
12/26/1971	**Baltimore Colts**	@	Cleveland Browns	20	3	W	-4.0	W			AFC Divisional Play-offs
12/26/1971	**San Francisco**	vs	Washington	24	20	W	-5.5	L			NFC Divisional Play-offs
12/25/1971	**Dallas**	@	Minnesota	20	12	W	-1.0	W			NFC Divisional Play-offs
12/25/1971	**Miami**	@	Kansas City (OT)	27	24	W	3.0	W			AFC Divisional Play-offs
1/17/1971	**Baltimore Colts**	vs	Dallas	16	13	W	2.5	W	36.0	U	Super Bowl V @ Miami, FL
1/3/1971	**Dallas**	@	San Francisco	17	10	W	4.0	W			NFC CHAMPIONSHIP
1/3/1971	**Baltimore Colts**	vs	Oakland Raiders	27	17	W	1.5	W			AFC CHAMPIONSHIP
12/27/1970	**Oakland Raiders**	vs	Miami	21	14	W	-6.0	W			AFC Divisional Play-offs
12/27/1970	**San Francisco**	@	Minnesota	17	14	W	7.0	W			NFC Divisional Play-offs
12/26/1970	**Dallas**	vs	Detroit	5	0	W	3.0	W			NFC Divisional Play-offs
12/26/1970	**Baltimore Colts**	vs	Cincinnati	17	0	W	-7.0	W			AFC Divisional Play-offs

Playoffs History

Date	Team 1		Team 2	Score 1	Score 2	Result	Spread	ATS	Total	O/U	Notes
1/11/1970	Kansas City	vs	Minnesota	23	7	W	12.0	W	39.0	U	Super Bowl IV @ New Orleans, LA
1/4/1970	Kansas City	@	Oakland Raiders	17	7	W	5.0	W			AFL Championship
1/4/1970	Minnesota	vs	Cleveland	27	7	W	-9.0	W			NFL CHAMPIONSHIP
1/3/1970	Los Angeles Rams	vs	Dallas	31	0	W					NFL Play-off Bowl @ Miami, FL
12/28/1969	Cleveland Browns	@	Dallas	38	14	W	7.0	W			NFL Divisional Play-offs
12/27/1969	Minnesota	vs	Los Angeles Rams	23	20	W	-4.0	L			NFL Divisional Play-offs
12/21/1969	Oakland Raiders	vs	Houston Oilers	56	7	W	-13.0	W			AFL Divisional Play-offs
12/20/1969	Kansas City	@	New York Jets	13	6	W	-2.5	W			AFL Divisional Play-offs
1/12/1969	New York Jets	vs	Baltimore Colts	16	7	W	18.0	W	40.0	U	Super Bowl III @ Miami, FL
1/5/1969	Dallas	vs	Minnesota	17	13	W					NFL Play-off Bowl @ Miami, FL
12/29/1968	Baltimore Colts	@	Cleveland Browns	34	0	W	-6.0	W			NFL Championship
12/29/1968	New York Jets	vs	Oakland Raiders	27	23	W	-2.0	W			AFL Championship
12/22/1968	Baltimore Colts	vs	Minnesota	24	14	W	-11.0	L			NFL Divisional Play-offs
12/22/1968	Oakland Raiders	vs	Kansas City	41	6	W	3.5	W			AFL Divisional Play-offs
12/21/1968	Cleveland Browns	vs	Dallas	31	20	W	3.0	W			NFL Divisional Play-offs
1/14/1968	Green Bay	vs	Oakland Raiders	33	14	W	-13.5	W	43.0	O	Super Bowl II @ Miami, FL
1/7/1968	Los Angeles Rams	vs	Cleveland Browns	30	6	W					NFL Play-off Bowl @ Miami, FL
12/31/1967	Green Bay	vs	Dallas	21	17	W	-6.5	L			NFL CHAMPIONSHIP
12/31/1967	Oakland Raiders	vs	Houston Oilers	40	7	W	-10.5	W			AFL Championship
12/24/1967	Dallas	vs	Cleveland	52	14	W	5.0	L			NFL Divisional Play-offs
12/23/1967	Green Bay	vs	Los Angeles Rams (Milw)	28	7	W	3.0	W			NFL Divisional Play-offs
1/15/1967	Green Bay	vs	Kansas City	35	10	W	-14.0	W			Super Bowl I @ Los Angeles, CA
1/8/1967	Baltimore Colts	vs	Philadelphia	20	14	W					NFL Play-off Bowl @ Miami, FL
1/1/1967	Green Bay	@	Dallas	34	27	W	-7.0	T			NFL CHAMPIONSHIP
1/1/1967	Kansas City	@	Buffalo	31	7	W	-3.0	W			AFL Championship
1/9/1966	Baltimore Colts	vs	Dallas	35	3	W					NFL Play-off Bowl @ Miami, FL
1/2/1966	Green Bay	vs	Cleveland Browns	23	12	W					NFL CHAMPIONSHIP
12/26/1965	Buffalo	@	San Diego	23	0	W	6.5	W			AFL Championship
12/26/1965	Green Bay	vs	Baltimore Colts (OT)	13	10	W					NFL Divisional Play-offs
1/3/1965	St. Louis Cardinals	vs	Green Bay	24	17	W	7.0	W			NFL Play-off Bowl @ Miami, FL
12/27/1964	Cleveland Browns	vs	Baltimore Colts	27	0	W	7.0	W			NFL Championship
12/26/1964	Buffalo	vs	San Diego	20	7	W					AFL Championship
1/5/1964	Green Bay	vs	Cleveland Browns	40	23	W					NFL Play-off Bowl @ Miami, FL
1/5/1964	San Diego	vs	Boston Patriots	51	10	W					AFL Championship
12/29/1963	Chicago	vs	New York Giants	14	10	W	1.0	W			NFL CHAMPIONSHIP
12/28/1963	Boston Patriots	@	Buffalo	26	8	W					AFL Play-offs
1/6/1963	Detroit	vs	Pittsburgh	17	10	W					NFL Play-off Bowl @ Miami, FL
12/30/1962	Green Bay	@	New York Giants	16	7	W	-6.5	W			NFL CHAMPIONSHIP
12/23/1962	Dallas Texans	@	Houston Oilers {2 OT}	20	17	W	6.5	W			AFL Championship
1/6/1962	Detroit	vs	Philadelphia	38	10	W					NFL Play-off Bowl @ Miami, FL
12/31/1961	Green Bay	vs	New York Giants	37	0	W	-3.5	W			NFL CHAMPIONSHIP
12/24/1961	Houston Oilers	@	San Diego	10	3	W	-3.0	W			AFL Championship
1/7/1961	Detroit	vs	Cleveland Browns	17	16	W					NFL Play-off Bowl @ Miami, FL
1/1/1961	Houston Oilers	vs	La Chargers	24	16	W	-6.5	W			AFL Championship
12/26/1960	Philadelphia	vs	Green Bay	17	13	W	2.0	W			NFL CHAMPIONSHIP
12/27/1959	Baltimore Colts	vs	New York Giants	31	16	W	-3.5	W			NFL Championship
12/28/1958	Baltimore Colts	@	New York Giants (OT)	23	17	W	-3.5	W			NFL Championship
12/21/1958	New York Giants	vs	Cleveland Browns	10	0	W					NFL Play-offs
12/29/1957	Detroit	vs	Cleveland	59	14	W	3.0	W			NFL CHAMPIONSHIP
12/22/1957	Detroit	@	San Francisco	31	27	W					NFL Divisional Play-offs
12/30/1956	New York Giants	@	Chicago	47	7	W	2.0	W			NFL CHAMPIONSHIP
12/26/1955	Cleveland Browns	@	Los Angeles Rams	38	14	W	-6.0	W			NFL Championship
12/26/1954	Cleveland Browns	vs	Detroit	56	10	W	3.0	W			NFL Championship
12/27/1953	Detroit	vs	Cleveland	17	16	W	3.0	W			NFL CHAMPIONSHIP

Playoffs History

12/28/1952	**Detroit**	vs	Cleveland	17	7	W	-3.5	W		NFL CHAMPIONSHIP
12/21/1952	**Detroit**	vs	Los Angeles Rams	31	21	W				NFL Divisional Play-offs
12/23/1951	**Los Angeles Rams**	vs	Cleveland Browns	24	17	W	6.0	W		NFL CHAMPIONSHIP
12/24/1950	**Cleveland Browns**	vs	Los Angeles Rams	30	28	W	-4.0	L		NFL Championship
12/17/1950	**Cleveland Browns**	vs	New York Giants	8	3	W				NFL Divisional Play-offs
12/17/1950	**Los Angeles Rams**	vs	Chicago	24	14	W				NFL Divisional Play-offs
12/18/1949	**Philadelphia**	@	Los Angeles Rams	14	0	W	-7.0	W		NFL CHAMPIONSHIP
12/11/1949	*Cleveland Browns*	vs	*San Francisco*	*21*	*7*	*W*				*AAFC CHAMPIONSHIP*
12/4/1949	*Cleveland Browns*	vs	*Buffalo*	*31*	*21*	*W*				*AAFC Play-offs*
12/4/1949	*San Francisco*	vs	*New York Yankees*	*17*	*7*	*W*				*AAFC Divisional Play-offs*
12/19/1948	*Cleveland Browns*	vs	*Buffalo*	*49*	*7*	*W*				*AAFC CHAMPIONSHIP*
12/19/1948	**Philadelphia**	vs	Chicago Cardinals	7	0	W	3.5	W		NFL CHAMPIONSHIP
12/12/1948	*Baltimore Colts*	@	*Buffalo*	*17*	*28*	*L*				*AAFC Play-offs*
12/28/1947	**Chicago Cardinals**	vs	Philadelphia	28	21	W	-12.0	L		NFL CHAMPIONSHIP
12/21/1947	**Philadelphia**	@	Pittsburgh	21	0	W				NFL Divisional Play-offs
12/14/1947	*Cleveland Browns*	@	*New York Yankees*	*14*	*3*	*W*				*AAFC CHAMPIONSHIP*
12/22/1946	*Cleveland Browns*	vs	*New York Yankees*	*14*	*9*	*W*				*AAFC CHAMPIONSHIP*
12/15/1946	**Chicago**	@	New York Giants	24	14	W	-7.0	W		NFL CHAMPIONSHIP
12/16/1945	**Cleveland Rams**	vs	Washington	15	14	W				NFL CHAMPIONSHIP
12/17/1944	**Green Bay**	@	New York Giants	14	7	W	-1.0	W		NFL CHAMPIONSHIP
12/26/1943	**Chicago**	@	Washington	41	21	W	-7.0	W		NFL CHAMPIONSHIP
12/19/1943	**Washington**	@	New York Giants	28	0	W				NFL Play-offs
12/13/1942	**Washington**	vs	Chicago	14	6	W	21.0	W		NFL Championship
12/21/1941	**Chicago**	vs	New York Giants	37	9	W	-14.0	W		NFL CHAMPIONSHIP
12/14/1941	**Chicago**	vs	Green Bay	33	14	W				NFL Divisional Play-offs
12/8/1940	**Chicago**	@	Washington	73	0	W	-1.0	W		NFL CHAMPIONSHIP
12/10/1939	**Green Bay**	vs	New York Giants (Milw)	27	0	W	-10.0	W		NFL CHAMPIONSHIP
12/11/1938	**New York Giants**	vs	Green Bay	23	17	W				NFL CHAMPIONSHIP
12/12/1937	**Washington**	@	Chicago	28	21	W				NFL Championship
12/13/1936	**Green Bay**	@	Boston Redskins (NYC)	7	3	W				NFL CHAMPIONSHIP
12/15/1935	**Detroit**	vs	New York Giants	26	7	W				NFL CHAMPIONSHIP
12/9/1934	**New York Giants**	@	Chicago	30	13	W				NFL CHAMPIONSHIP
12/17/1933	**Chicago**	vs	New York Giants	23	21	W				NFL CHAMPIONSHIP
12/18/1932	**Chicago**	vs	Portsmouth	9	0	W				NFL CHAMPIONSHIP

Did you know? Only four teams in the NFL haven't made the Super Bowl. They are:
Detroit Lions
Cleveland Browns
Houston Texans
Jacksonville Jaguars

The following teams have played 50 or more playoff games in their history.
Dallas Cowboys – 69
*Baltimore Ravens – 66 (includes AAFC Playoffs)
Pittsburgh Steelers – 64
Green Bay Packers – 63
New England Patriots – 59
*San Francisco 49ers – 61 (includes AAFC Playoffs)
Los Angeles Rams - 54
Minnesota Vikings – 52
Philadelphia Eagles – 52
New York Giants - 51

Interesting Playoffs facts

Dallas Cowboys are 1-9 on road in Playoffs since 1994

Denver is 0-6 on the road in AFC Wild Card game since 1979

Detroit is 0-11 on the road in Playoffs since 1970

Detroit 0-9 in NFC Wild Card game since 1983

Indianapolis is 0-5 vs Pittsburgh in the Playoffs since 1975

Miami is 0-7 on road in AFC Divisional Playoff games since 1974

Minnesota is 0-6 in NFC Championship game since 1977

New England is 13-1 at home in AFC Divisional Playoffs games since 1996

New York Giants are 5-0 in NFC Championship game since 1986

Las Vegas Raiders are 0-7 on road in Playoffs since 1984

Philadelphia is 6-0 at home in Divisional Playoff games since 1980

Pittsburgh is 12-2 at home in Divisional Playoff games since 1972

San Francisco is 11-1 at home in Divisional Playoff games since 1988

Seattle is 10-1 at home in Playoffs since 2005

Seattle is 0-9 on road in Divisional Playoffs since 1984

Tennessee vs Baltimore in Playoffs – ROAD team is 6-0 since 1988

Washington vs Los Angeles Rams in Playoffs – HOME team is 4-0 since 1945

Dallas is 0-4 on road on Saturday in Playoffs since 1986

Detroit is 0-9 on Saturday in Playoffs since 1970

Green Bay is 7-2 at home on Saturday in Playoffs since 1967

Miami is 0-6 on road on Saturday in Playoffs since 1974

Miami is 6-0 at home on Saturday in Playoffs since 1984

New England is 10-1 at home on Saturday in Playoffs since 2002

New Orleans is 4-0 at home on Saturday in Playoffs since 2000

Las Vegas Raiders are 0-6 on road on Saturday in Playoffs since 1984

San Francisco is 12-2 at home on Saturday in Playoffs since 1983

Seattle is 0-6 on road on Saturday in Playoffs since 1984

Seattle is 7-1 at home on Saturday in Playoffs since 2006

Tennessee is 6-0 on Saturday in AFC Wild Card games since 1988

NFL Football Series available at: www.stevesfootballbible.com (NFL)

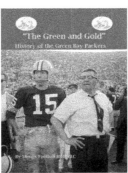
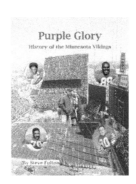
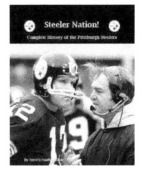

| DALLAS | GREEN BAY | MINNESOTA | PITTSBURGH |

All books are available in Paperback and Hardcover

These books are available from numerous online bookstores

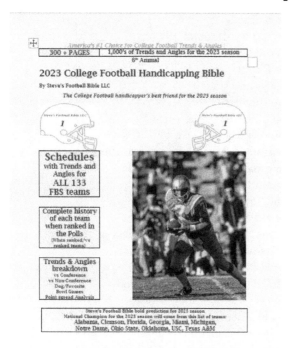

The 2023 College Football Trends and Angles Bible has every FBS teams 2023 schedule with trends and angles for each game, plus the most comprehensive pointspread analysis for each team. It has trends and angles for Conference opponents, Non-Conference opponents and Bowl Games. It includes the last 4 years schedules with S/U, ATS and O/U results for each team. It also has each teams history in the Polls, when ranked and versus ranked teams. Plus, it has Trophy games and Rivalry games highlighted as well. It truly is the College Football handicappers best friend for the 2023 College Football season. It's the most informative book on handicapping for the

2023 College Football Bible .8.5" x 11" {312 pages} {Paperback}

$29.95 -- Available at numerous online retailers

The 2023 FCS College Football Bible has every FCS teams 2023 schedule, plus the last 2 years S/U results. It has series trends/history for each 2023 opponent. It includes Post-season history for each FCS team. Plus, it has Trophy games and Rivalry games highlighted as well. It is the most comprehensive FCS College Football publication for the 2021 season. It is the FCS College Football fan's best friend for the 2023 College Football season.

2023 FCS College Football Bible

8.5" x 11" {176 pages}

$19.95 -- Available at numerous online retailers

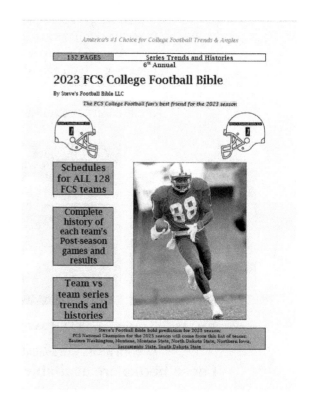

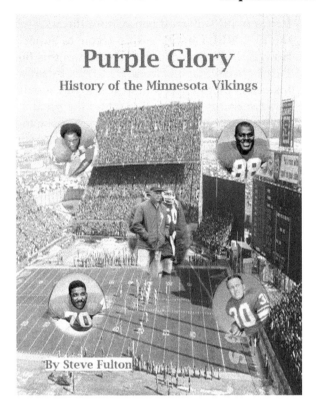

If you love Football, then you will enjoy reading about the history of the Minnesota Vikings. Inside you will read about every season in Vikings history. Since 1961 the Vikings have been a staple of the Upper Midwest, drawing fans from all over Minnesota, Iowa and the Dakotas. Relive some of the great seasons, games and moments in Vikings history.

"Purple Glory" – History of the Minnesota Vikings

8.5" x 11" {298 pages} {Paperback}

$29.95

Available in Hardcover from Barnes & Noble at: https://www.barnesandnoble.com/w/purple-glory-history-of-the-minnesota-vikings-steve-fulton/1136923139?ean=9781393422082

If you love football, then you will enjoy reading about the history of the Green Bay Packers. Inside you will read about every season in Green Bay Packers history. Since 1919, the Packers have been a staple of Wisconsin lore. Relive some of the great seasons, games and moments in Packers history.

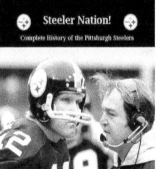

If you love Football, then you will enjoy reading about the history of the Pittsburgh Steelers. Inside you will read about every season in Steelers history. Since 1933 the Steelers have been a staple of Western Pennsylvania lore and one of the most successful teams in NFL history. Relive some of the great seasons, games and moments in Steelers history.

"The Green & Gold" History of the Green Bay Packers

8.5" x 11" {305 pages} {Paperback & Hardcover}

$29.95 PB - $34.95 HC

Available at numerous online retailers

Steeler Nation! History of the Pittsburgh Steelers

8.5" x 11" {260 pages} {Paperback}

$29.95 PB - $36.95 HC

Available at numerous online retailers

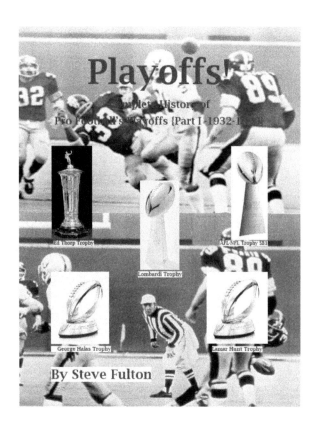

Everything you wanted to know about the history of the NFL Playoffs is here. Game recaps for every NFL Playoff game, from the start with the 1932 NFL Championship Game to Super Bowl XXXIV, you can read about it in this book. Part I covers Playoffs from 1932-1999. Filled with historical pictures as well, you can take a stroll down memory lane reading about the great games, great teams and great players past and present. It is a must read for all NFL fans young and old alike.

PLAYOFFS! – Complete History of Pro Football's Playoffs Part I {1932-1999}

8.5" x 11" {407 pages} {Paperback}

$34.95

Available at numerous online retailers

More Books available from https://stevesfootballbible.com/paperback-bookstore/

Everything you wanted to know about the history of the NFL Playoffs is here in Part II {2000-2022} of this book. Game recaps for every NFL Playoff game, from the 2000 Playoffs to Super Bowl LVI, you can read about it in this book. Filled with historical pictures as well, you can take a stroll down memory lane reading about the great games, great teams and great players past and present. It is a must read for all NFL fans young and old alike.

Playoffs! Complete History of Pro Football's Playoffs {Part II – 2000-2022}

8.5" x 11" {287 pages}

$34.95

Available at numerous online retailers

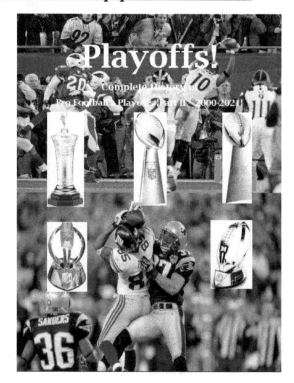

This book is for football fans of all ages. It is both educational and entertaining as you can read nostalgically about former great College teams and players, as well as some of the great Bowl Games from the past. This book covers all the Bowl Games of the 20th Century (1902-1999), so you can read about your football heroes, past and present.

College Football History "Bowl Games of the 20th Century"

8.5" x 11" {596 pages}

$39.95

Available at numerous online retailers

More Books available from https://stevesfootballbible.com/paperback-bookstore/

This book takes a comprehensive look at College Football's most memorable plays and memorable moments throughout the years. You will read about games most people have never heard of but have played an important role in shaping College Football as we know it today. It is a must read for fans of College Football. Games include all divisions of College Football (FBS, FCS, Division II and Division III). It is truly a walk down memory lane for fans who enjoy the rich traditions and history of college football.

College Football History "Memorable Plays and Memorable Moments" {8.5" x 11"} {156 pages}

$24.95 -- Available at numerous online retailers

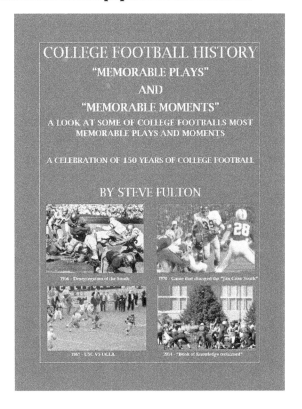

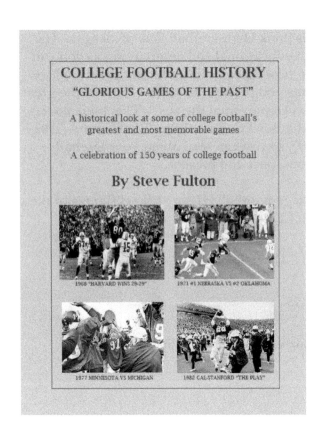

This book takes a Historical look at past College Football games. Game of the Century, Memorable games, Great comebacks, great games of the 20th Century, when number 1 played number 2, when number #1 ranked teams lost to an unranked team. Everything for the College Football fan.

College Football "Glorious Games of the Past" {8.5" x 11"} {293 pages}

$34.95 - Available at numerous online retailers

More Books available from https://stevesfootballbible.com/paperback-bookstore/

This book is a definitive account of College Football Trophy games across all divisions in FBS, FCS, Division 2 and Division 3. Full of historical information and game recaps of some of the memorable and notable games for each trophy game/rivalry. This book is for College Football fans of all ages, being both entertaining and educational, it is a must read if you love college football.

College Football History "Trophy Games"

{8.5" x 11"} {430 pages}

$34.95

Available at numerous online retailers

All these books are available in Paperback or Hardcover at www.stevesfootballbible.com and numerous online retailers

Boston Red Sox	Los Angeles Dodgers	Minnesota Twins
$32.95 PB/$37.95 HC	$34.95 PB/$39.95 HC	$29.95 PB/$34.95 HC

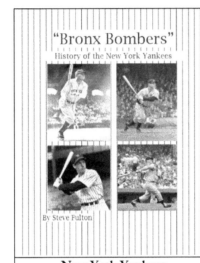

New York Yankees	Philadelphia Phillies
$39.95 PB/$44.95 HC	$32.95/$36.95

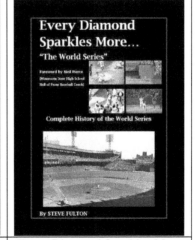

Every Diamond Does Sparkle {Part I-1901-1999}	Every Diamond Does Sparkle {Part II-2000-present}	Every Diamond Sparkles More {The World Series}
$29.95 PB/$34.95 HC	$34.95/$34.95 HC	$39.95 PB/$44.95 HC

Printed in the USA
CPSIA information can be obtained
at www.ICGtesting.com
LVHW070932270124
770126LV00011B/1313